fushigi yûgi™

The Mysterious Play
VOL. 13: GODDESS

Story & Art By
YÛ WATASE

FUSHIGI YÛGI
THE MYSTERIOUS PLAY
VOL. 13: GODDESS
SHÔJO EDITION

This volume contains the FUSHIGI YÛGI installments from Animerica Extra Vol. 7, No. 8 through Vol. 7, No. 10 in their entirety.

STORY AND ART BY YÛ WATASE

English Adaptation/William Flanagan
Translation/Yuji Oniki and William Flanagan
Touch-up & Lettering/Bill Spicer
Touch-up Assistance/Walden Wong
Design/Hidemi Sahara
Editors/Elizabeth Kawasaki and Frances E. Wall

Managing Editor/Annette Roman
Editorial Director/Alvin Lu
Director of Production/Noboru Watanabe
Sr. Director of Licensing & Acquisitions/Rika Inouye
Vice President of Sales & Marketing/Liza Coppola
Executive Vice President/Hyoe Narita
Publisher/Seiji Horibuchi

Printed in Canada

Published by VIZ, LLC
P.O. Box 77010
San Francisco, CA 94107

Shôjo Edition
10 9 8 7 6 5 4 3 2 1
First printing, December 2004

www.viz.com store.viz.com

CONTENTS

STORY THUS FAR

Miaka is a cheerful junior high school girl who's physically drawn into the world of a strange book – THE UNIVERSE OF THE FOUR GODS – where she is offered the role of the lead character, the Priestess of the god Suzaku. Miaka is charged with saving the nation of Hong-Nan, and in the process will be granted three wishes. While Miaka makes a short trip back to the real world, her best friend Yui is sucked into the book only to suffer rape and manipulation, which drives her to attempt suicide. Now, Yui has become the Priestess of the god Seiryu, the bitter enemy of Suzaku and Miaka.

Yui blames Miaka for the torments that she has experienced, and the only way for Miaka to gain back the trust of her former friend is to summon the god Suzaku and wish to be reconciled, so she re-enters the world of the book. It doesn't hurt that going back into the book also grants Miaka the chance to see more of the dreamy Suzaku warrior Tamahome! Unfortunately, Miaka's attempts to summon Suzaku are repeatedly thwarted by the Seiryu Celestial Warriors. Yui, still furious at Miaka and terribly jealous of her budding romance with Tamahome, is bent on revenge and manages to perform the Seiryu summoning ceremony before Miaka can stop her. Yui's first wish seals away Suzaku, leaving the Suzaku Celestial Warriors stripped of their power and forced to fight like normal humans when they come face-to-face with the Seiryu warriors. In the middle of battle, Yui, still determined to separate Miaka and Tamahome, makes her second wish, sending herself and Miaka back to the real world… but Tamahome emerges from the book world with them!

When Yui learns that Tamahome and Miaka have been reunited, she is furious and pledges again to destroy their relationship, calling Suboshi, one of her Seiryu warriors, into the real world to help her. Tamahome is enjoying learning about life in the modern world, but his heart is divided between reveling in Miaka's company and needing to be back in the world of the book, helping to defend Hong-Nan. Miaka learns that even if Tamahome is able to return to Hong-Nan, Yui's second wish to Seiryu means that she will never be able to enter THE UNIVERSE OF THE FOUR GODS again! Tamahome overhears Miaka and Keisuke talking about how he is just a fictional character, and is sent into a tailspin of confusion and self-doubt. But then, with his faith in his loyalty and love for Miaka renewed, Tamahome runs to her side to help her fight Suboshi....

THE UNIVERSE OF THE FOUR GODS is based on ancient Chinese legend, but Japanese pronunciation of Chinese names differs slightly from their Chinese equivalents. Here is a short glossary of the Japanese pronunciation of the Chinese names in this graphic novel:

CHINESE	JAPANESE	PERSON OR PLACE	MEANING
Hong-Nan	Konan	Southern Kingdom	Crimson South
Qu-Dong	Kutô	Eastern Kingdom	Gathered East
Bei-Jia	Hokkan	Northern Kingdom	Armored North
Xi-Lang	Sairô	Western Kingdom	West Tower
Tai Yi-Jun	Tai Itsukun	An Oracle	Preeminent Person
Feng-Qi	Hôki	Hotohori's Bride	Rare Phoenix

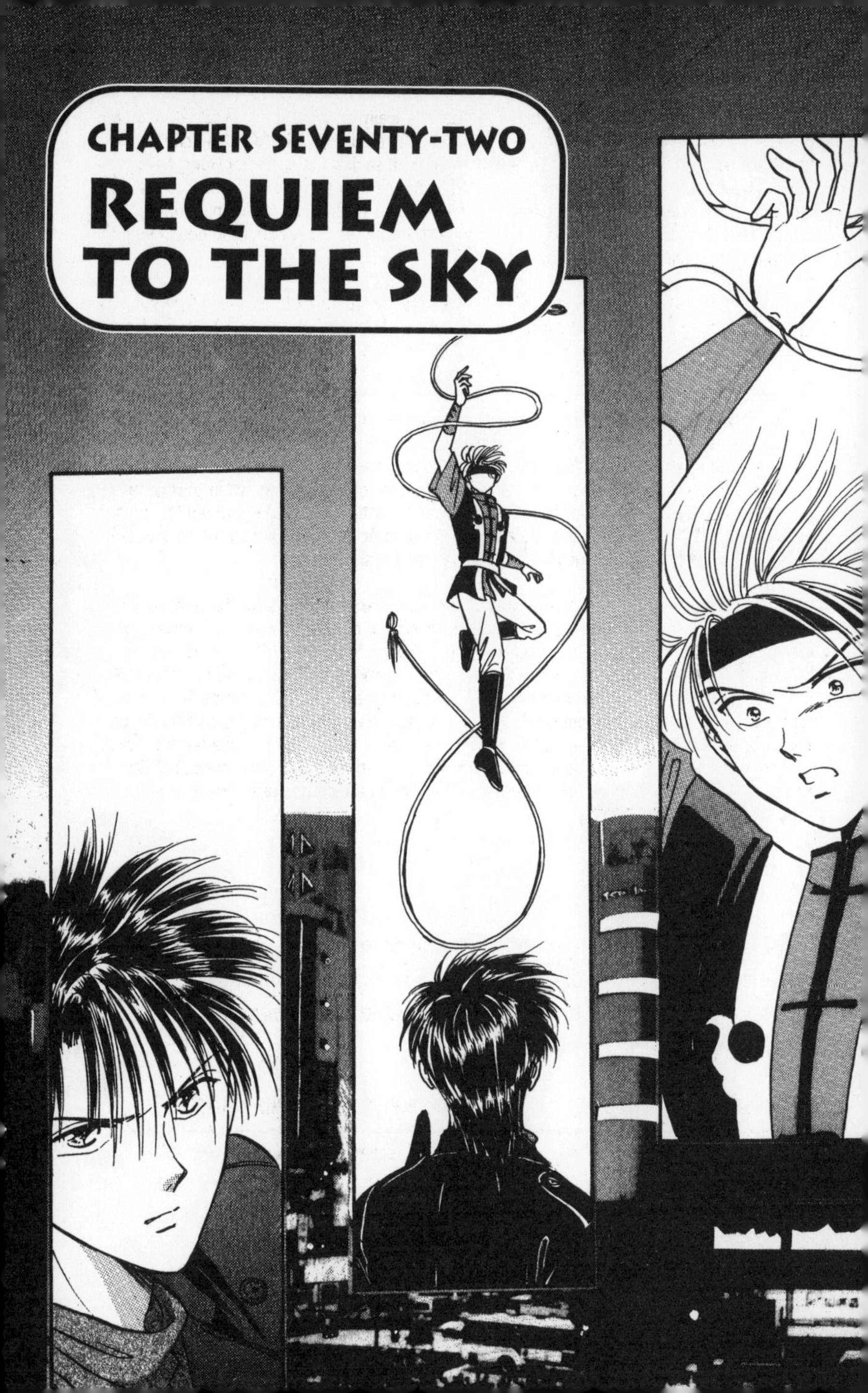
CHAPTER SEVENTY-TWO
REQUIEM TO THE SKY

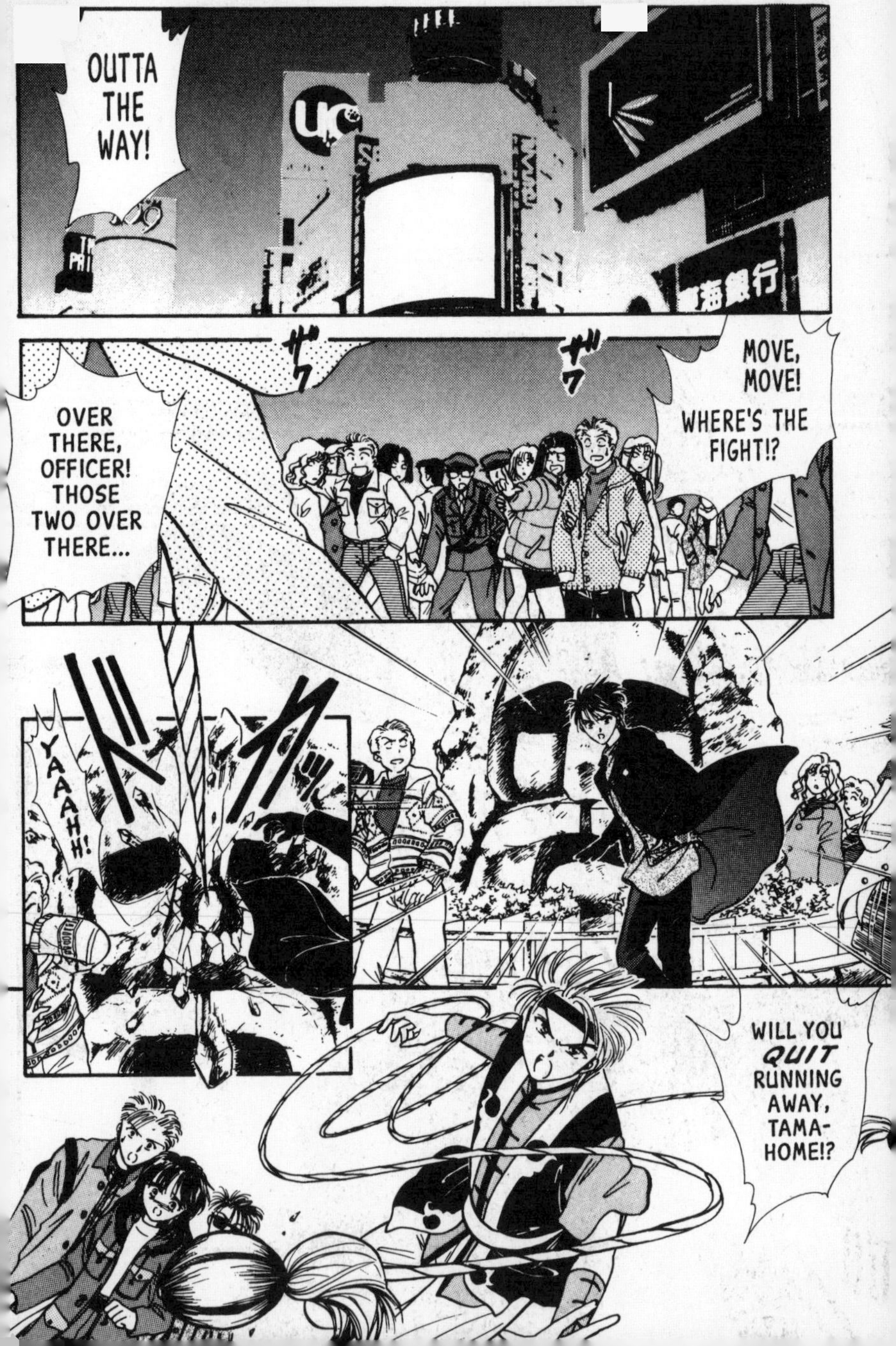
OUTTA THE WAY!
ザワ
ザワ
MOVE, MOVE! WHERE'S THE FIGHT!?
OVER THERE, OFFICER! THOSE TWO OVER THERE...
WILL YOU QUIT RUNNING AWAY, TAMA-HOME!?
YAAAHH!

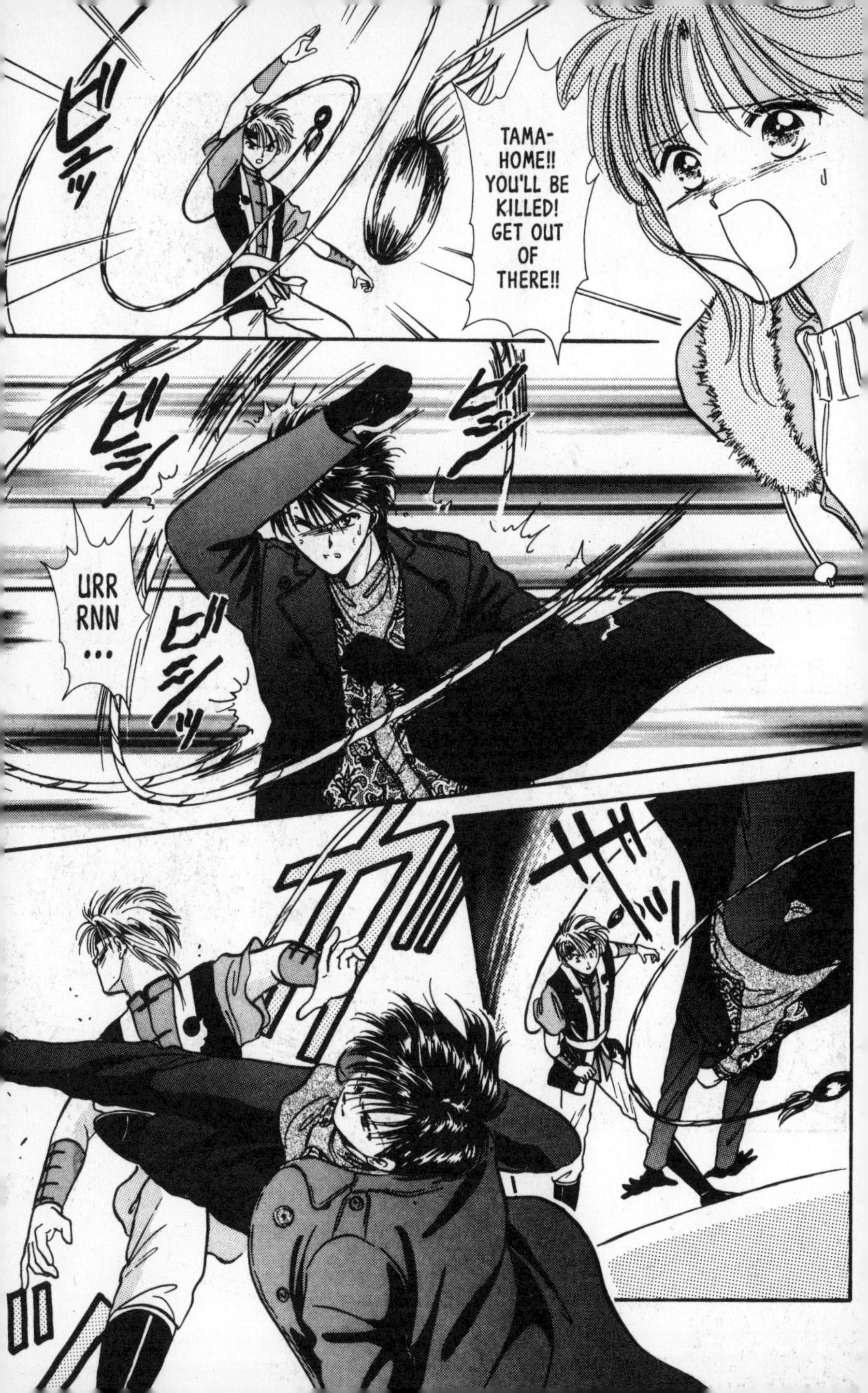
TAMA-HOME!! YOU'LL BE KILLED! GET OUT OF THERE!!
URR RNN ...

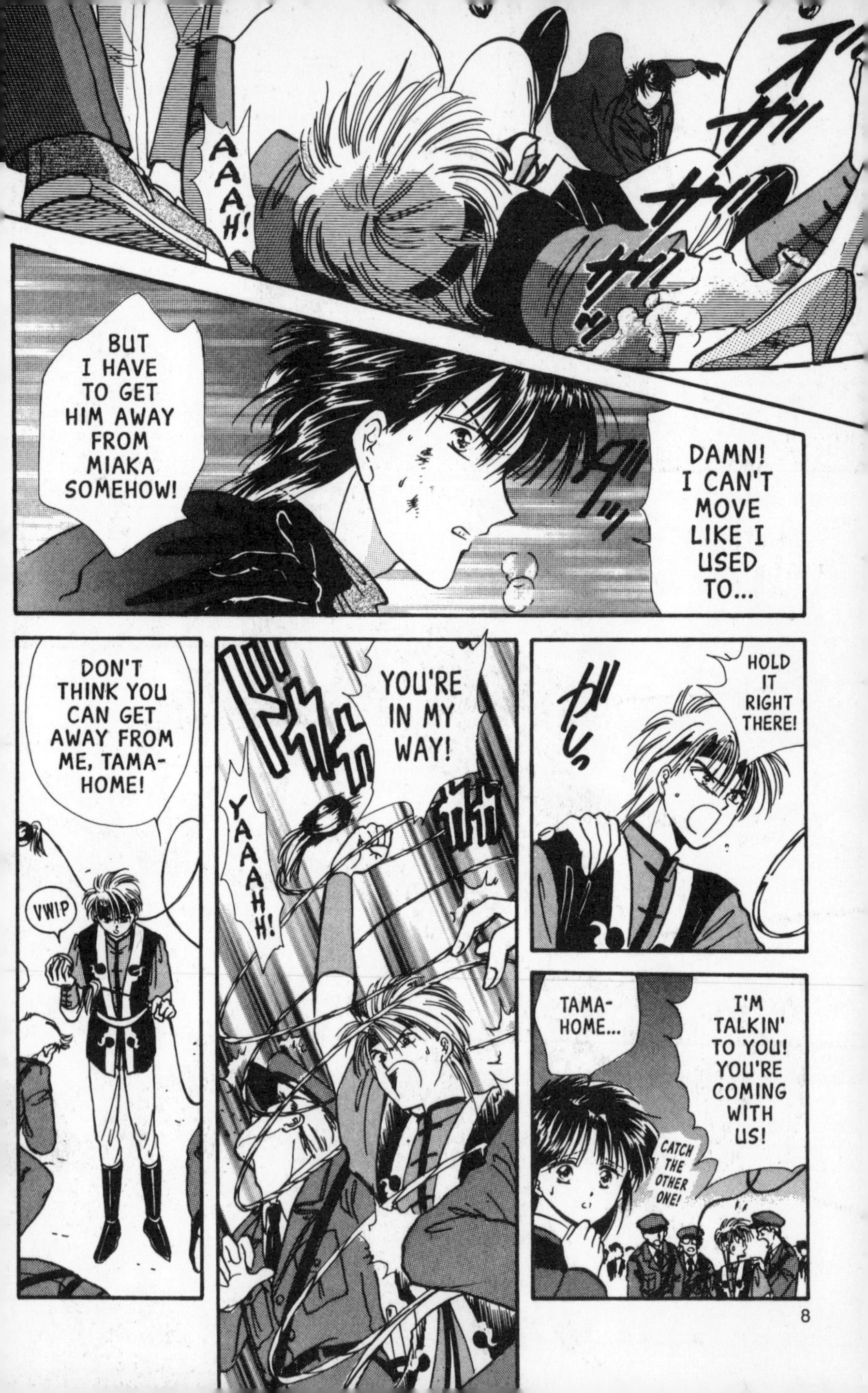
AAAAH!
DAMN! I CAN'T MOVE LIKE I USED TO...
BUT I HAVE TO GET HIM AWAY FROM MIAKA SOMEHOW!
HOLD IT RIGHT THERE!
TAMA-HOME...
I'M TALKIN' TO YOU! YOU'RE COMING WITH US!
CATCH THE OTHER ONE!
YOU'RE IN MY WAY!
YAAAAHH!
DON'T THINK YOU CAN GET AWAY FROM ME, TAMA-HOME!
VWIP

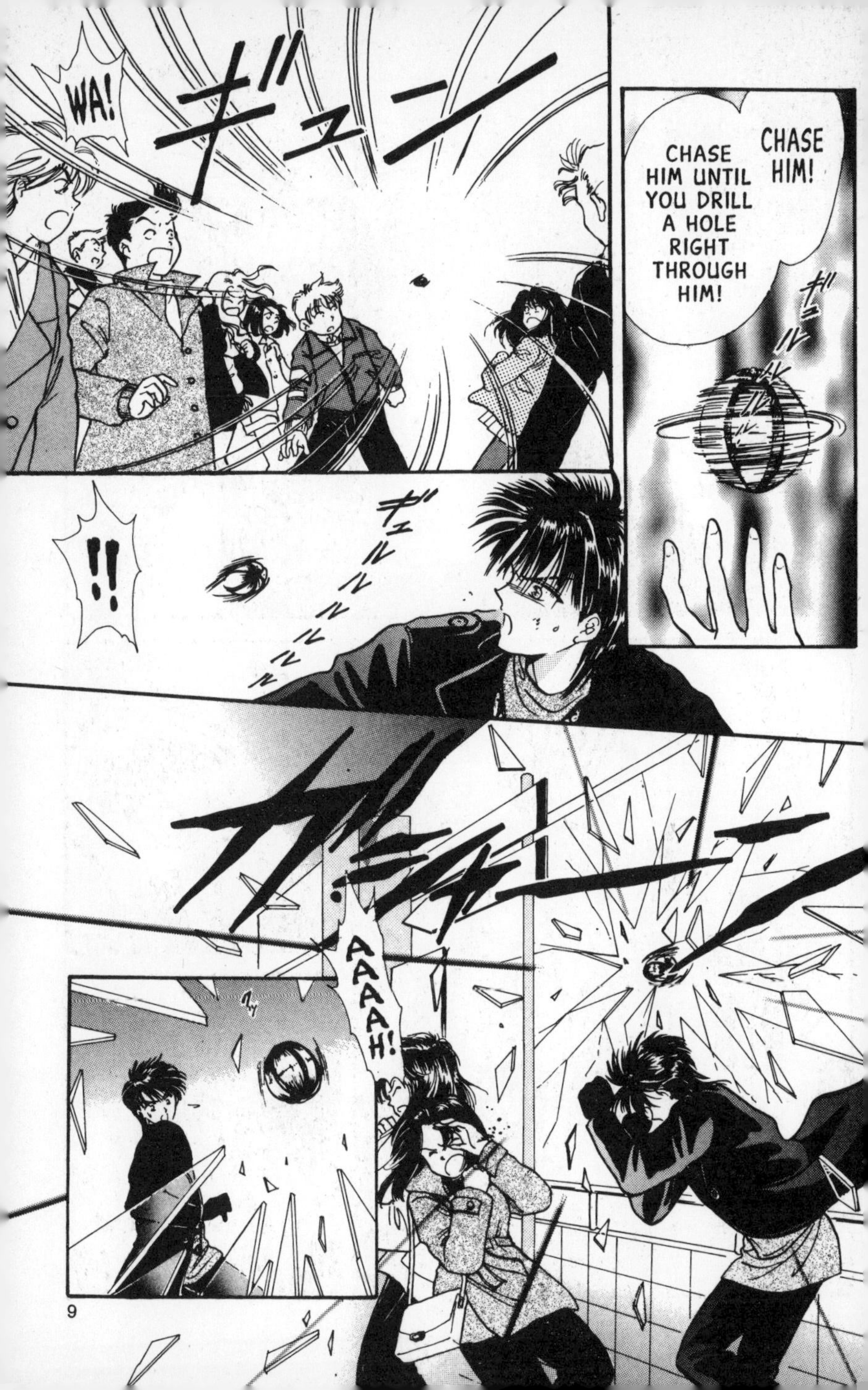
CHASE HIM!
CHASE HIM UNTIL YOU DRILL A HOLE RIGHT THROUGH HIM!
WA!
ギューン
!!
AAAAH!

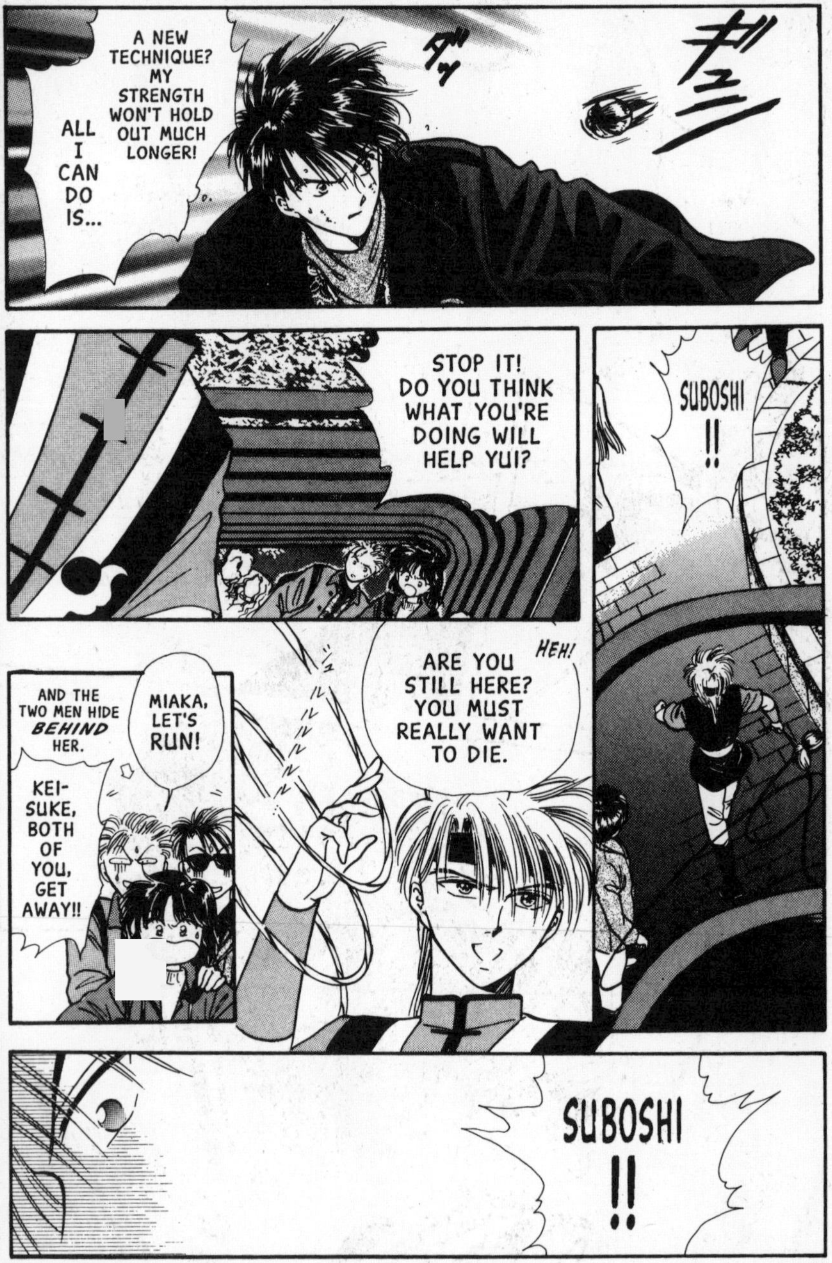
ギュン
ダッ
A NEW TECHNIQUE? MY STRENGTH WON'T HOLD OUT MUCH LONGER!
ALL I CAN DO IS...
SUBOSHI !!
STOP IT! DO YOU THINK WHAT YOU'RE DOING WILL HELP YUI?
HEH!
ARE YOU STILL HERE? YOU MUST REALLY WANT TO DIE.
MIAKA, LET'S RUN!
AND THE TWO MEN HIDE ***BEHIND*** HER.
KEI-SUKE, BOTH OF YOU, GET AWAY!!
SUBOSHI !!

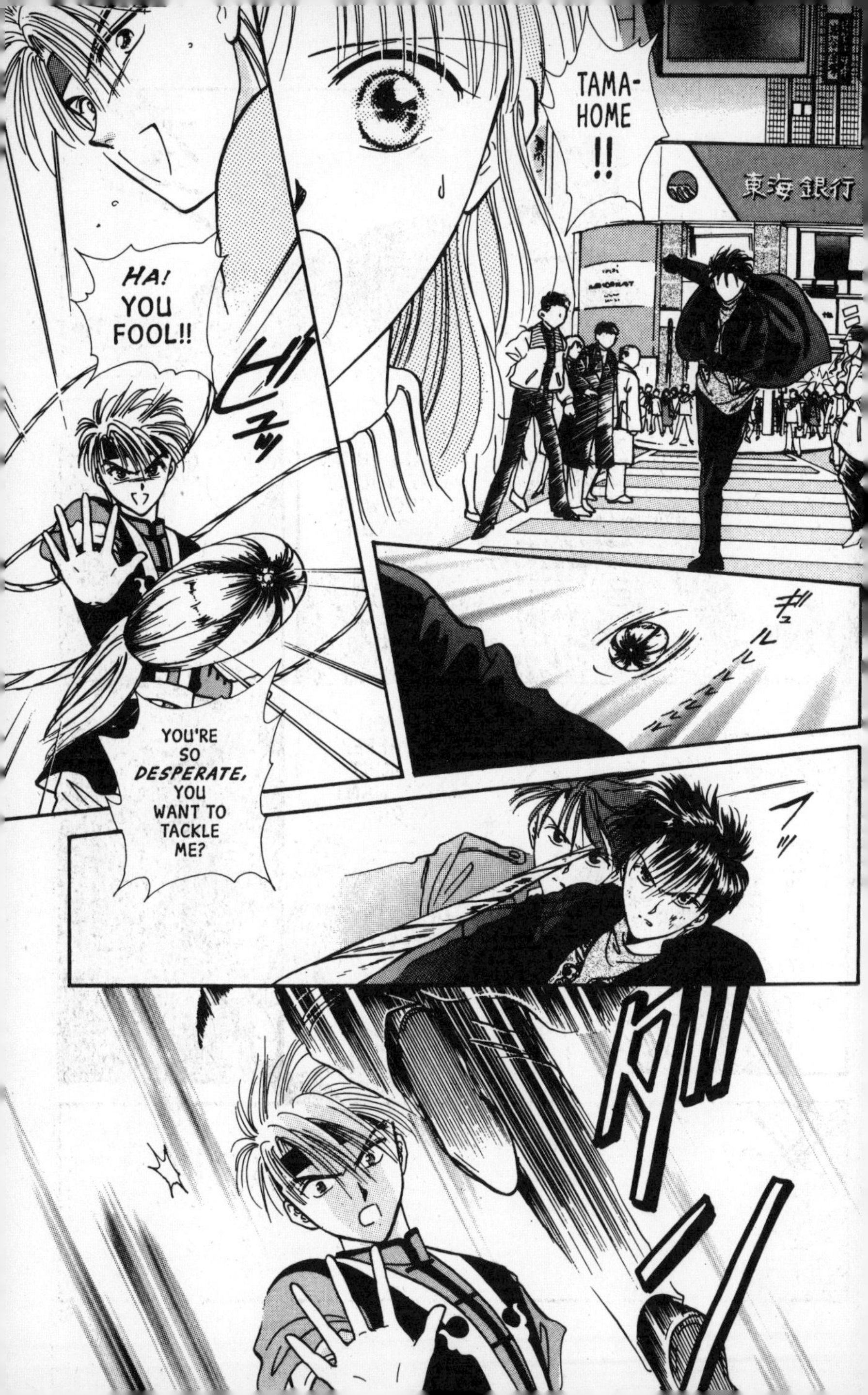
TAMA-HOME !!
東海銀行
HA! YOU FOOL!!
YOU'RE SO *DESPERATE,* YOU WANT TO TACKLE ME?

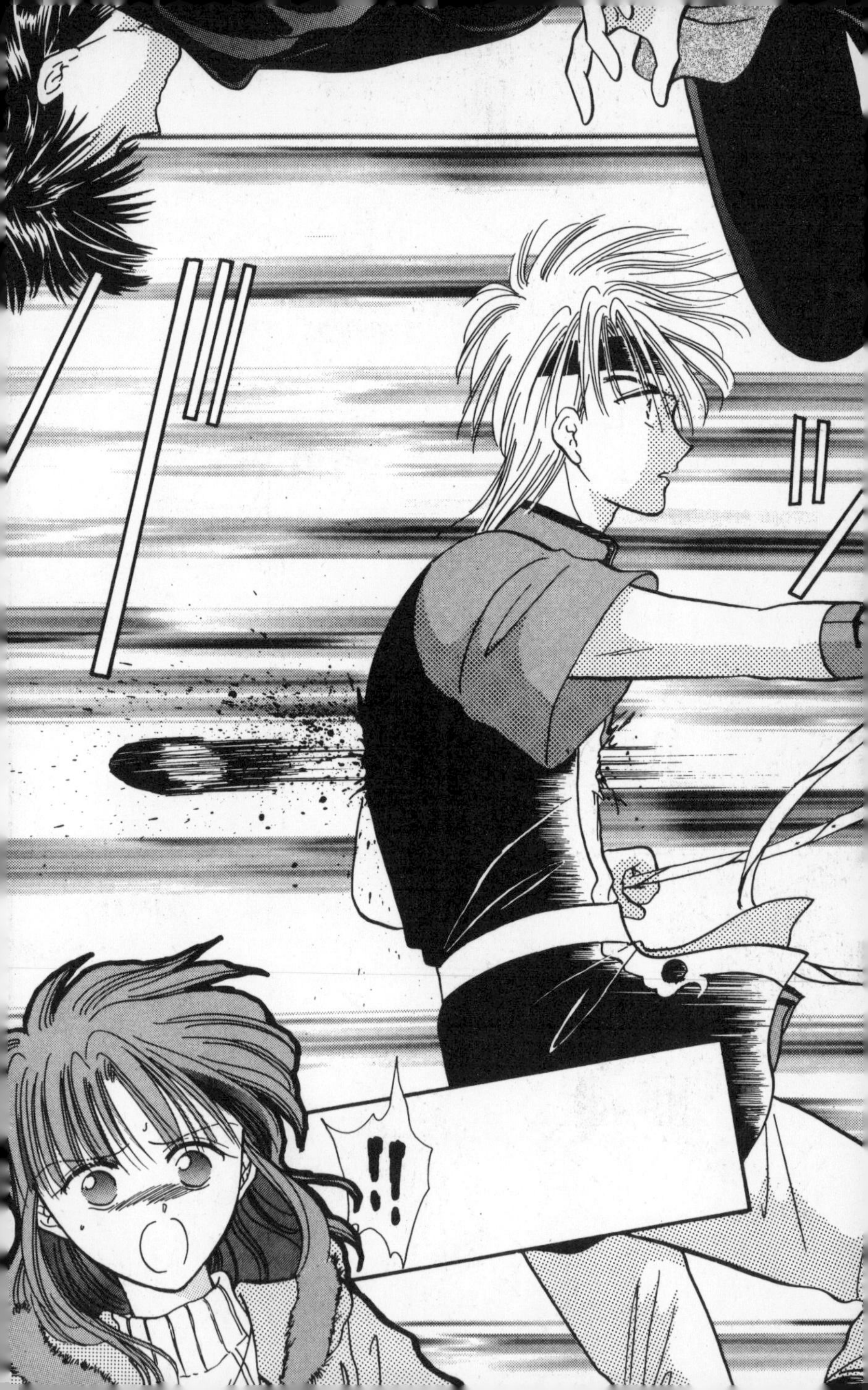
!!

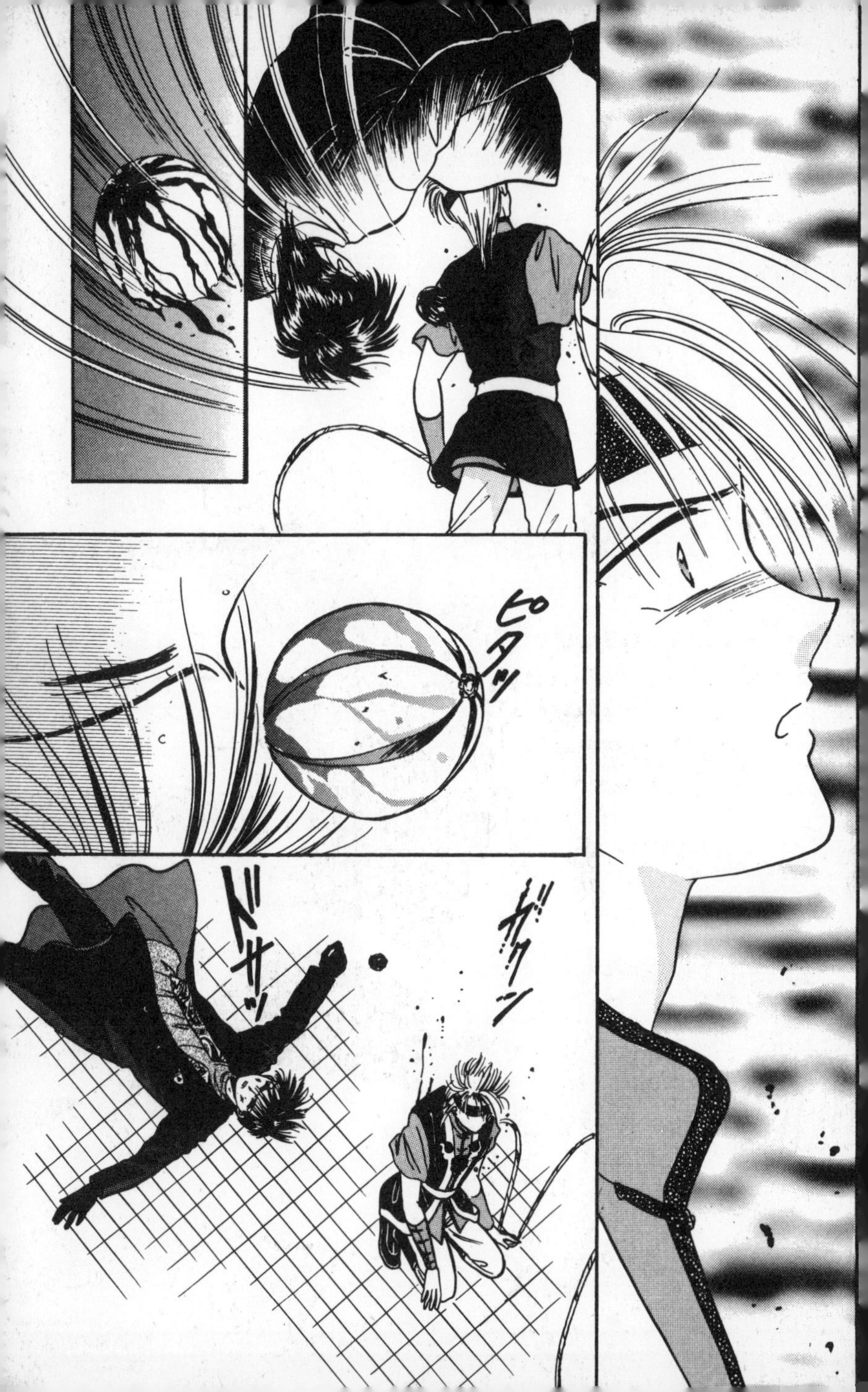
ピタッ
ガクーン!!
ドサッ

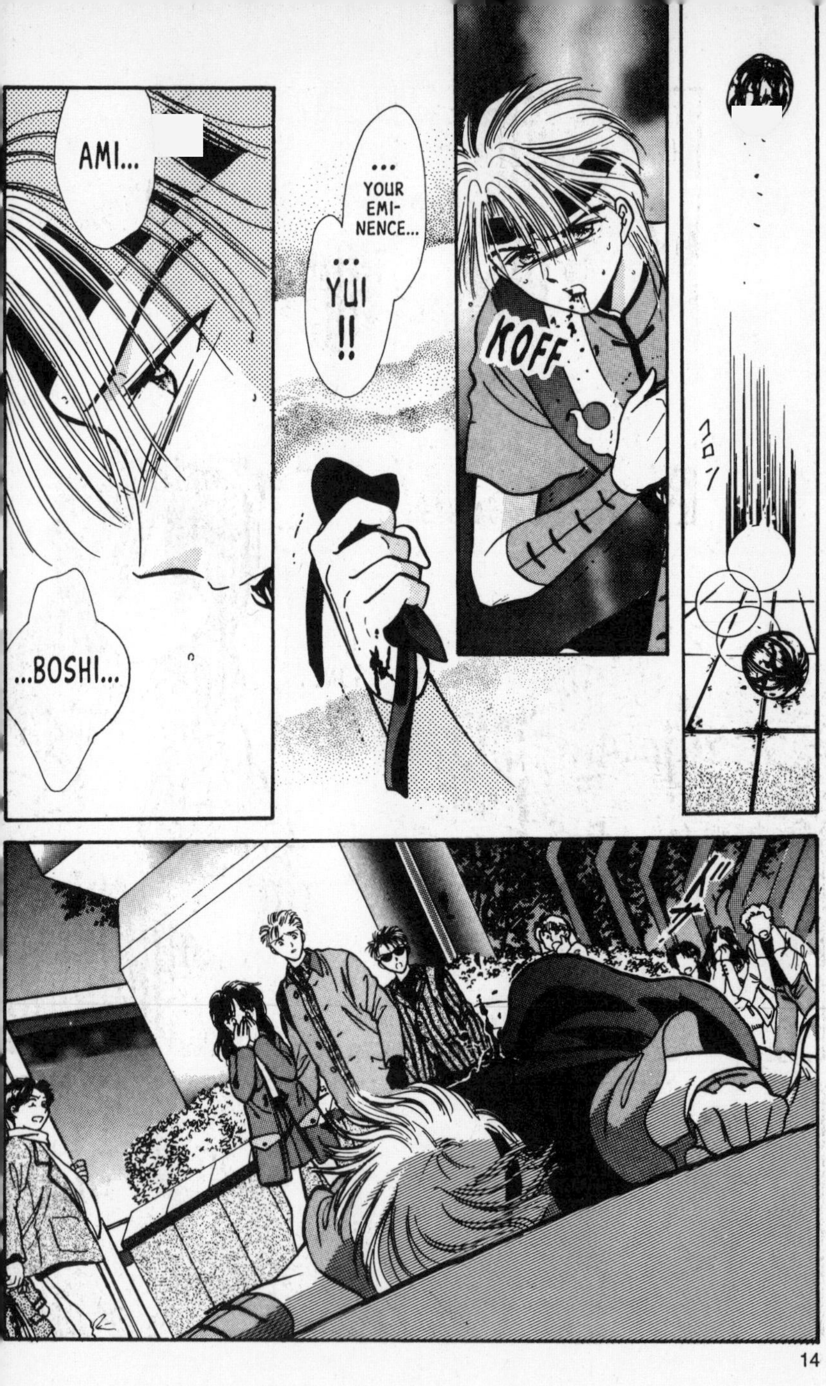
コロン
KOFF
... YOUR EMI-NENCE...
... YUI !!
AMI...
...BOSHI...

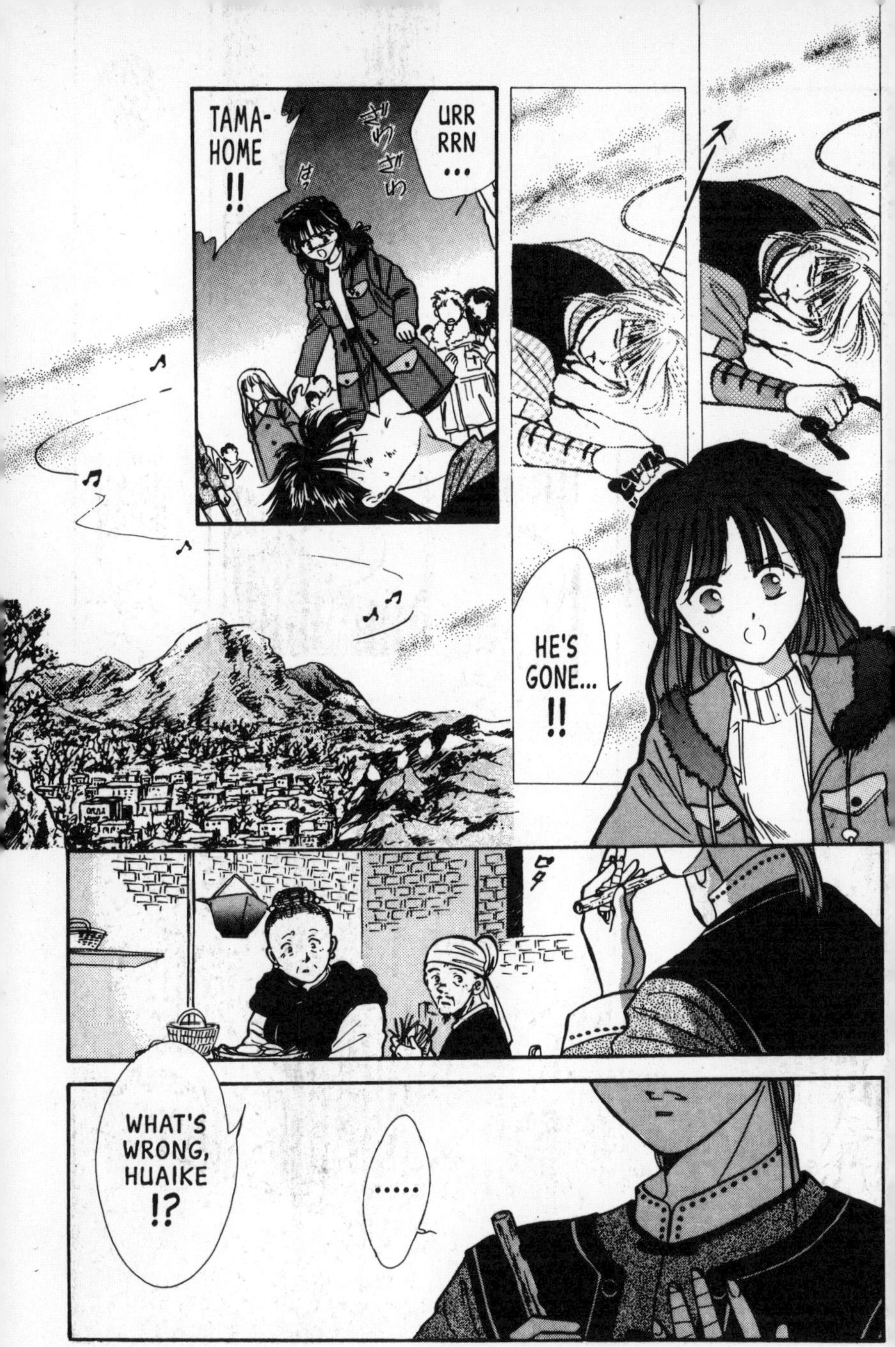
HE'S GONE... !!
URR RRN ...
ざわざわ
TAMA-HOME !!
ピタ
WHAT'S WRONG, HUAIKE !?
.....

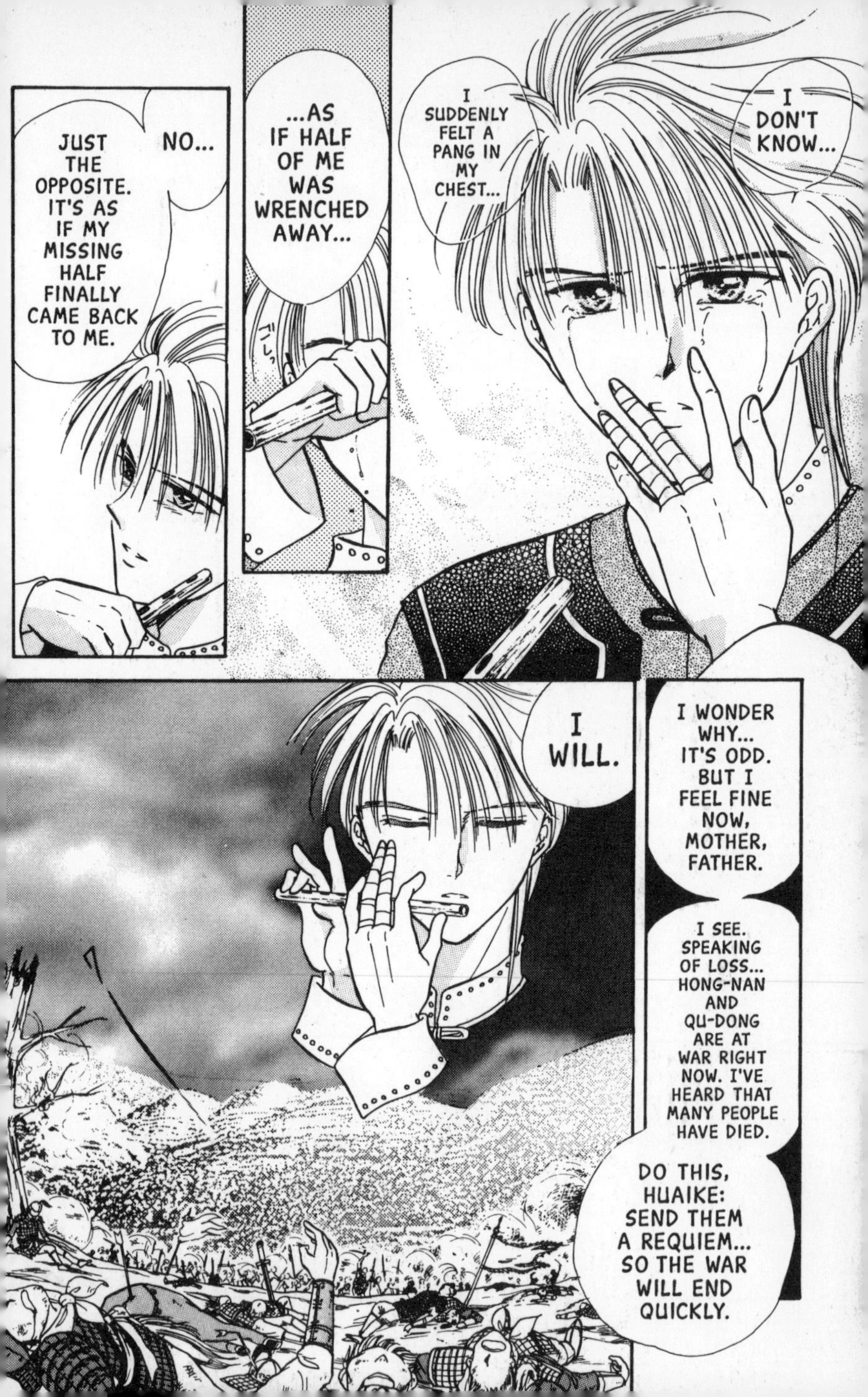
I DON'T KNOW...
I SUDDENLY FELT A PANG IN MY CHEST...
...AS IF HALF OF ME WAS WRENCHED AWAY...
NO...
JUST THE OPPOSITE. IT'S AS IF MY MISSING HALF FINALLY CAME BACK TO ME.
I WONDER WHY... IT'S ODD. BUT I FEEL FINE NOW, MOTHER, FATHER.
I SEE. SPEAKING OF LOSS... HONG-NAN AND QU-DONG ARE AT WAR RIGHT NOW. I'VE HEARD THAT MANY PEOPLE HAVE DIED.
DO THIS, HUAIKE: SEND THEM A REQUIEM... SO THE WAR WILL END QUICKLY.
I WILL.

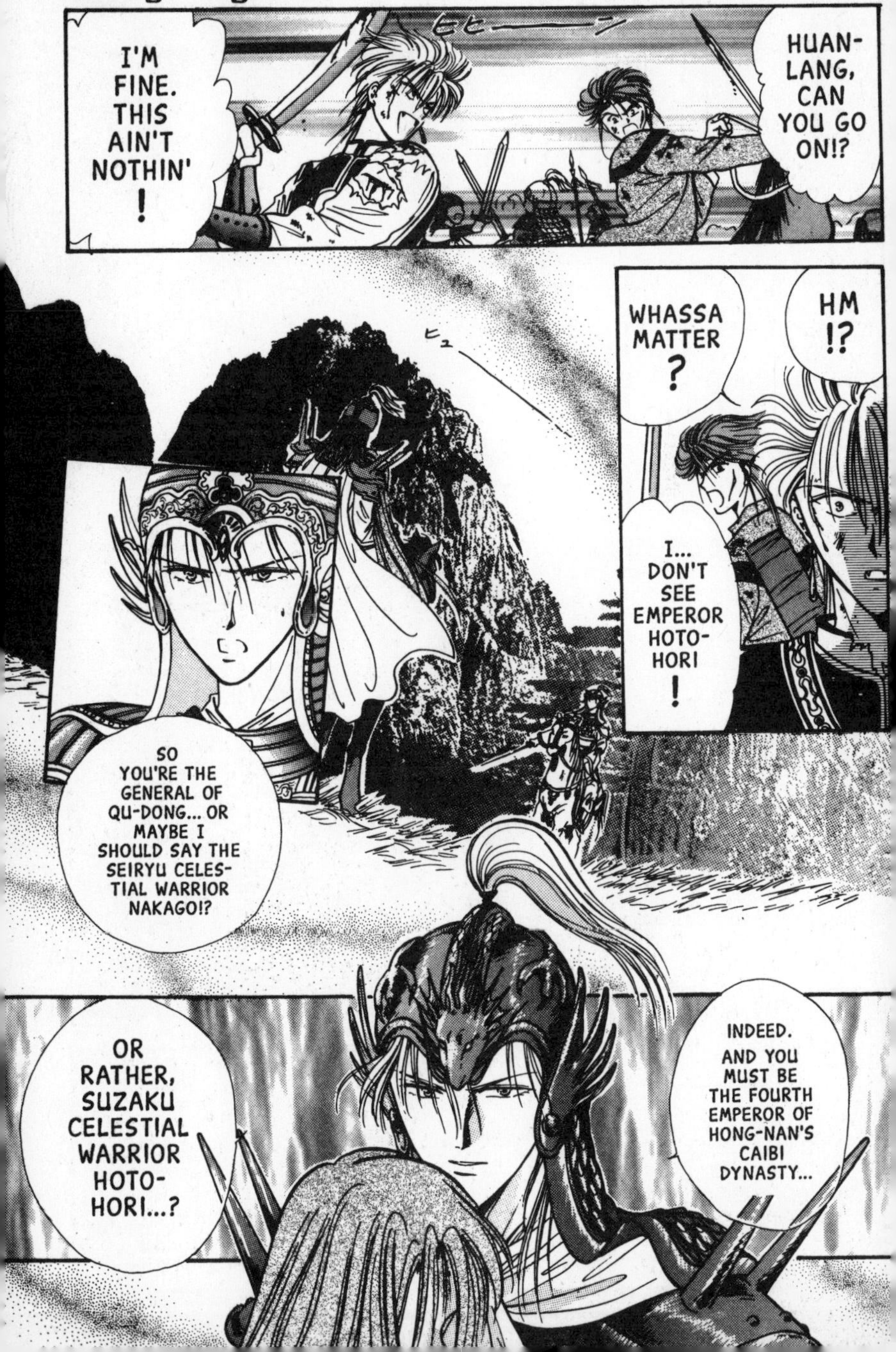
HUAN-LANG, CAN YOU GO ON!?
I'M FINE. THIS AIN'T NOTHIN'!
HM !?
WHASSA MATTER ?
I... DON'T SEE EMPEROR HOTO-HORI !
SO YOU'RE THE GENERAL OF QU-DONG... OR MAYBE I SHOULD SAY THE SEIRYU CELES-TIAL WARRIOR NAKAGO!?
INDEED. AND YOU MUST BE THE FOURTH EMPEROR OF HONG-NAN'S CAIBI DYNASTY...
OR RATHER, SUZAKU CELESTIAL WARRIOR HOTO-HORI...?

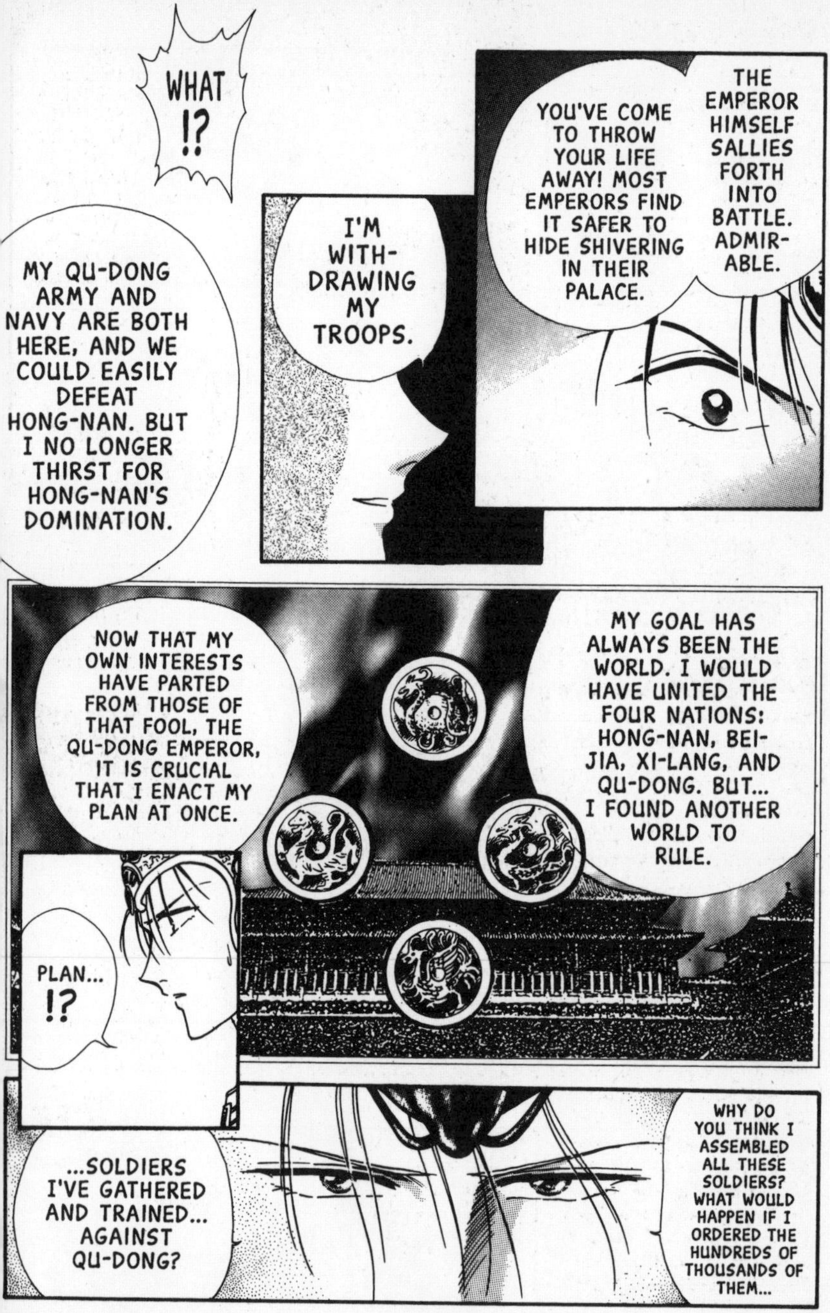
THE EMPEROR HIMSELF SALLIES FORTH INTO BATTLE. ADMIRABLE.
YOU'VE COME TO THROW YOUR LIFE AWAY! MOST EMPERORS FIND IT SAFER TO HIDE SHIVERING IN THEIR PALACE.
WHAT !?
I'M WITH-DRAWING MY TROOPS.
MY QU-DONG ARMY AND NAVY ARE BOTH HERE, AND WE COULD EASILY DEFEAT HONG-NAN. BUT I NO LONGER THIRST FOR HONG-NAN'S DOMINATION.
MY GOAL HAS ALWAYS BEEN THE WORLD. I WOULD HAVE UNITED THE FOUR NATIONS: HONG-NAN, BEI-JIA, XI-LANG, AND QU-DONG. BUT... I FOUND ANOTHER WORLD TO RULE.
NOW THAT MY OWN INTERESTS HAVE PARTED FROM THOSE OF THAT FOOL, THE QU-DONG EMPEROR, IT IS CRUCIAL THAT I ENACT MY PLAN AT ONCE.
PLAN... !?
WHY DO YOU THINK I ASSEMBLED ALL THESE SOLDIERS? WHAT WOULD HAPPEN IF I ORDERED THE HUNDREDS OF THOUSANDS OF THEM...
...SOLDIERS I'VE GATHERED AND TRAINED... AGAINST QU-DONG?

Goddess

Hello, everyone... it's Watase.
I'm praying for the victims of the Great Hanshin (Kobe) earthquake!! ➔(I was down with a cold at the time.)
Now, it seems I ended my last volume with a lie to you readers. I rambled on in volume 12 about how "the next volume will be the last," and how the story was coming to an end. But I only meant the end of Part One! (I said the same thing on CD3!)
Unlike "Prepubescence" which was a sequel series, Fushigi Yûgi is going to continue with Part Two in the next volume, volume 14.

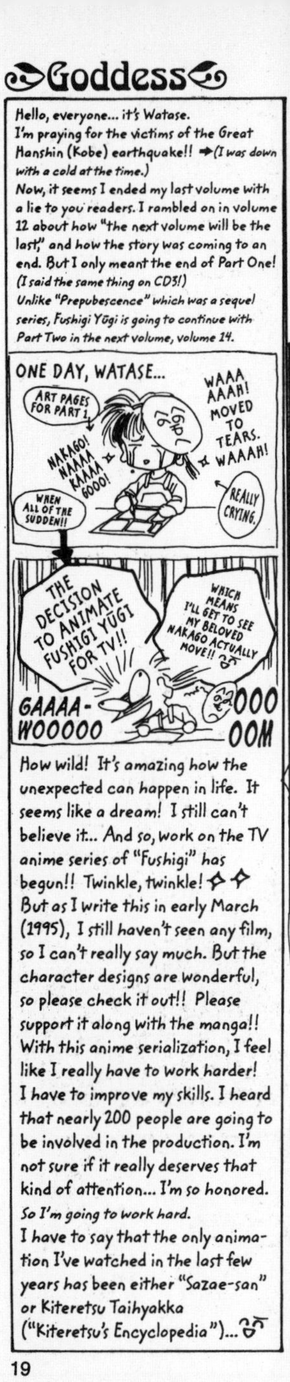
ONE DAY, WATASE...
ART PAGES FOR PART 1
WAAA AAAH! MOVED TO TEARS. WAAAH!
NAKAGO! NAAAA KAAAA GOOO!
REALLY CRYING.
WHEN ALL OF THE SUDDEN!!
THE DECISION TO ANIMATE FUSHIGI YÛGI FOR TV!!
WHICH MEANS I'LL GET TO SEE MY BELOVED NAKAGO ACTUALLY MOVE!!
GAAAA-WOOOOO
OOOOOM

How wild! It's amazing how the unexpected can happen in life. It seems like a dream! I still can't believe it... And so, work on the TV anime series of "Fushigi" has begun!! Twinkle, twinkle! ✧✧ But as I write this in early March (1995), I still haven't seen any film, so I can't really say much. But the character designs are wonderful, so please check it out!! Please support it along with the manga!! With this anime serialization, I feel like I really have to work harder! I have to improve my skills. I heard that nearly 200 people are going to be involved in the production. I'm not sure if it really deserves that kind of attention... I'm so honored. So I'm going to work hard.
I have to say that the only animation I've watched in the last few years has been either "Sazae-san" or Kiteretsu Taihyakka ("Kiteretsu's Encyclopedia")...

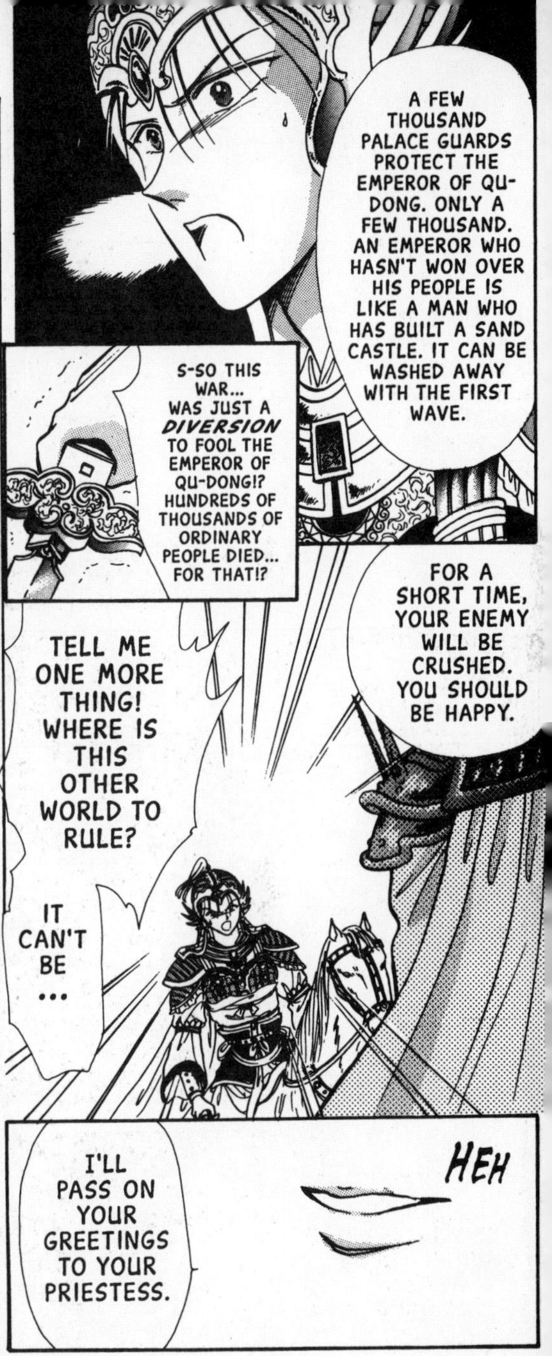
A FEW THOUSAND PALACE GUARDS PROTECT THE EMPEROR OF QU-DONG. ONLY A FEW THOUSAND. AN EMPEROR WHO HASN'T WON OVER HIS PEOPLE IS LIKE A MAN WHO HAS BUILT A SAND CASTLE. IT CAN BE WASHED AWAY WITH THE FIRST WAVE.
S-SO THIS WAR... WAS JUST A DIVERSION TO FOOL THE EMPEROR OF QU-DONG!? HUNDREDS OF THOUSANDS OF ORDINARY PEOPLE DIED... FOR THAT!?
FOR A SHORT TIME, YOUR ENEMY WILL BE CRUSHED. YOU SHOULD BE HAPPY.
TELL ME ONE MORE THING! WHERE IS THIS OTHER WORLD TO RULE?
IT CAN'T BE ...
HEH
I'LL PASS ON YOUR GREETINGS TO YOUR PRIESTESS.

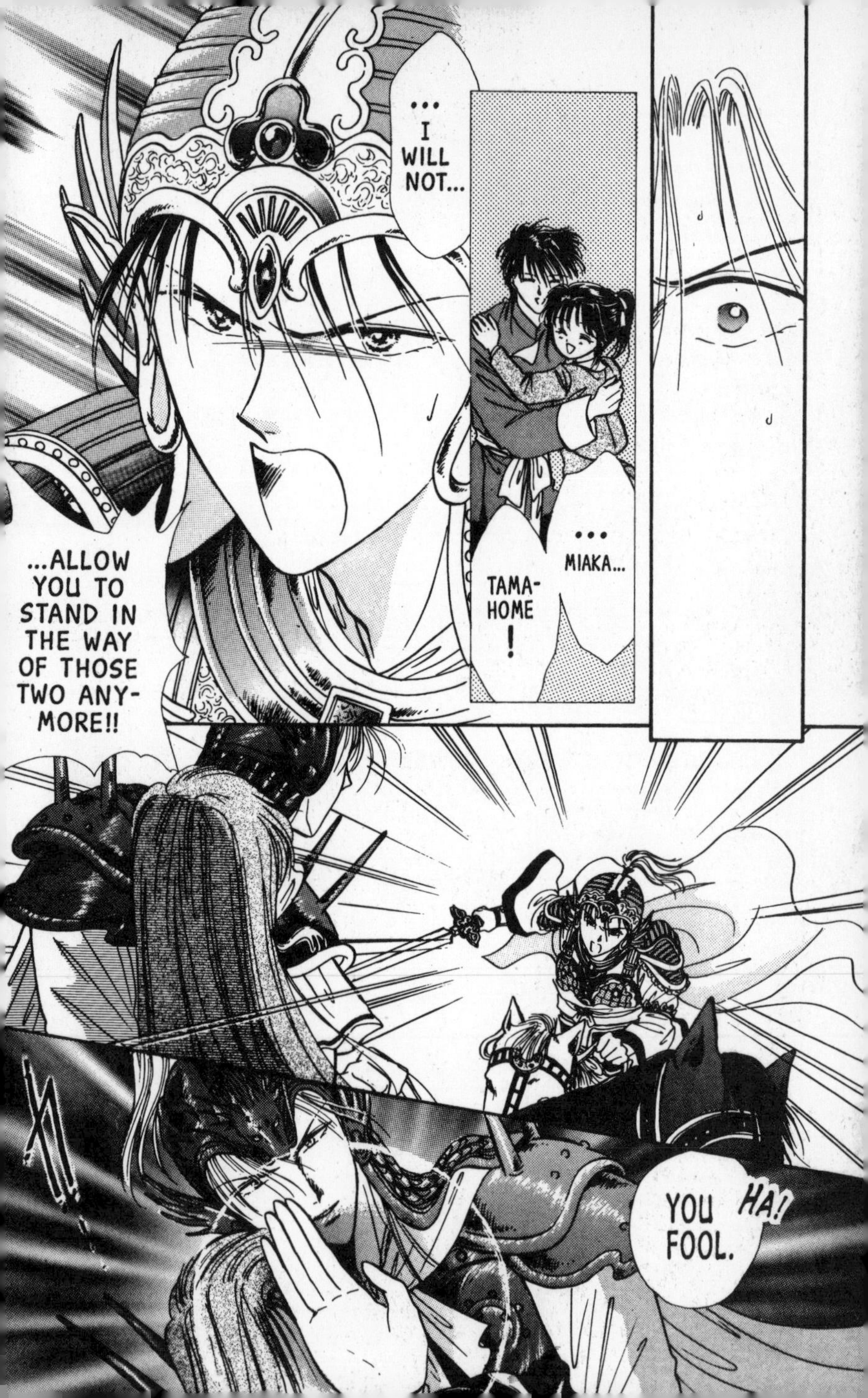

... MIAKA...
TAMA-HOME!
... I WILL NOT...
...ALLOW YOU TO STAND IN THE WAY OF THOSE TWO ANYMORE!!
HA!
YOU FOOL.

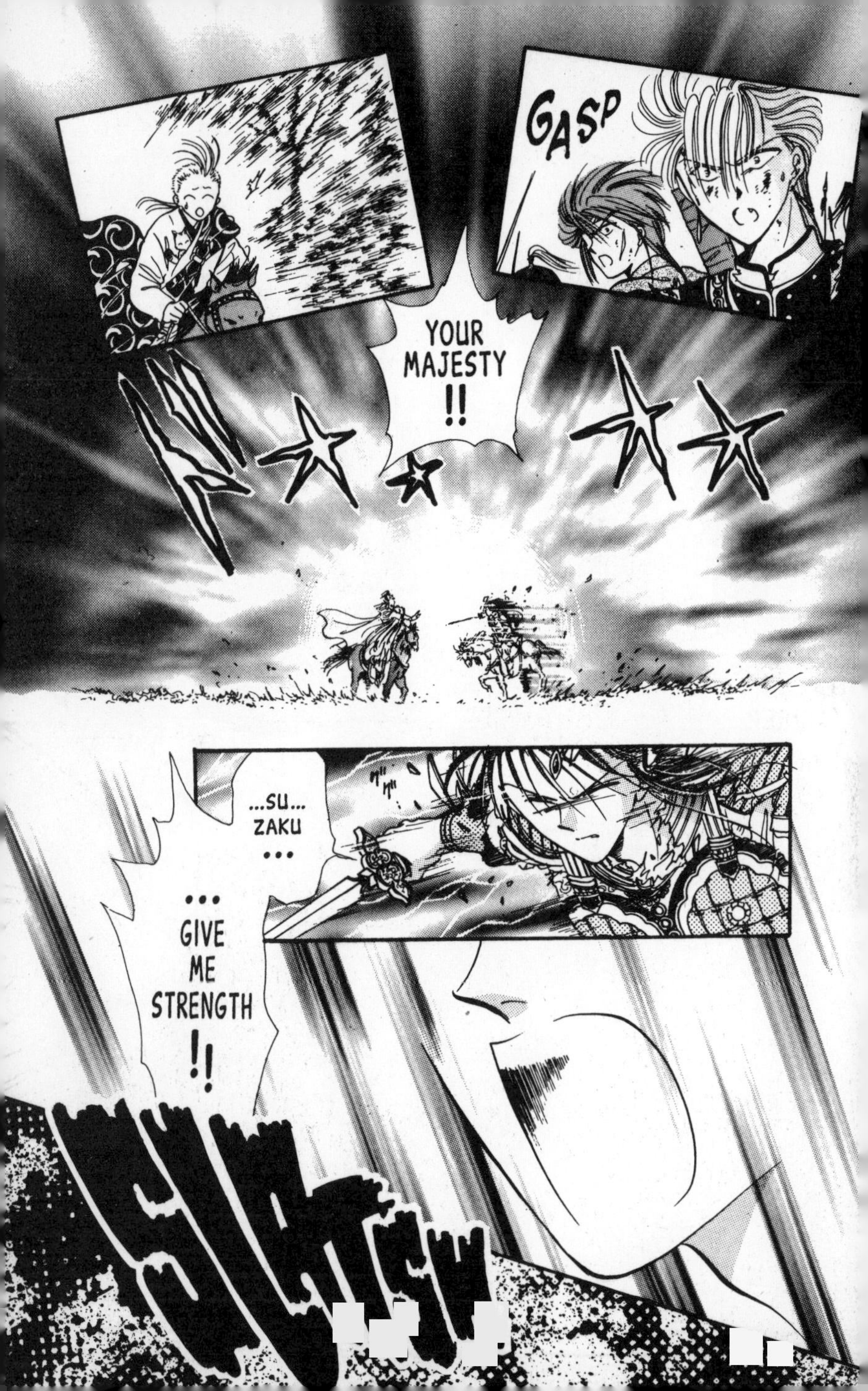
GASP
YOUR MAJESTY !!
...SU... ZAKU ...
... GIVE ME STRENGTH !!

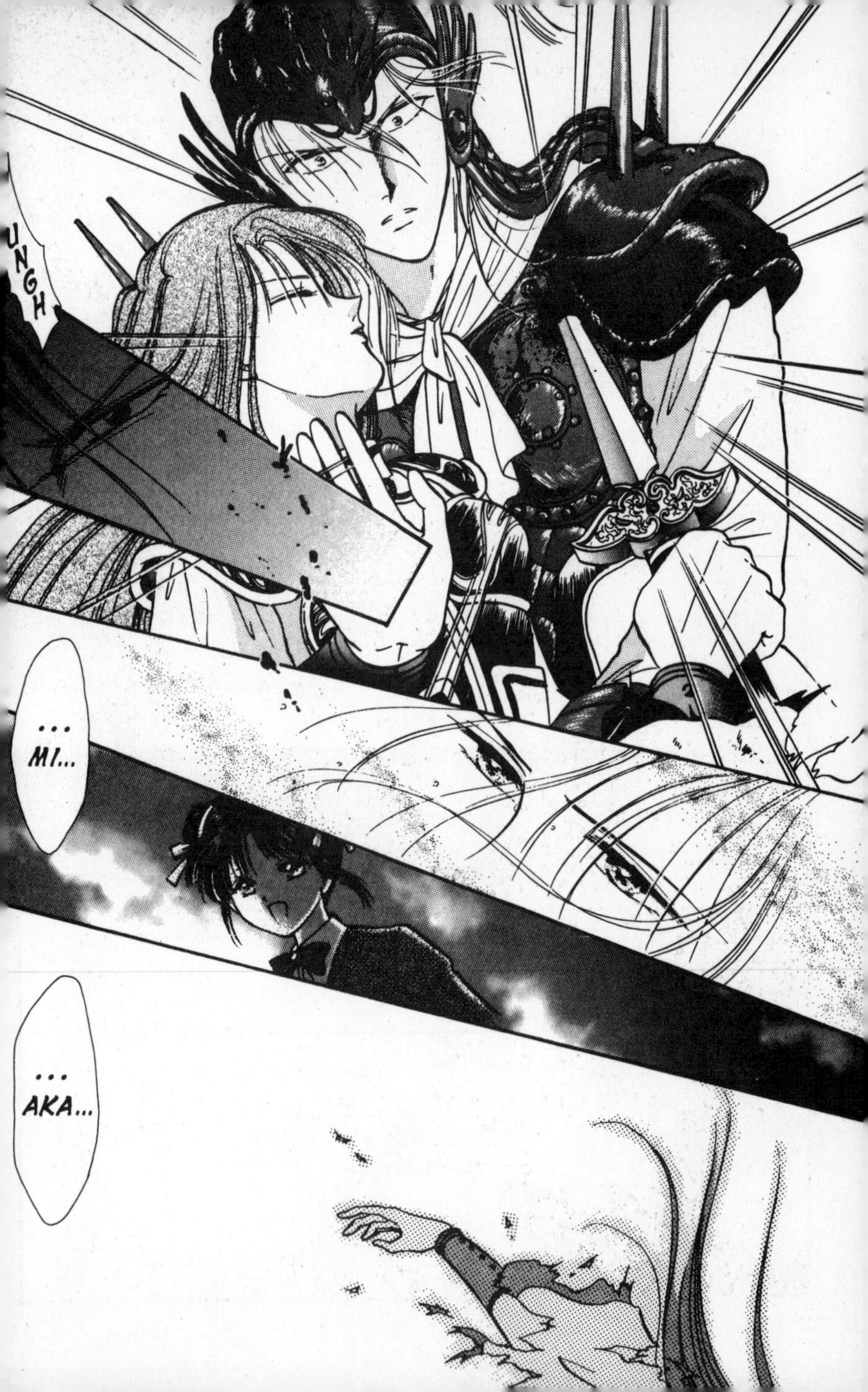
UNGH
... MI...
... AKA...

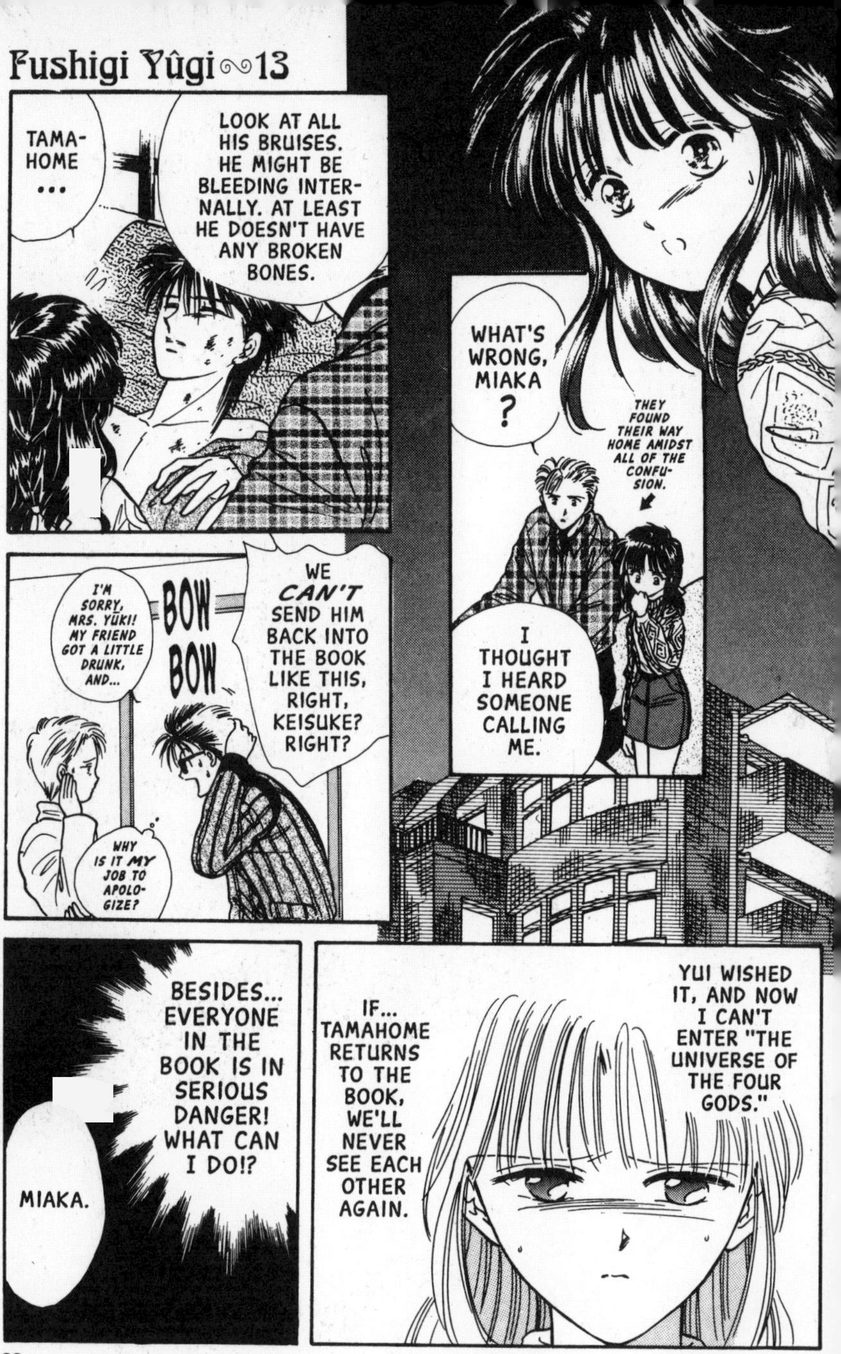
WHAT'S WRONG, MIAKA ?
THEY FOUND THEIR WAY HOME AMIDST ALL OF THE CONFUSION.
I THOUGHT I HEARD SOMEONE CALLING ME.
LOOK AT ALL HIS BRUISES. HE MIGHT BE BLEEDING INTERNALLY. AT LEAST HE DOESN'T HAVE ANY BROKEN BONES.
TAMAHOME ...
WE *CAN'T* SEND HIM BACK INTO THE BOOK LIKE THIS, RIGHT, KEISUKE? RIGHT?
BOW BOW
I'M SORRY, MRS. YŪKI! MY FRIEND GOT A LITTLE DRUNK, AND...
WHY IS IT *MY* JOB TO APOLOGIZE?
YUI WISHED IT, AND NOW I CAN'T ENTER "THE UNIVERSE OF THE FOUR GODS."
IF... TAMAHOME RETURNS TO THE BOOK, WE'LL NEVER SEE EACH OTHER AGAIN.
BESIDES... EVERYONE IN THE BOOK IS IN SERIOUS DANGER! WHAT CAN I DO!?
MIAKA.

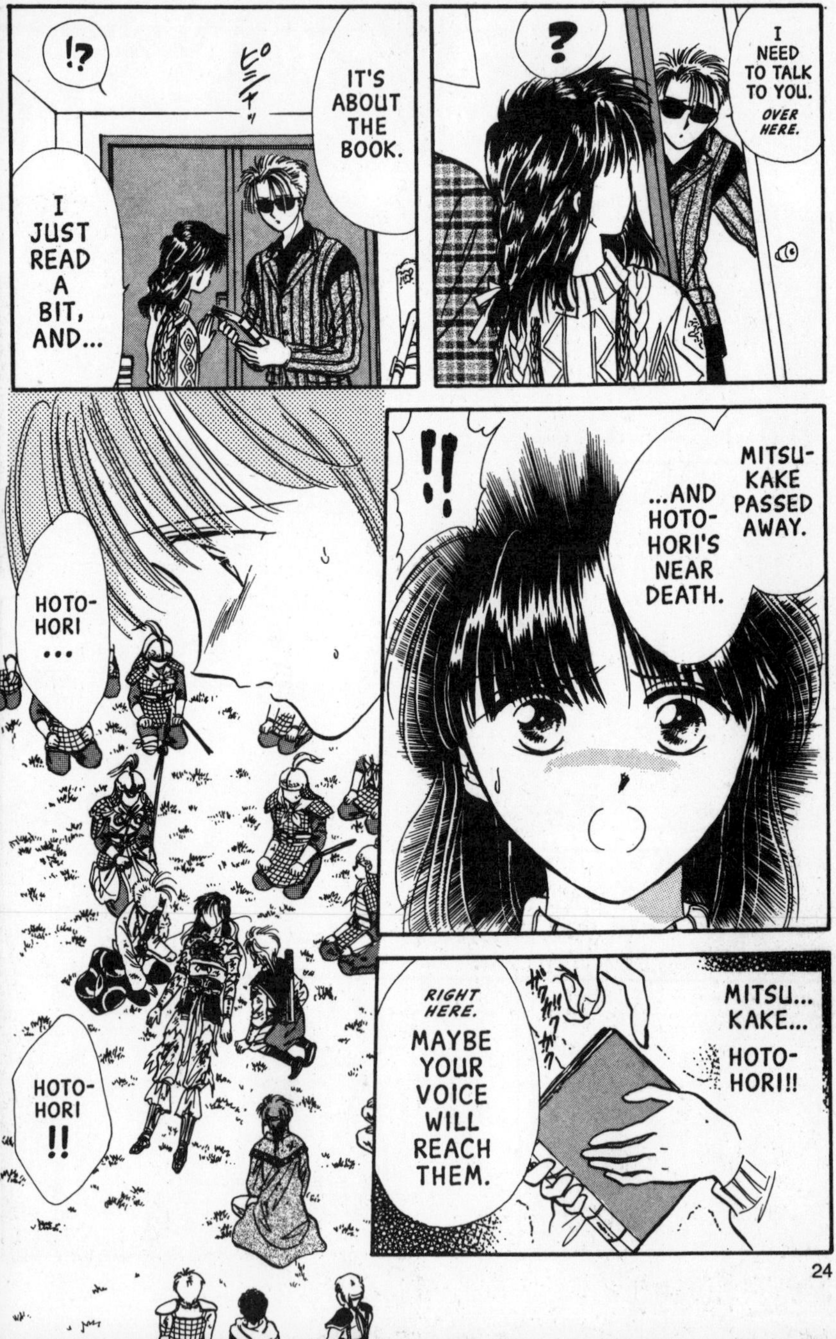
I NEED TO TALK TO YOU.
OVER HERE.
?
IT'S ABOUT THE BOOK.
ピシャッ
!?
I JUST READ A BIT, AND...
MITSUKAKE PASSED AWAY.
...AND HOTOHORI'S NEAR DEATH.
!!
MITSU... KAKE...
HOTOHORI!!
RIGHT HERE.
MAYBE YOUR VOICE WILL REACH THEM.
HOTOHORI...
HOTOHORI!!

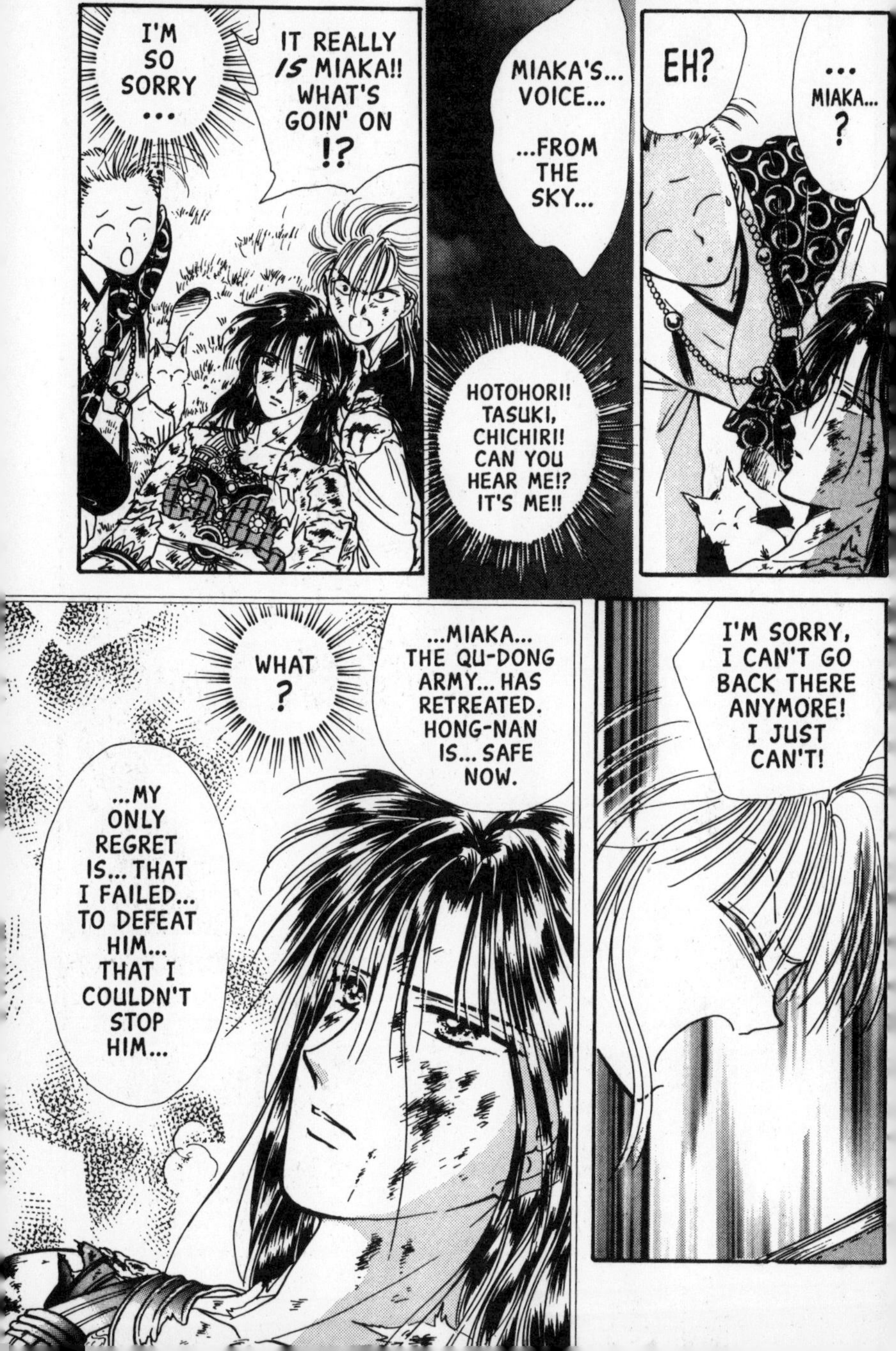
... MIAKA... ?
EH?
MIAKA'S... VOICE... ...FROM THE SKY...
HOTOHORI! TASUKI, CHICHIRI! CAN YOU HEAR ME!? IT'S ME!!
IT REALLY *IS* MIAKA!! WHAT'S GOIN' ON !?
I'M SO SORRY ...
I'M SORRY, I CAN'T GO BACK THERE ANYMORE! I JUST CAN'T!
...MIAKA... THE QU-DONG ARMY... HAS RETREATED. HONG-NAN IS... SAFE NOW.
WHAT ?
...MY ONLY REGRET IS... THAT I FAILED... TO DEFEAT HIM... THAT I COULDN'T STOP HIM...

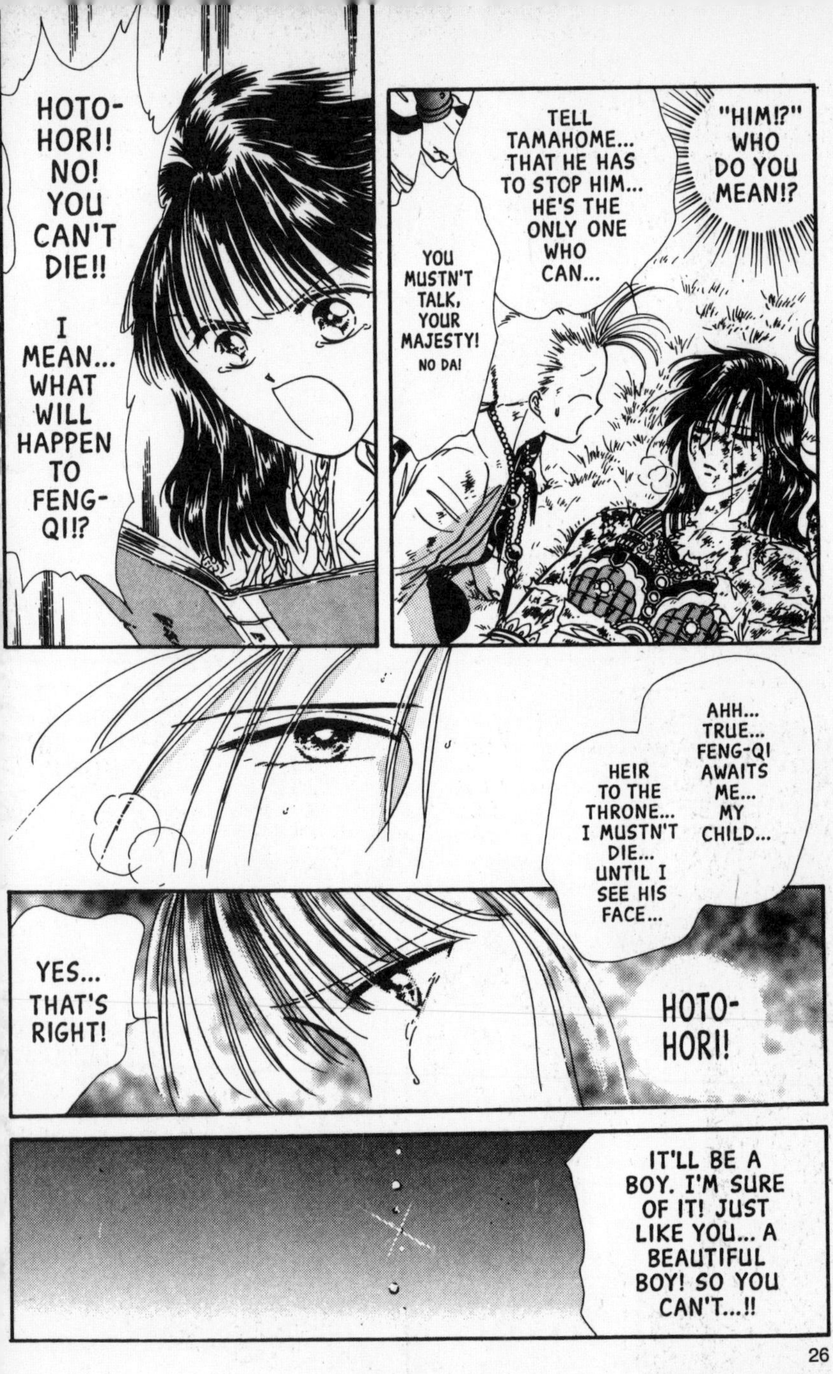
"HIM!?" WHO DO YOU MEAN!?
TELL TAMAHOME... THAT HE HAS TO STOP HIM... HE'S THE ONLY ONE WHO CAN...
YOU MUSTN'T TALK, YOUR MAJESTY! NO DA!
HOTO-HORI! NO! YOU CAN'T DIE!!
I MEAN... WHAT WILL HAPPEN TO FENG-QI!?
AHH... TRUE... FENG-QI AWAITS ME... MY CHILD...
HEIR TO THE THRONE... I MUSTN'T DIE... UNTIL I SEE HIS FACE...
HOTO-HORI!
YES... THAT'S RIGHT!
IT'LL BE A BOY. I'M SURE OF IT! JUST LIKE YOU... A BEAUTIFUL BOY! SO YOU CAN'T...!!

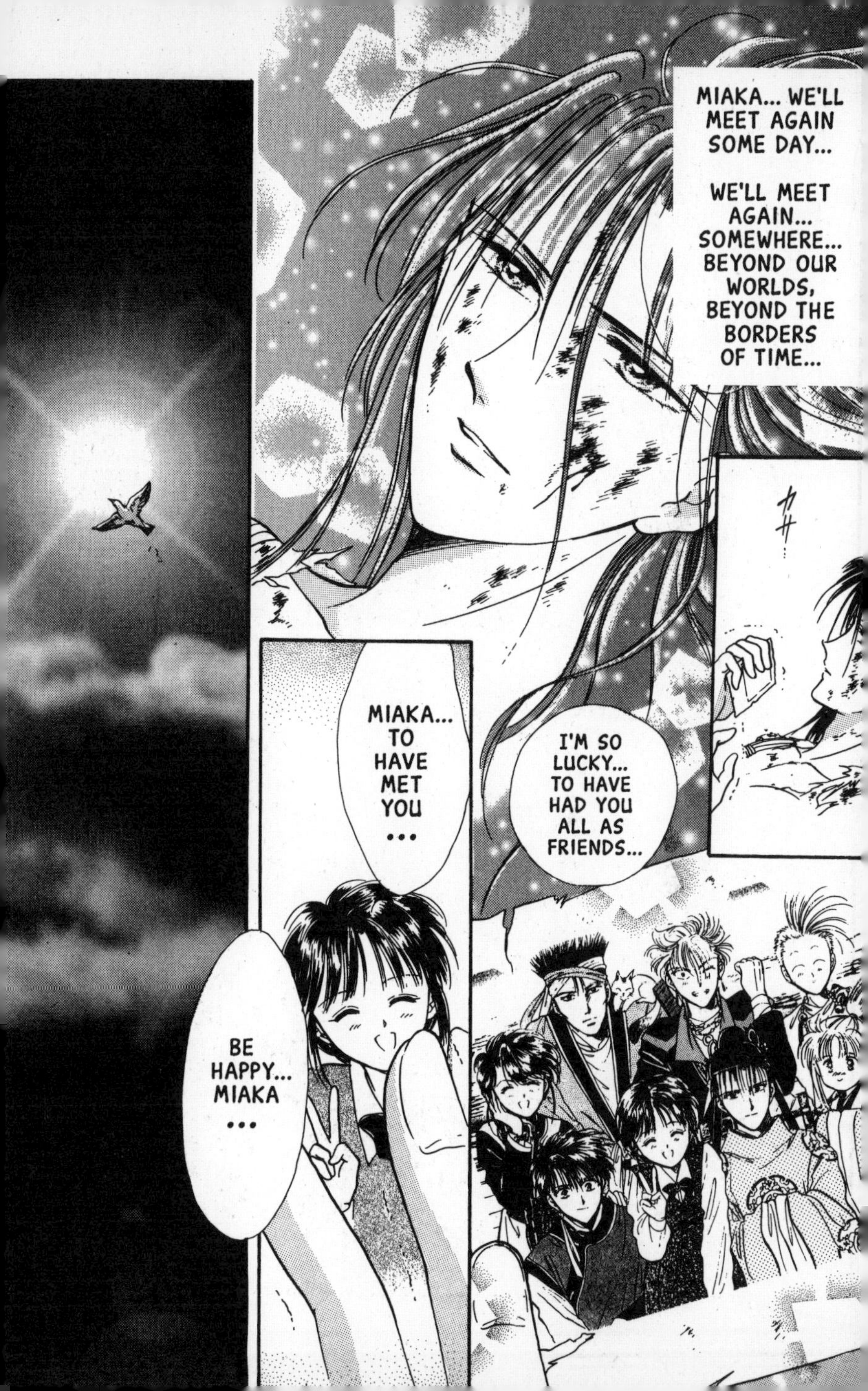
MIAKA... WE'LL MEET AGAIN SOME DAY...
WE'LL MEET AGAIN... SOMEWHERE... BEYOND OUR WORLDS, BEYOND THE BORDERS OF TIME...
I'M SO LUCKY... TO HAVE HAD YOU ALL AS FRIENDS...
MIAKA... TO HAVE MET YOU ...
BE HAPPY... MIAKA ...

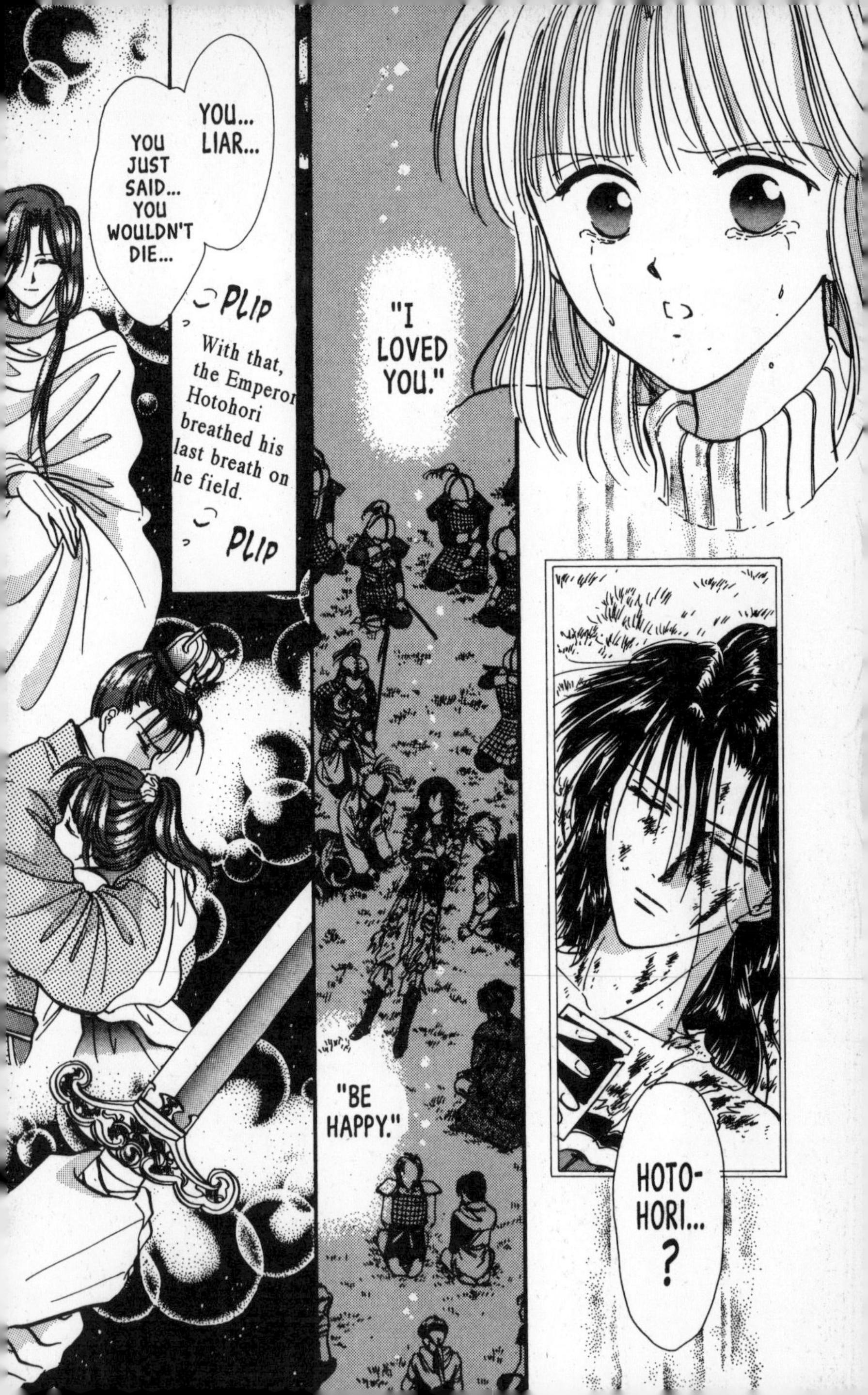
HOTO-HORI...?
"I LOVED YOU."
"BE HAPPY."
YOU... LIAR...
YOU JUST SAID... YOU WOULDN'T DIE...
PLIP
With that, the Emperor Hotohori breathed his last breath on he field.
PLIP

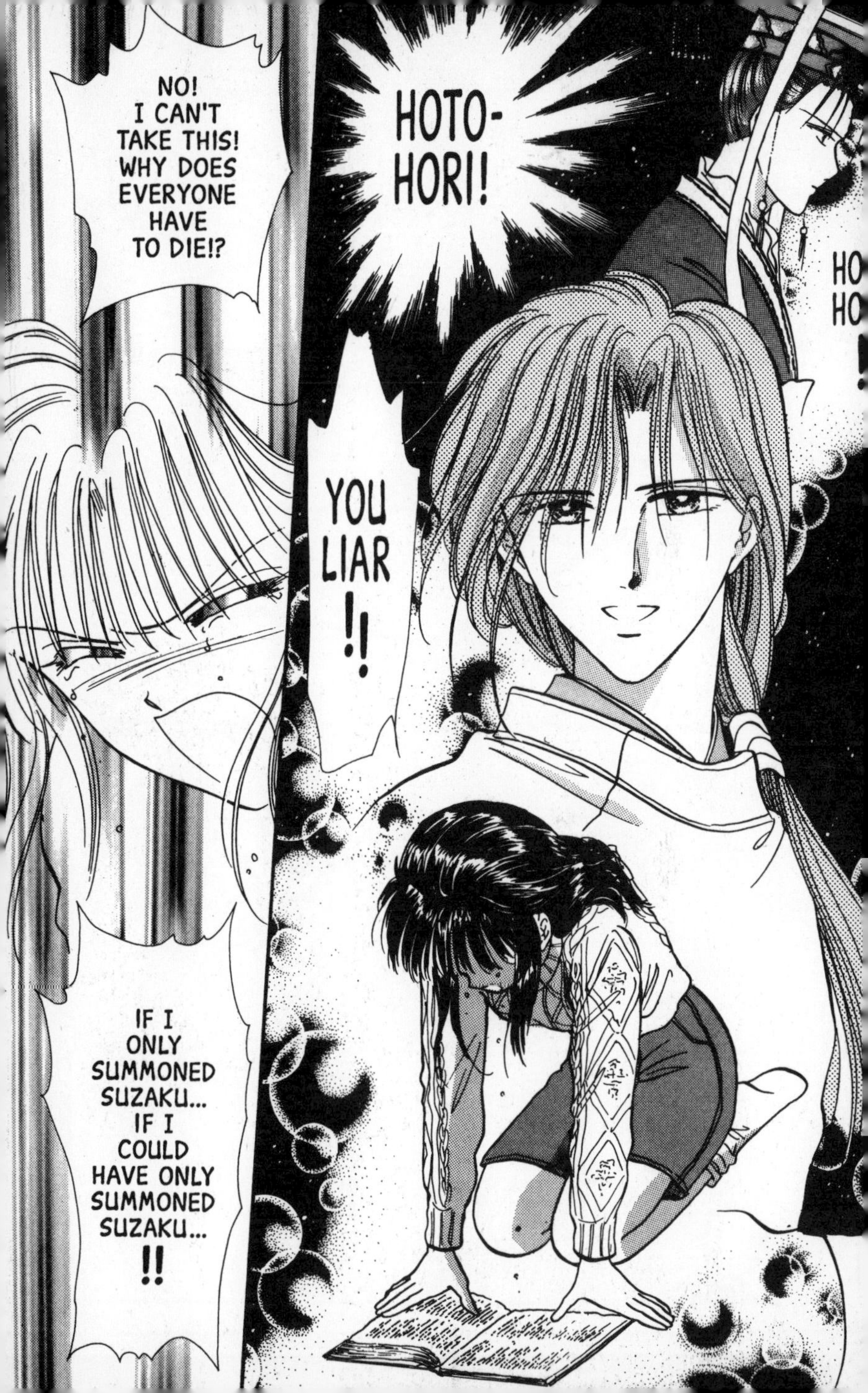
HOTO-HORI!
YOU LIAR !!
NO! I CAN'T TAKE THIS! WHY DOES EVERYONE HAVE TO DIE!?
IF I ONLY SUMMONED SUZAKU... IF I COULD HAVE ONLY SUMMONED SUZAKU... !!

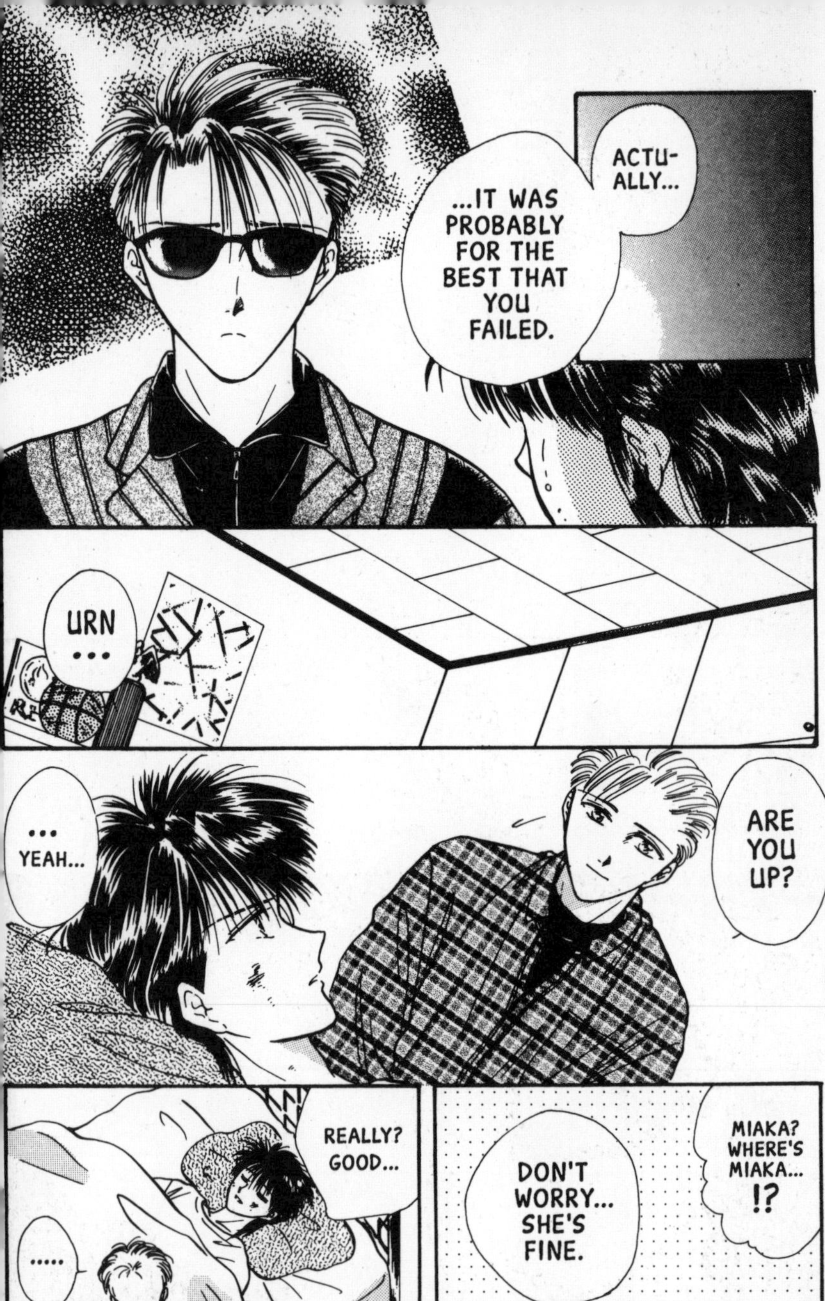
ACTU-ALLY...
...IT WAS PROBABLY FOR THE BEST THAT YOU FAILED.
URN ...
ARE YOU UP?
... YEAH...
MIAKA? WHERE'S MIAKA... !?
DON'T WORRY... SHE'S FINE.
REALLY? GOOD...
......

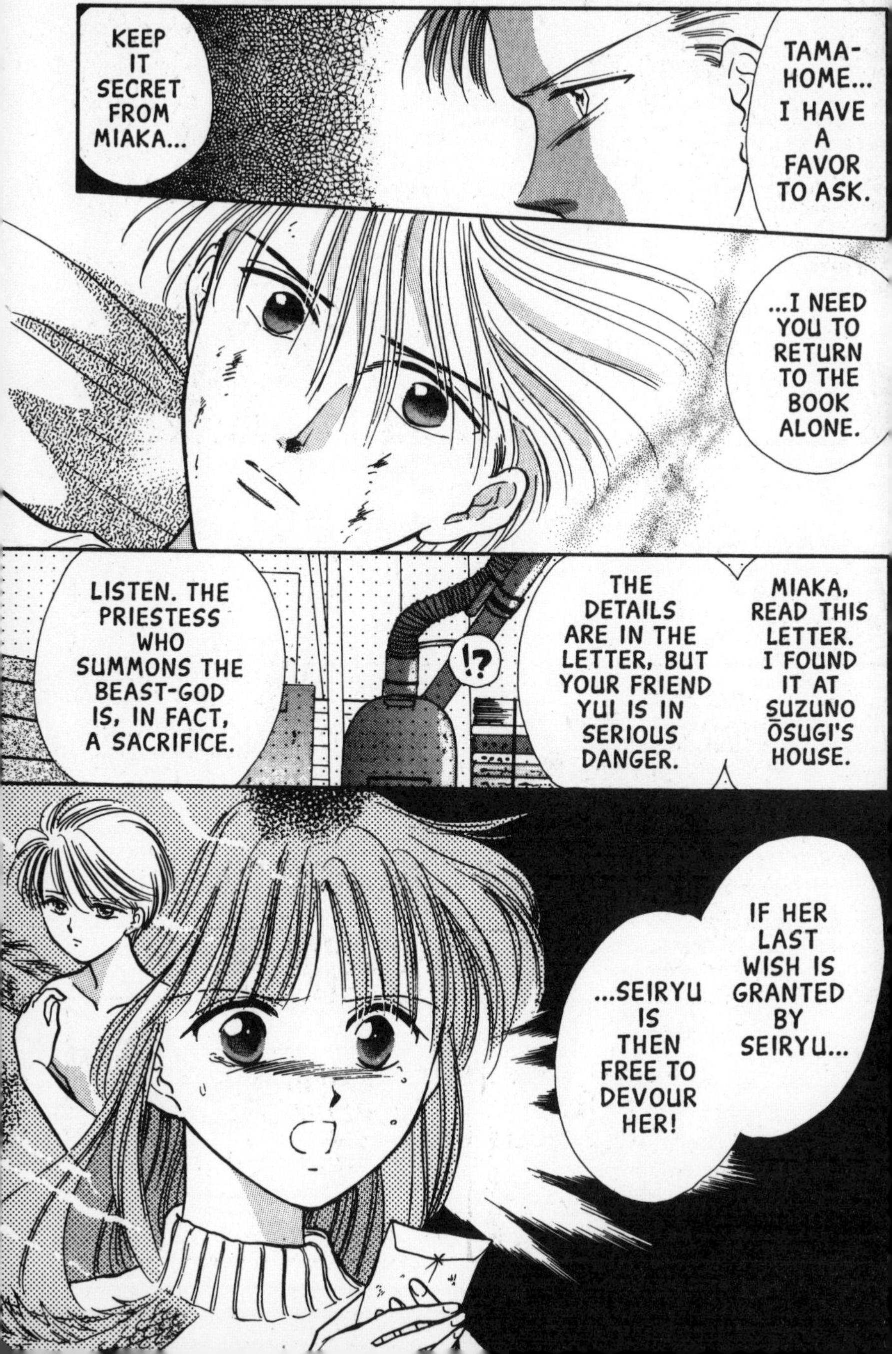
TAMA-HOME... I HAVE A FAVOR TO ASK.
KEEP IT SECRET FROM MIAKA...
...I NEED YOU TO RETURN TO THE BOOK ALONE.
MIAKA, READ THIS LETTER. I FOUND IT AT SUZUNO ŌSUGI'S HOUSE.
THE DETAILS ARE IN THE LETTER, BUT YOUR FRIEND YUI IS IN SERIOUS DANGER.
!?
LISTEN. THE PRIESTESS WHO SUMMONS THE BEAST-GOD IS, IN FACT, A SACRIFICE.
IF HER LAST WISH IS GRANTED BY SEIRYU...
...SEIRYU IS THEN FREE TO DEVOUR HER!

This is the only bonus page for this volume, so I crammed a lot in here. *(The page count was pretty tight.)*

- I heard that "Nakago, Shikkari Shinasai" ("Get it Together, Nakago") in the short-story anthology manga "Mint de Kiss Me" ("Kiss Me with Mint") was really popular! I drew that comic after my assistants and I came up with the basic concept. Consider it a longer version of the infamous Fushigi Akugi, Malicious Play series. *I really wouldn't want anyone to take it too seriously (it was a gag manga, after all), but I guess some readers did... Some of them actually got upset! I guess it shows how much they care about the characters, huh?*

- Previously, I included illustrations from readers without any permission. Regardless *(of whether or not I include them or not)*, keep on sending those portraits to me. A lot of fans apologize that their drawings don't look like mine. But actually, I prefer the unique ones that aren't trying to copy my style! *Don't worry about your skill level!!*

- By the way, I know everyone hates him, but I'm realizing how much I love Nakago! My editor was showing me the anime character designs (someone else is in charge of character design for the animation). I was admiring the designs, and the last one was Nakago! Suddenly, I felt this surge from deep inside (No, it wasn't vomit!) of emotion... I almost burst into tears. The thing that makes me happiest about the anime show is how he'll be animated and colored. *This kind of thing makes me blush a little.*

- Changing the subject, I received a lot of mail from readers pointing out how characters from a certain popular series appeared in the background of Fushigi Yûgi Vol. 8 and the second Prepubescence series Vol. 3. I wasn't responsible. My assistant, who is a big fan, drew those in. I haven't seen much recent anime, so I don't know much about it. *Sorry!*

- Have you had a chance to listen to CD Book 3? I love, love, love Yoko Ueno's "Deai no Page kara" ("From the Encounter Page"). Of course, the same applies to all the songs up until now, but this song (lyrically and melodically) is a perfect match!! She said that she wants to sing it at her concerts. It's such a pretty song. (I was just astounded how perfect it was for Chapter 77!)

THIS IS TURNING INTO A REGULAR FEATURE.

THANK YOU FOR THIS YEAR'S VALENTINE'S DAY GIFTS!!

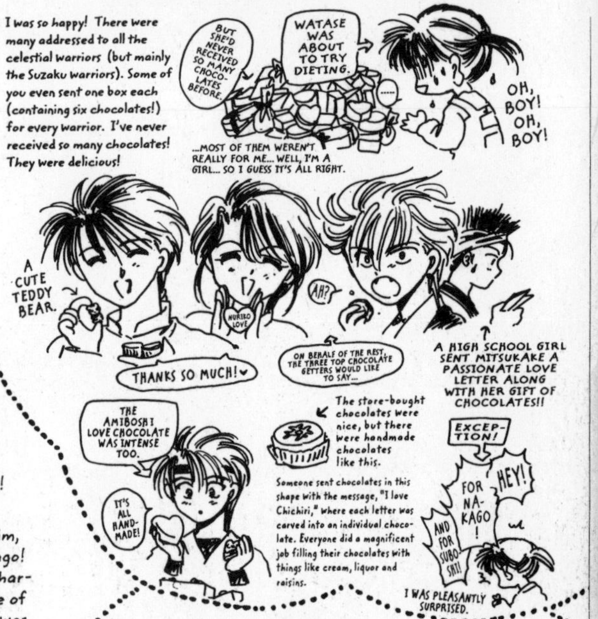
I was so happy! There were many addressed to all the celestial warriors (but mainly the Suzaku warriors). Some of you even sent one box each (containing six chocolates!) for every warrior. I've never received so many chocolates! They were delicious!
WATASE WAS ABOUT TO TRY DIETING.
BUT SHE'D NEVER RECEIVED SO MANY CHOCOLATES BEFORE.
OH, BOY! OH, BOY!
...MOST OF THEM WEREN'T REALLY FOR ME... WELL, I'M A GIRL... SO I GUESS IT'S ALL RIGHT.
A CUTE TEDDY BEAR.
AH?
HURIKO LOVE
THANKS SO MUCH!
ON BEHALF OF THE REST, THE THREE TOP CHOCOLATE GETTERS WOULD LIKE TO SAY...
A HIGH SCHOOL GIRL SENT MITSUKAKE A PASSIONATE LOVE LETTER ALONG WITH HER GIFT OF CHOCOLATES!!
THE AMIBOSHI LOVE CHOCOLATE WAS INTENSE TOO.
IT'S ALL HAND-MADE!
The store-bought chocolates were nice, but there were handmade chocolates like this.
Someone sent chocolates in this shape with the message, "I love Chichiri," where each letter was carved into an individual chocolate. Everyone did a magnificent job filling their chocolates with things like cream, liquor and raisins.
EXCEPTION!
HEY!
FOR NAKAGO!
AND FOR SUBOSHI!
I WAS PLEASANTLY SURPRISED.

BONUS!

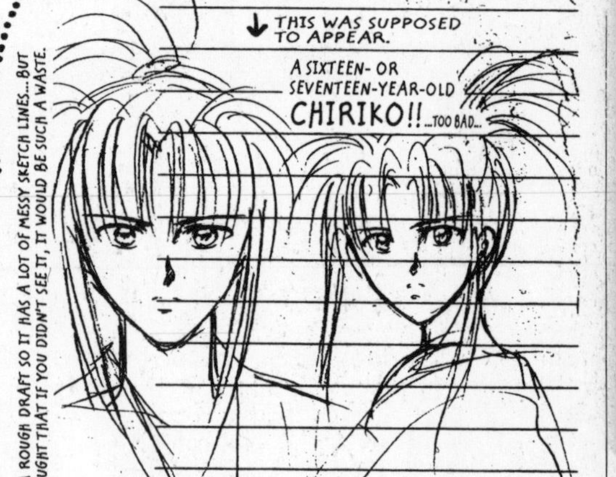
THIS WAS SUPPOSED TO APPEAR.
A SIXTEEN- OR SEVENTEEN-YEAR-OLD CHIRIKO!! ...TOO BAD...
IT'S A ROUGH DRAFT SO IT HAS A LOT OF MESSY SKETCH LINES... BUT I THOUGHT THAT IF YOU DIDN'T SEE IT, IT WOULD BE SUCH A WASTE.

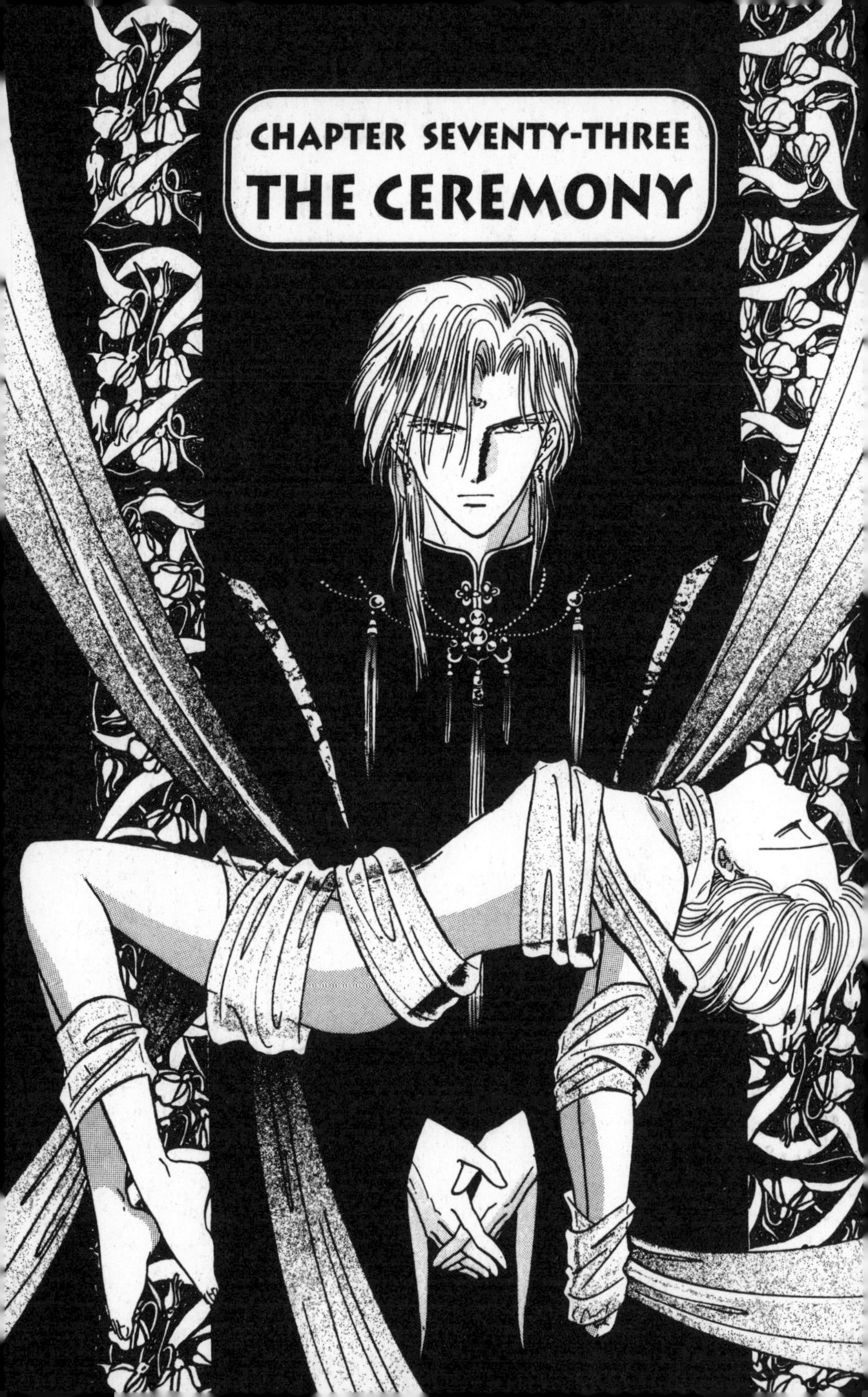
CHAPTER SEVENTY-THREE
THE CEREMONY

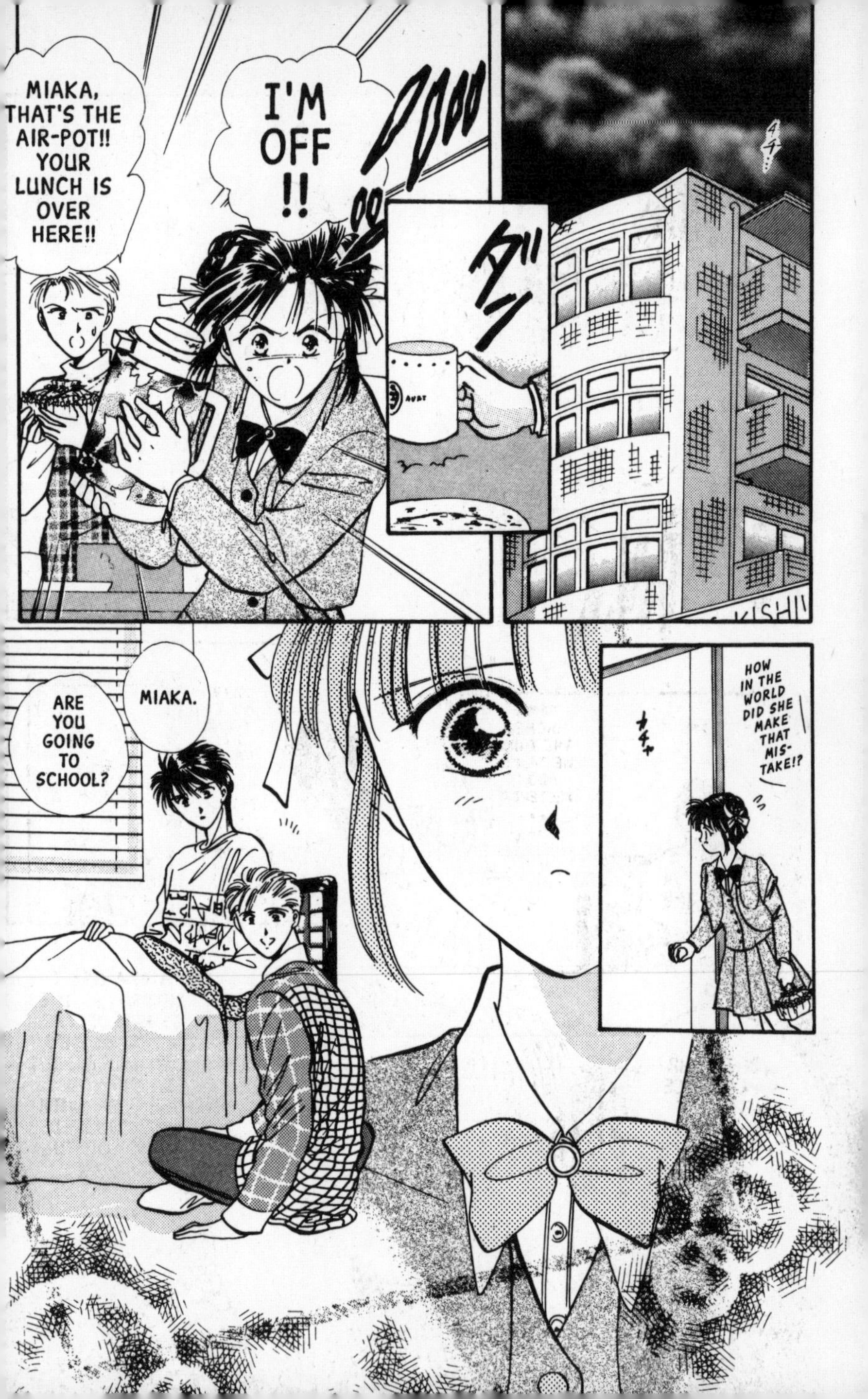
I'M OFF !!
MIAKA, THAT'S THE AIR-POT!! YOUR LUNCH IS OVER HERE!!
HOW IN THE WORLD DID SHE MAKE THAT MIS-TAKE!?
MIAKA.
ARE YOU GOING TO SCHOOL?

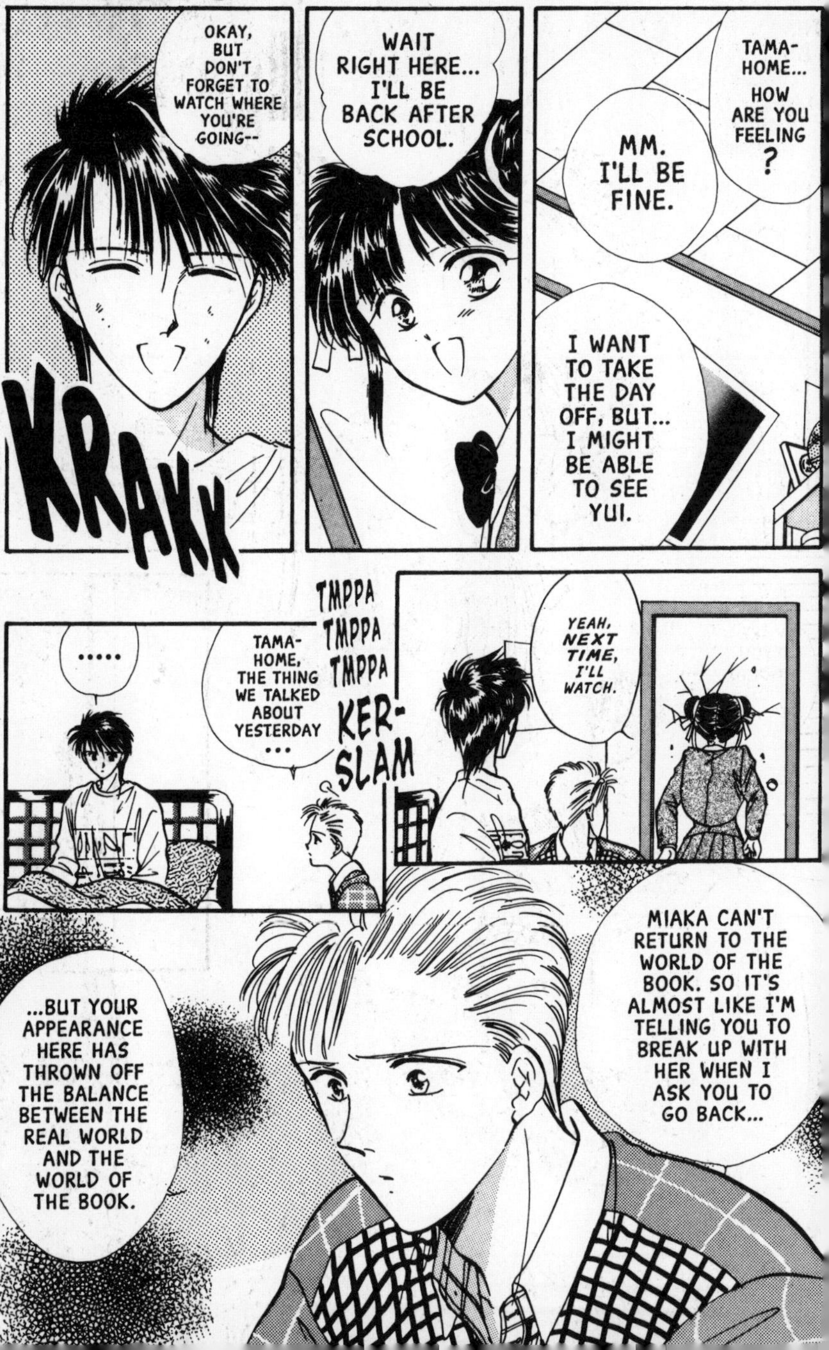
TAMA-HOME... HOW ARE YOU FEELING?
MM. I'LL BE FINE.
I WANT TO TAKE THE DAY OFF, BUT... I MIGHT BE ABLE TO SEE YUI.
WAIT RIGHT HERE... I'LL BE BACK AFTER SCHOOL.
OKAY, BUT DON'T FORGET TO WATCH WHERE YOU'RE GOING--
KRAKK
YEAH, NEXT TIME, I'LL WATCH.
TMPPA TMPPA TMPPA
KER-SLAM
TAMA-HOME, THE THING WE TALKED ABOUT YESTERDAY...
.....
MIAKA CAN'T RETURN TO THE WORLD OF THE BOOK. SO IT'S ALMOST LIKE I'M TELLING YOU TO BREAK UP WITH HER WHEN I ASK YOU TO GO BACK...
...BUT YOUR APPEARANCE HERE HAS THROWN OFF THE BALANCE BETWEEN THE REAL WORLD AND THE WORLD OF THE BOOK.

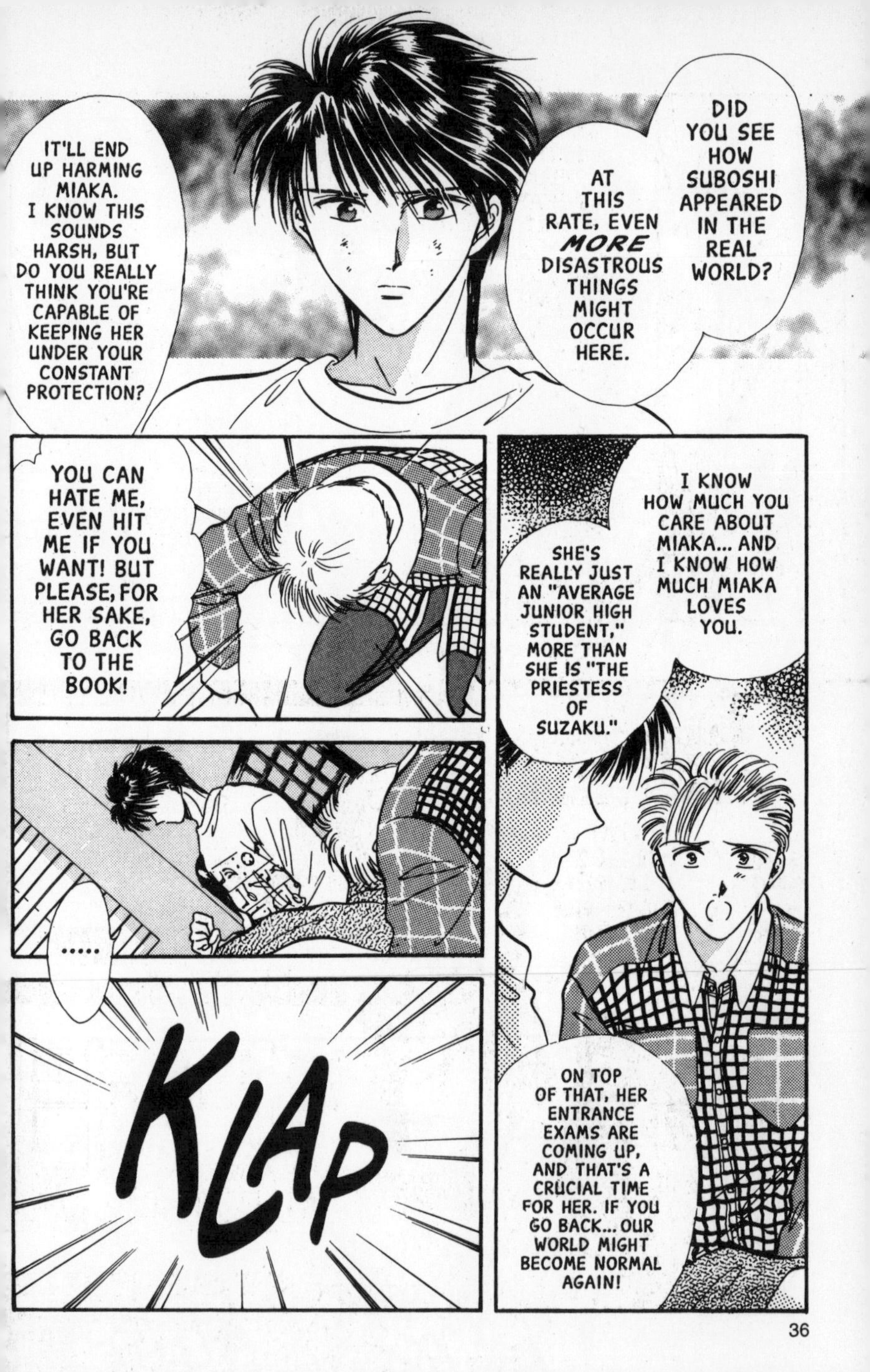
DID YOU SEE HOW SUBOSHI APPEARED IN THE REAL WORLD?
AT THIS RATE, EVEN *MORE* DISASTROUS THINGS MIGHT OCCUR HERE.
IT'LL END UP HARMING MIAKA. I KNOW THIS SOUNDS HARSH, BUT DO YOU REALLY THINK YOU'RE CAPABLE OF KEEPING HER UNDER YOUR CONSTANT PROTECTION?
I KNOW HOW MUCH YOU CARE ABOUT MIAKA... AND I KNOW HOW MUCH MIAKA LOVES YOU.
SHE'S REALLY JUST AN "AVERAGE JUNIOR HIGH STUDENT," MORE THAN SHE IS "THE PRIESTESS OF SUZAKU."
ON TOP OF THAT, HER ENTRANCE EXAMS ARE COMING UP, AND THAT'S A CRUCIAL TIME FOR HER. IF YOU GO BACK... OUR WORLD MIGHT BECOME NORMAL AGAIN!
YOU CAN HATE ME, EVEN HIT ME IF YOU WANT! BUT PLEASE, FOR HER SAKE, GO BACK TO THE BOOK!
.....
KLAP

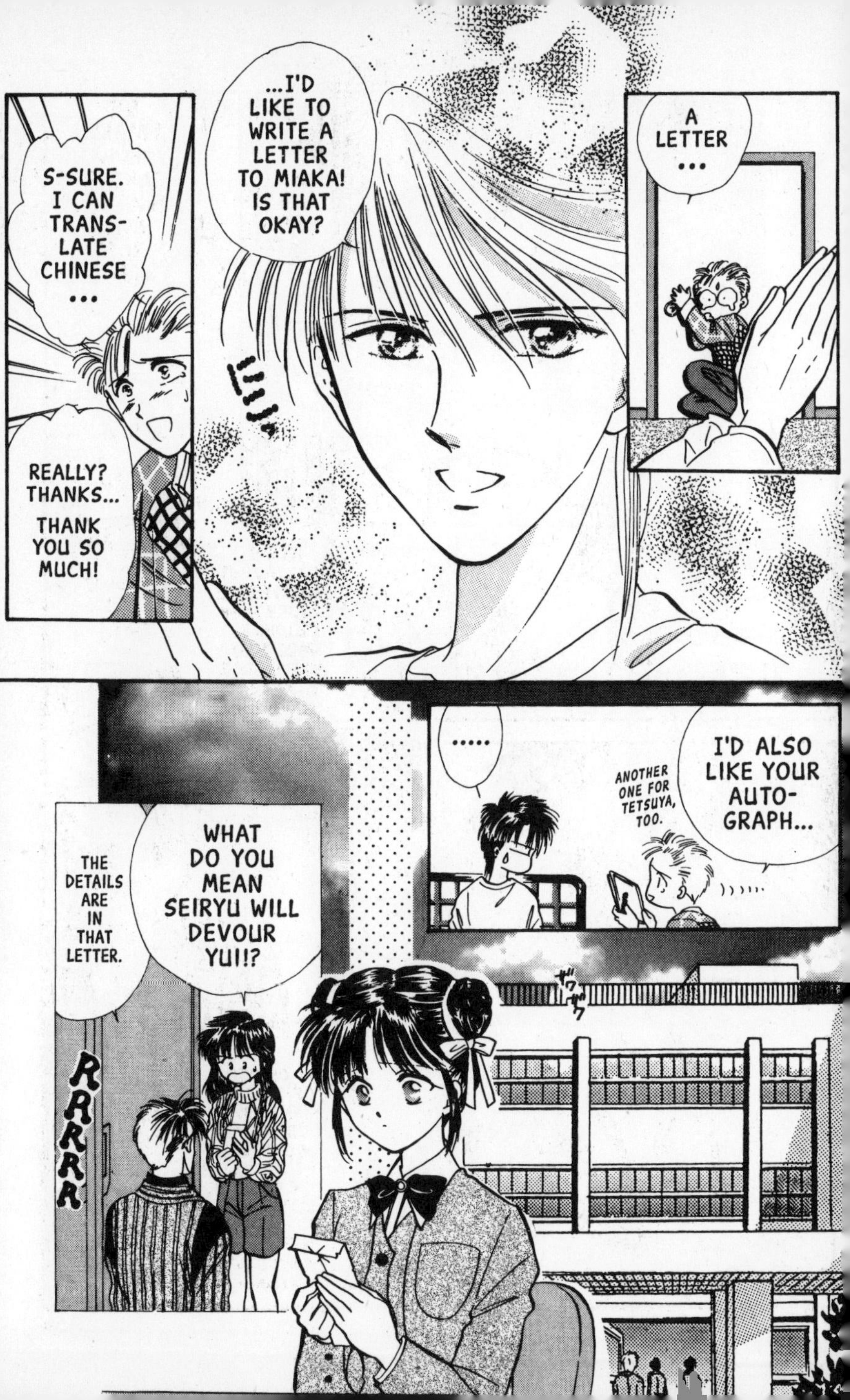
A LETTER ...
...I'D LIKE TO WRITE A LETTER TO MIAKA! IS THAT OKAY?
S-SURE. I CAN TRANS-LATE CHINESE ...
REALLY? THANKS...
THANK YOU SO MUCH!
I'D ALSO LIKE YOUR AUTO-GRAPH...
ANOTHER ONE FOR TETSUYA, TOO.
.....
WHAT DO YOU MEAN SEIRYU WILL DEVOUR YUI!?
THE DETAILS ARE IN THAT LETTER.
RRRRR

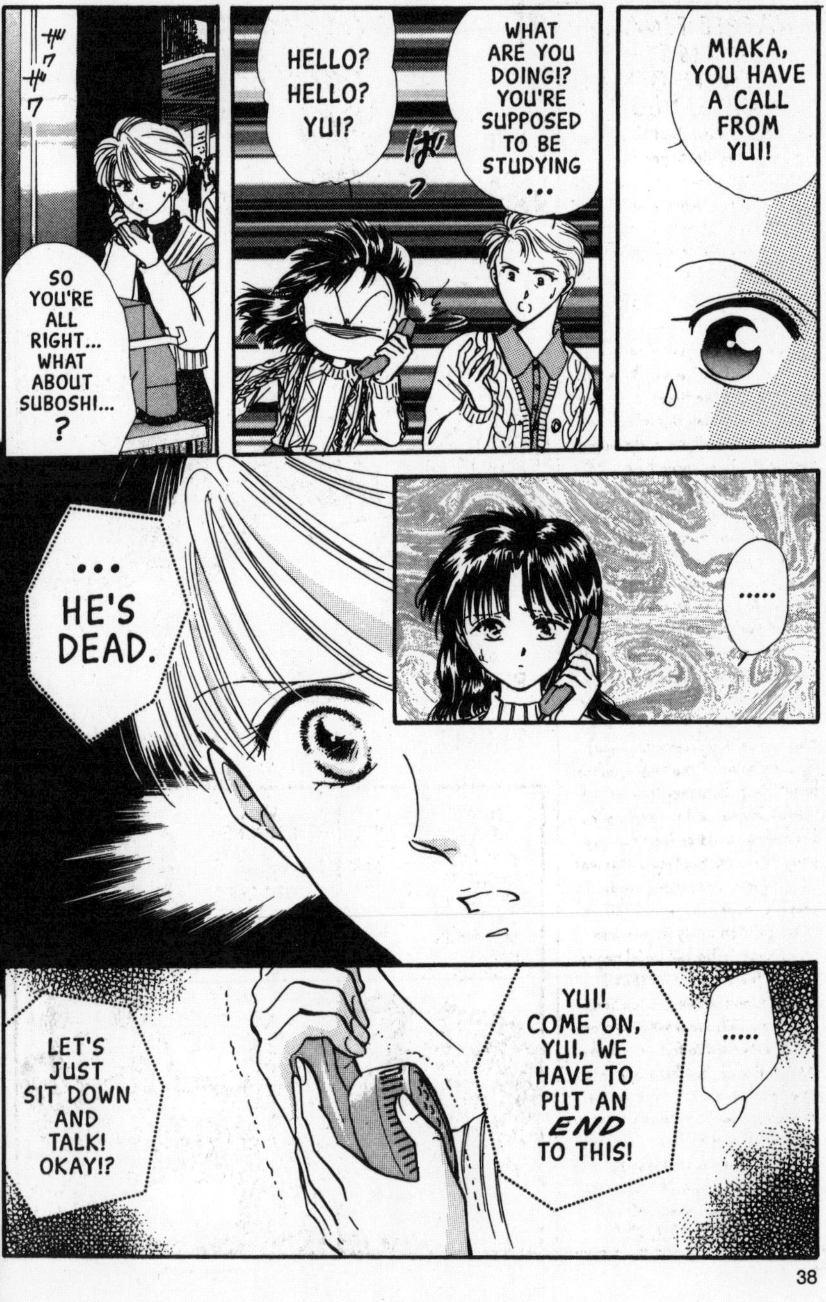
MIAKA, YOU HAVE A CALL FROM YUI!
WHAT ARE YOU DOING!? YOU'RE SUPPOSED TO BE STUDYING ...
ばっ
HELLO? HELLO? YUI?
ザワザワ
SO YOU'RE ALL RIGHT... WHAT ABOUT SUBOSHI... ?
.....
... HE'S DEAD.
.....
YUI! COME ON, YUI, WE HAVE TO PUT AN *END* TO THIS!
LET'S JUST SIT DOWN AND TALK! OKAY!?

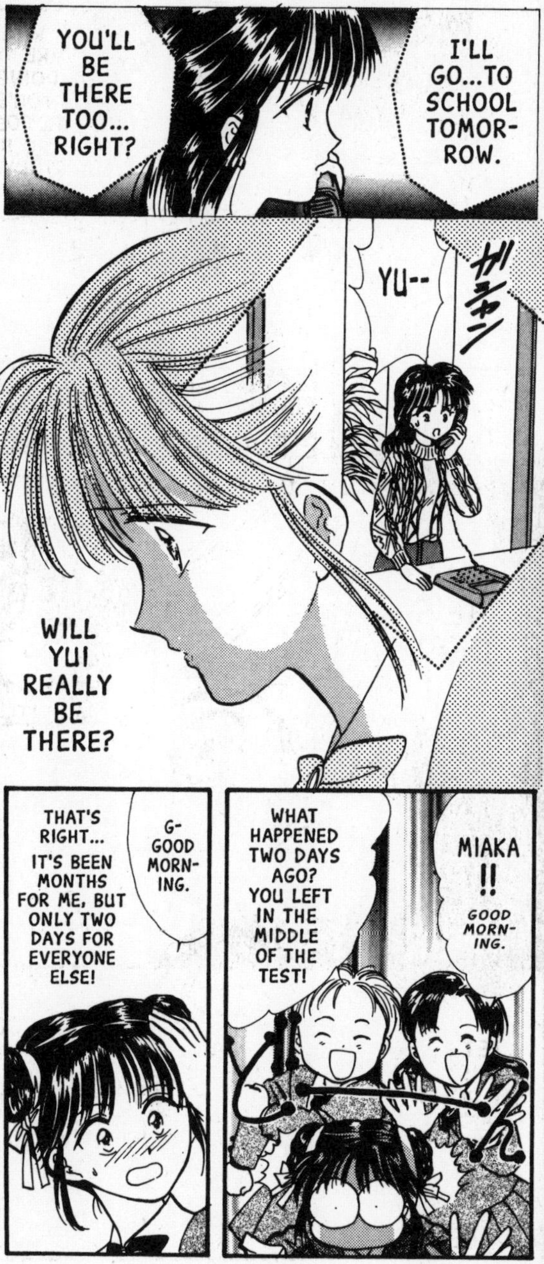
I'LL GO...TO SCHOOL TOMOR-ROW.
YOU'LL BE THERE TOO... RIGHT?
YU--
ガチャン
WILL YUI REALLY BE THERE?
MIAKA!!
GOOD MORN-ING.
WHAT HAPPENED TWO DAYS AGO? YOU LEFT IN THE MIDDLE OF THE TEST!
G-GOOD MORN-ING.
THAT'S RIGHT... IT'S BEEN MONTHS FOR ME, BUT ONLY TWO DAYS FOR EVERYONE ELSE!

WATASE FINALLY SPILLS IT! THE TRUTH BEHIND FUSHIGI YŪGI!!

...by which I mean that I'd like to cover some in-depth personal material this time round. Oh! With regard to Yui, I talked about her in my interview in the Fushigi Yūgi Artbook (available in English!), so please refer to that. *Says Watase as she pushes the book on her readers.* "Fushigi" was a problem manga that actually made me sick (case of nerves?) when it began. Back then, my editor (at the time) said, "To be blunt, I don't think this will do very well." I still recall it clearly. In fact, he said it two or three times. It was a shock, but at the same time, I also thought that it made sense. I mean, it was serialized in a shōjo manga magazine where school dramas and love stories were right on target. Besides, there were other gifted artists working on inventive stories while I was hardly three years into my career as a manga artist. A rookie with little talent in drawing and story structure (some things never change). (笑) On top of that, my previous serial "Prepubescence" was a school drama, so it seemed unlikely those fans would go for a fantasy story. I realize that my editor was warning me in advance in order to prepare me for the serial's failure. But I got sick to my stomach so many times after the serial began. I'd feel so nauseous that I couldn't look at the publications. It's very painful to work on a story that's expected to fail even before it's serialized! But I really wanted to do it. I wanted to take on the challenge. So if anyone's surprised about this story's massive success, it's me! I was half joking when I said it would go past 10 volumes. Try and you shall succeed! Ha ha ha ha ha! ♫♫ ♫♫

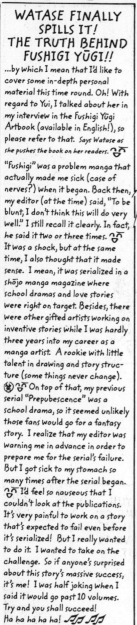

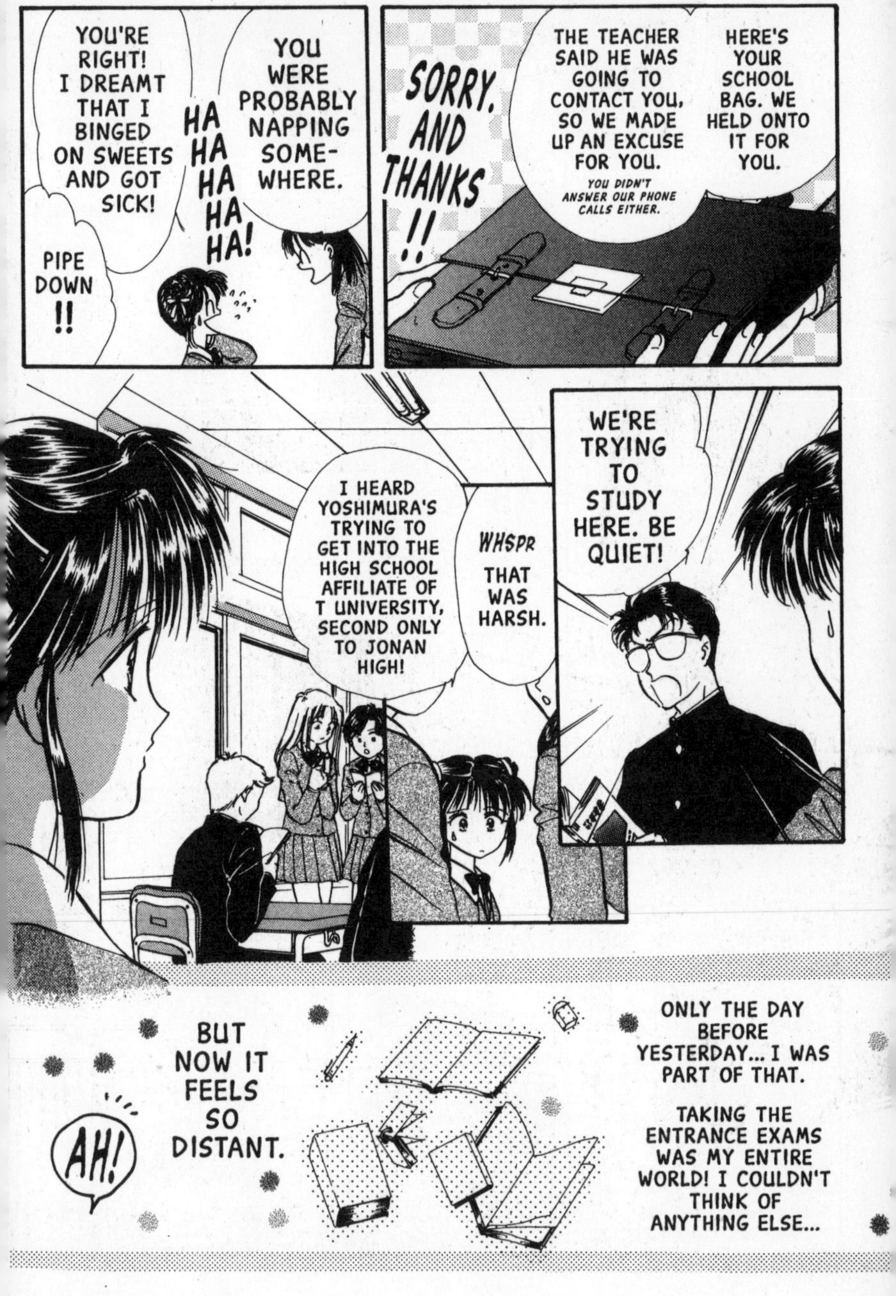
HERE'S YOUR SCHOOL BAG. WE HELD ONTO IT FOR YOU.
THE TEACHER SAID HE WAS GOING TO CONTACT YOU, SO WE MADE UP AN EXCUSE FOR YOU.
YOU DIDN'T ANSWER OUR PHONE CALLS EITHER.
SORRY, AND THANKS!!
YOU WERE PROBABLY NAPPING SOME-WHERE.
HA HA HA HA HA!
YOU'RE RIGHT! I DREAMT THAT I BINGED ON SWEETS AND GOT SICK!
PIPE DOWN!!
WE'RE TRYING TO STUDY HERE. BE QUIET!
WHSPR
THAT WAS HARSH.
I HEARD YOSHIMURA'S TRYING TO GET INTO THE HIGH SCHOOL AFFILIATE OF T UNIVERSITY, SECOND ONLY TO JONAN HIGH!
ONLY THE DAY BEFORE YESTERDAY... I WAS PART OF THAT.
TAKING THE ENTRANCE EXAMS WAS MY ENTIRE WORLD! I COULDN'T THINK OF ANYTHING ELSE...
BUT NOW IT FEELS SO DISTANT.
AH!

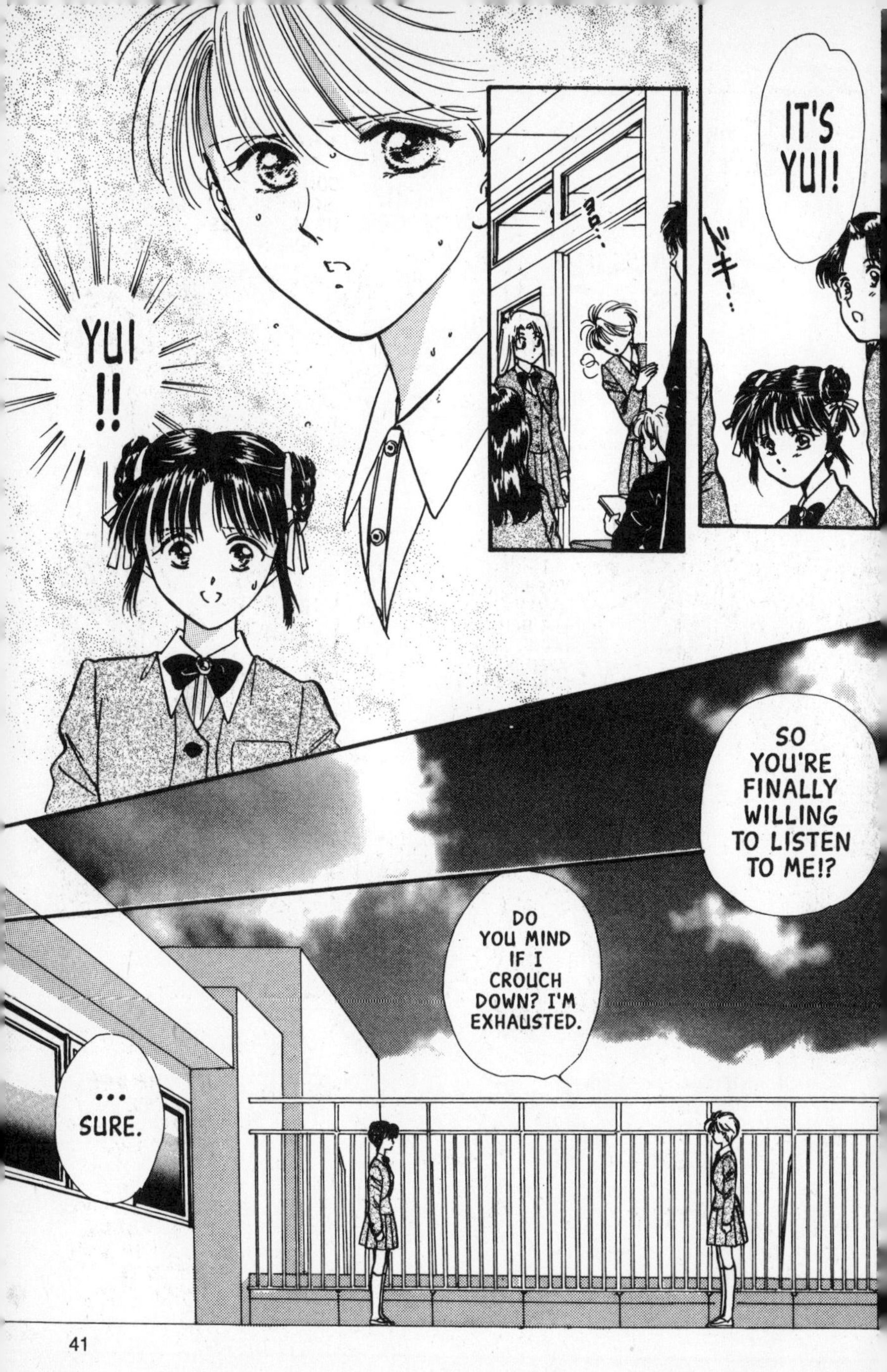
IT'S YUI!
ドキ…
ヨロ…
YUI !!
SO YOU'RE FINALLY WILLING TO LISTEN TO ME!?
DO YOU MIND IF I CROUCH DOWN? I'M EXHAUSTED.
... SURE.

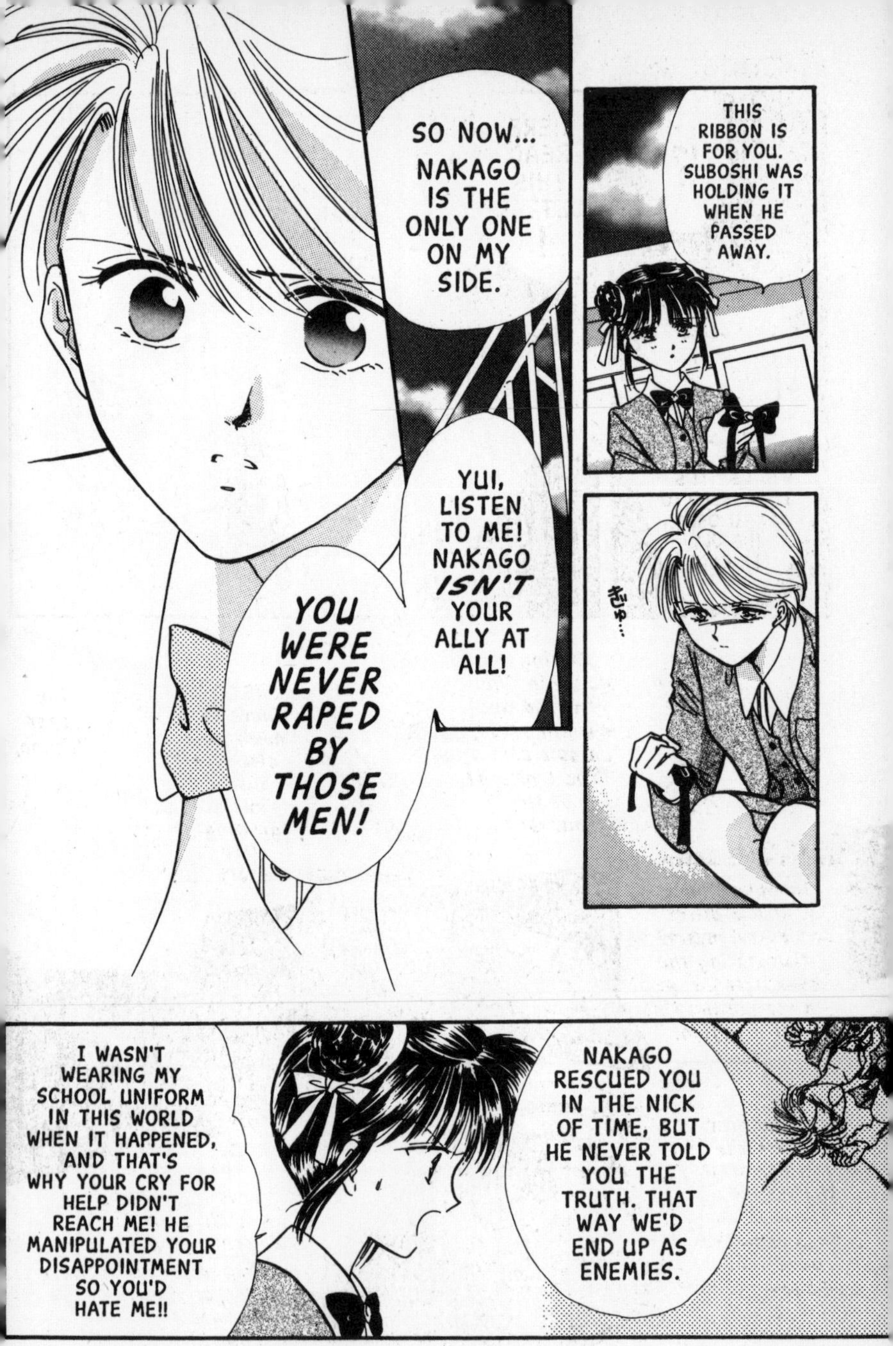
THIS RIBBON IS FOR YOU. SUBOSHI WAS HOLDING IT WHEN HE PASSED AWAY.
ぎゅ…
SO NOW... NAKAGO IS THE ONLY ONE ON MY SIDE.
YUI, LISTEN TO ME! NAKAGO *ISN'T* YOUR ALLY AT ALL!
YOU WERE NEVER RAPED BY THOSE MEN!
NAKAGO RESCUED YOU IN THE NICK OF TIME, BUT HE NEVER TOLD YOU THE TRUTH. THAT WAY WE'D END UP AS ENEMIES.
I WASN'T WEARING MY SCHOOL UNIFORM IN THIS WORLD WHEN IT HAPPENED, AND THAT'S WHY YOUR CRY FOR HELP DIDN'T REACH ME! HE MANIPULATED YOUR DISAPPOINTMENT SO YOU'D HATE ME!!

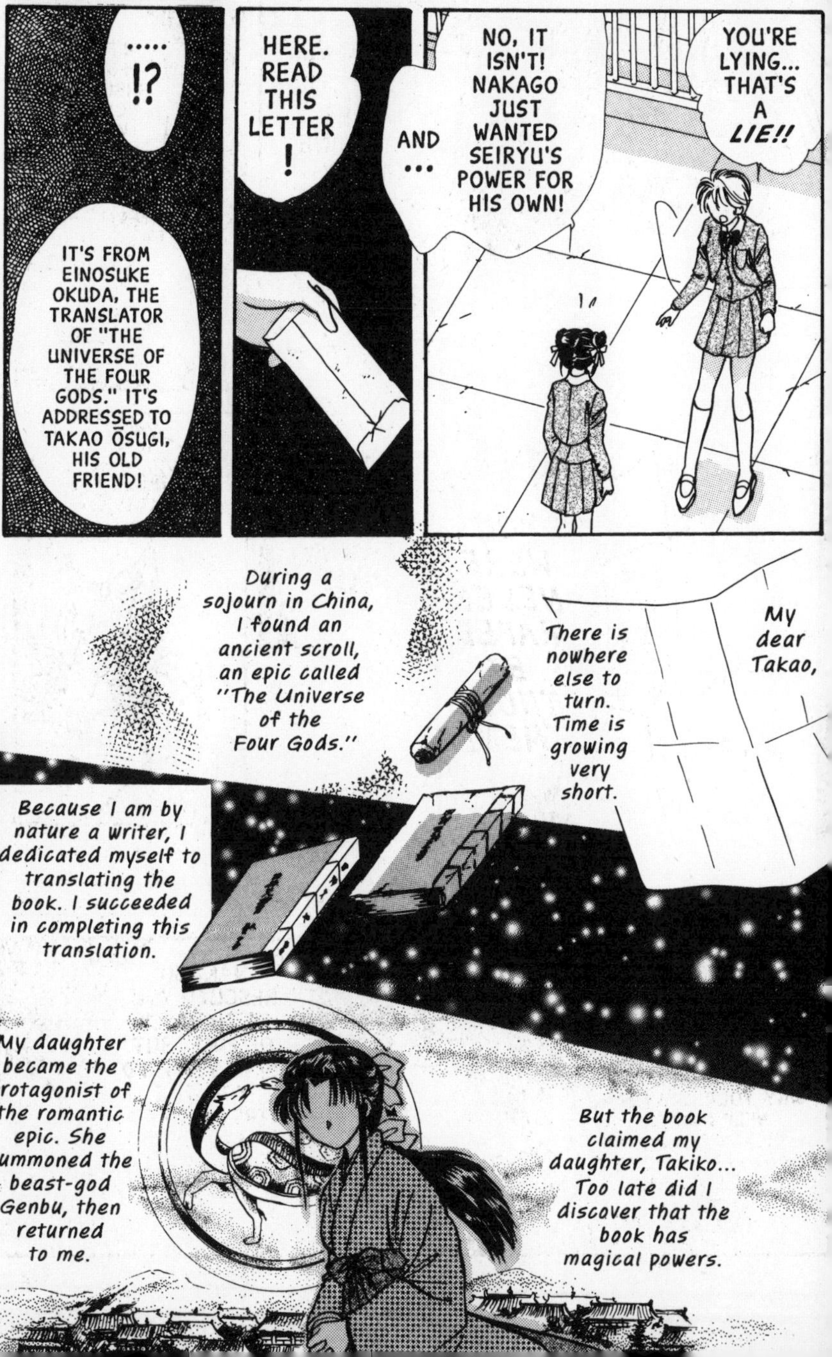
YOU'RE LYING... THAT'S A LIE!!
NO, IT ISN'T! NAKAGO JUST WANTED SEIRYU'S POWER FOR HIS OWN!
AND ...
HERE. READ THIS LETTER!
..... !?
IT'S FROM EINOSUKE OKUDA, THE TRANSLATOR OF "THE UNIVERSE OF THE FOUR GODS." IT'S ADDRESSED TO TAKAO ŌSUGI, HIS OLD FRIEND!
My dear Takao,
There is nowhere else to turn. Time is growing very short.
During a sojourn in China, I found an ancient scroll, an epic called "The Universe of the Four Gods."
Because I am by nature a writer, I dedicated myself to translating the book. I succeeded in completing this translation.
But the book claimed my daughter, Takiko... Too late did I discover that the book has magical powers.
My daughter became the protagonist of the romantic epic. She summoned the beast-god Genbu, then returned to me.

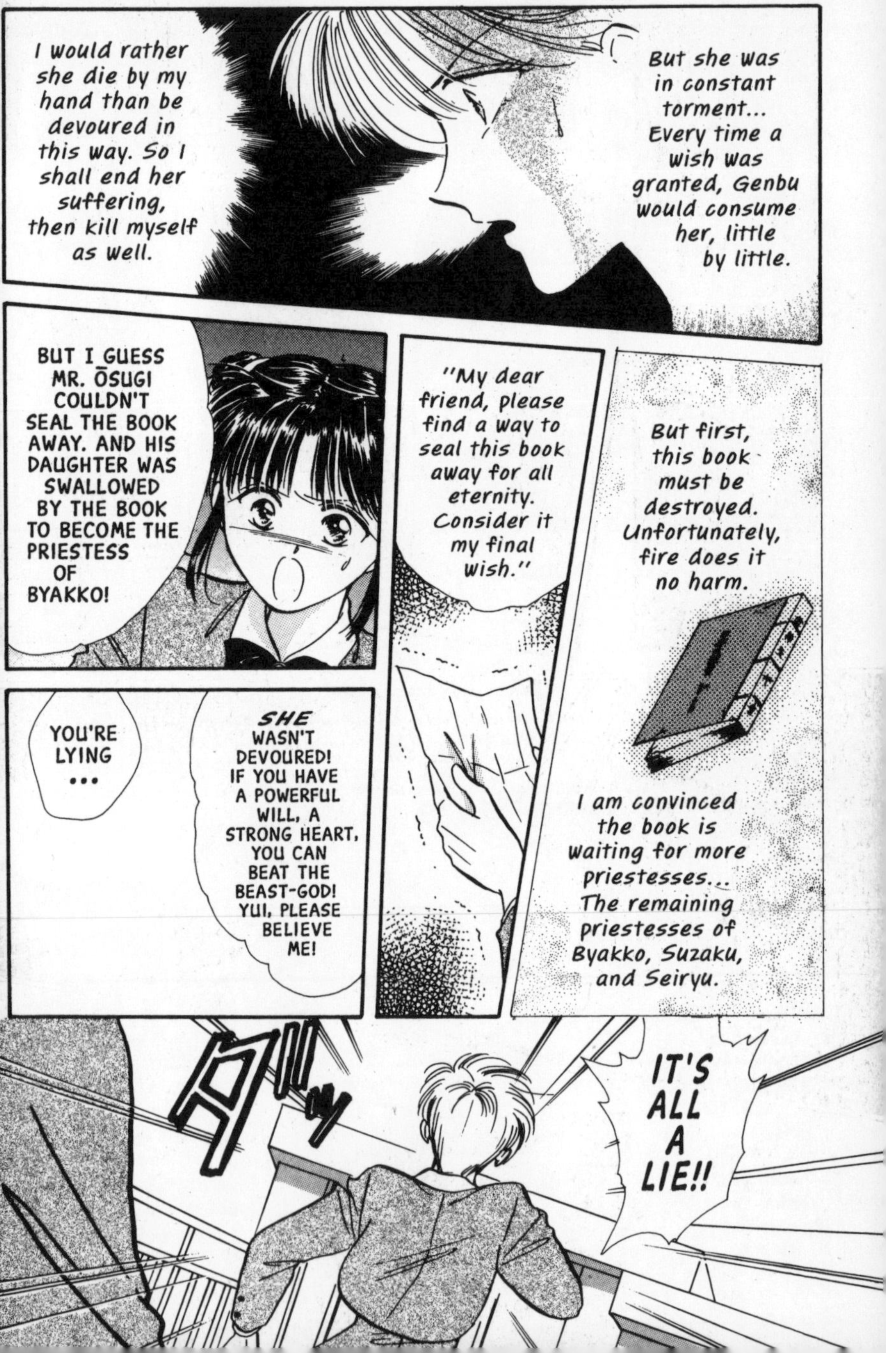
But she was in constant torment... Every time a wish was granted, Genbu would consume her, little by little.
I would rather she die by my hand than be devoured in this way. So I shall end her suffering, then kill myself as well.
But first, this book must be destroyed. Unfortunately, fire does it no harm.
I am convinced the book is waiting for more priestesses... The remaining priestesses of Byakko, Suzaku, and Seiryu.
"My dear friend, please find a way to seal this book away for all eternity. Consider it my final wish."
BUT I GUESS MR. ŌSUGI COULDN'T SEAL THE BOOK AWAY. AND HIS DAUGHTER WAS SWALLOWED BY THE BOOK TO BECOME THE PRIESTESS OF BYAKKO!
SHE WASN'T DEVOURED! IF YOU HAVE A POWERFUL WILL, A STRONG HEART, YOU CAN BEAT THE BEAST-GOD! YUI, PLEASE BELIEVE ME!
YOU'RE LYING...
IT'S ALL A LIE!!

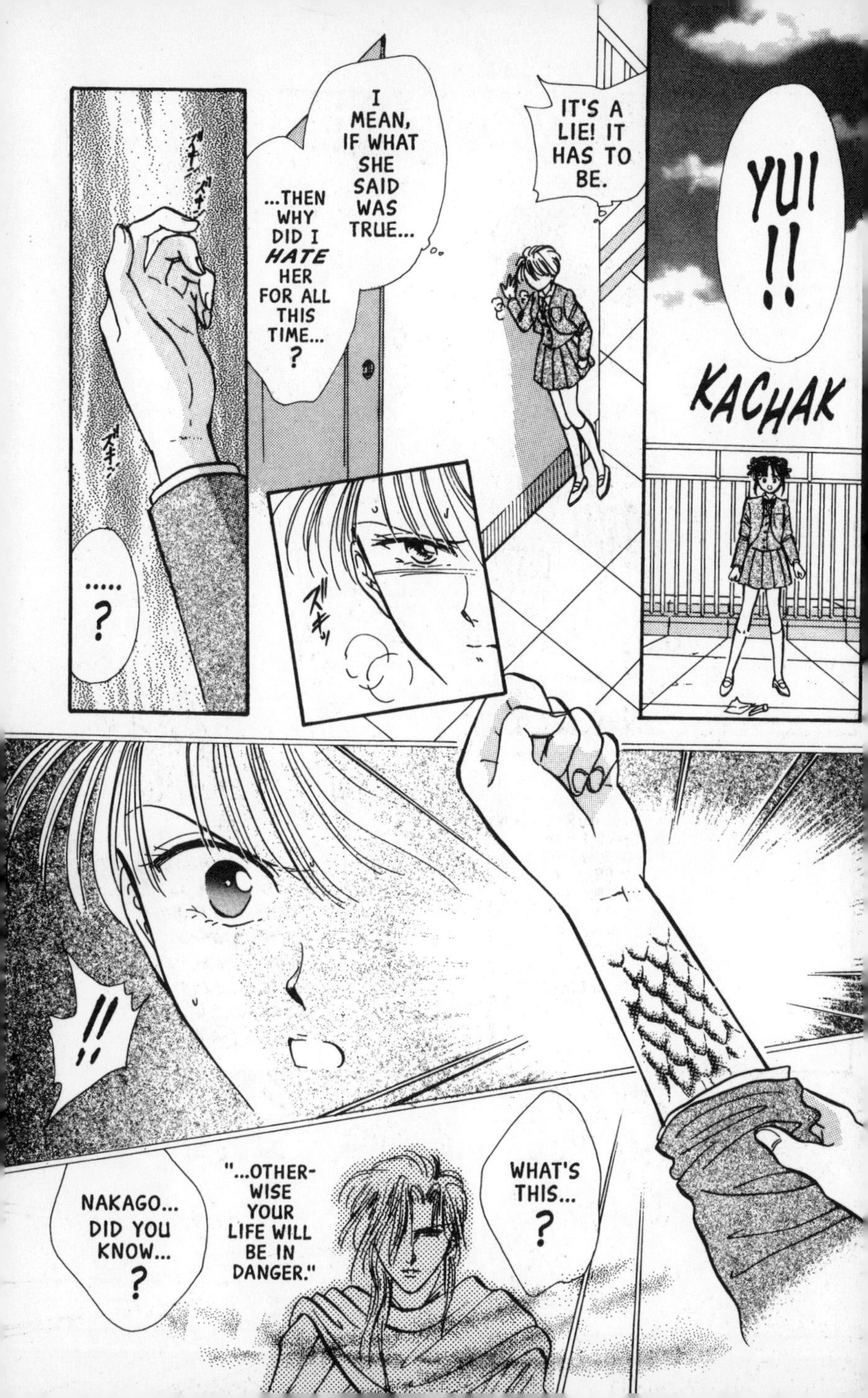
YUI!!
KACHAK
IT'S A LIE! IT HAS TO BE.
I MEAN, IF WHAT SHE SAID WAS TRUE...
...THEN WHY DID I HATE HER FOR ALL THIS TIME...?
.....?
!!
WHAT'S THIS...?
"...OTHER-WISE YOUR LIFE WILL BE IN DANGER."
NAKAGO... DID YOU KNOW...?

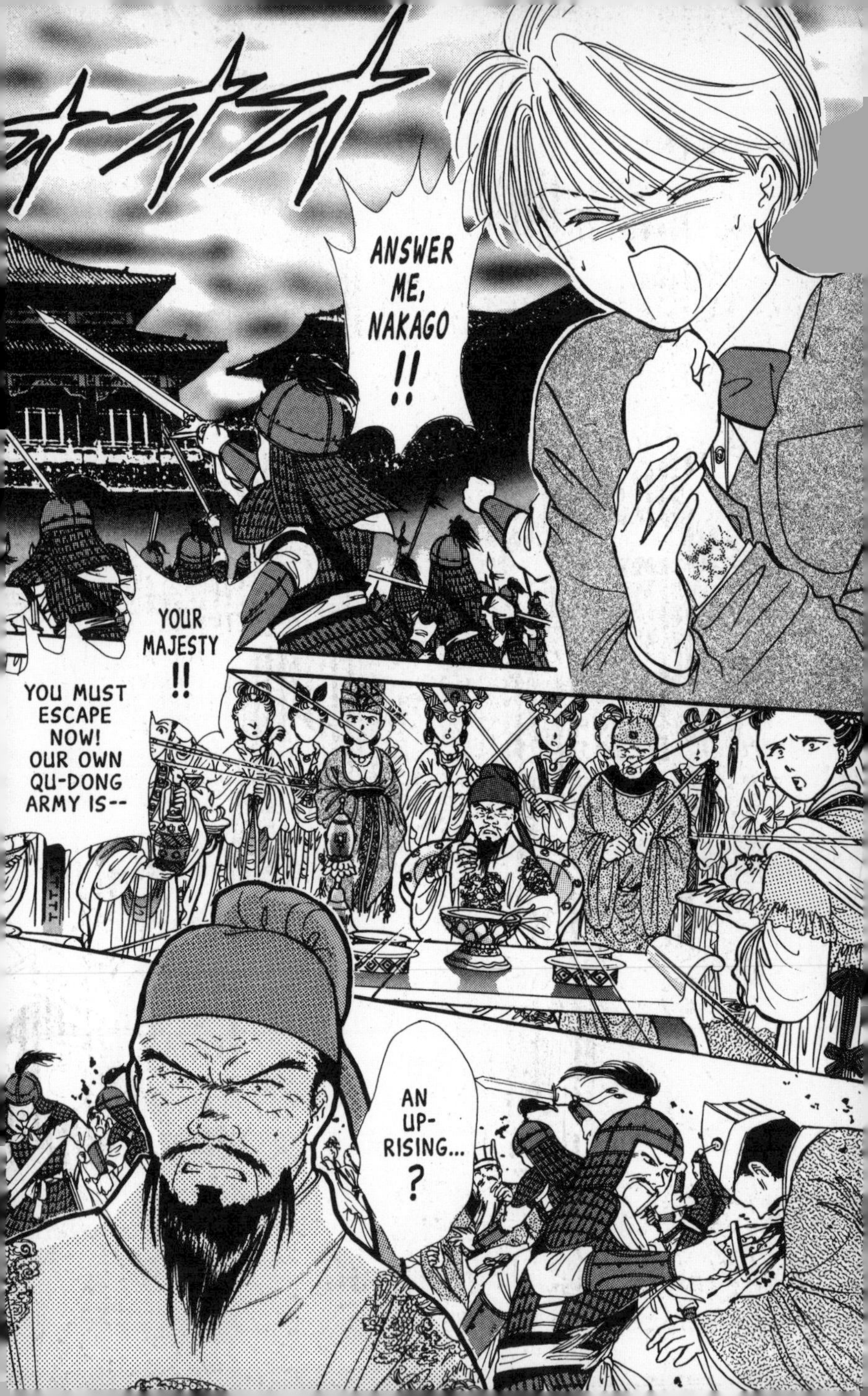
ANSWER ME, NAKAGO!!
YOUR MAJESTY!!
YOU MUST ESCAPE NOW! OUR OWN QU-DONG ARMY IS--
AN UP-RISING...?

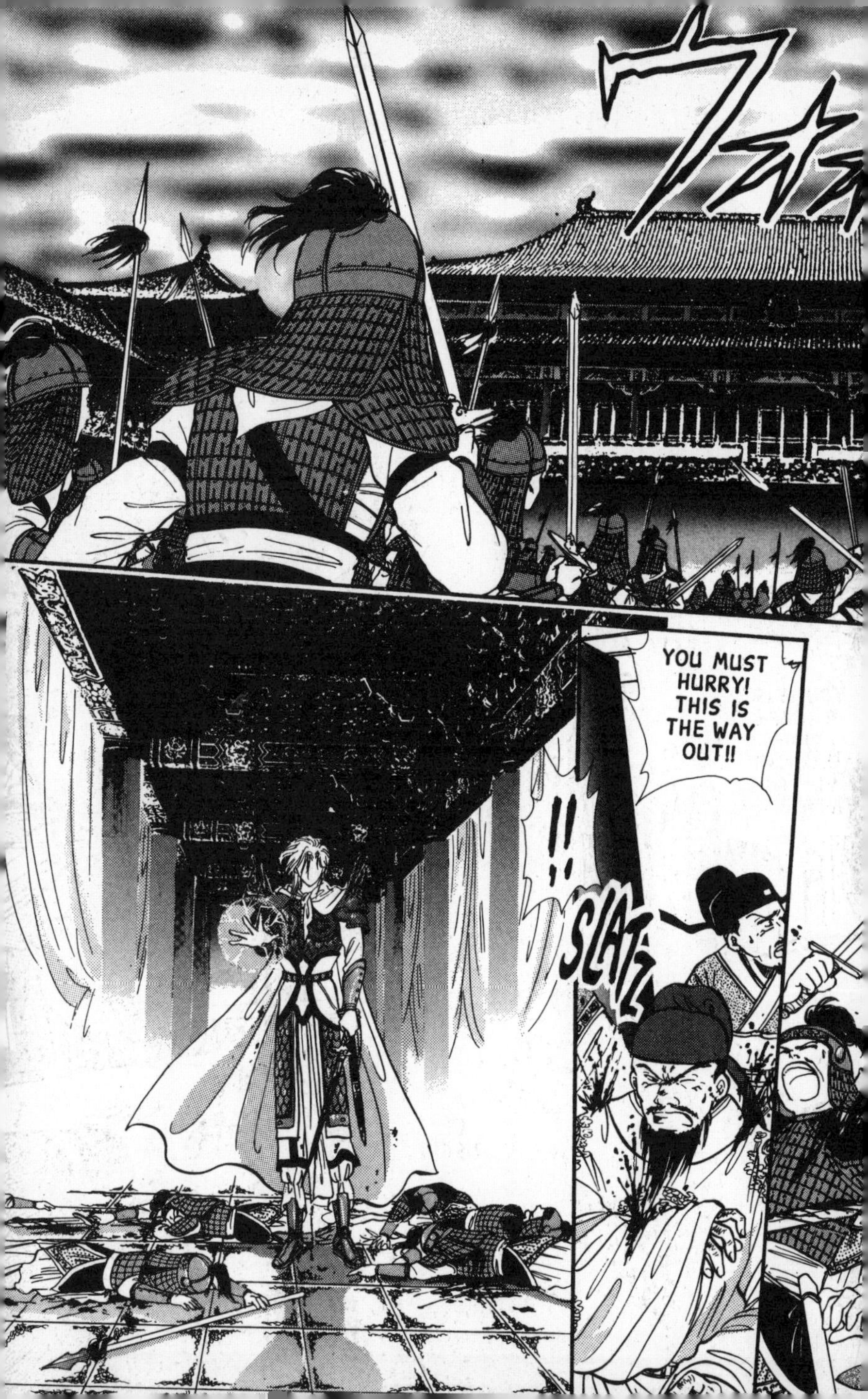
YOU MUST HURRY! THIS IS THE WAY OUT!!
!!
SLASH

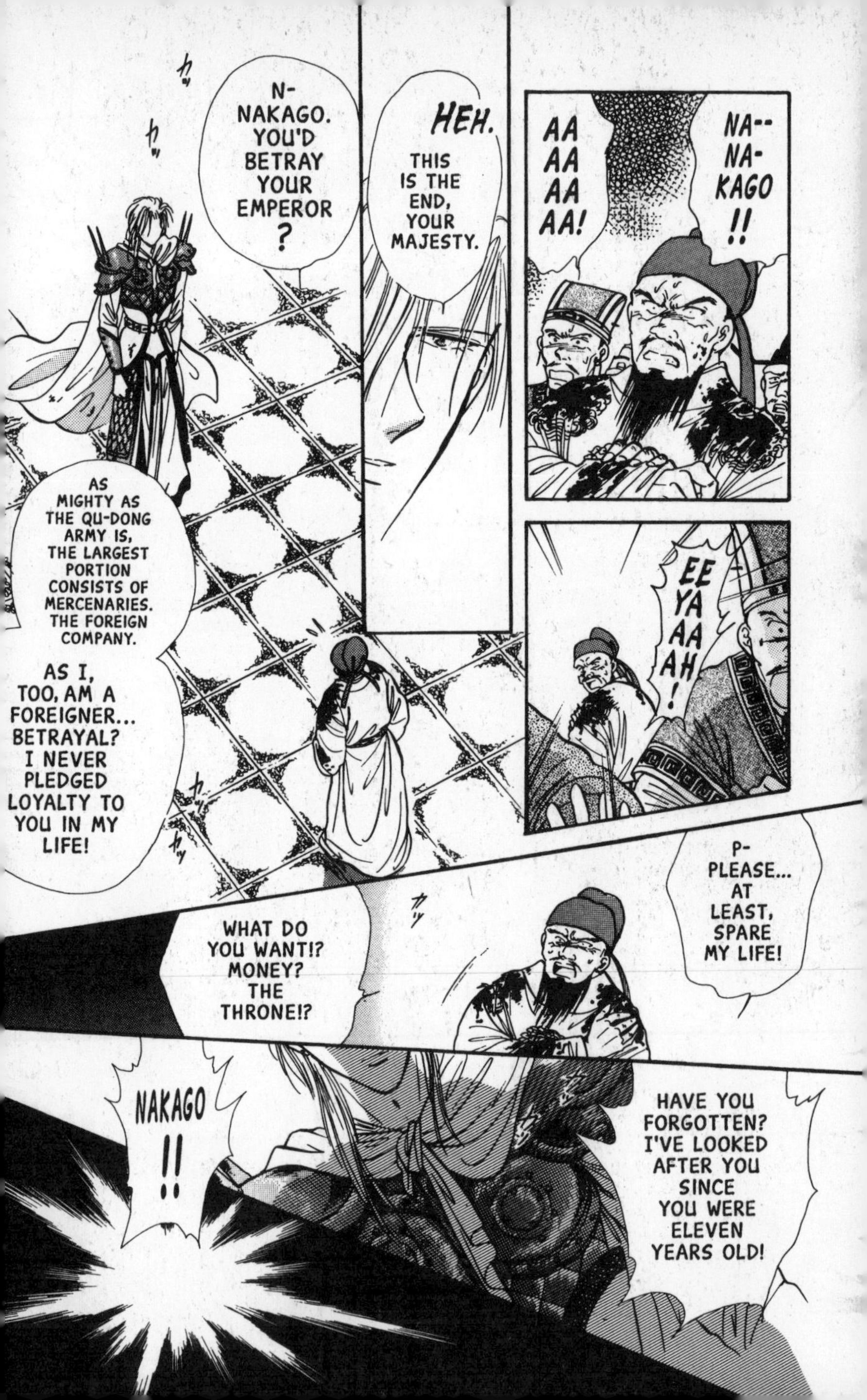
NA--NA-KAGO!!
AAAAAAAA!
EEYAAAAH!
HEH.
THIS IS THE END, YOUR MAJESTY.
N-NAKAGO. YOU'D BETRAY YOUR EMPEROR?
AS MIGHTY AS THE QU-DONG ARMY IS, THE LARGEST PORTION CONSISTS OF MERCENARIES. THE FOREIGN COMPANY.
AS I, TOO, AM A FOREIGNER... BETRAYAL? I NEVER PLEDGED LOYALTY TO YOU IN MY LIFE!
P-PLEASE... AT LEAST, SPARE MY LIFE!
WHAT DO YOU WANT!? MONEY? THE THRONE!?
HAVE YOU FORGOTTEN? I'VE LOOKED AFTER YOU SINCE YOU WERE ELEVEN YEARS OLD!
NAKAGO!!

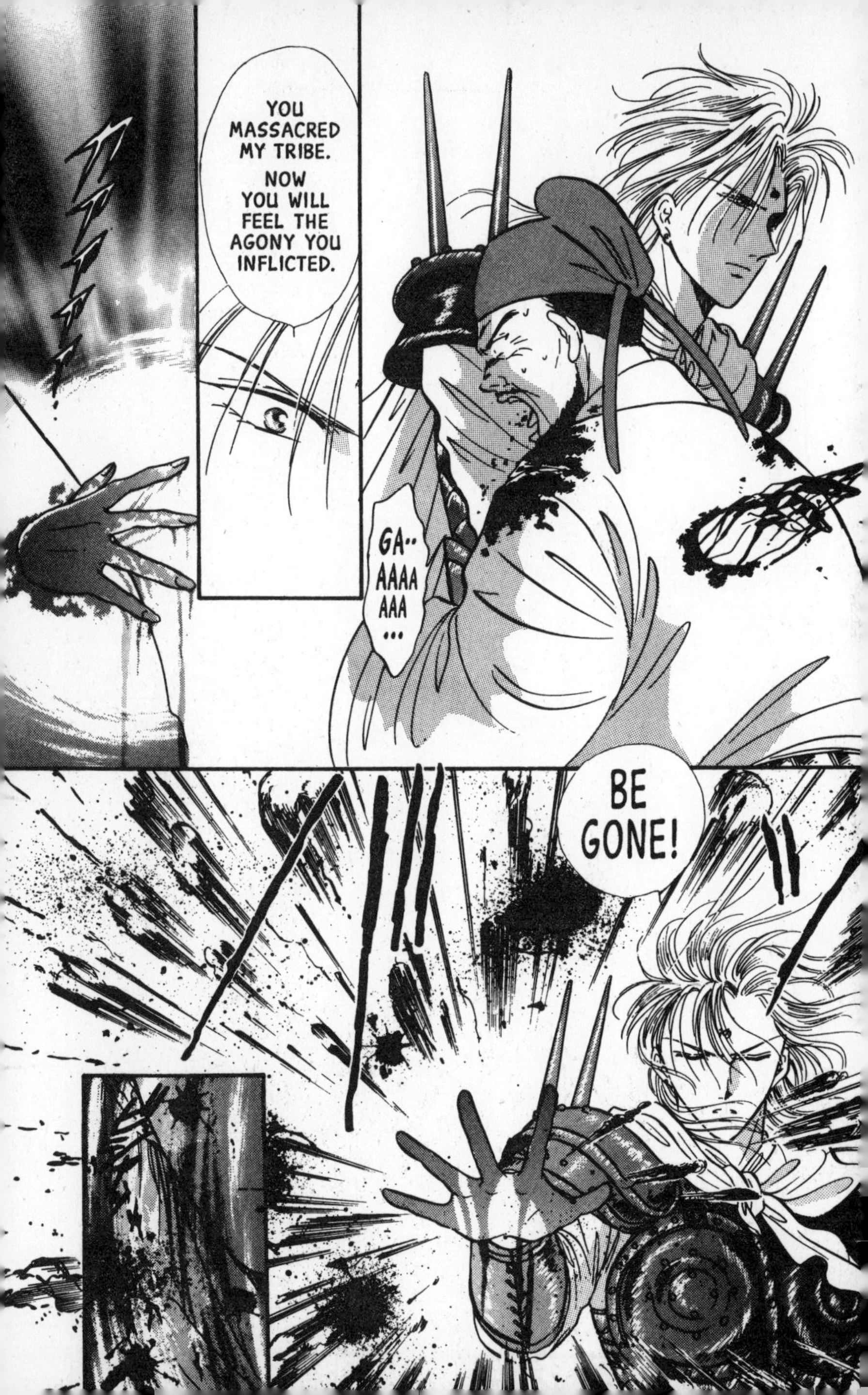
GA.. AAAA AAA ...
YOU MASSACRED MY TRIBE.
NOW YOU WILL FEEL THE AGONY YOU INFLICTED.
BE GONE!

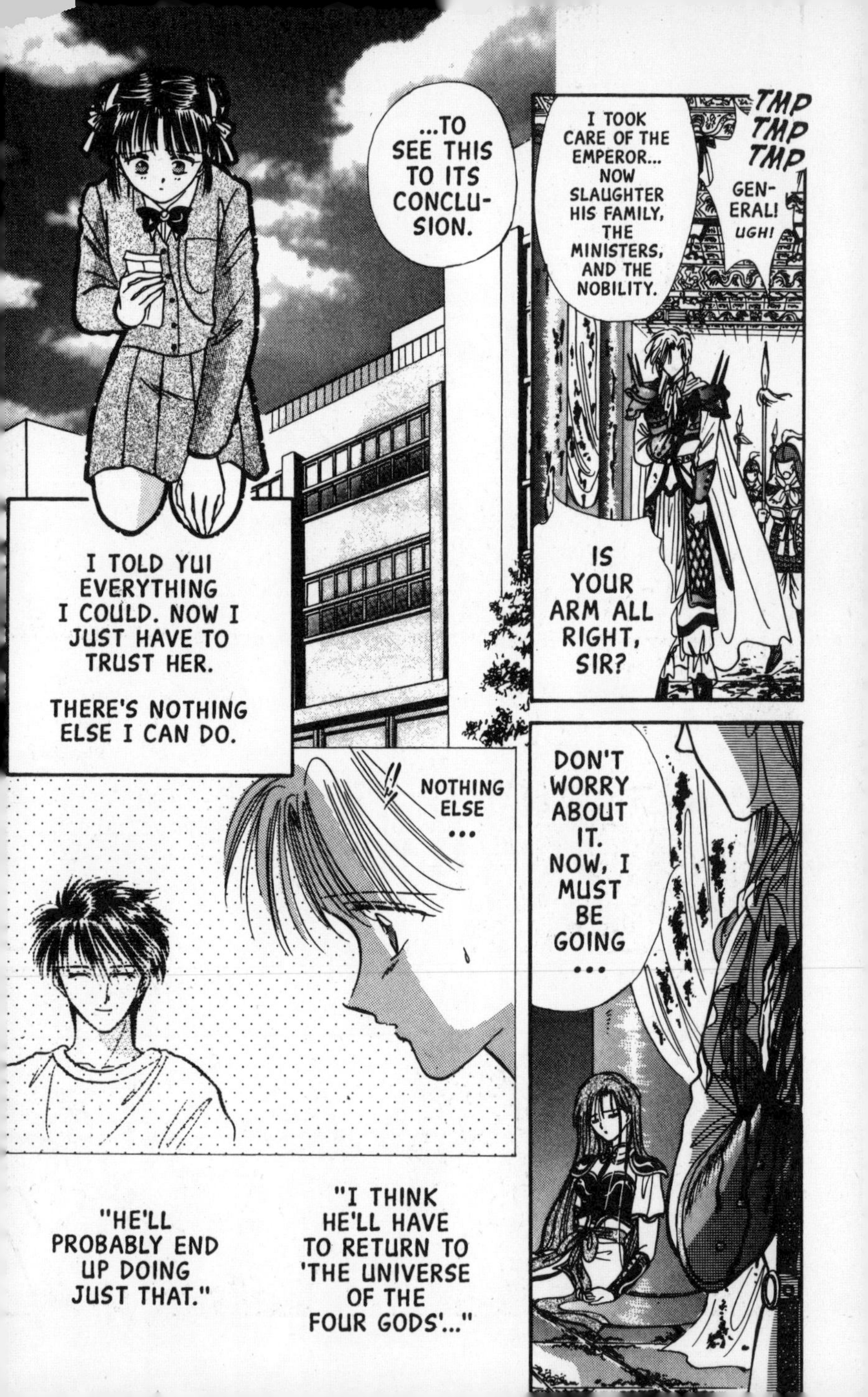
TMP TMP TMP
I TOOK CARE OF THE EMPEROR... NOW SLAUGHTER HIS FAMILY, THE MINISTERS, AND THE NOBILITY.
GEN-ERAL!
UGH!
IS YOUR ARM ALL RIGHT, SIR?
DON'T WORRY ABOUT IT. NOW, I MUST BE GOING...
...TO SEE THIS TO ITS CONCLU-SION.
I TOLD YUI EVERYTHING I COULD. NOW I JUST HAVE TO TRUST HER.
THERE'S NOTHING ELSE I CAN DO.
NOTHING ELSE...
"I THINK HE'LL HAVE TO RETURN TO 'THE UNIVERSE OF THE FOUR GODS'..."
"HE'LL PROBABLY END UP DOING JUST THAT."

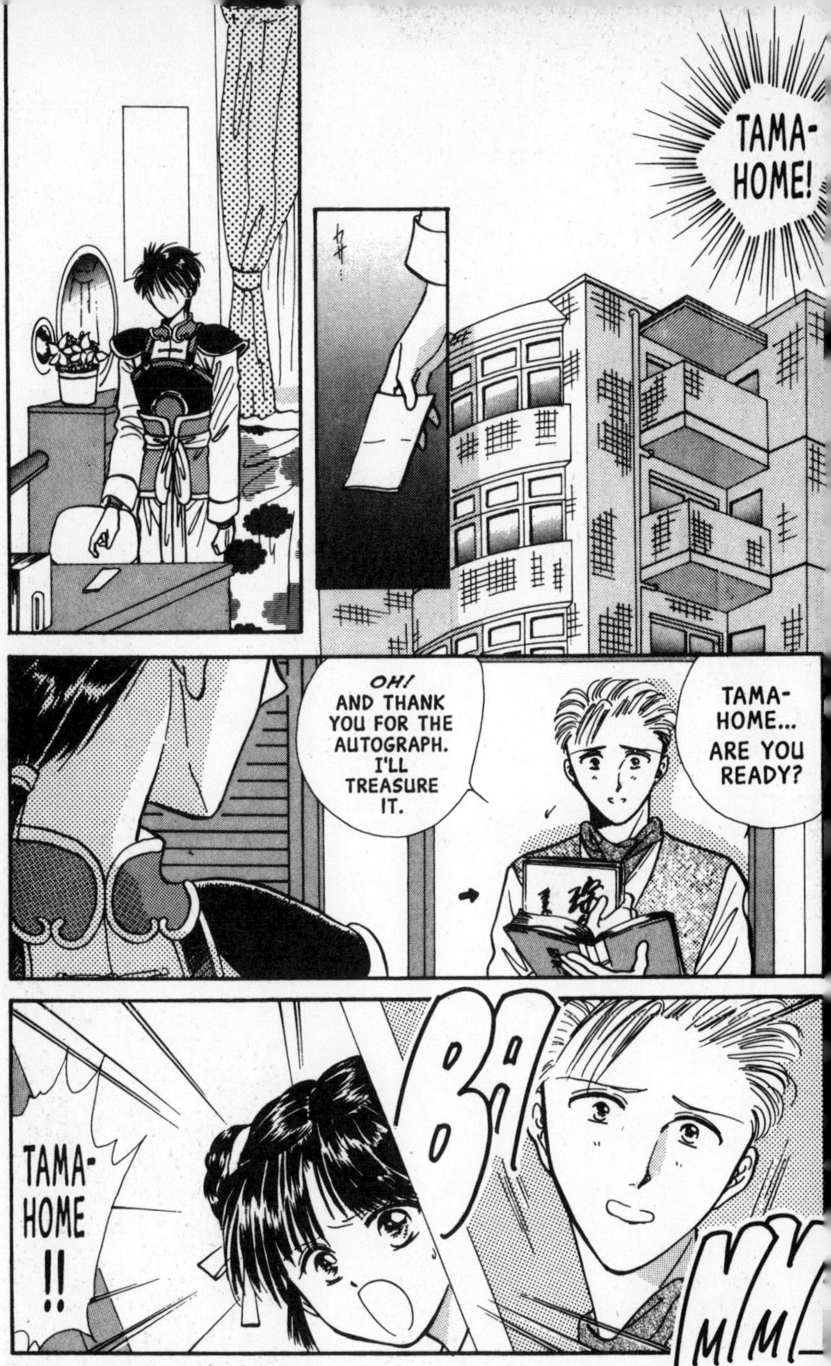
TAMA-HOME!
TAMA-HOME... ARE YOU READY?
OH! AND THANK YOU FOR THE AUTOGRAPH. I'LL TREASURE IT.
BA
MMM
TAMA-HOME !!

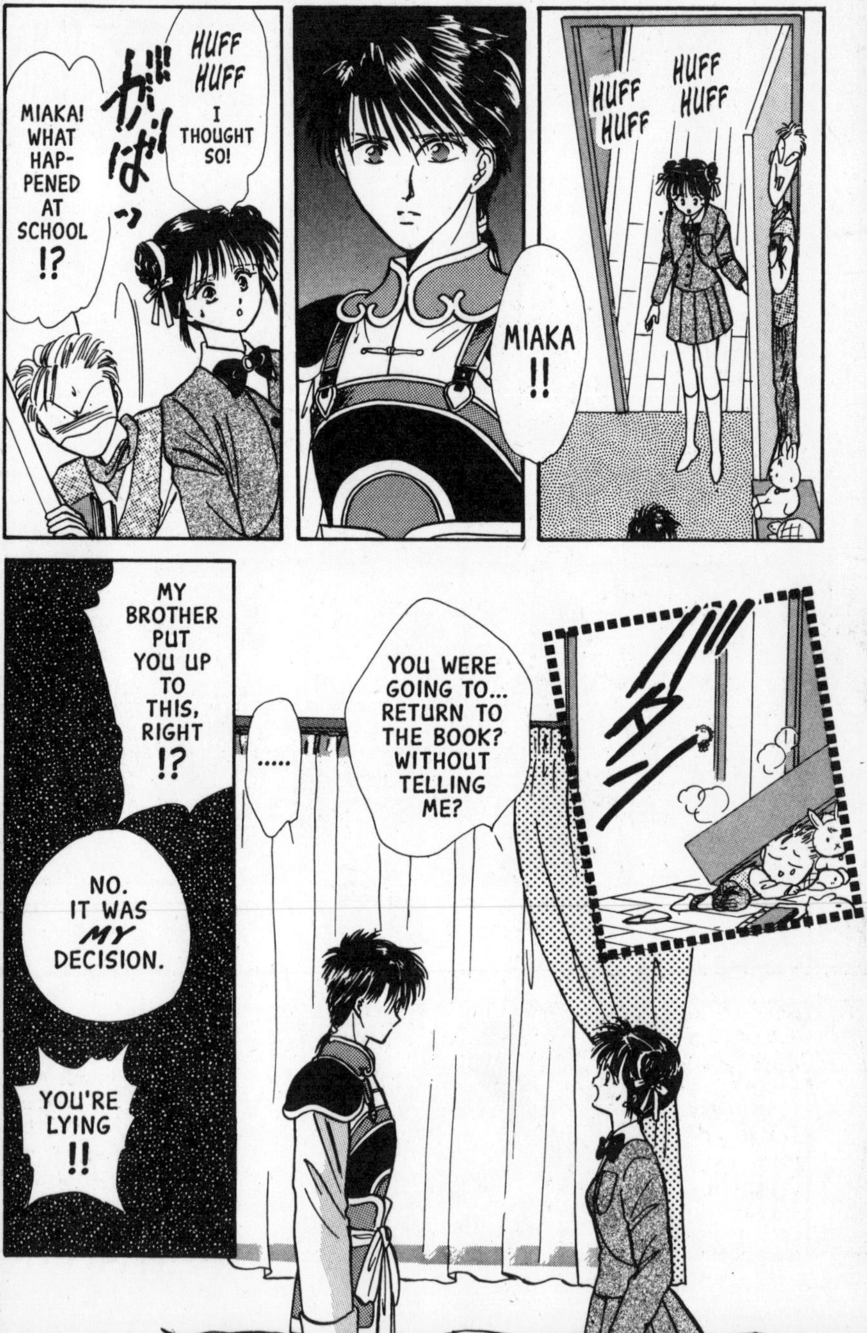
HUFF HUFF
HUFF HUFF
MIAKA!!
HUFF HUFF
I THOUGHT SO!
がばっ
MIAKA! WHAT HAP-PENED AT SCHOOL!?
ガタン
YOU WERE GOING TO... RETURN TO THE BOOK? WITHOUT TELLING ME?
.....
MY BROTHER PUT YOU UP TO THIS, RIGHT!?
NO. IT WAS MY DECISION.
YOU'RE LYING!!

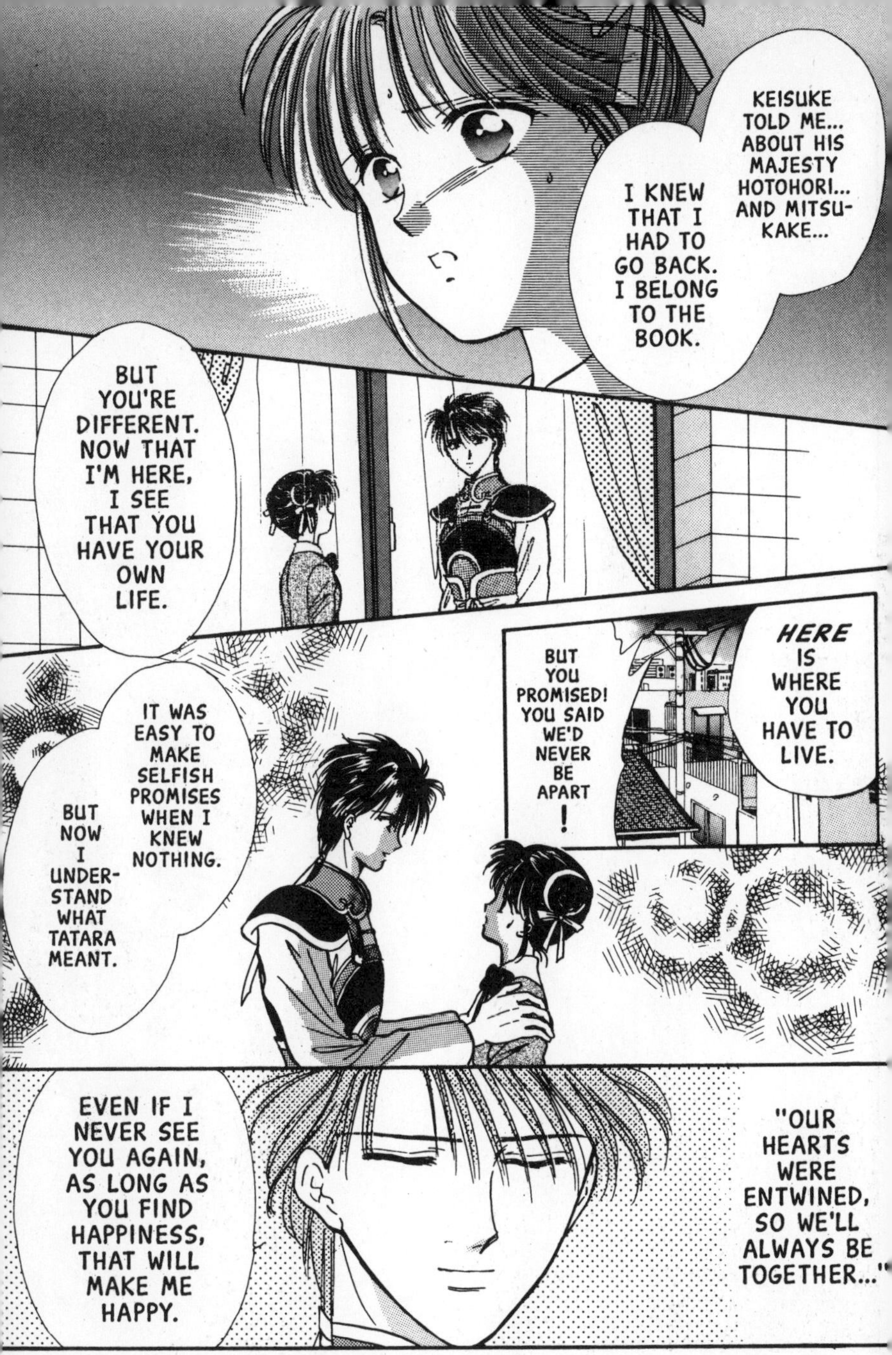
KEISUKE TOLD ME... ABOUT HIS MAJESTY HOTOHORI... AND MITSU-KAKE...
I KNEW THAT I HAD TO GO BACK. I BELONG TO THE BOOK.
BUT YOU'RE DIFFERENT. NOW THAT I'M HERE, I SEE THAT YOU HAVE YOUR OWN LIFE.
HERE IS WHERE YOU HAVE TO LIVE.
BUT YOU PROMISED! YOU SAID WE'D NEVER BE APART!
IT WAS EASY TO MAKE SELFISH PROMISES WHEN I KNEW NOTHING.
BUT NOW I UNDER-STAND WHAT TATARA MEANT.
"OUR HEARTS WERE ENTWINED, SO WE'LL ALWAYS BE TOGETHER..."
EVEN IF I NEVER SEE YOU AGAIN, AS LONG AS YOU FIND HAPPINESS, THAT WILL MAKE ME HAPPY.

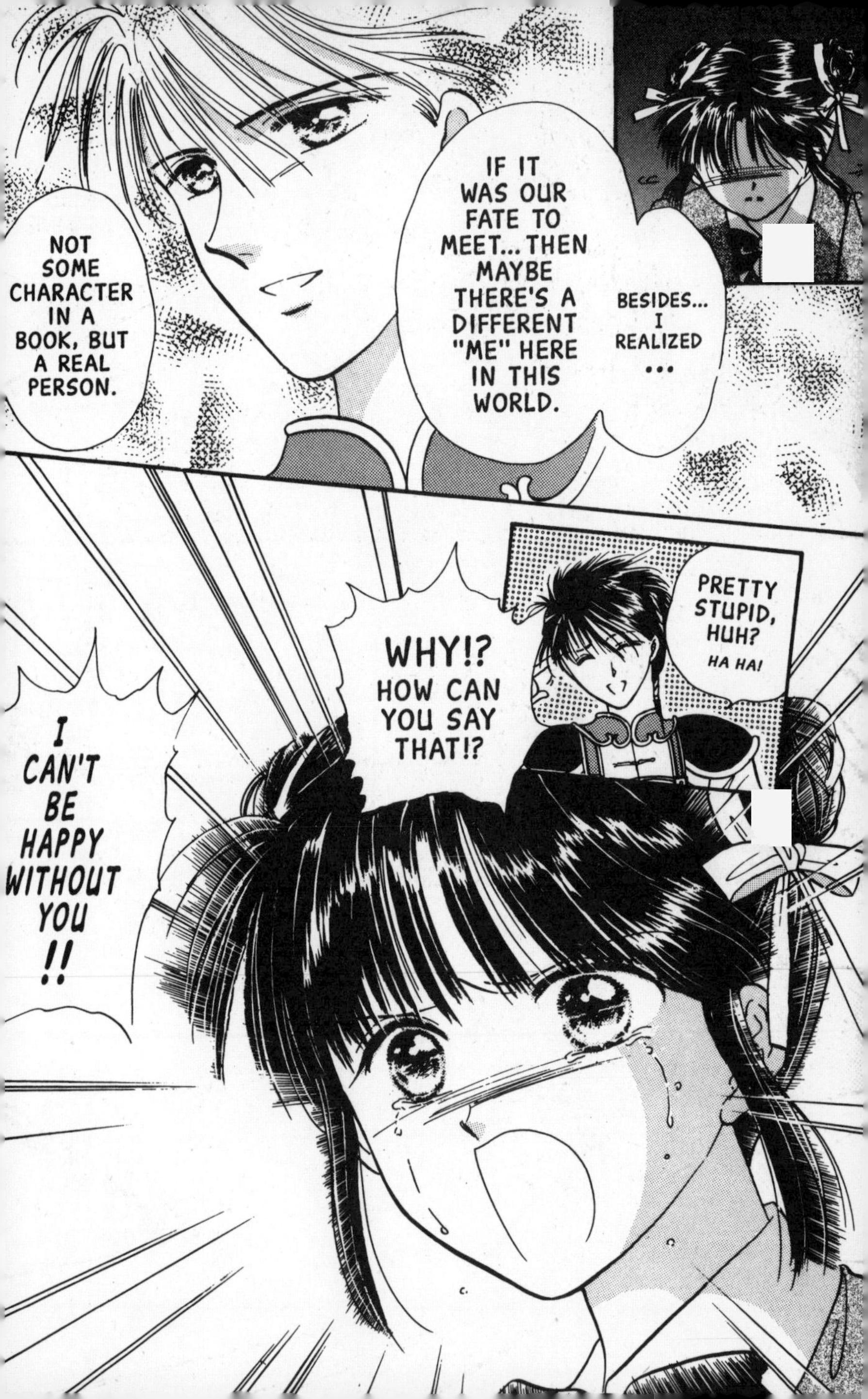
BESIDES... I REALIZED ...
IF IT WAS OUR FATE TO MEET... THEN MAYBE THERE'S A DIFFERENT "ME" HERE IN THIS WORLD.
NOT SOME CHARACTER IN A BOOK, BUT A REAL PERSON.
PRETTY STUPID, HUH? HA HA!
WHY!? HOW CAN YOU SAY THAT!?
I CAN'T BE HAPPY WITHOUT YOU!!

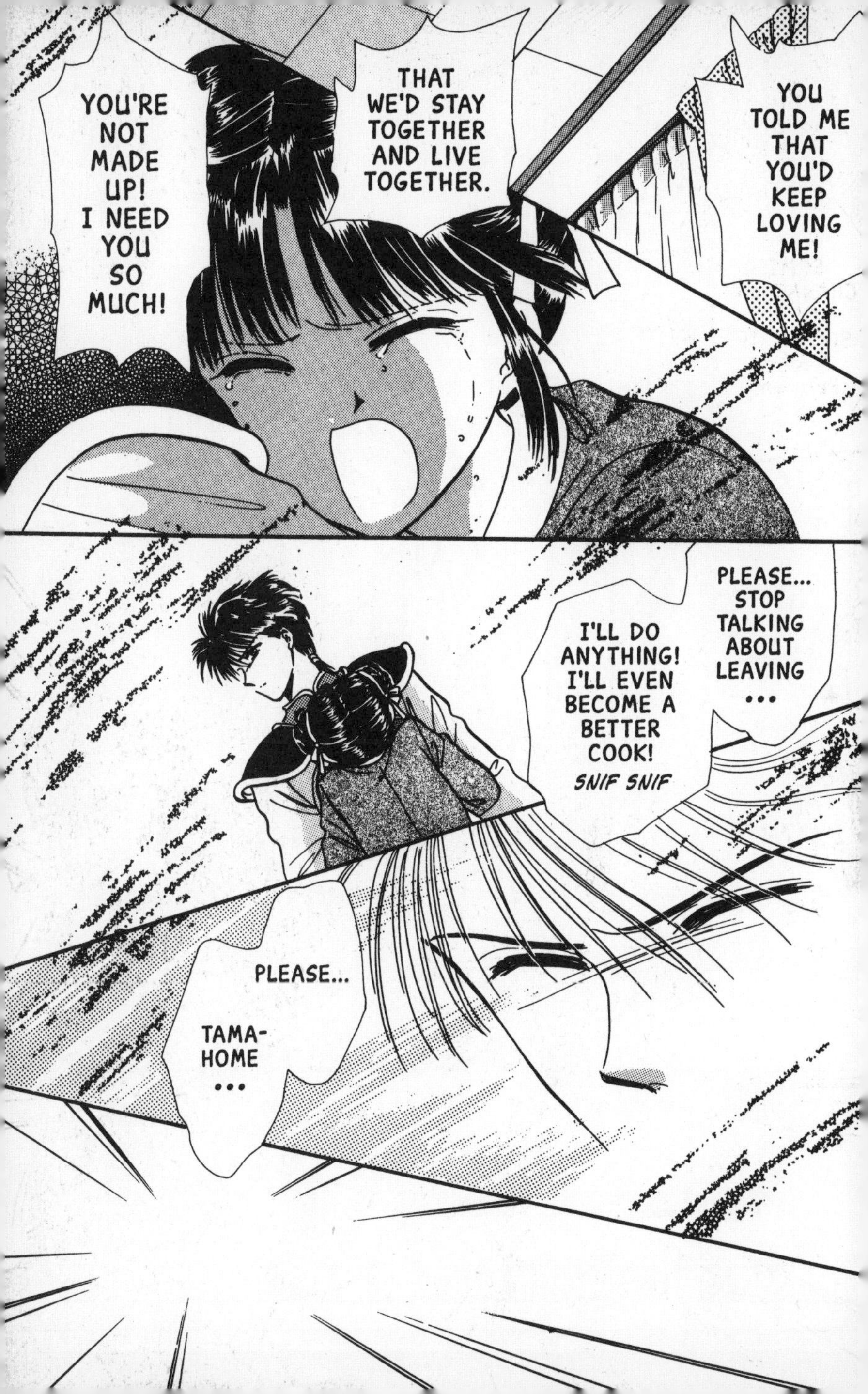
YOU TOLD ME THAT YOU'D KEEP LOVING ME!
THAT WE'D STAY TOGETHER AND LIVE TOGETHER.
YOU'RE NOT MADE UP! I NEED YOU SO MUCH!
PLEASE... STOP TALKING ABOUT LEAVING...
I'LL DO ANYTHING! I'LL EVEN BECOME A BETTER COOK!
SNIF SNIF
PLEASE...
TAMA-HOME...

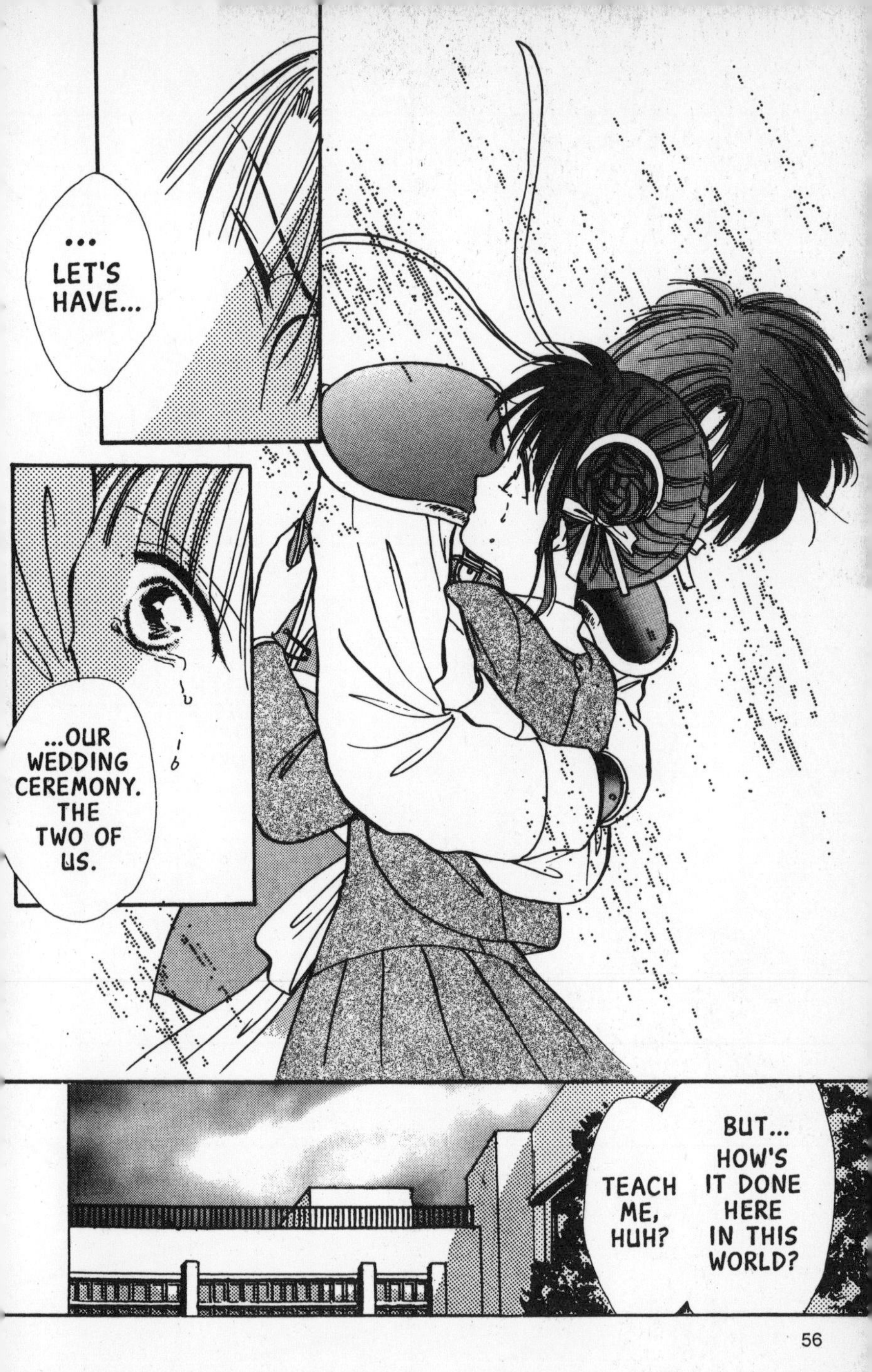
...LET'S HAVE...
...OUR WEDDING CEREMONY. THE TWO OF US.
BUT... HOW'S IT DONE HERE IN THIS WORLD?
TEACH ME, HUH?

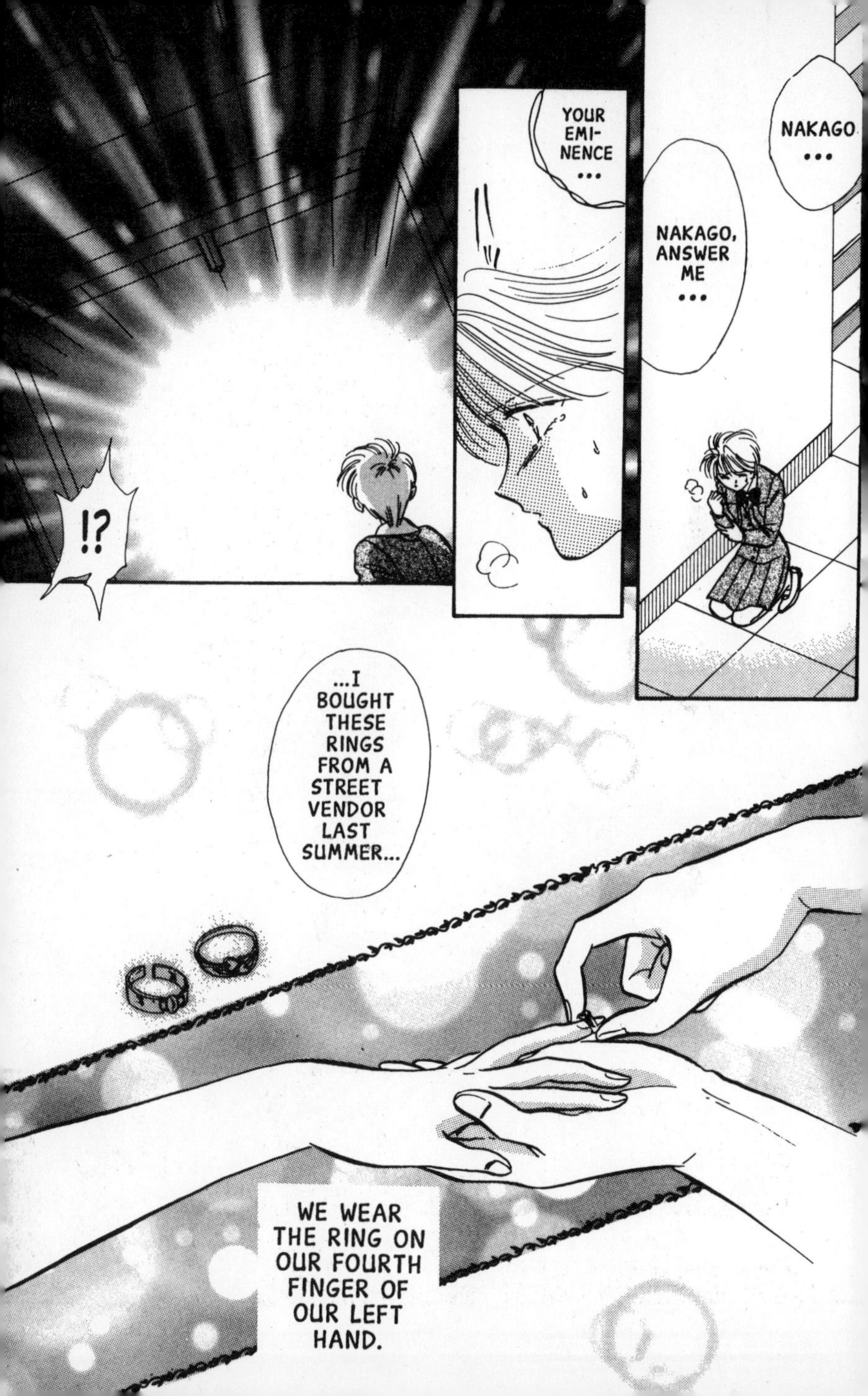
NAKAGO...
NAKAGO, ANSWER ME...
YOUR EMI-NENCE...
!?
...I BOUGHT THESE RINGS FROM A STREET VENDOR LAST SUMMER...
WE WEAR THE RING ON OUR FOURTH FINGER OF OUR LEFT HAND.

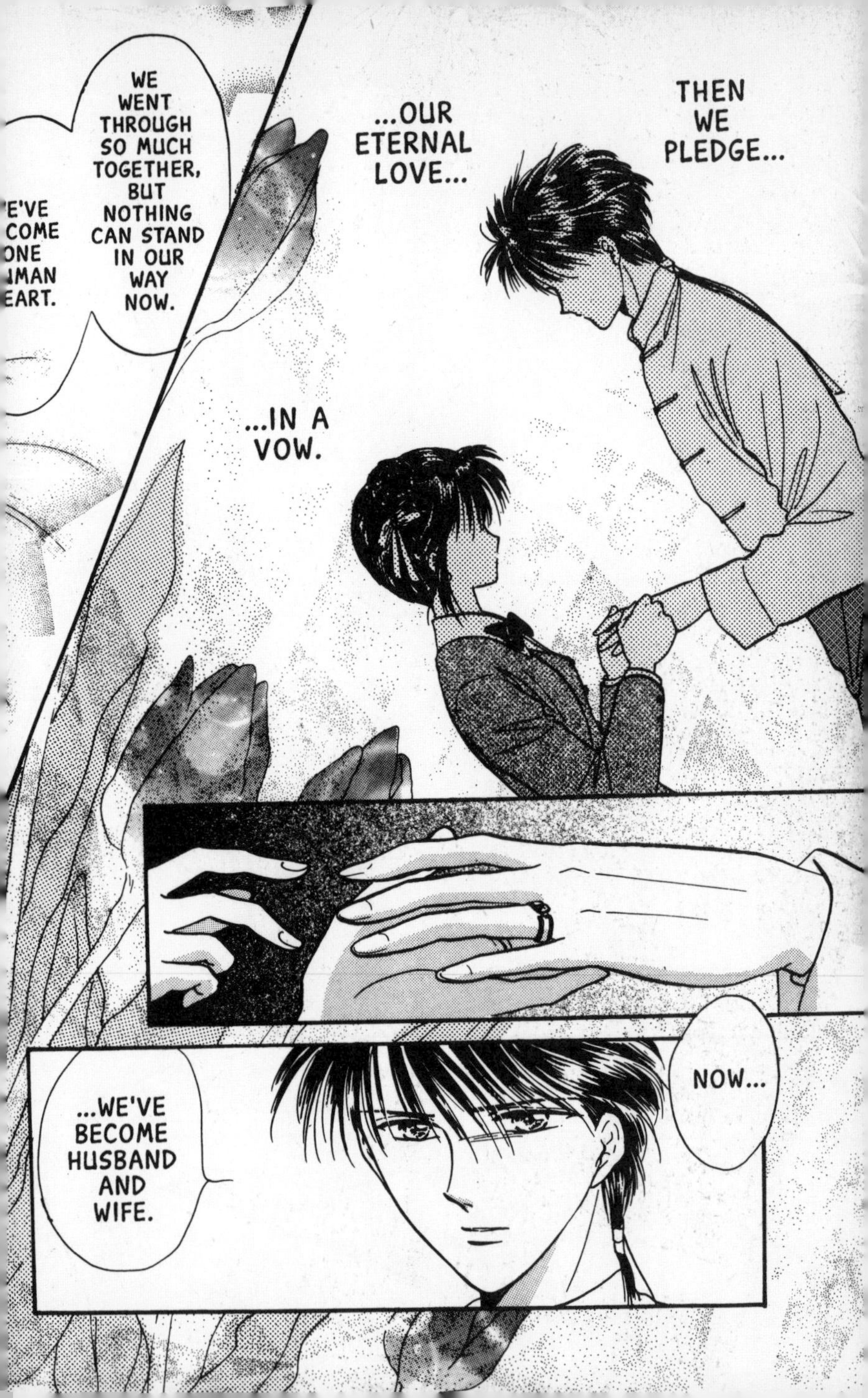
THEN WE PLEDGE...
...OUR ETERNAL LOVE...
...IN A VOW.
WE WENT THROUGH SO MUCH TOGETHER, BUT NOTHING CAN STAND IN OUR WAY NOW.
E'VE COME ONE MAN EART.
NOW...
...WE'VE BECOME HUSBAND AND WIFE.

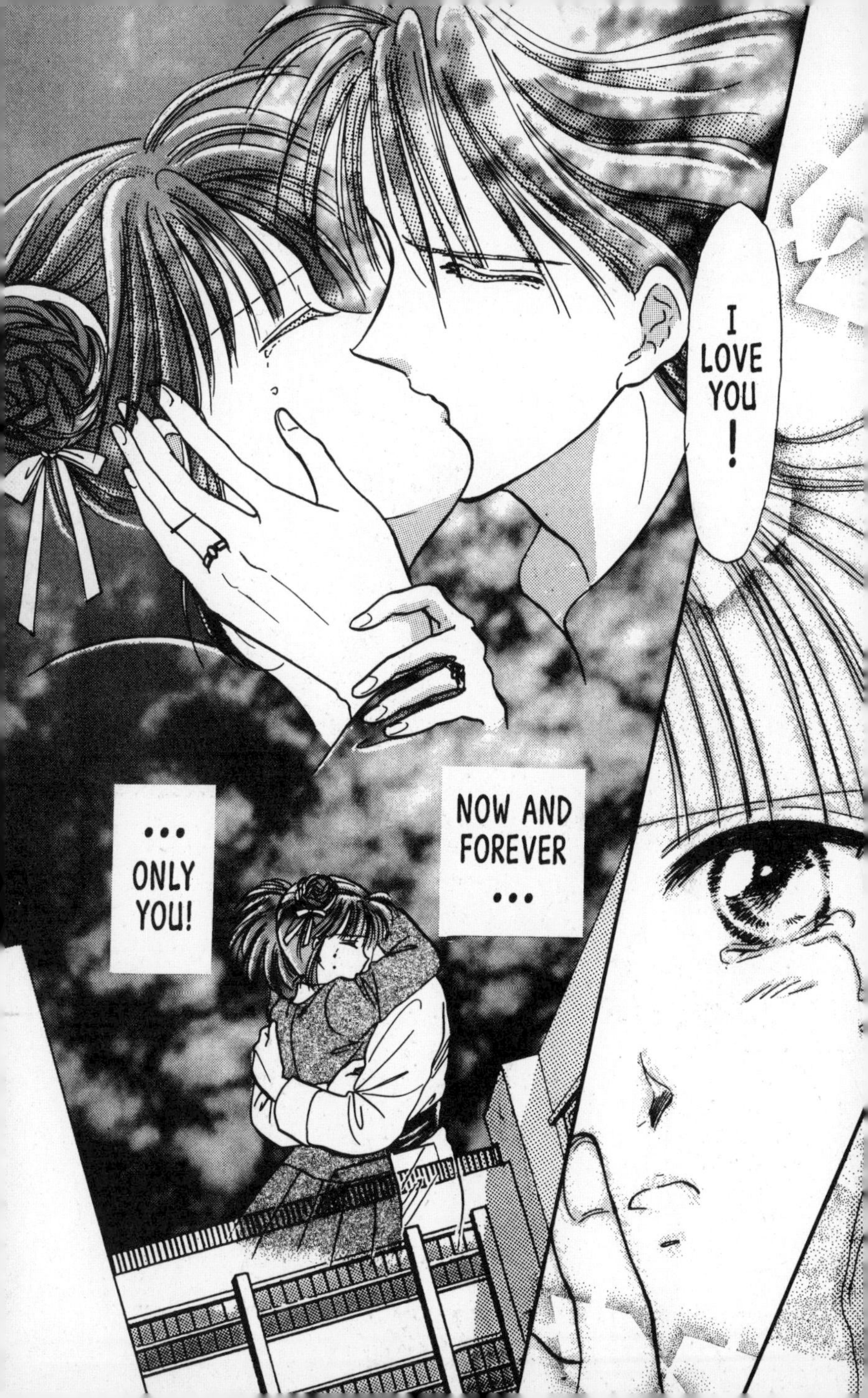
I LOVE YOU!
NOW AND FOREVER...
...ONLY YOU!

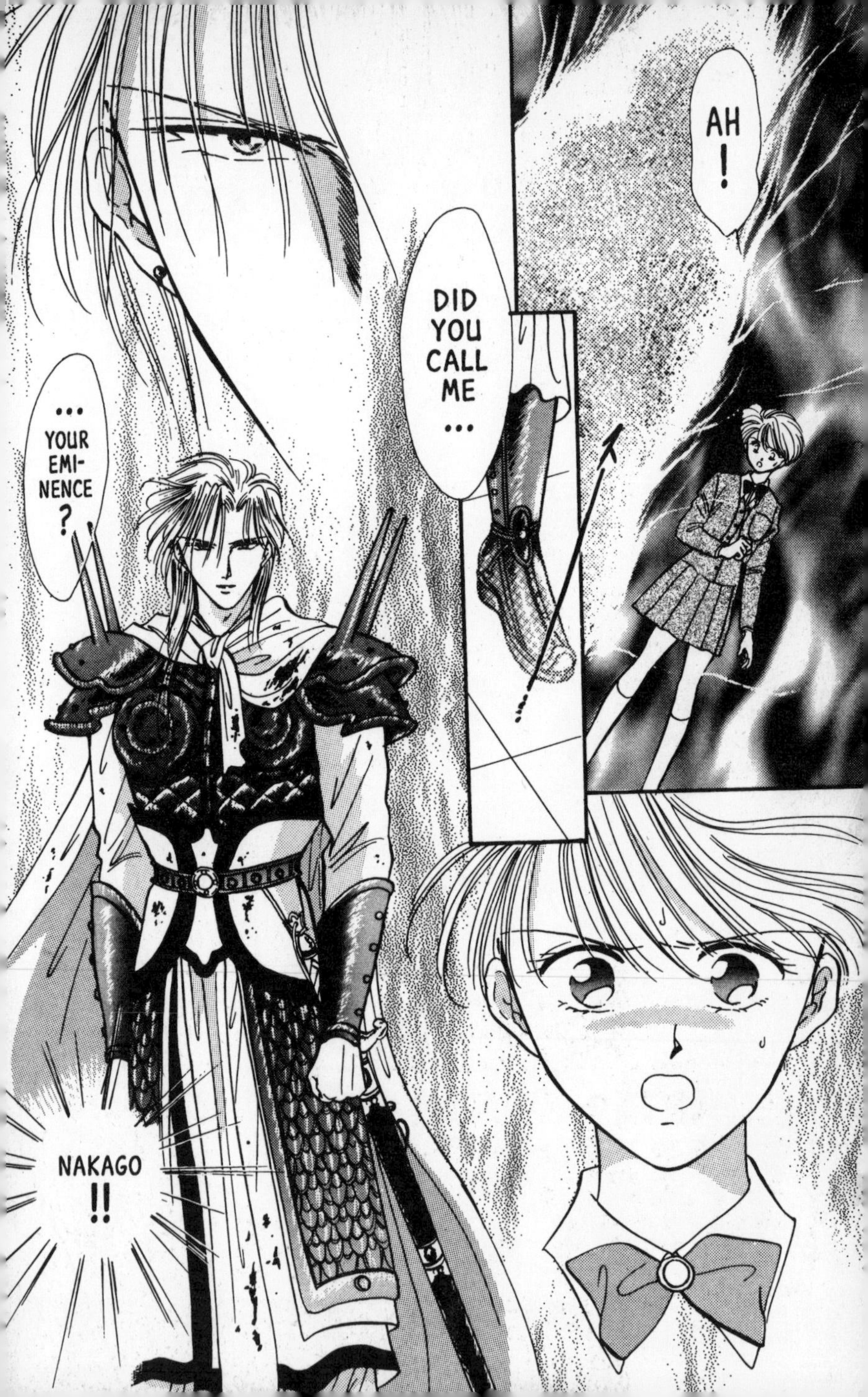
AH!
DID YOU CALL ME ...
... YOUR EMINENCE?
NAKAGO!!

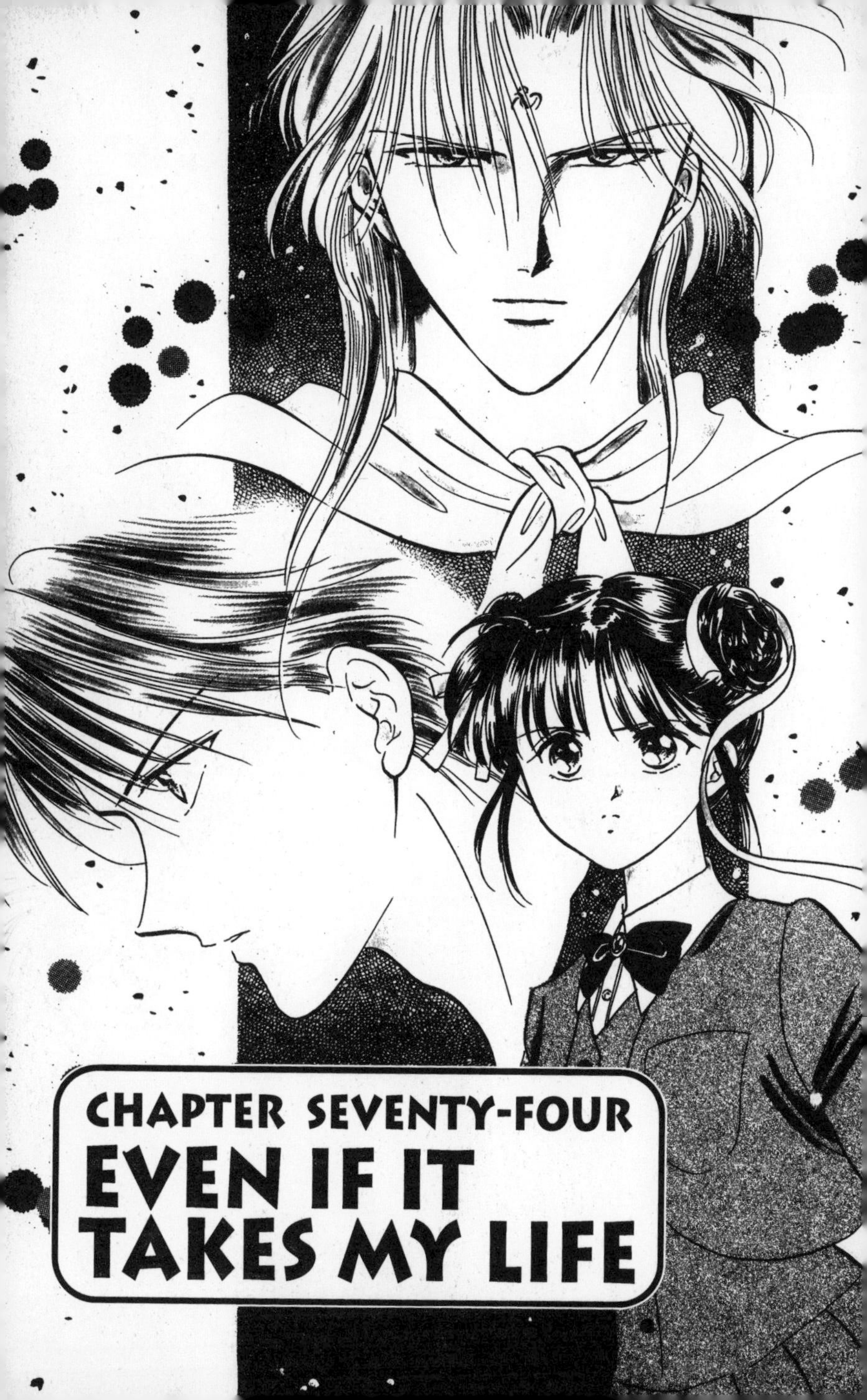
CHAPTER SEVENTY-FOUR
EVEN IF IT TAKES MY LIFE

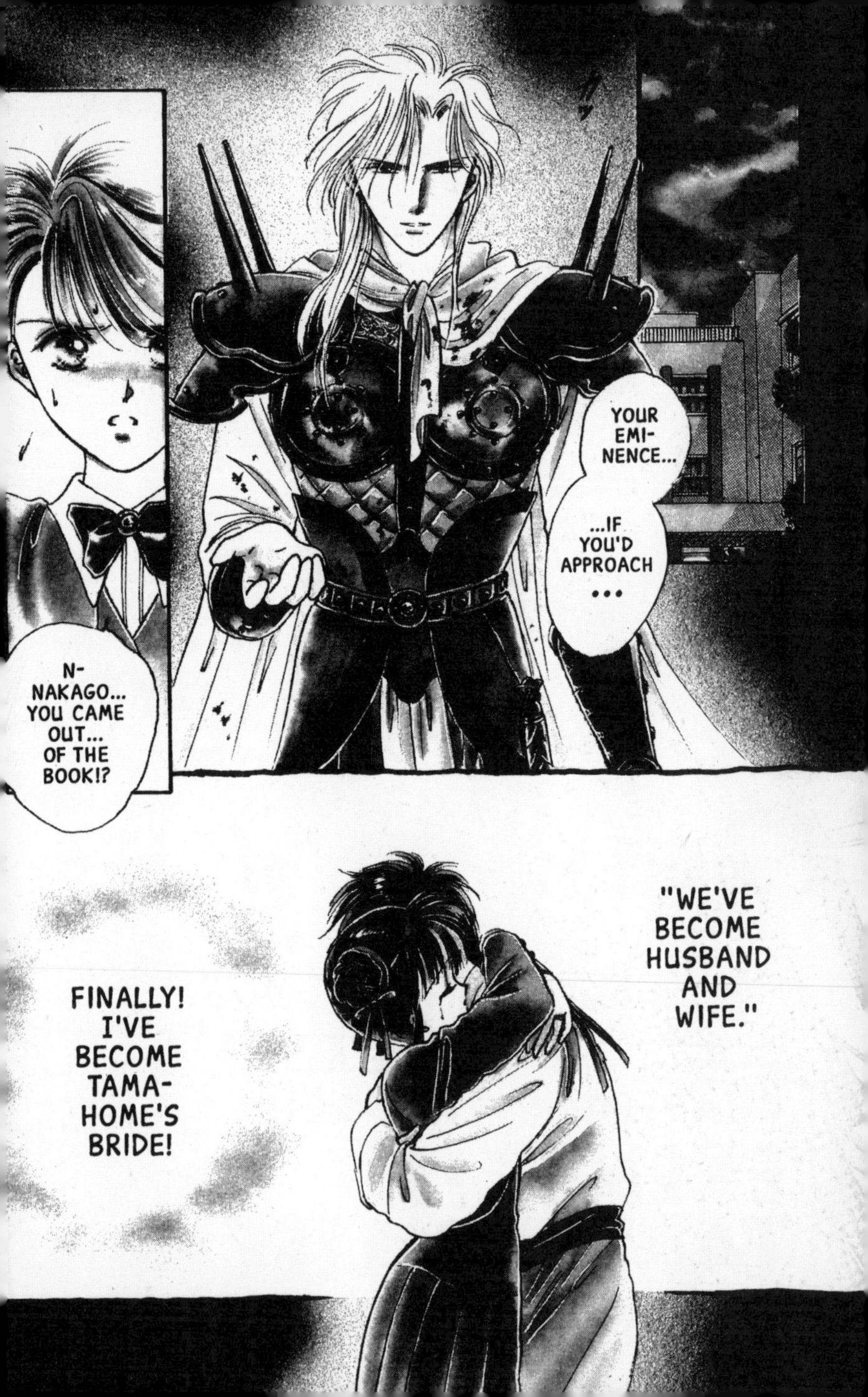
YOUR EMI-NENCE...
...IF YOU'D APPROACH...
N-NAKAGO... YOU CAME OUT... OF THE BOOK!?
"WE'VE BECOME HUSBAND AND WIFE."
FINALLY! I'VE BECOME TAMA-HOME'S BRIDE!

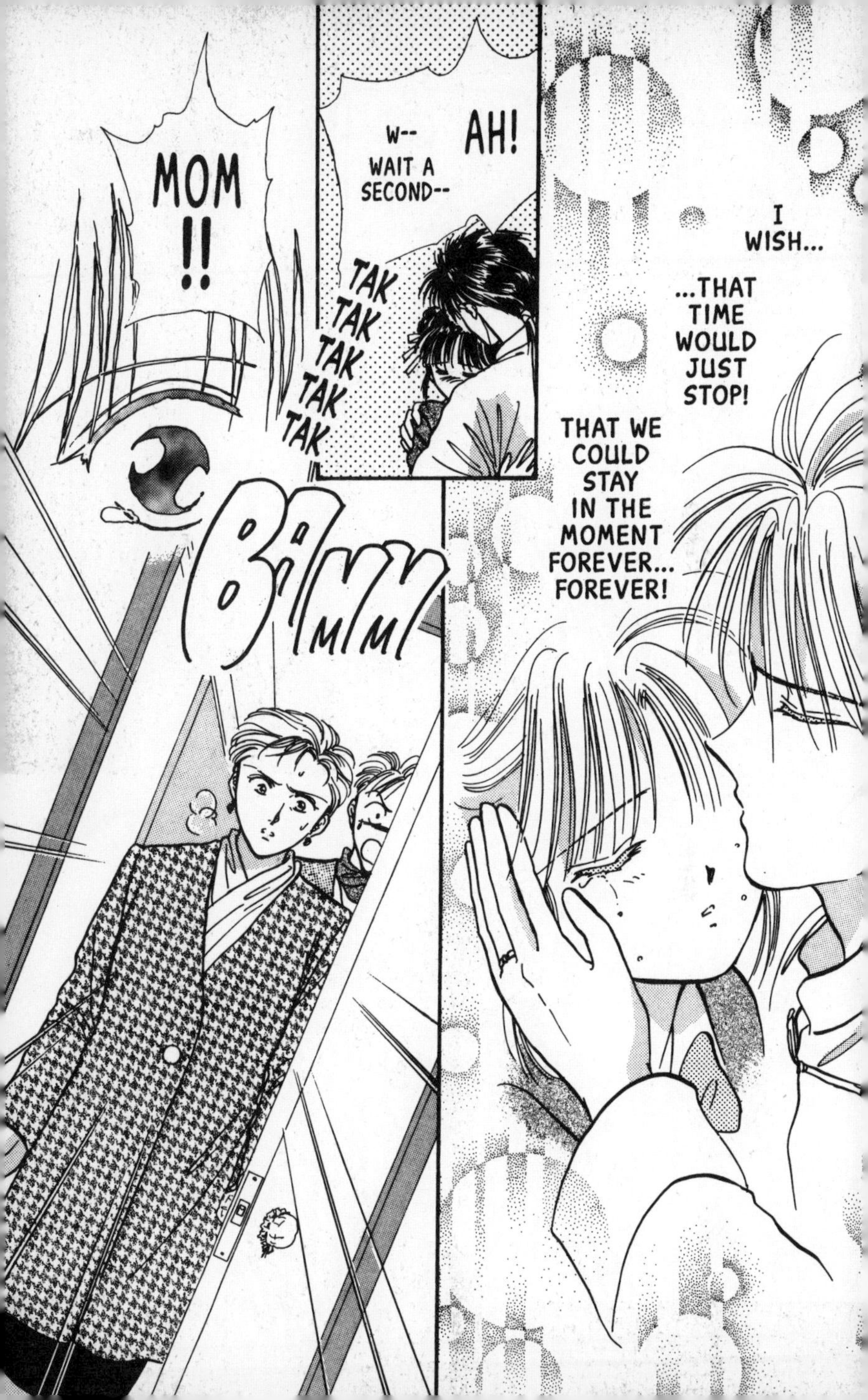

I WISH...
...THAT TIME WOULD JUST STOP!
THAT WE COULD STAY IN THE MOMENT FOREVER... FOREVER!
AH!
W-- WAIT A SECOND--
TAK TAK TAK TAK TAK
MOM !!
BAMMM

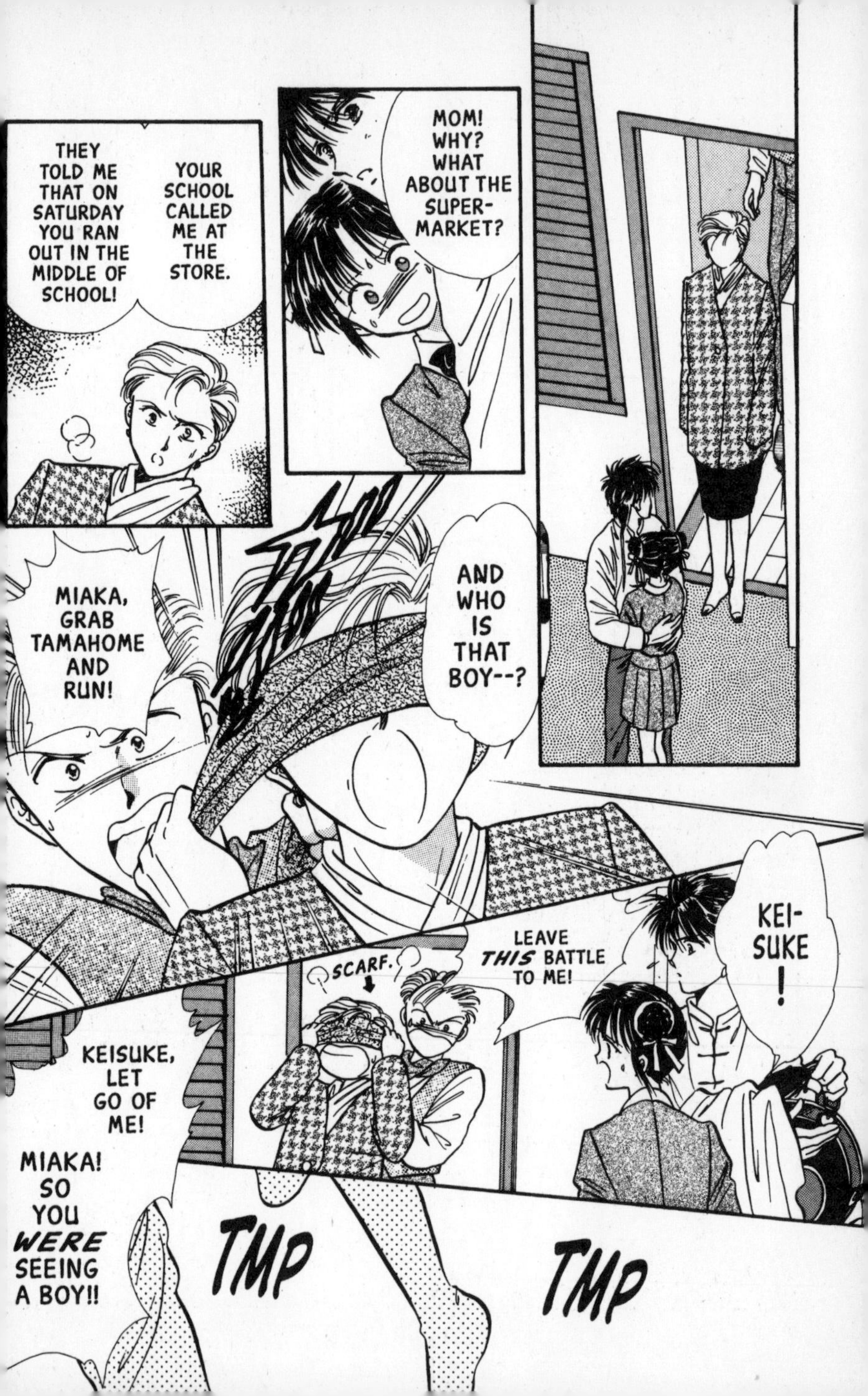
MOM! WHY? WHAT ABOUT THE SUPER-MARKET?
YOUR SCHOOL CALLED ME AT THE STORE.
THEY TOLD ME THAT ON SATURDAY YOU RAN OUT IN THE MIDDLE OF SCHOOL!
AND WHO IS THAT BOY--?
MIAKA, GRAB TAMAHOME AND RUN!
KEI-SUKE!
LEAVE *THIS* BATTLE TO ME!
SCARF.
KEISUKE, LET GO OF ME!
MIAKA! SO YOU *WERE* SEEING A BOY!!
TMP
TMP

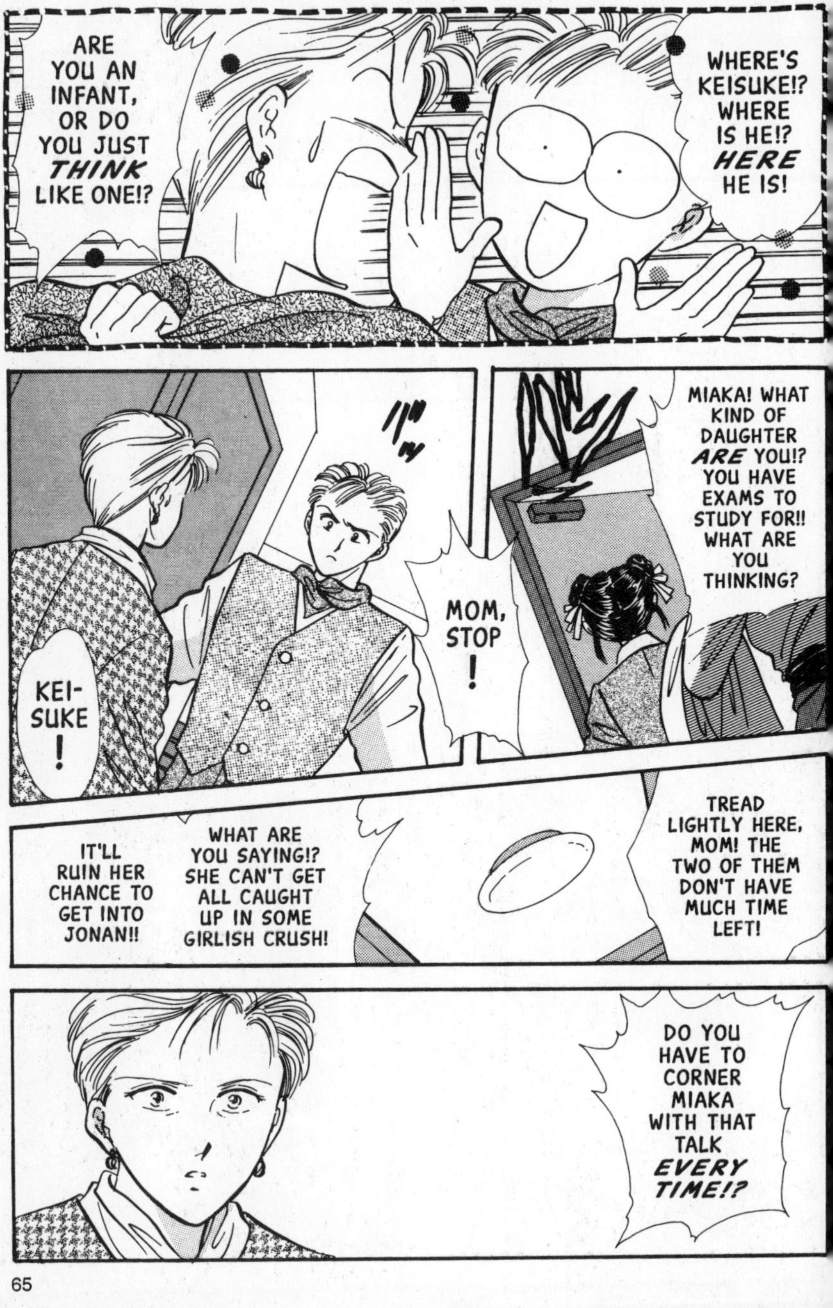
WHERE'S KEISUKE!? WHERE IS HE!? *HERE* HE IS!
ARE YOU AN INFANT, OR DO YOU JUST *THINK* LIKE ONE!?
MIAKA! WHAT KIND OF DAUGHTER *ARE* YOU!? YOU HAVE EXAMS TO STUDY FOR!! WHAT ARE YOU THINKING?
MOM, STOP!
KEI-SUKE!
TREAD LIGHTLY HERE, MOM! THE TWO OF THEM DON'T HAVE MUCH TIME LEFT!
WHAT ARE YOU SAYING!? SHE CAN'T GET ALL CAUGHT UP IN SOME GIRLISH CRUSH!
IT'LL RUIN HER CHANCE TO GET INTO JONAN!!
DO YOU HAVE TO CORNER MIAKA WITH THAT TALK *EVERY TIME!?*

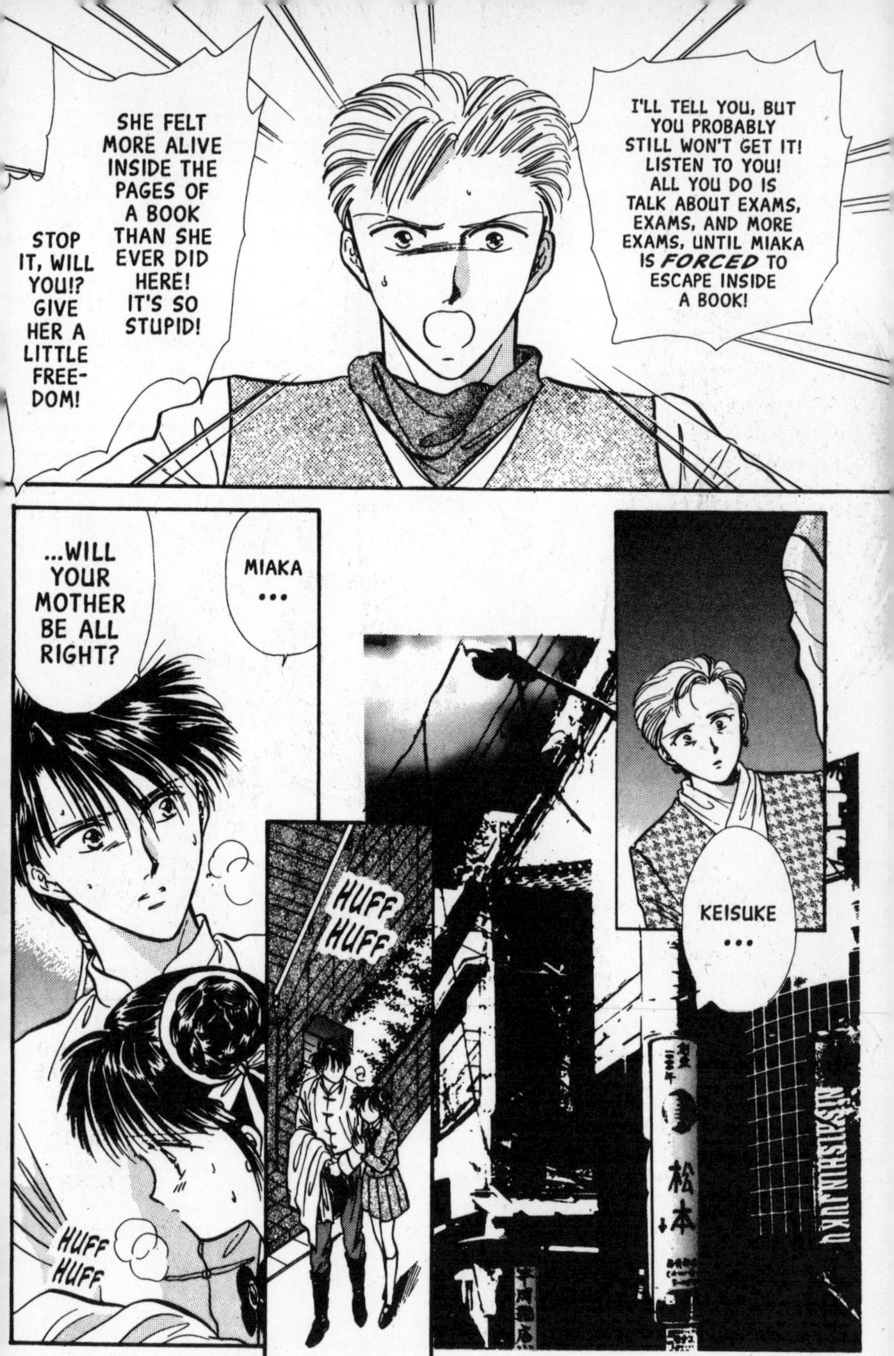
I'LL TELL YOU, BUT YOU PROBABLY STILL WON'T GET IT! LISTEN TO YOU! ALL YOU DO IS TALK ABOUT EXAMS, EXAMS, AND MORE EXAMS, UNTIL MIAKA IS *FORCED* TO ESCAPE INSIDE A BOOK!
SHE FELT MORE ALIVE INSIDE THE PAGES OF A BOOK THAN SHE EVER DID HERE! IT'S SO STUPID!
STOP IT, WILL YOU!? GIVE HER A LITTLE FREE-DOM!
KEISUKE ...
松本
HUFF HUFF
MIAKA ...
...WILL YOUR MOTHER BE ALL RIGHT?
HUFF HUFF

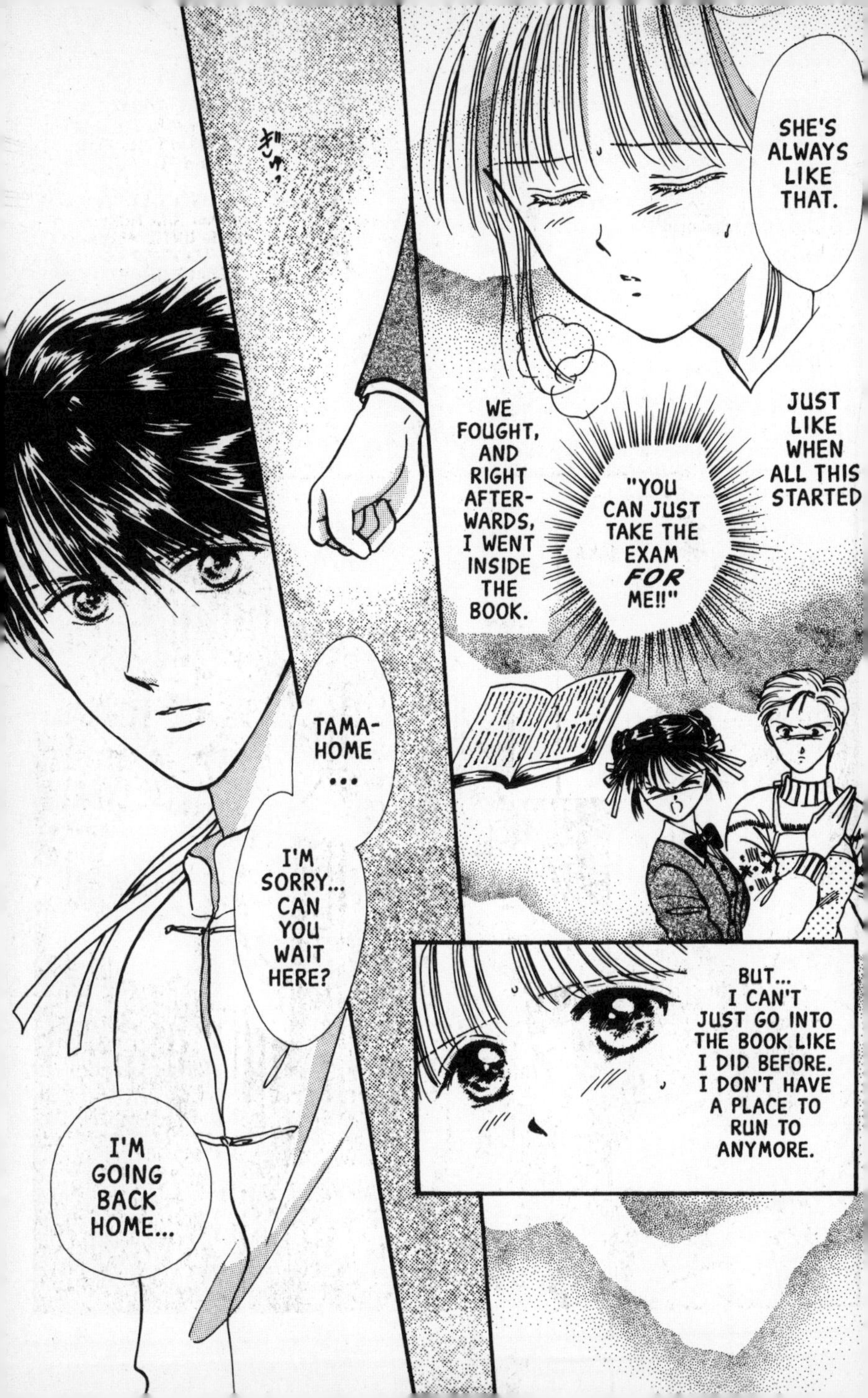
SHE'S ALWAYS LIKE THAT.
JUST LIKE WHEN ALL THIS STARTED
"YOU CAN JUST TAKE THE EXAM FOR ME!!"
WE FOUGHT, AND RIGHT AFTERWARDS, I WENT INSIDE THE BOOK.
BUT... I CAN'T JUST GO INTO THE BOOK LIKE I DID BEFORE. I DON'T HAVE A PLACE TO RUN TO ANYMORE.
TAMAHOME ...
I'M SORRY... CAN YOU WAIT HERE?
I'M GOING BACK HOME...

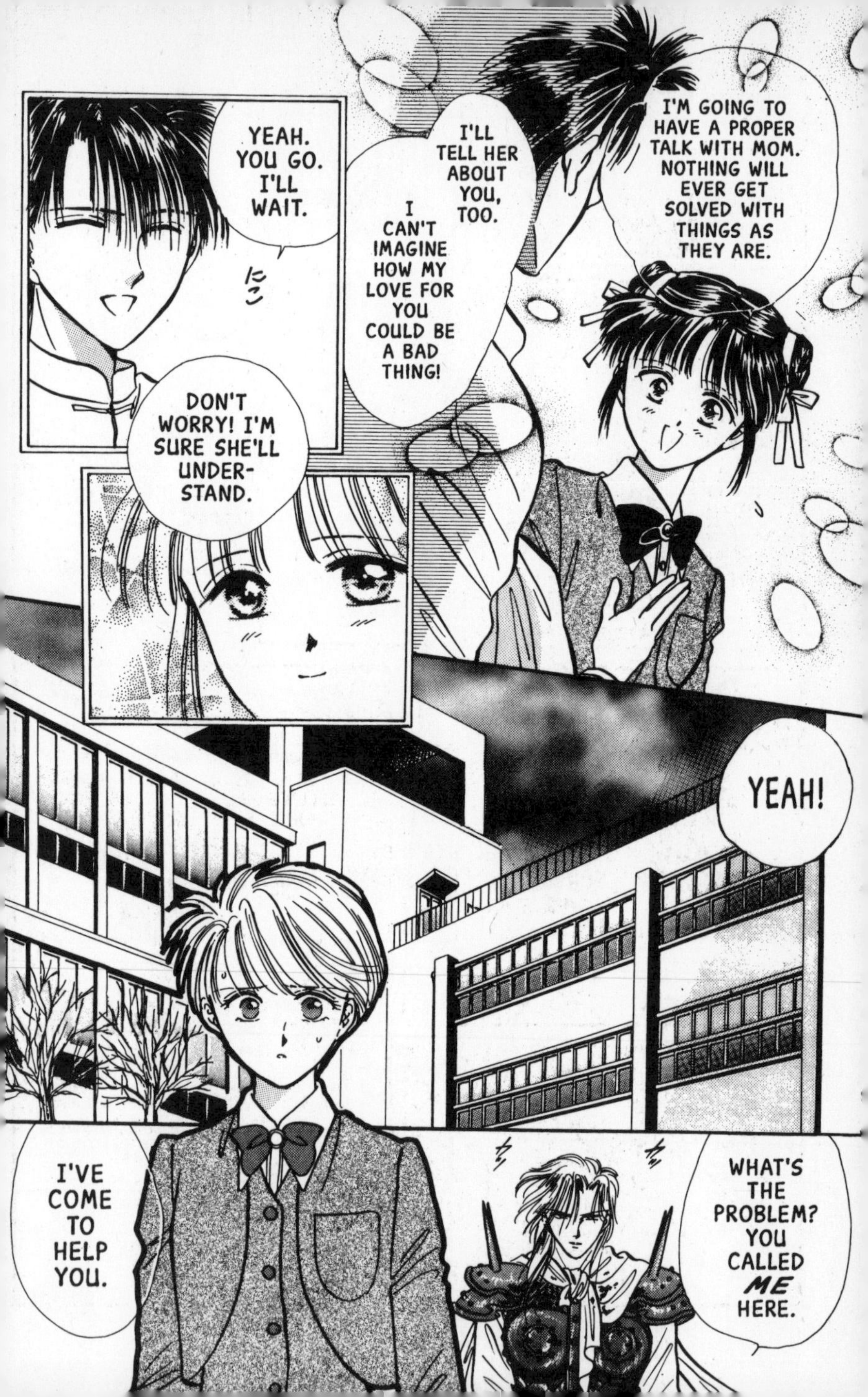
I'M GOING TO HAVE A PROPER TALK WITH MOM. NOTHING WILL EVER GET SOLVED WITH THINGS AS THEY ARE.
I'LL TELL HER ABOUT YOU, TOO.
I CAN'T IMAGINE HOW MY LOVE FOR YOU COULD BE A BAD THING!
YEAH. YOU GO. I'LL WAIT.
にこ
DON'T WORRY! I'M SURE SHE'LL UNDER-STAND.
YEAH!
WHAT'S THE PROBLEM? YOU CALLED *ME* HERE.
I'VE COME TO HELP YOU.

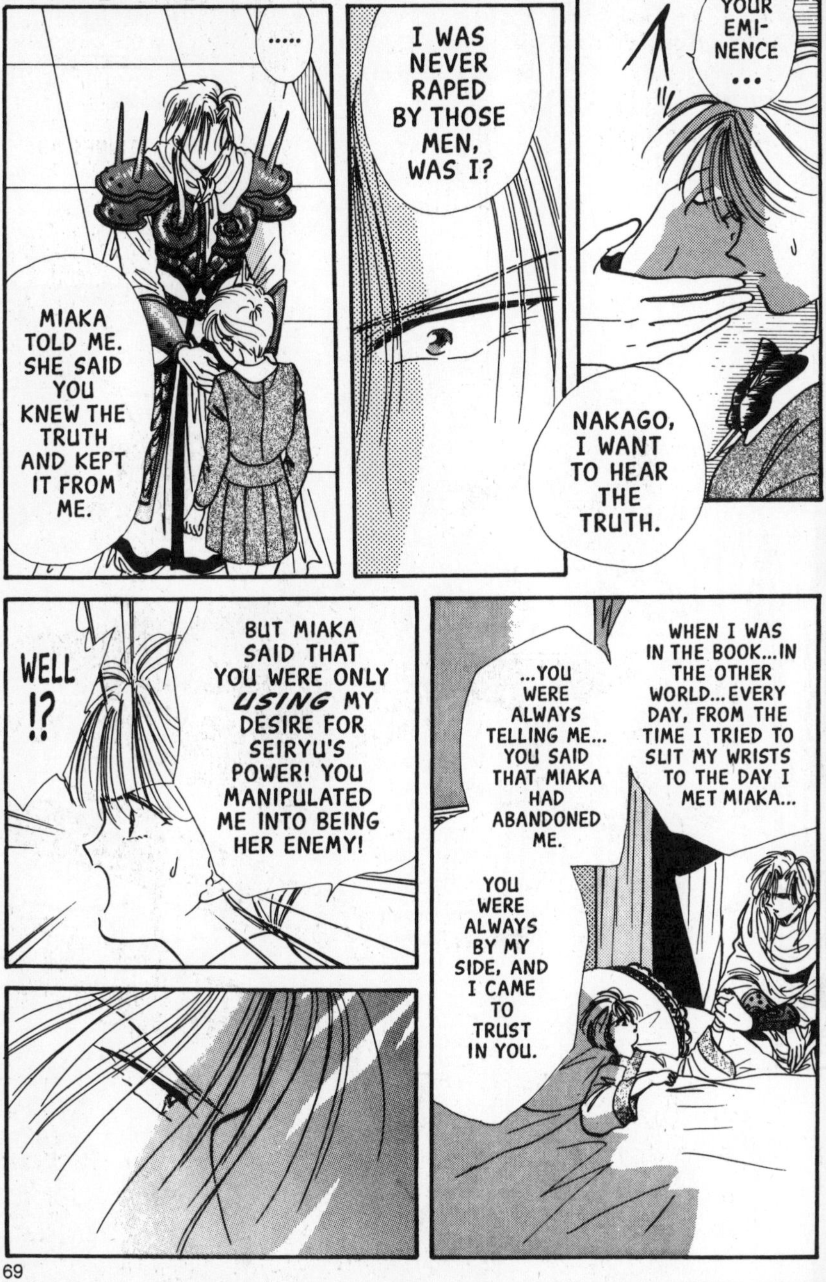
YOUR EMINENCE...
NAKAGO, I WANT TO HEAR THE TRUTH.
I WAS NEVER RAPED BY THOSE MEN, WAS I?
.....
MIAKA TOLD ME. SHE SAID YOU KNEW THE TRUTH AND KEPT IT FROM ME.
WHEN I WAS IN THE BOOK...IN THE OTHER WORLD...EVERY DAY, FROM THE TIME I TRIED TO SLIT MY WRISTS TO THE DAY I MET MIAKA...
...YOU WERE ALWAYS TELLING ME... YOU SAID THAT MIAKA HAD ABANDONED ME.
YOU WERE ALWAYS BY MY SIDE, AND I CAME TO TRUST IN YOU.
BUT MIAKA SAID THAT YOU WERE ONLY *USING* MY DESIRE FOR SEIRYU'S POWER! YOU MANIPULATED ME INTO BEING HER ENEMY!
WELL !?

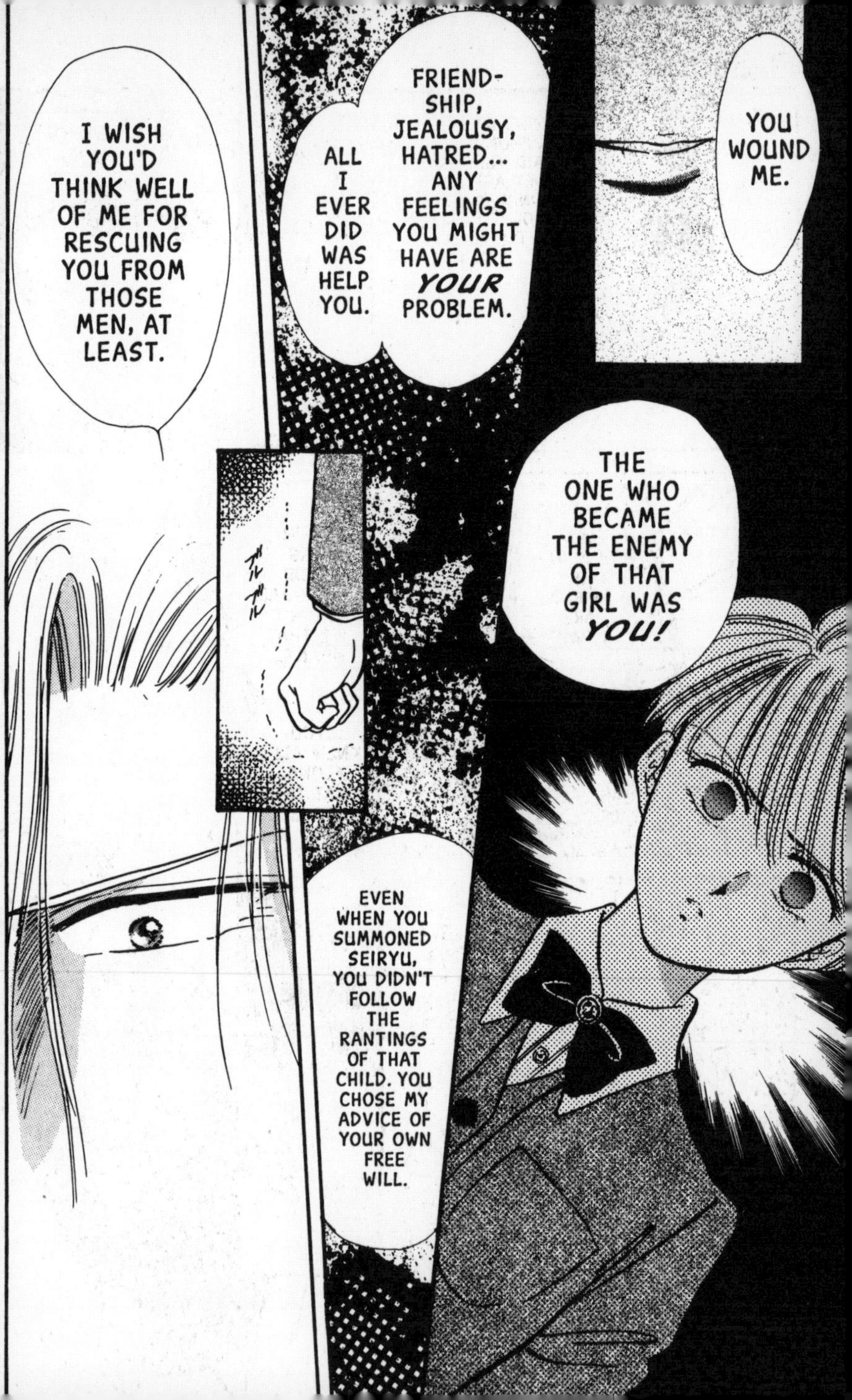
YOU WOUND ME.
ALL I EVER DID WAS HELP YOU.
FRIEND-SHIP, JEALOUSY, HATRED... ANY FEELINGS YOU MIGHT HAVE ARE *YOUR* PROBLEM.
THE ONE WHO BECAME THE ENEMY OF THAT GIRL WAS *YOU!*
ブルブル
EVEN WHEN YOU SUMMONED SEIRYU, YOU DIDN'T FOLLOW THE RANTINGS OF THAT CHILD. YOU CHOSE MY ADVICE OF YOUR OWN FREE WILL.
I WISH YOU'D THINK WELL OF ME FOR RESCUING YOU FROM THOSE MEN, AT LEAST.

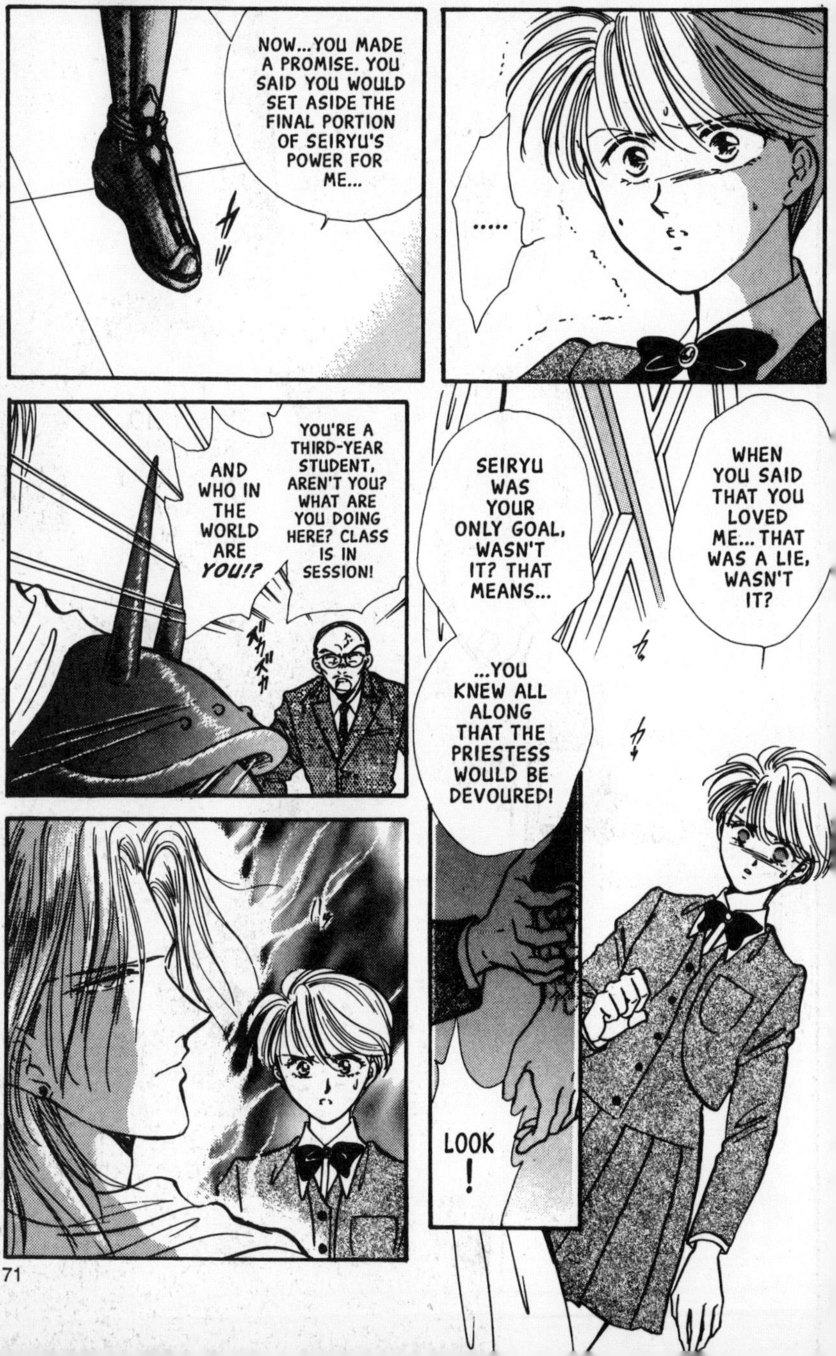
.....
NOW...YOU MADE A PROMISE. YOU SAID YOU WOULD SET ASIDE THE FINAL PORTION OF SEIRYU'S POWER FOR ME...
WHEN YOU SAID THAT YOU LOVED ME... THAT WAS A LIE, WASN'T IT?
SEIRYU WAS YOUR ONLY GOAL, WASN'T IT? THAT MEANS...
...YOU KNEW ALL ALONG THAT THE PRIESTESS WOULD BE DEVOURED!
LOOK!
YOU'RE A THIRD-YEAR STUDENT, AREN'T YOU? WHAT ARE YOU DOING HERE? CLASS IS IN SESSION!
AND WHO IN THE WORLD ARE *YOU!?*

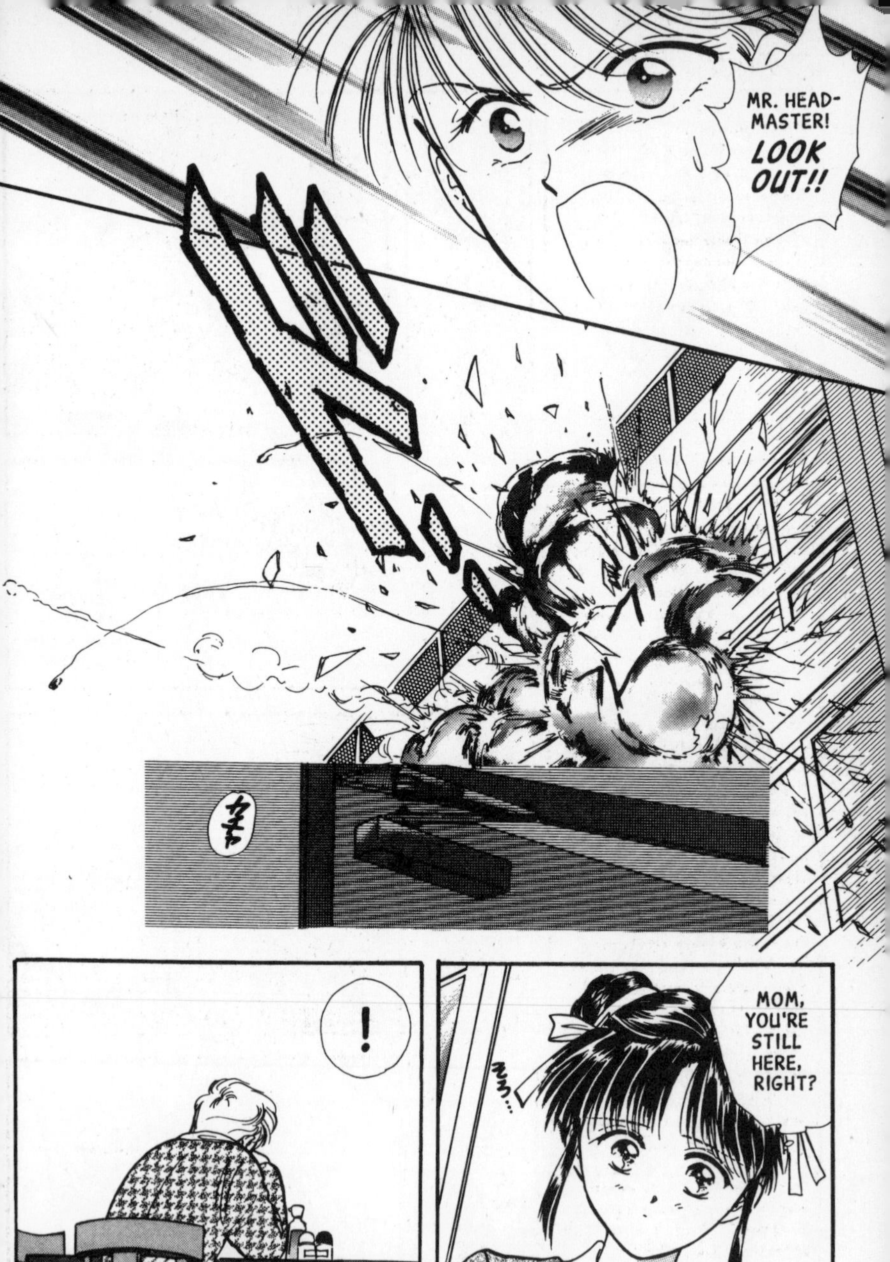
MR. HEAD-MASTER! LOOK OUT!!
カチャ
MOM, YOU'RE STILL HERE, RIGHT?
!

So you see that I started Fushigi with real apprehension.
And now that I think of it, there were quite a few comments that Nuriko seems a lot like Yoko from "Prepubescence." And at first, many of those similarities were there on purpose. I wanted the fans of "Prepubescence" to read and enjoy Fushigi. I was single-minded about it! No kidding! ☺ But soon, little by little, Nuriko's character changed by itself until Nuriko was completely different from Yoko.
But no matter how hard I worked, I kept on hearing complaints and grumbles! ☺ "If I had only continued 'Prepubescence,' I wouldn't be feeling this pressure," I said to myself, but now, I think I was being naive. There are certain loyalties that you can't import from one series to another. But I wanted everyone to shout at me, "Wow, you seem like you are having a lot of fun creating this series!" or, "Boy, is this different!" ☺ And soon, I did start to have fun.
"Prepubescence" was a character-driven comedy, so the characters were most important. So for this one, I thought it would be best to make it story-driven. *Of course, that's a big exaggeration!* But I went with my personal tastes, so I wonder what kind of story it turned out to be. What are my tastes? Oh, come on! You know! Look at all the love scenes! One or two in every installment! Friendship! Fights! Adventure! ...and other staples of the shônen world. But throw sadness in there too. ☺ That's what makes it a shôjo manga! *But it's also fun!* A rip-roaring fantasy was one of my favorite things, but this story wasn't so much that. Human emotions were the basis. For magic and the like, you'll need a better storyteller than me! ☺ I love the saying of an editor, "No work ever became a major work without a love story!" But it's also said, "Don't be too self-indulgent." ☺
I was a little, huh?
But anyway, I put my whole heart into this story!

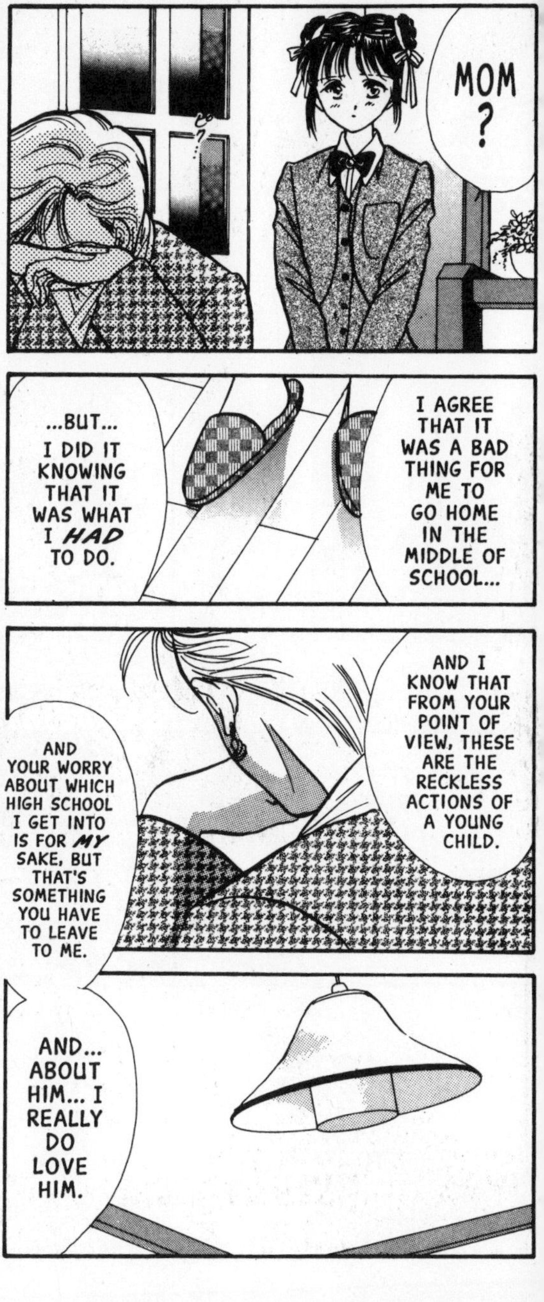
MOM?
I AGREE THAT IT WAS A BAD THING FOR ME TO GO HOME IN THE MIDDLE OF SCHOOL...
...BUT... I DID IT KNOWING THAT IT WAS WHAT I *HAD* TO DO.
AND I KNOW THAT FROM YOUR POINT OF VIEW, THESE ARE THE RECKLESS ACTIONS OF A YOUNG CHILD.
AND YOUR WORRY ABOUT WHICH HIGH SCHOOL I GET INTO IS FOR *MY* SAKE, BUT THAT'S SOMETHING YOU HAVE TO LEAVE TO ME.
AND... ABOUT HIM... I REALLY DO LOVE HIM.

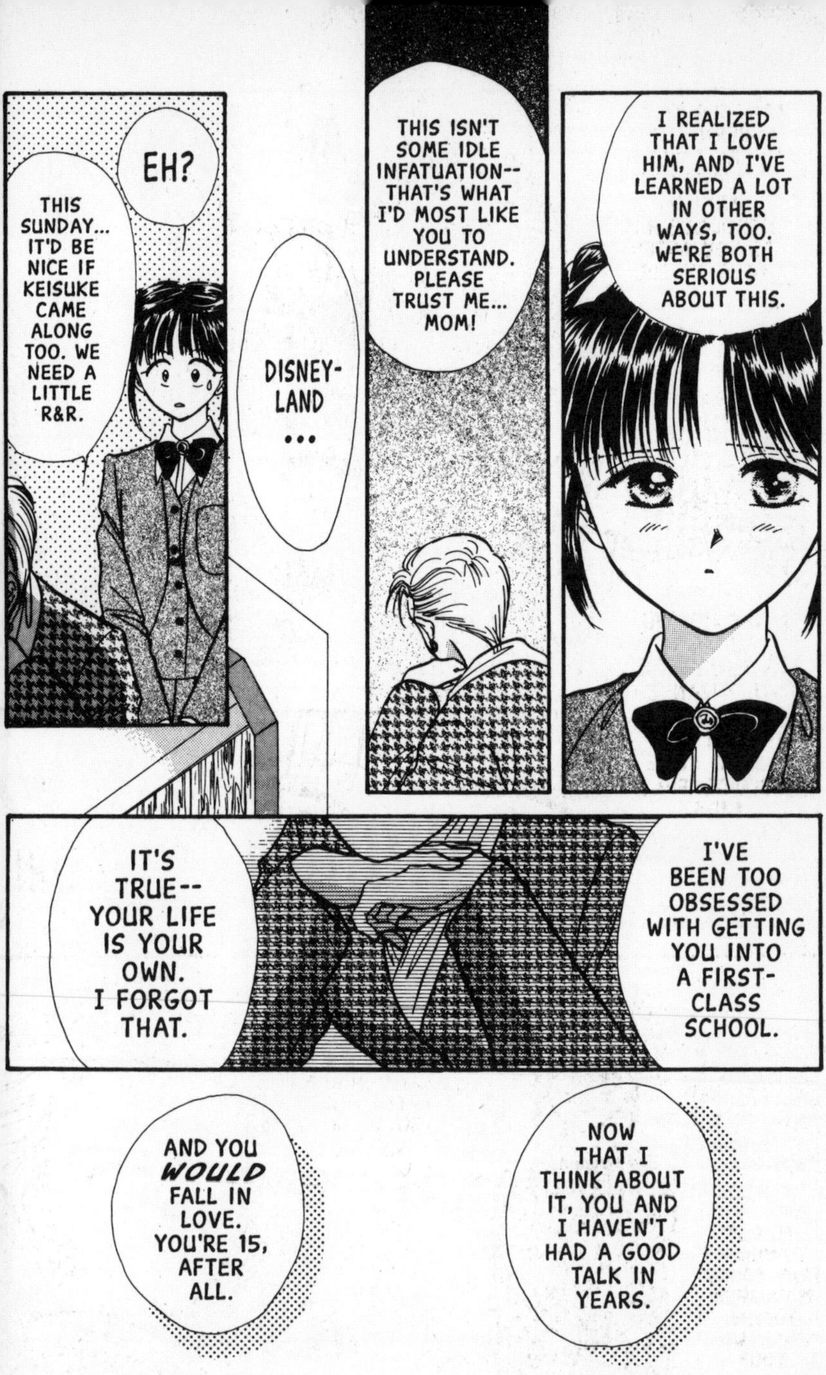
I REALIZED THAT I LOVE HIM, AND I'VE LEARNED A LOT IN OTHER WAYS, TOO. WE'RE BOTH SERIOUS ABOUT THIS.
THIS ISN'T SOME IDLE INFATUATION--THAT'S WHAT I'D MOST LIKE YOU TO UNDERSTAND. PLEASE TRUST ME... MOM!
DISNEY-LAND ...
EH?
THIS SUNDAY... IT'D BE NICE IF KEISUKE CAME ALONG TOO. WE NEED A LITTLE R&R.
I'VE BEEN TOO OBSESSED WITH GETTING YOU INTO A FIRST-CLASS SCHOOL.
IT'S TRUE--YOUR LIFE IS YOUR OWN. I FORGOT THAT.
NOW THAT I THINK ABOUT IT, YOU AND I HAVEN'T HAD A GOOD TALK IN YEARS.
AND YOU *WOULD* FALL IN LOVE. YOU'RE 15, AFTER ALL.

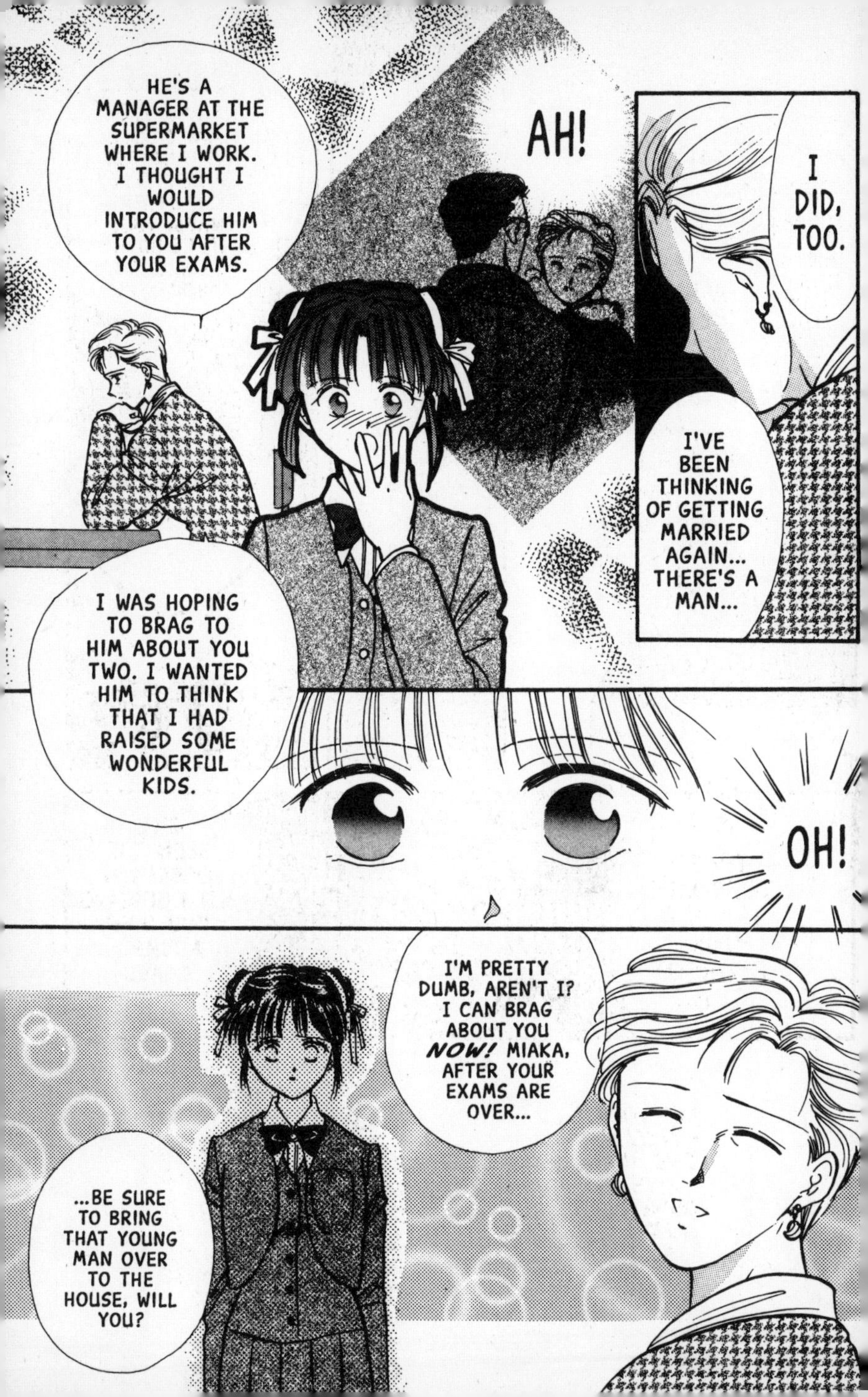
I DID, TOO.
I'VE BEEN THINKING OF GETTING MARRIED AGAIN... THERE'S A MAN...
AH!
HE'S A MANAGER AT THE SUPERMARKET WHERE I WORK. I THOUGHT I WOULD INTRODUCE HIM TO YOU AFTER YOUR EXAMS.
I WAS HOPING TO BRAG TO HIM ABOUT YOU TWO. I WANTED HIM TO THINK THAT I HAD RAISED SOME WONDERFUL KIDS.
OH!
I'M PRETTY DUMB, AREN'T I? I CAN BRAG ABOUT YOU *NOW!* MIAKA, AFTER YOUR EXAMS ARE OVER...
...BE SURE TO BRING THAT YOUNG MAN OVER TO THE HOUSE, WILL YOU?

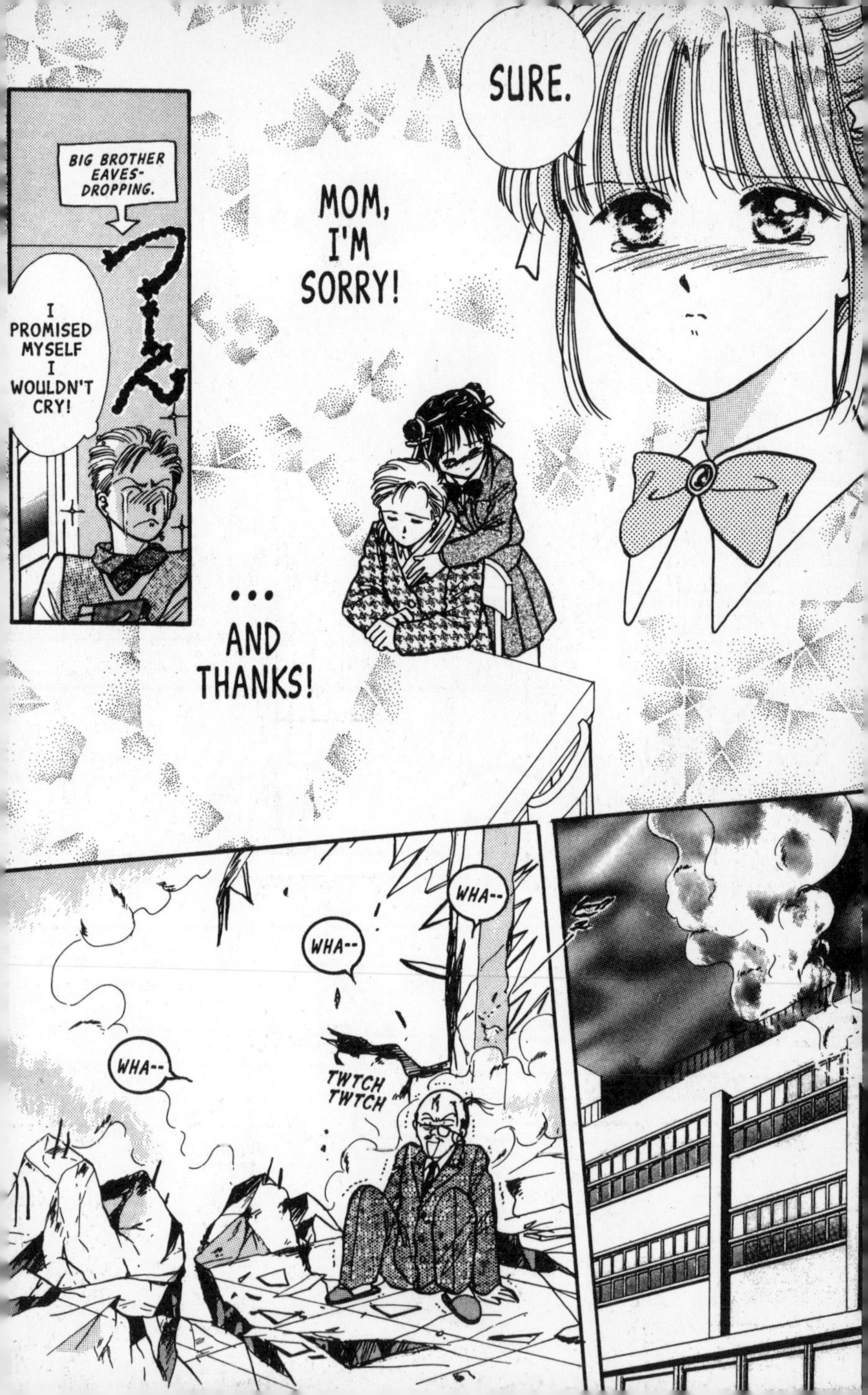
SURE.
MOM, I'M SORRY!
... AND THANKS!
BIG BROTHER EAVES-DROPPING.
I PROMISED MYSELF I WOULDN'T CRY!
WHA--
WHA--
TWTCH TWTCH
WHA--

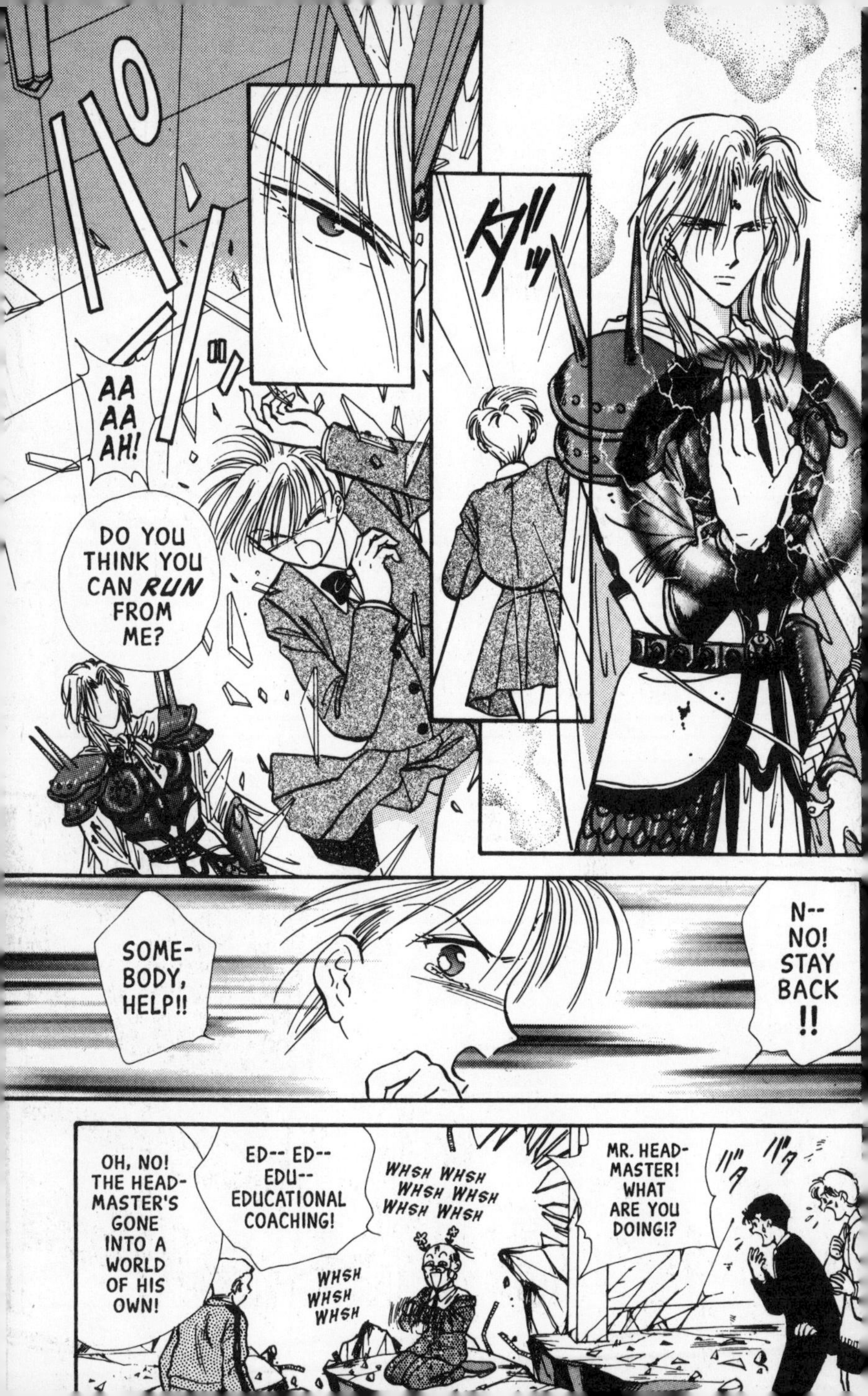

ダッ
AAAAAAH!
DO YOU THINK YOU CAN RUN FROM ME?
N-- NO! STAY BACK!!
SOME-BODY, HELP!!
バタ バタ
MR. HEAD-MASTER! WHAT ARE YOU DOING!?
WHSH WHSH WHSH WHSH WHSH WHSH
ED-- ED-- EDU-- EDUCATIONAL COACHING!
WHSH WHSH WHSH
OH, NO! THE HEAD-MASTER'S GONE INTO A WORLD OF HIS OWN!

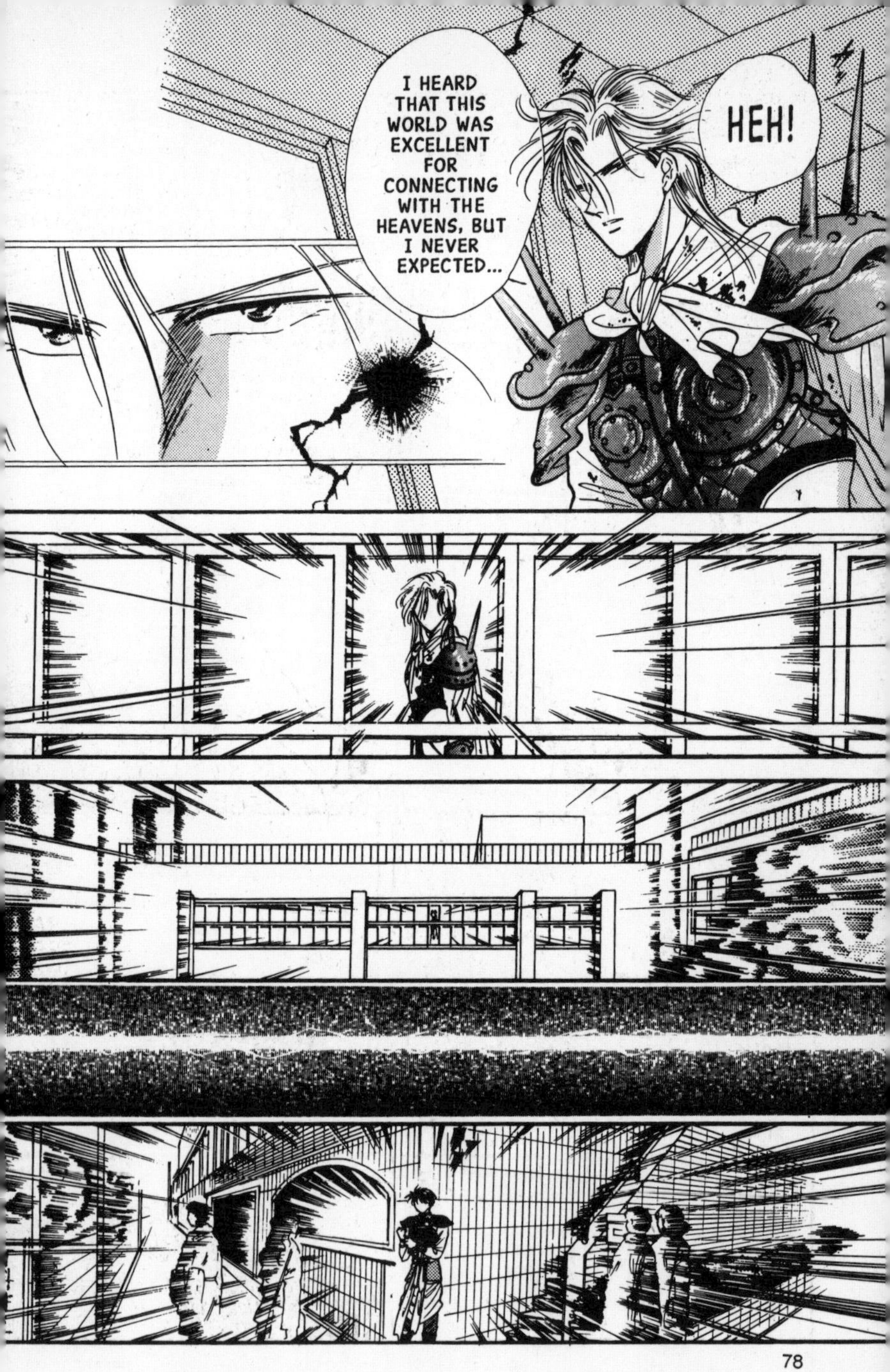
HEH!
I HEARD THAT THIS WORLD WAS EXCELLENT FOR CONNECTING WITH THE HEAVENS, BUT I NEVER EXPECTED...

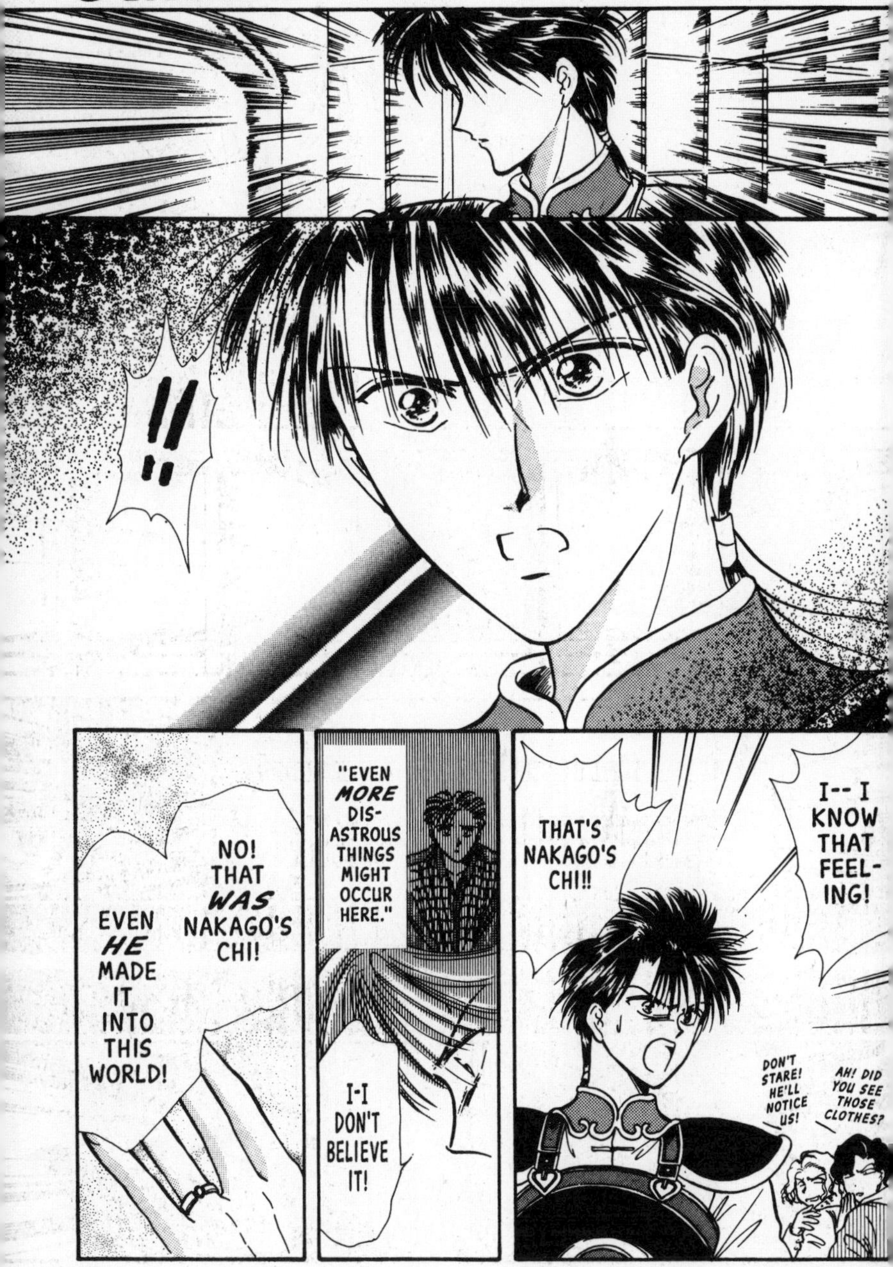
!!
I-- I KNOW THAT FEEL-ING!
THAT'S NAKAGO'S CHI!!
AH! DID YOU SEE THOSE CLOTHES?
DON'T STARE! HE'LL NOTICE US!
"EVEN *MORE* DIS-ASTROUS THINGS MIGHT OCCUR HERE."
I-I DON'T BELIEVE IT!
NO! THAT *WAS* NAKAGO'S CHI!
EVEN *HE* MADE IT INTO THIS WORLD!

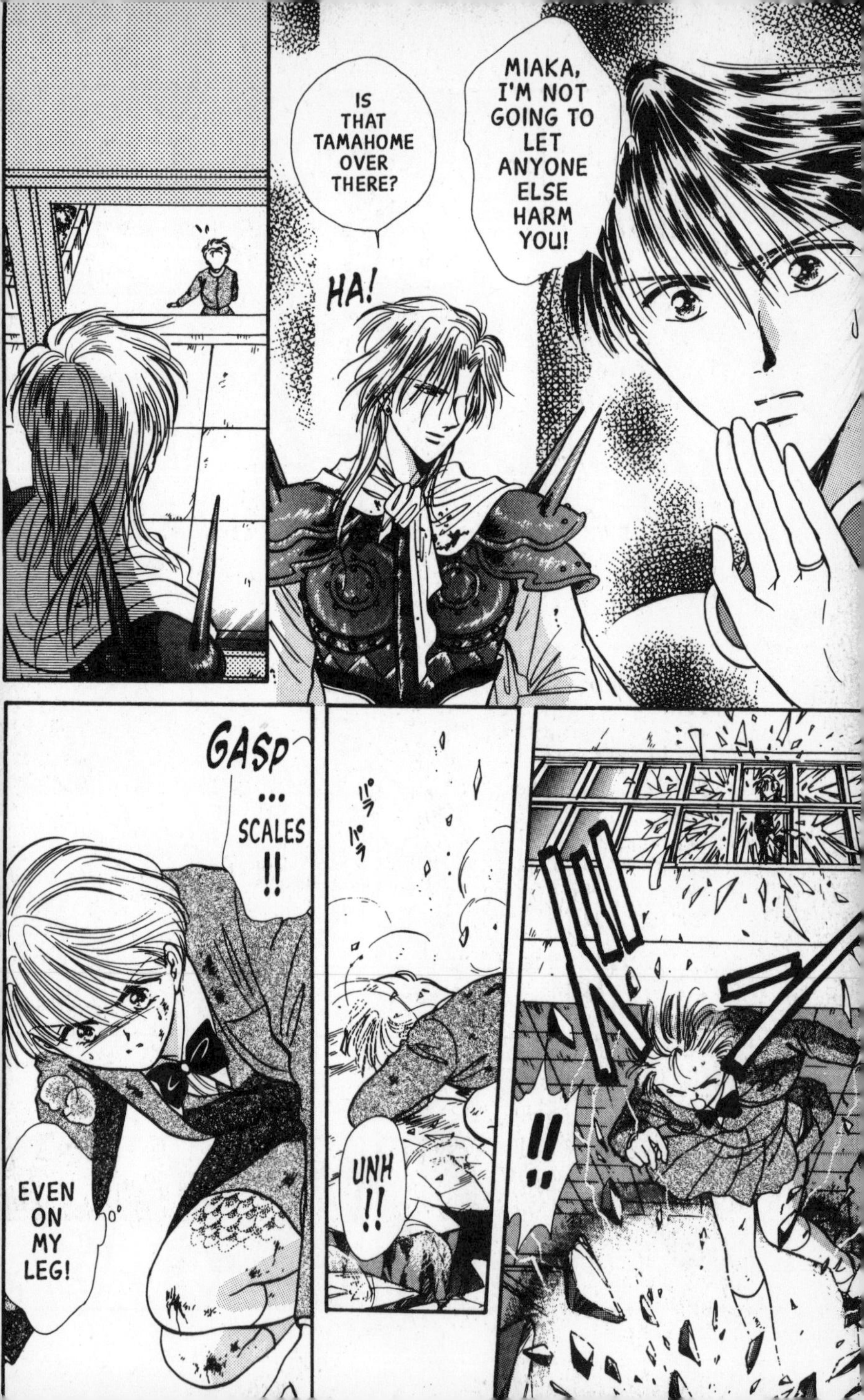

MIAKA, I'M NOT GOING TO LET ANYONE ELSE HARM YOU!
IS THAT TAMAHOME OVER THERE?
HA!
!!
パラ
パラ
UNH !!
GASP
... SCALES !!
EVEN ON MY LEG!

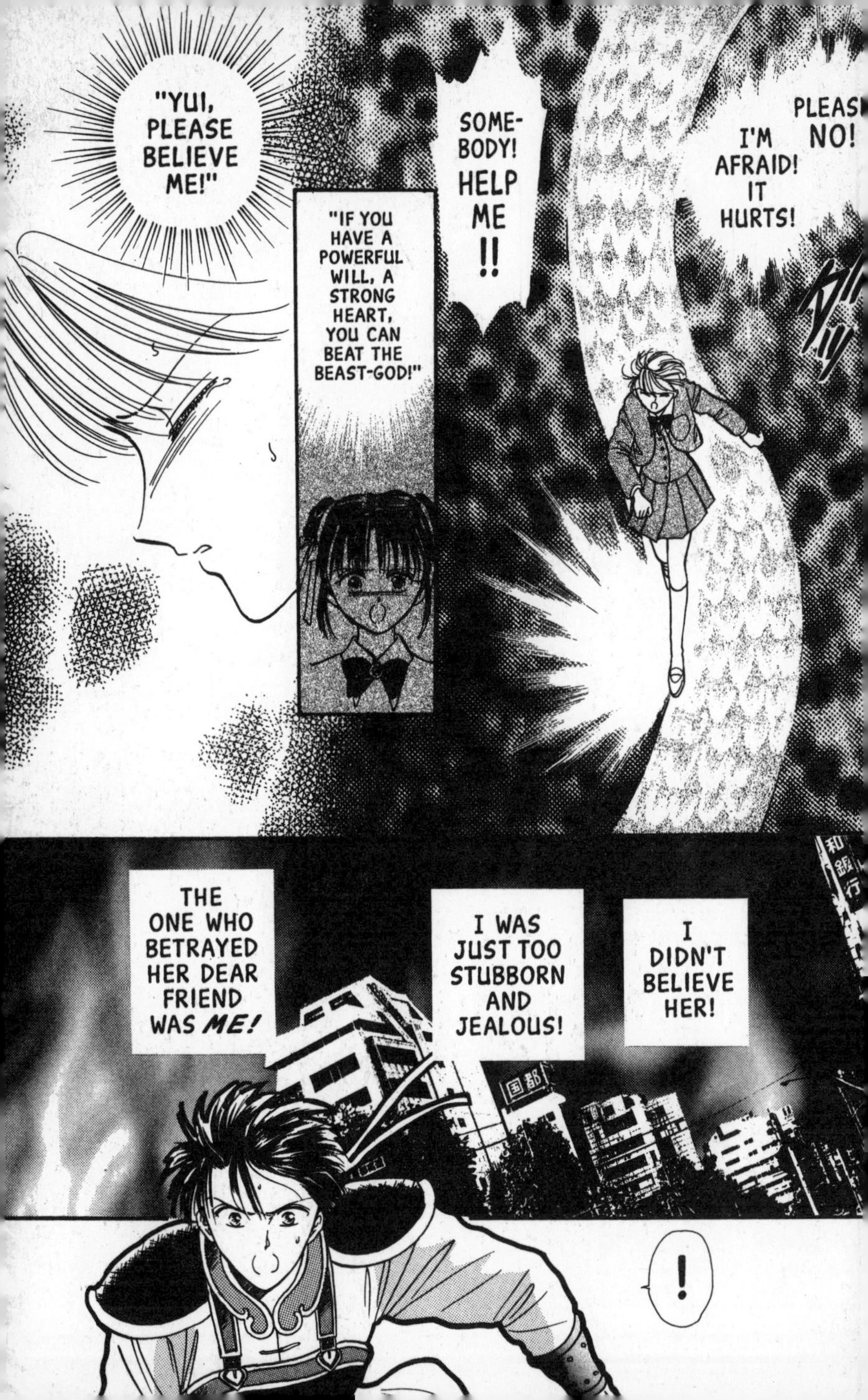
PLEAS NO!
I'M AFRAID! IT HURTS!
SOME-BODY! HELP ME !!
"IF YOU HAVE A POWERFUL WILL, A STRONG HEART, YOU CAN BEAT THE BEAST-GOD!"
"YUI, PLEASE BELIEVE ME!"
I DIDN'T BELIEVE HER!
I WAS JUST TOO STUBBORN AND JEALOUS!
THE ONE WHO BETRAYED HER DEAR FRIEND WAS *ME!*
!

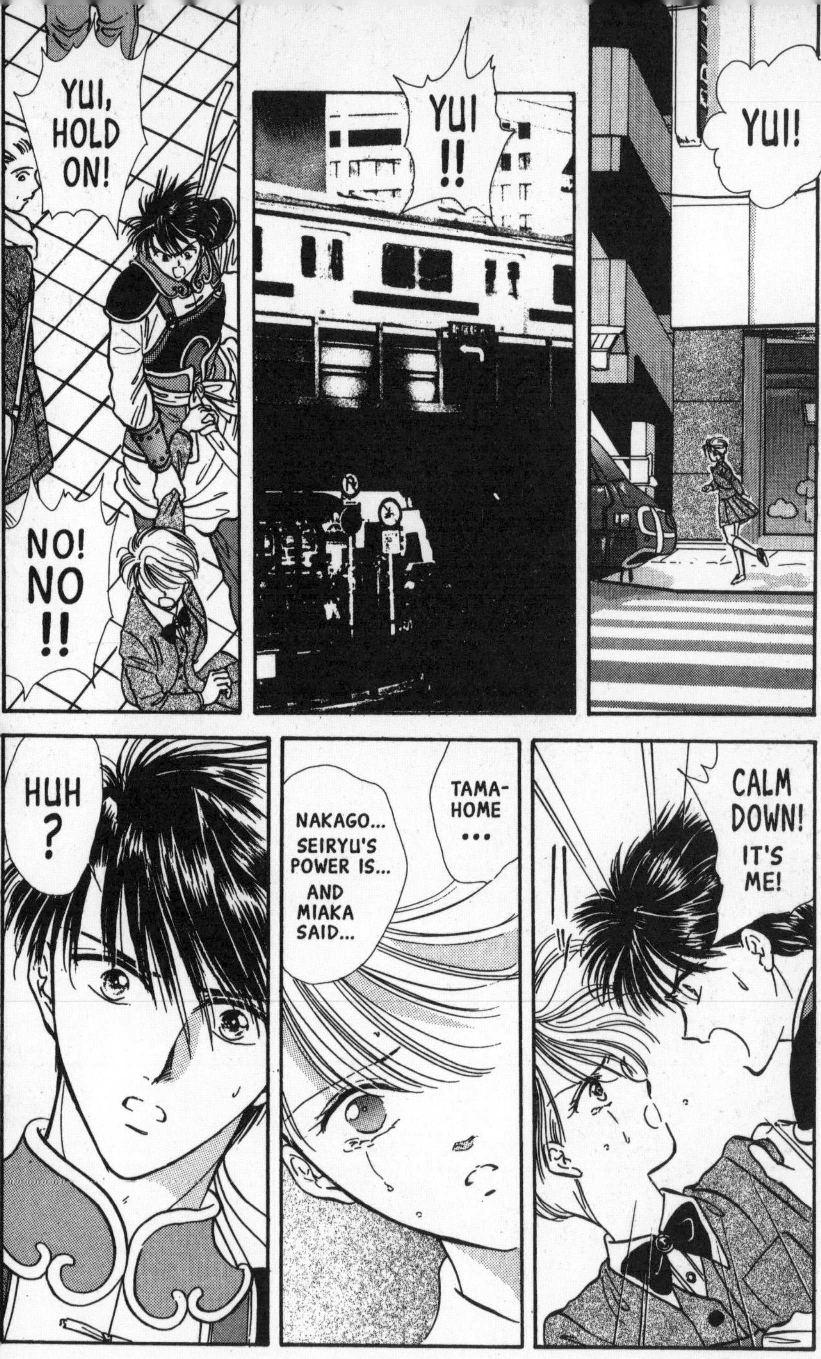
YUI!
YUI !!
YUI, HOLD ON!
NO! NO !!
CALM DOWN! IT'S ME!
TAMA-HOME ...
NAKAGO... SEIRYU'S POWER IS... AND MIAKA SAID...
HUH ?

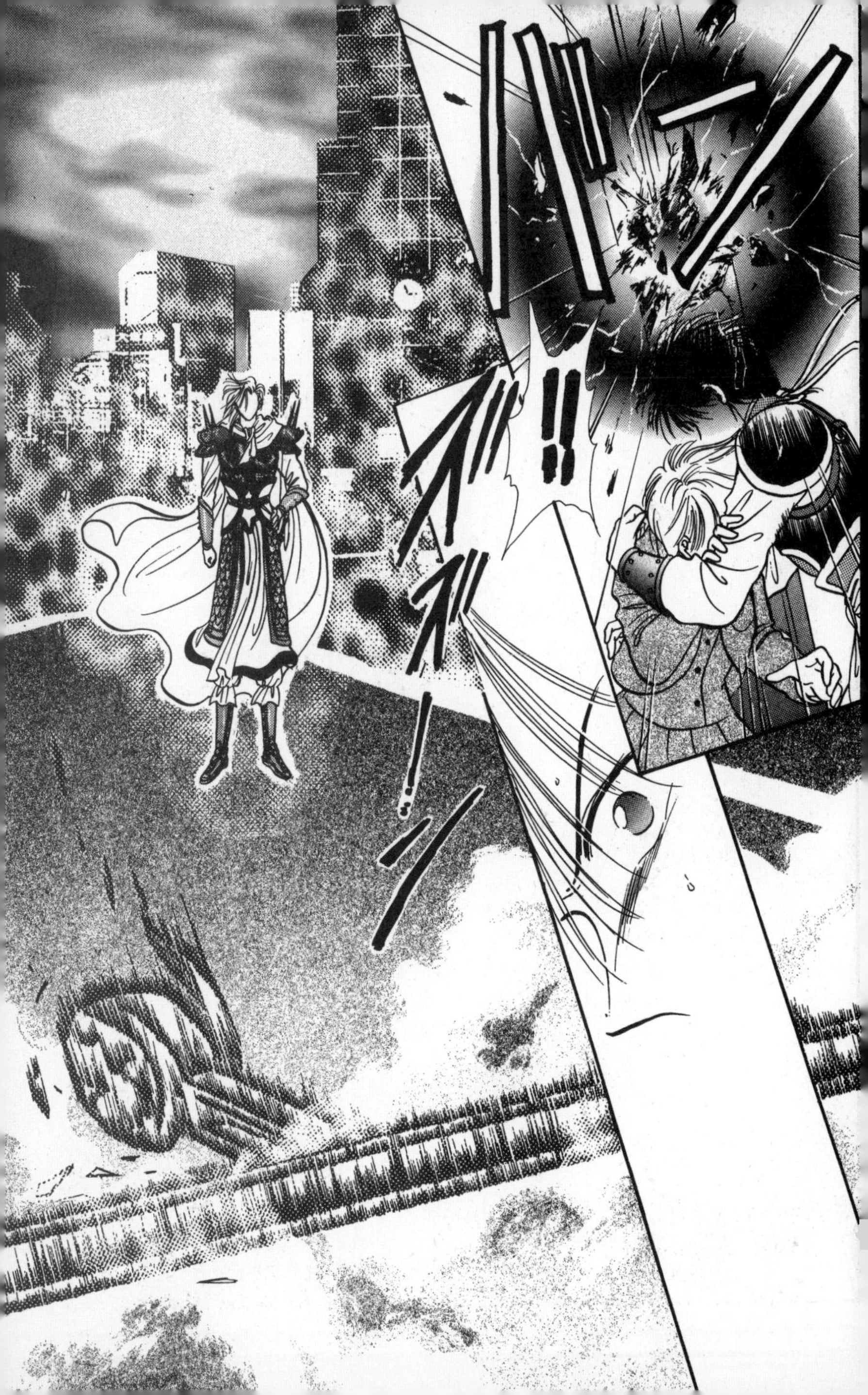
バーン
!!

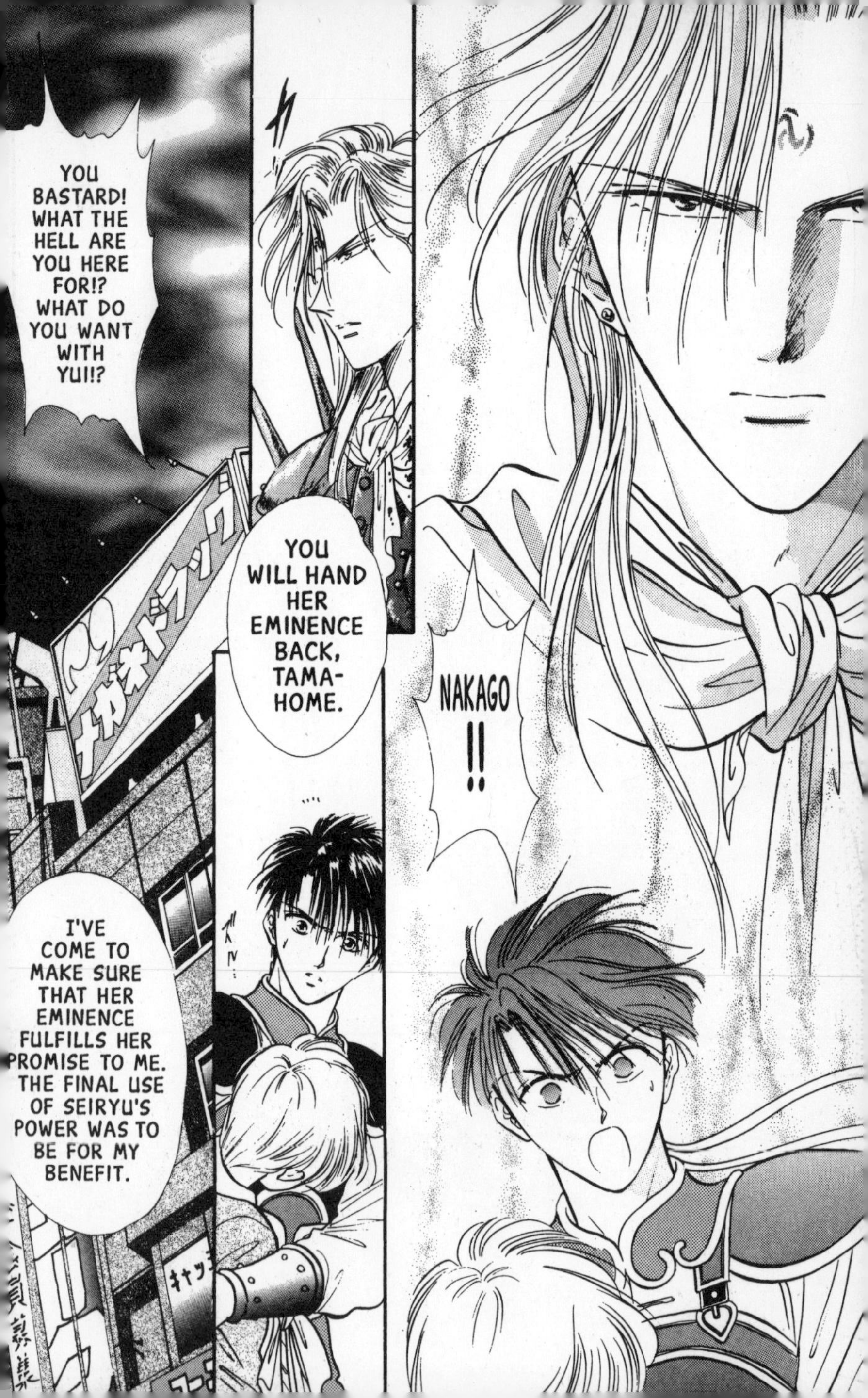
NAKAGO !!
YOU WILL HAND HER EMINENCE BACK, TAMA-HOME.
...
YOU BASTARD! WHAT THE HELL ARE YOU HERE FOR!? WHAT DO YOU WANT WITH YUI!?
I'VE COME TO MAKE SURE THAT HER EMINENCE FULFILLS HER PROMISE TO ME. THE FINAL USE OF SEIRYU'S POWER WAS TO BE FOR MY BENEFIT.

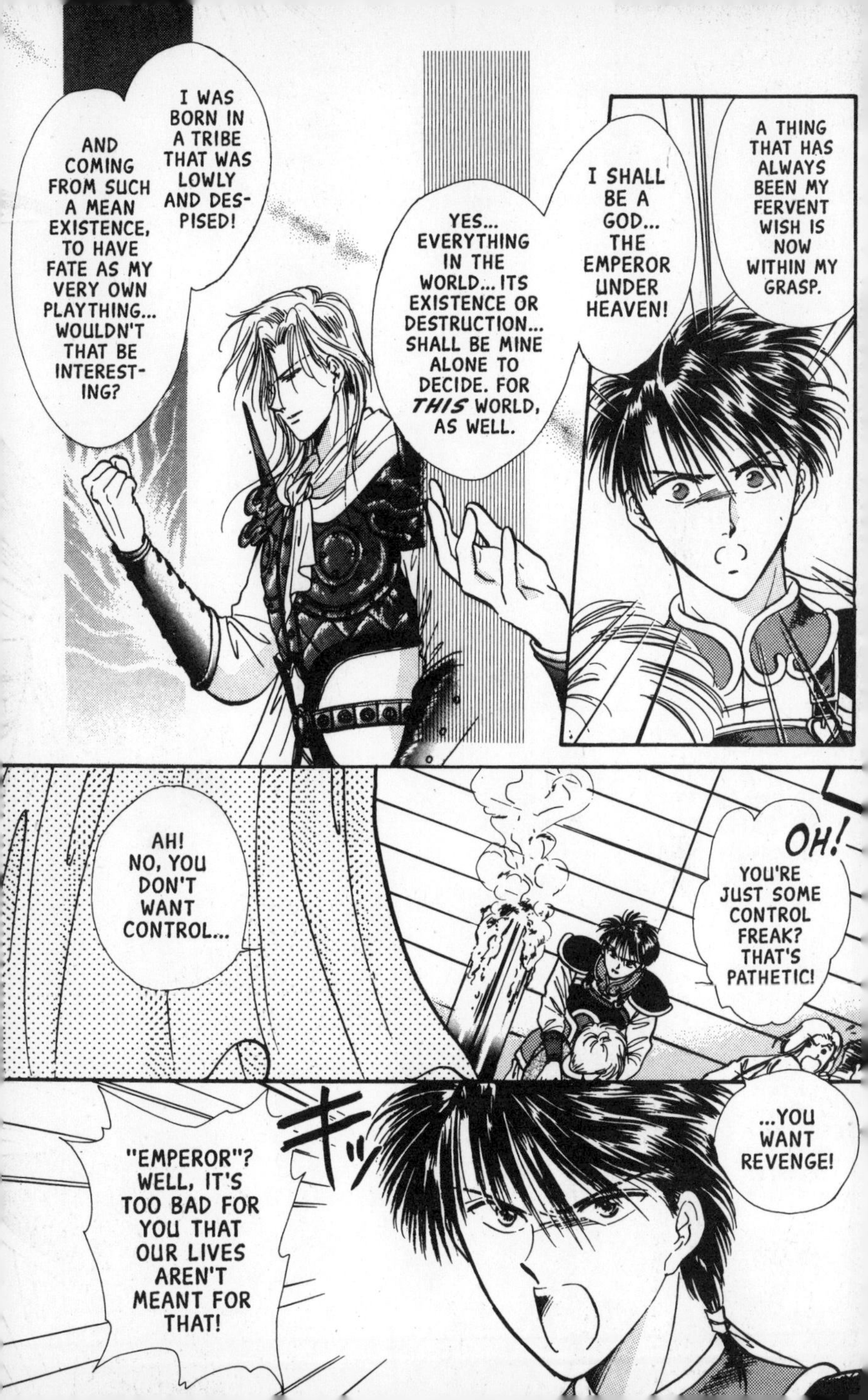
A THING THAT HAS ALWAYS BEEN MY FERVENT WISH IS NOW WITHIN MY GRASP.
I SHALL BE A GOD... THE EMPEROR UNDER HEAVEN!
YES... EVERYTHING IN THE WORLD... ITS EXISTENCE OR DESTRUCTION... SHALL BE MINE ALONE TO DECIDE. FOR *THIS* WORLD, AS WELL.
I WAS BORN IN A TRIBE THAT WAS LOWLY AND DES-PISED!
AND COMING FROM SUCH A MEAN EXISTENCE, TO HAVE FATE AS MY VERY OWN PLAYTHING... WOULDN'T THAT BE INTEREST-ING?
OH! YOU'RE JUST SOME CONTROL FREAK? THAT'S PATHETIC!
AH! NO, YOU DON'T WANT CONTROL...
...YOU WANT REVENGE!
キッ
"EMPEROR"? WELL, IT'S TOO BAD FOR YOU THAT OUR LIVES AREN'T MEANT FOR THAT!

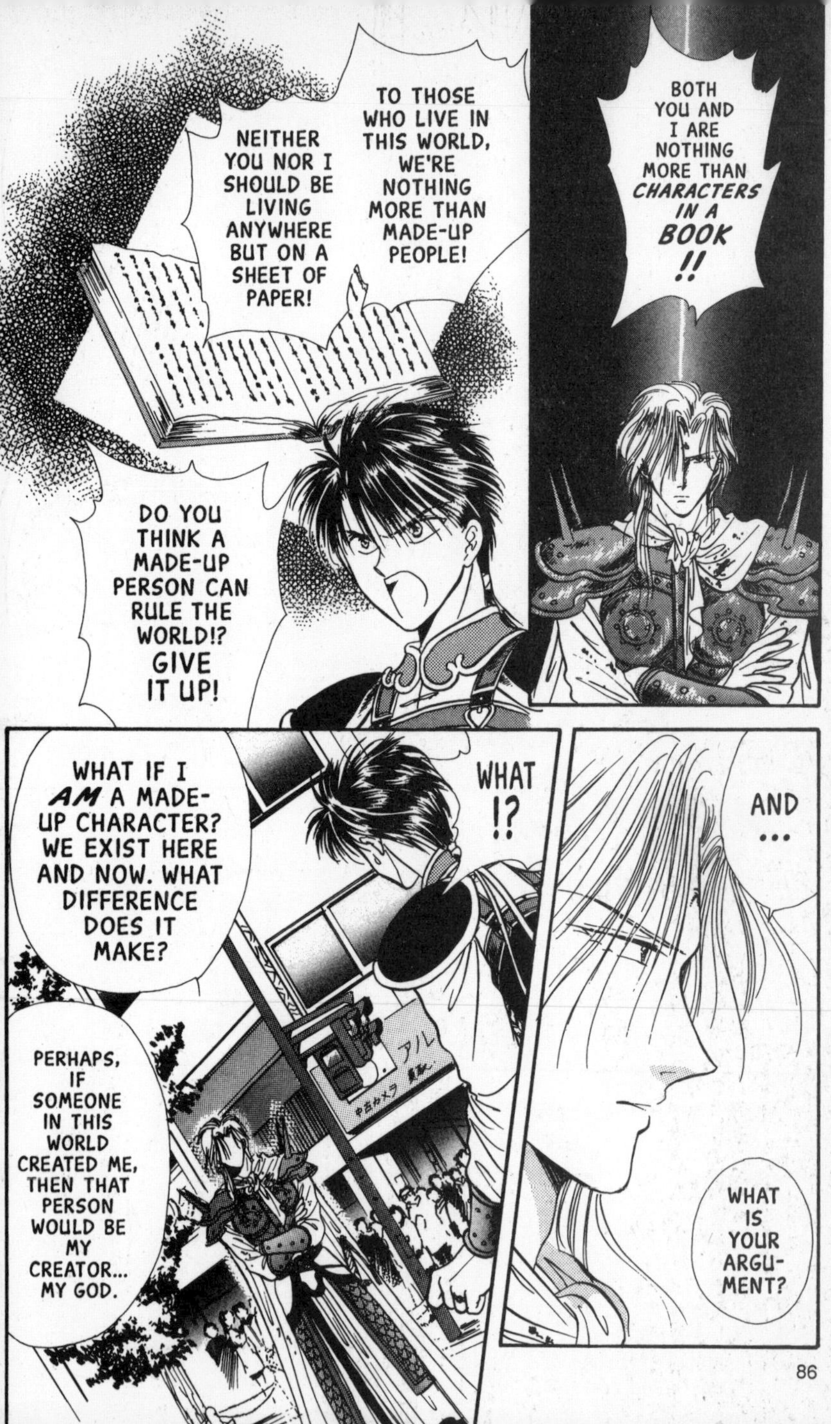
BOTH YOU AND I ARE NOTHING MORE THAN CHARACTERS IN A BOOK !!
TO THOSE WHO LIVE IN THIS WORLD, WE'RE NOTHING MORE THAN MADE-UP PEOPLE!
NEITHER YOU NOR I SHOULD BE LIVING ANYWHERE BUT ON A SHEET OF PAPER!
DO YOU THINK A MADE-UP PERSON CAN RULE THE WORLD!? GIVE IT UP!
AND ...
WHAT IS YOUR ARGU-MENT?
WHAT !?
WHAT IF I AM A MADE-UP CHARACTER? WE EXIST HERE AND NOW. WHAT DIFFERENCE DOES IT MAKE?
PERHAPS, IF SOMEONE IN THIS WORLD CREATED ME, THEN THAT PERSON WOULD BE MY CREATOR... MY GOD.

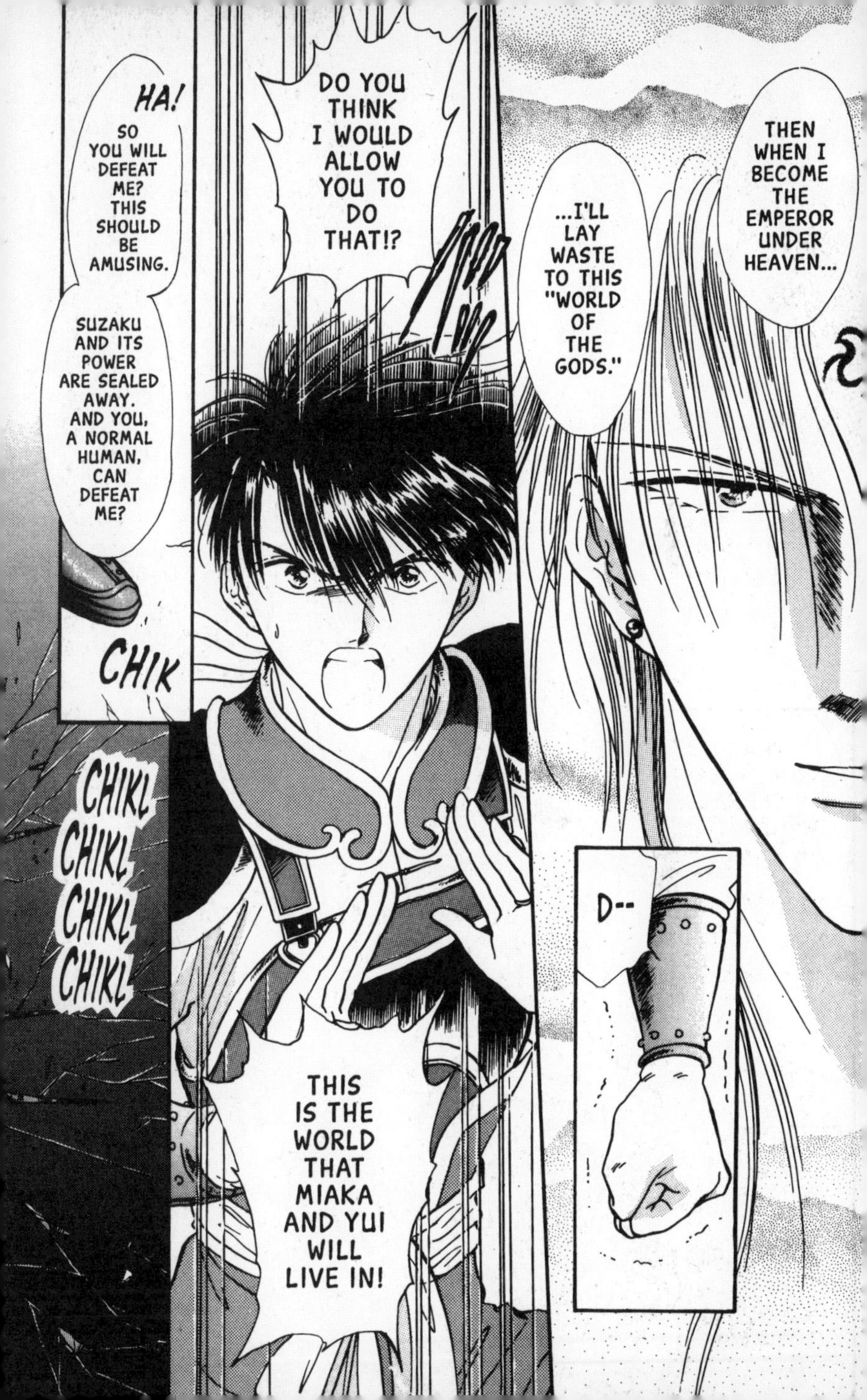

THEN WHEN I BECOME THE EMPEROR UNDER HEAVEN...
...I'LL LAY WASTE TO THIS "WORLD OF THE GODS."
D--
DO YOU THINK I WOULD ALLOW YOU TO DO THAT!?
THIS IS THE WORLD THAT MIAKA AND YUI WILL LIVE IN!
HA! SO YOU WILL DEFEAT ME? THIS SHOULD BE AMUSING.
SUZAKU AND ITS POWER ARE SEALED AWAY. AND YOU, A NORMAL HUMAN, CAN DEFEAT ME?
CHIK
CHIKL CHIKL CHIKL CHIKL

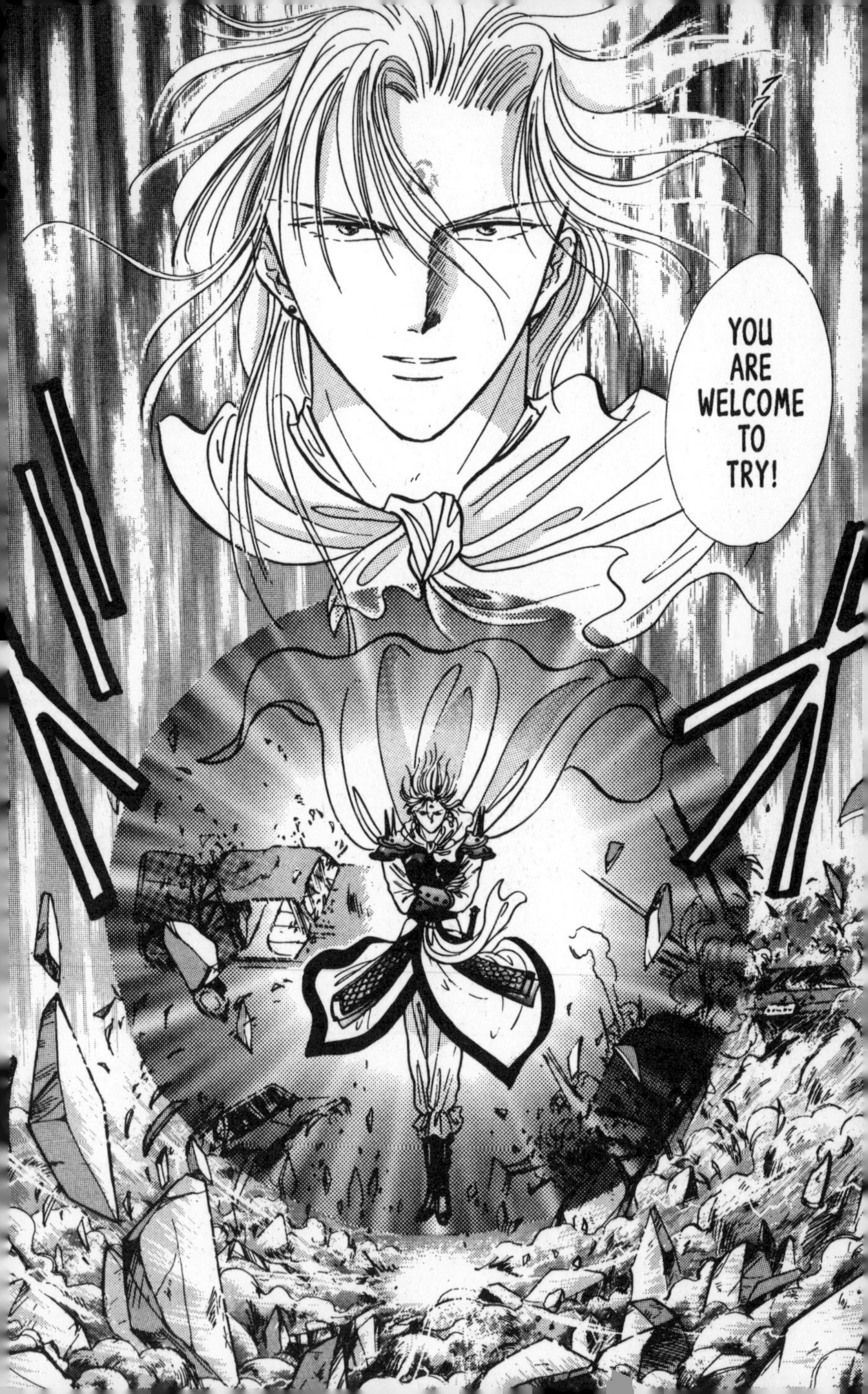
YOU ARE WELCOME TO TRY!

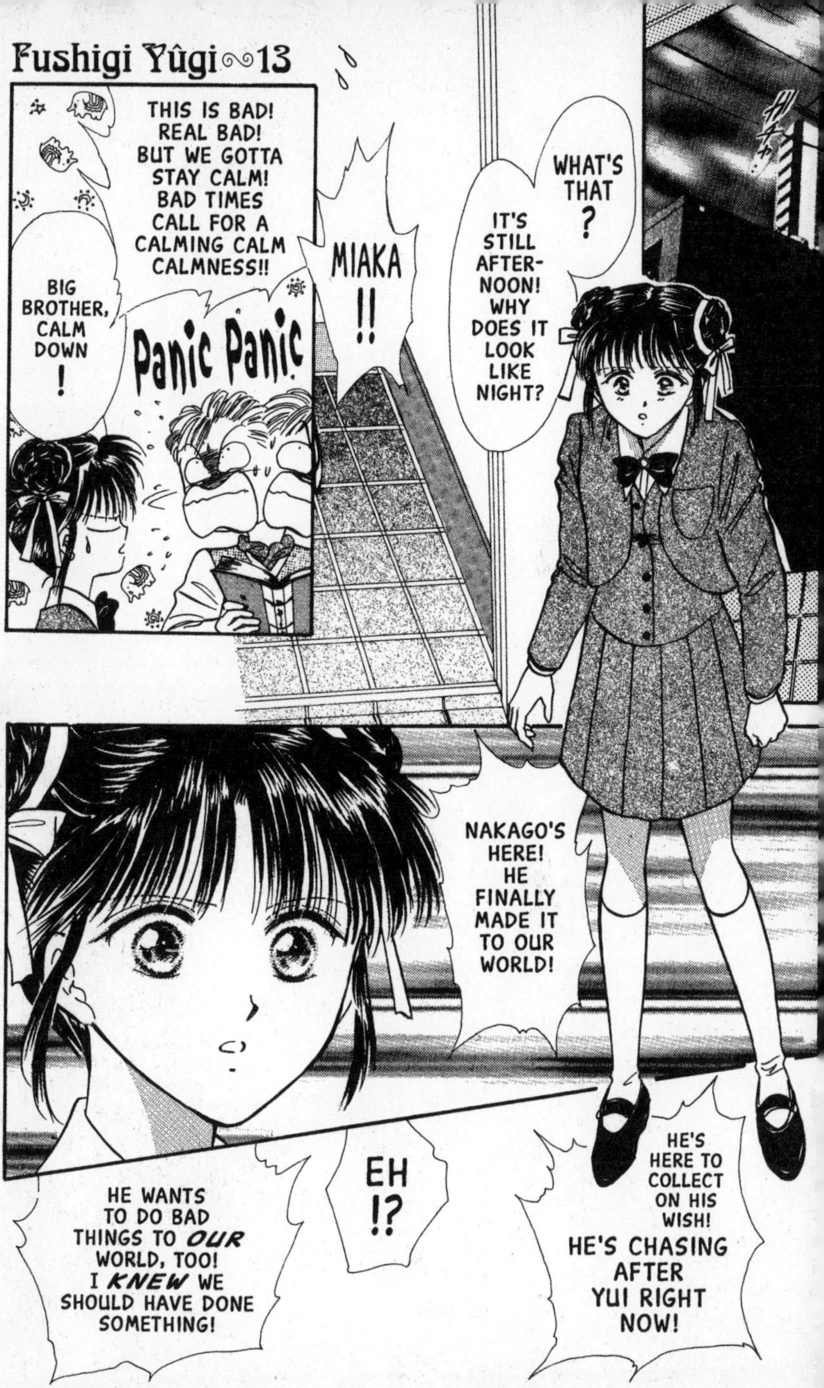
WHAT'S THAT ?
IT'S STILL AFTERNOON! WHY DOES IT LOOK LIKE NIGHT?
MIAKA !!
THIS IS BAD! REAL BAD! BUT WE GOTTA STAY CALM! BAD TIMES CALL FOR A CALMING CALM CALMNESS!!
Panic Panic
BIG BROTHER, CALM DOWN !
NAKAGO'S HERE! HE FINALLY MADE IT TO OUR WORLD!
HE'S HERE TO COLLECT ON HIS WISH! HE'S CHASING AFTER YUI RIGHT NOW!
EH !?
HE WANTS TO DO BAD THINGS TO *OUR* WORLD, TOO! I *KNEW* WE SHOULD HAVE DONE SOMETHING!

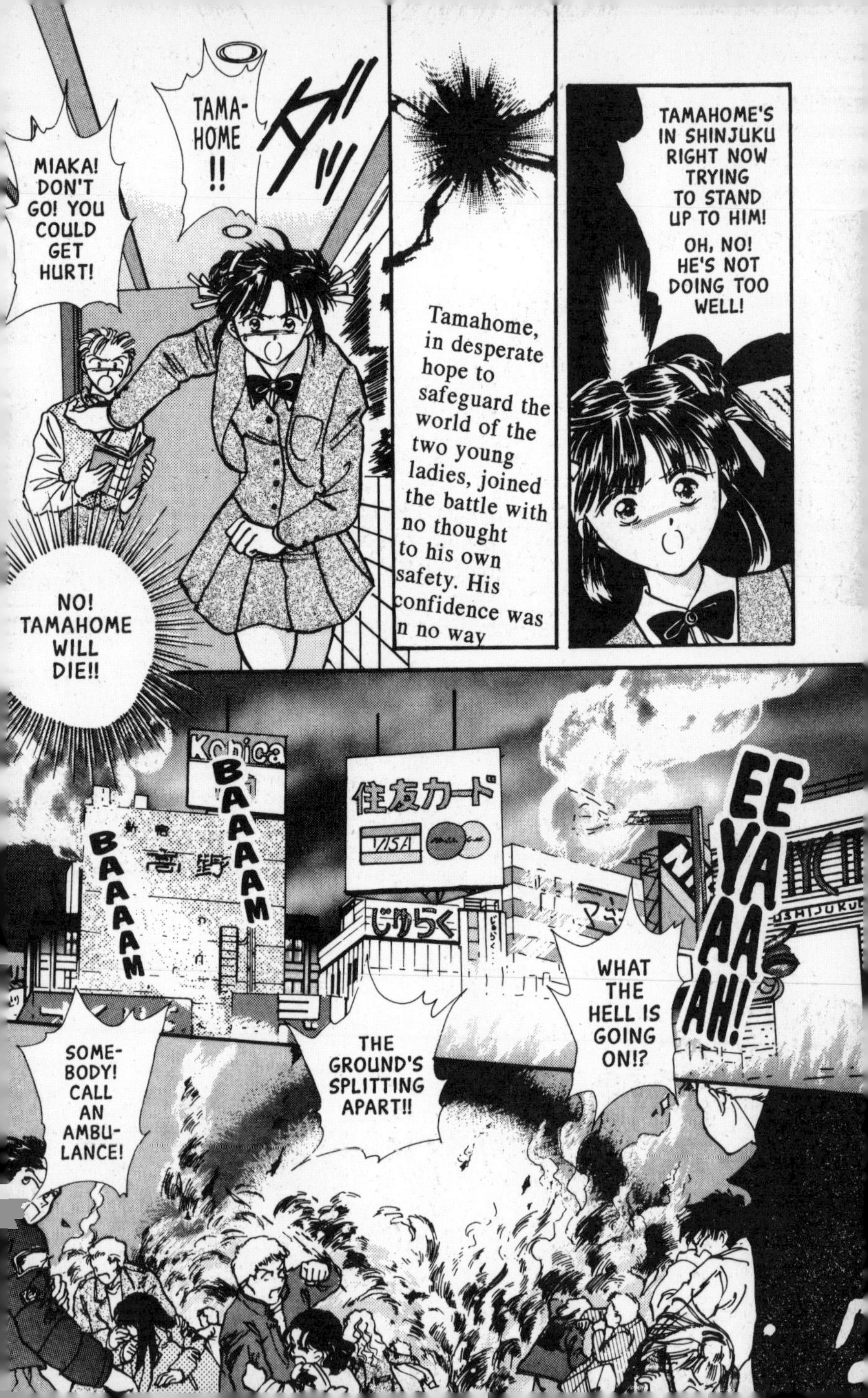
TAMAHOME'S IN SHINJUKU RIGHT NOW TRYING TO STAND UP TO HIM!
OH, NO! HE'S NOT DOING TOO WELL!
Tamahome, in desperate hope to safeguard the world of the two young ladies, joined the battle with no thought to his own safety. His confidence was n no way
ダッ
TAMA-HOME !!
MIAKA! DON'T GO! YOU COULD GET HURT!
NO! TAMAHOME WILL DIE!!
EEYAAAAH!
WHAT THE HELL IS GOING ON!?
住友カード
VISA
THE GROUND'S SPLITTING APART!!
Konica
BAAAAAM
BAAAAM
SOME-BODY! CALL AN AMBULANCE!

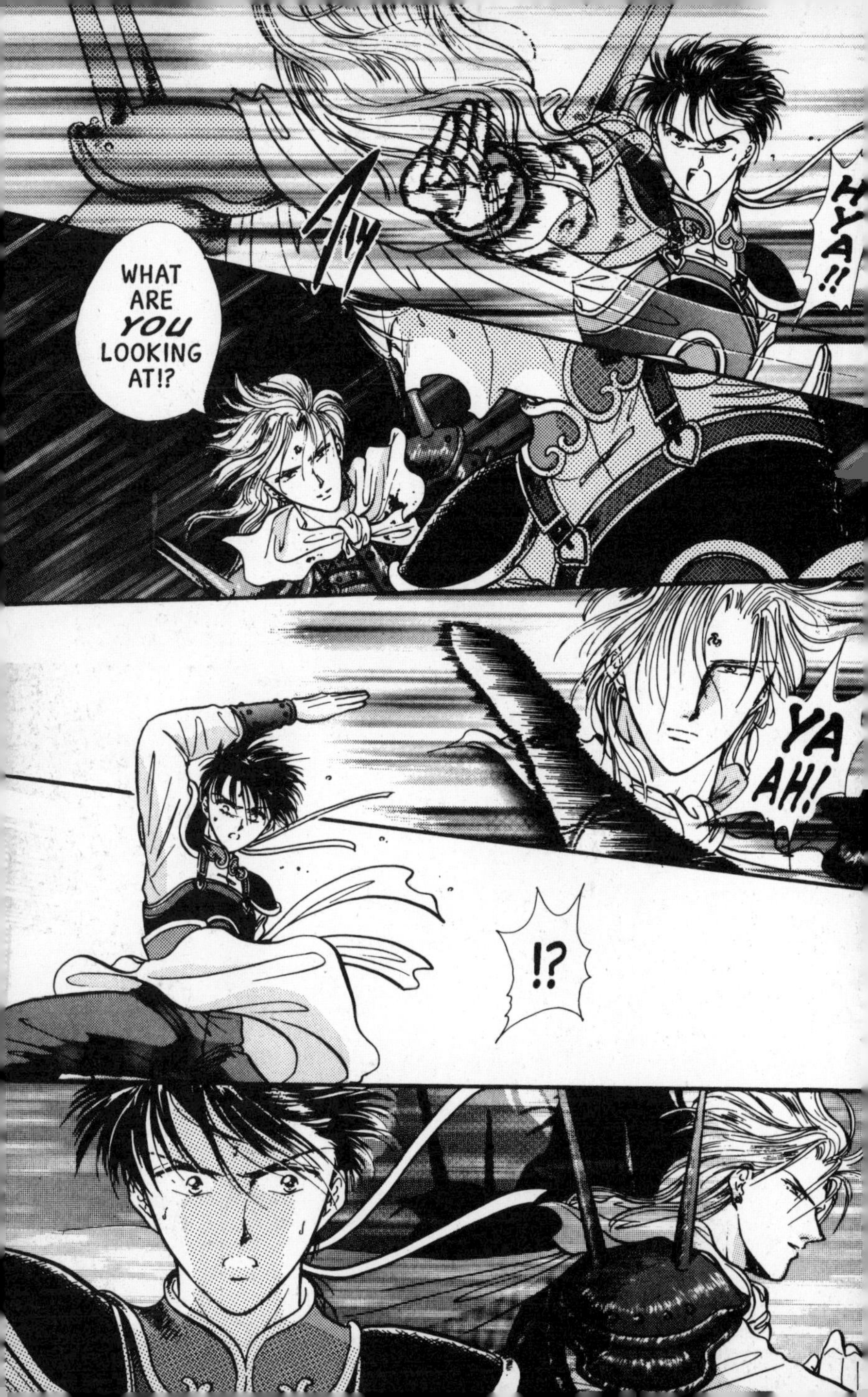
HYA!!
WHAT ARE YOU LOOKING AT!?
YA AH!
!?

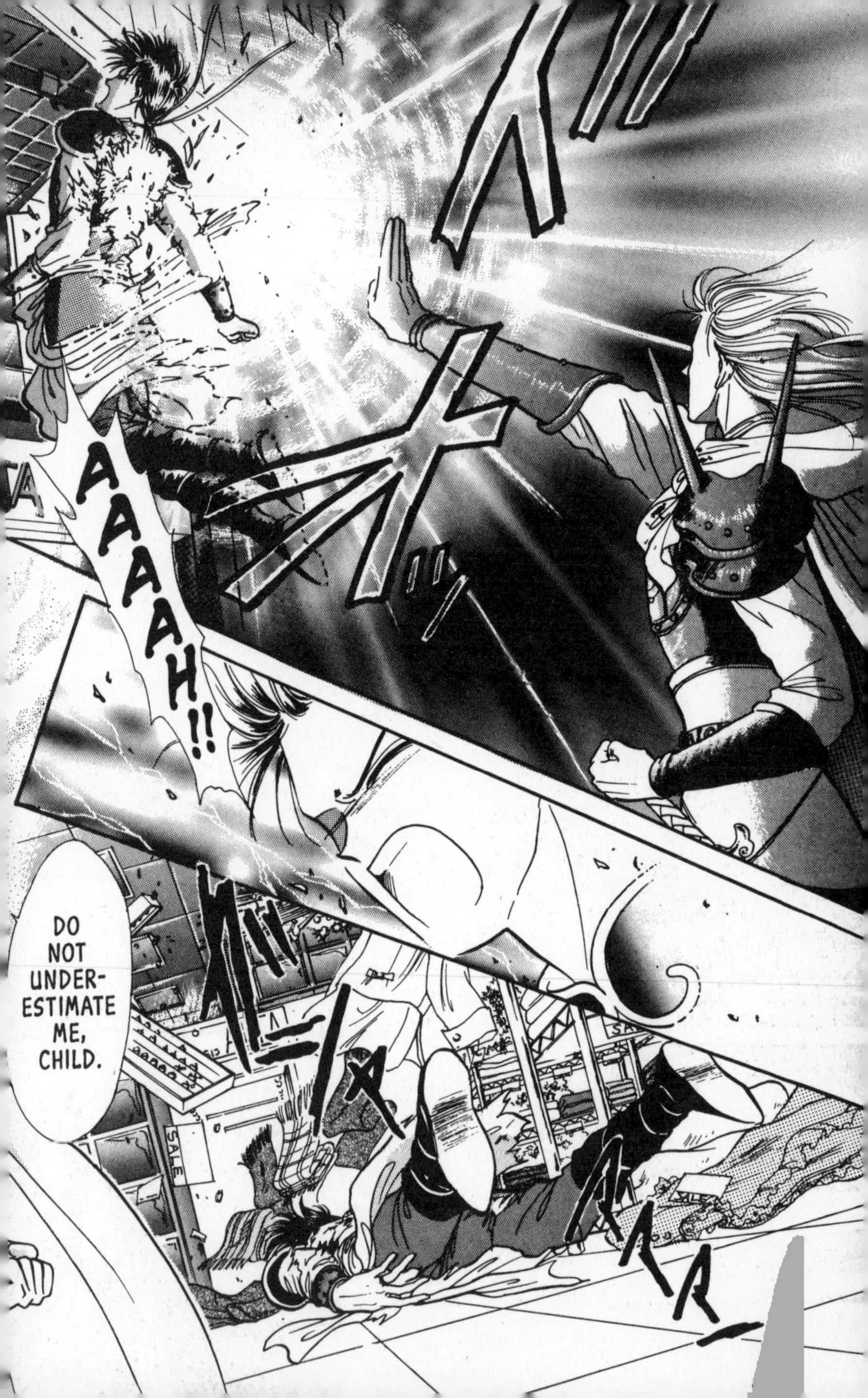
AAAAAH!!
DO NOT UNDER-ESTIMATE ME, CHILD.

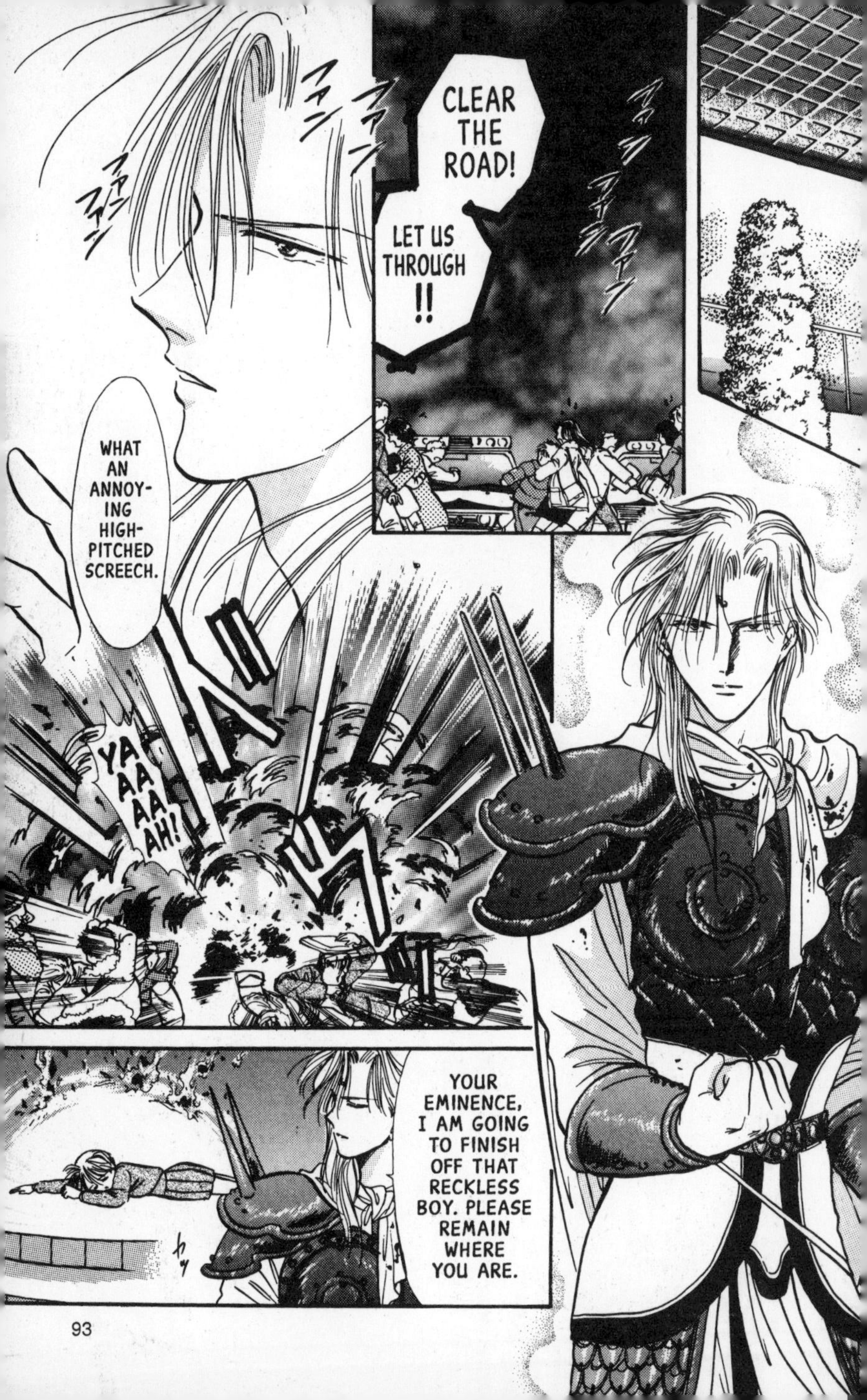
CLEAR THE ROAD!
LET US THROUGH !!
WHAT AN ANNOY-ING HIGH-PITCHED SCREECH.
YAAAAAH!
YOUR EMINENCE, I AM GOING TO FINISH OFF THAT RECKLESS BOY. PLEASE REMAIN WHERE YOU ARE.

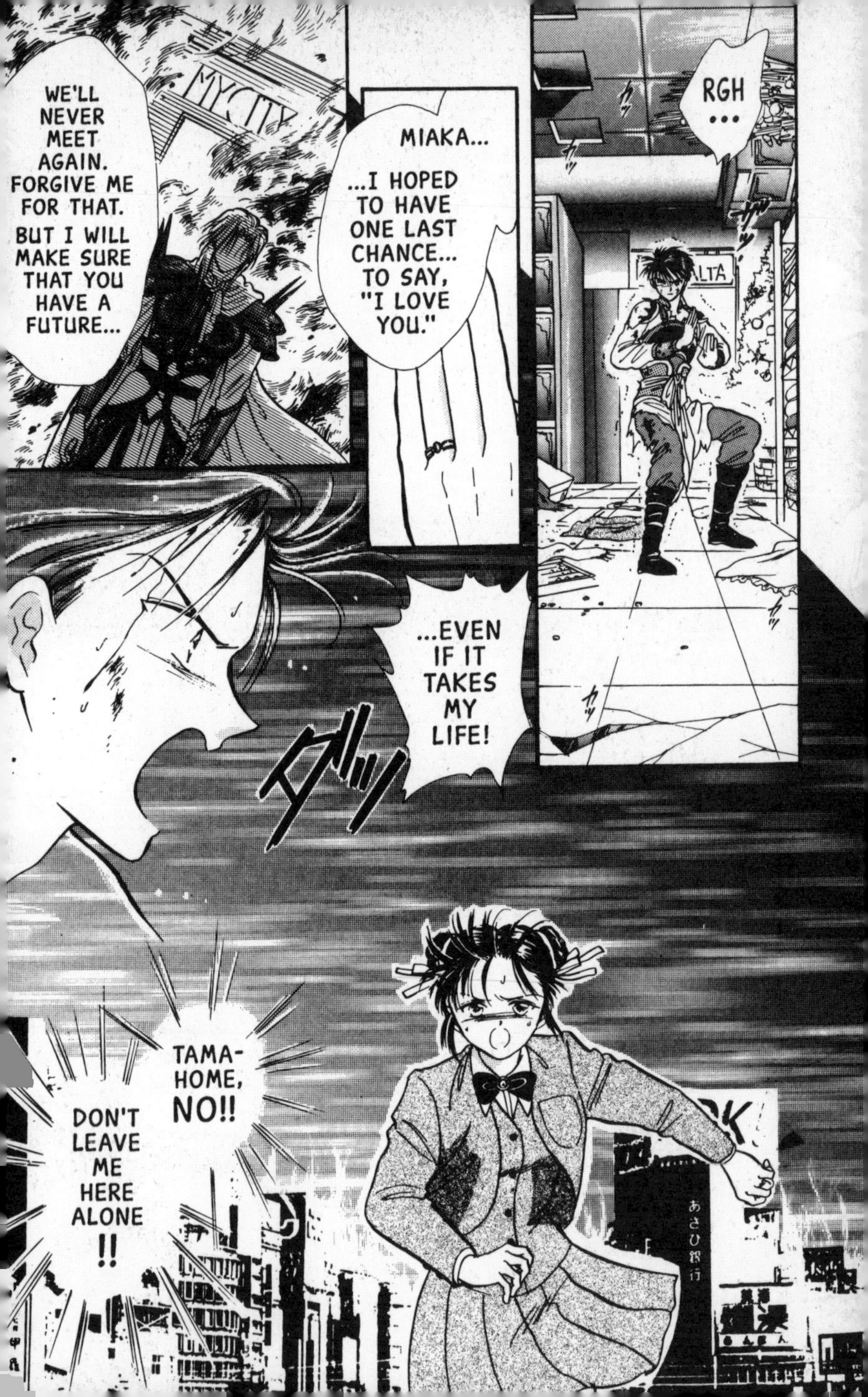
RGH ...
MIAKA...
...I HOPED TO HAVE ONE LAST CHANCE... TO SAY, "I LOVE YOU."
WE'LL NEVER MEET AGAIN. FORGIVE ME FOR THAT.
BUT I WILL MAKE SURE THAT YOU HAVE A FUTURE...
...EVEN IF IT TAKES MY LIFE!
TAMA-HOME, NO!!
DON'T LEAVE ME HERE ALONE!!

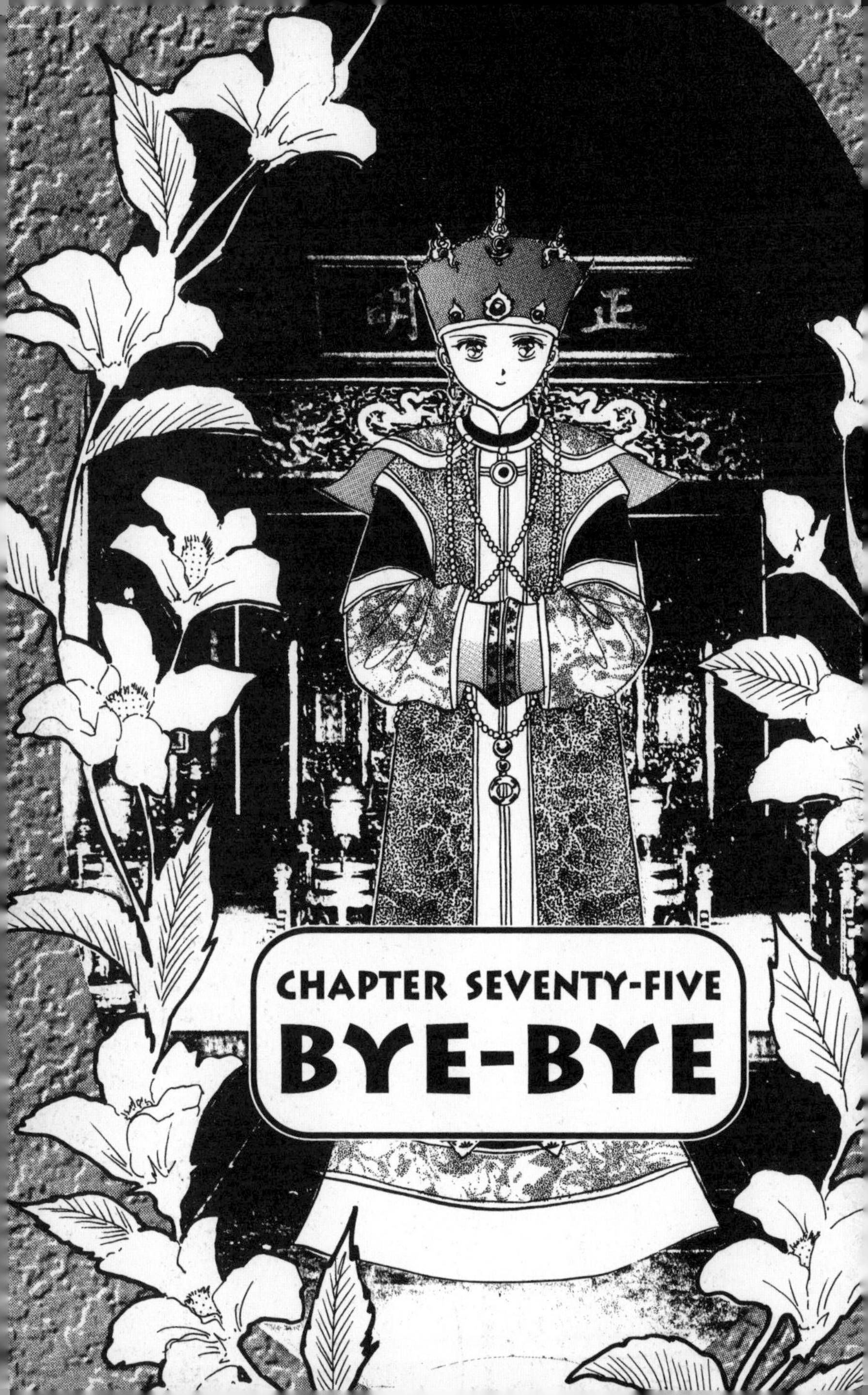
CHAPTER SEVENTY-FIVE
BYE-BYE

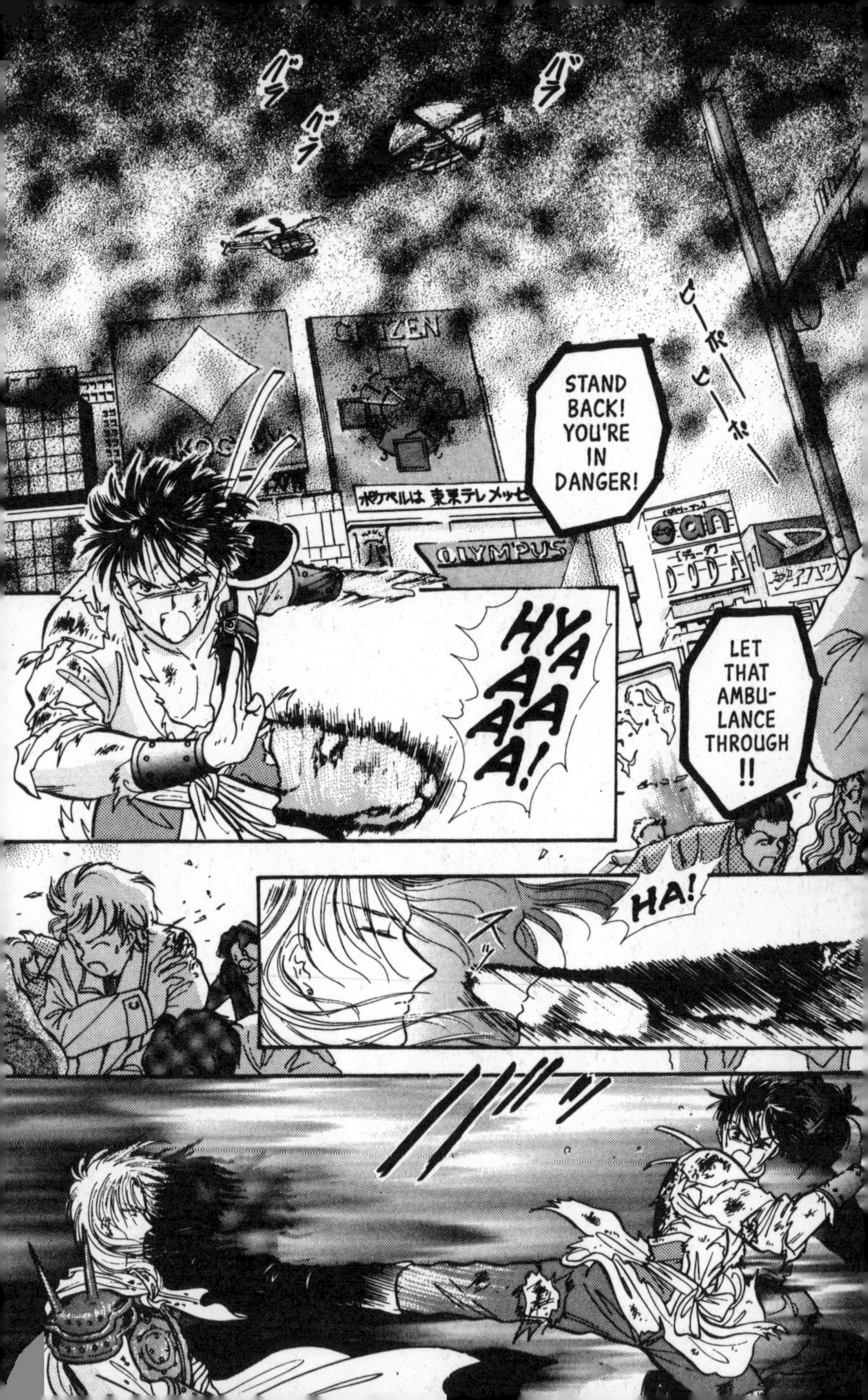
バラ
バラバラ
ピーポーピーポー
ポケベルは 東京テレメッセ
OLYMPUS
STAND BACK! YOU'RE IN DANGER!
HYAAAAA!
LET THAT AMBULANCE THROUGH!!
HA!

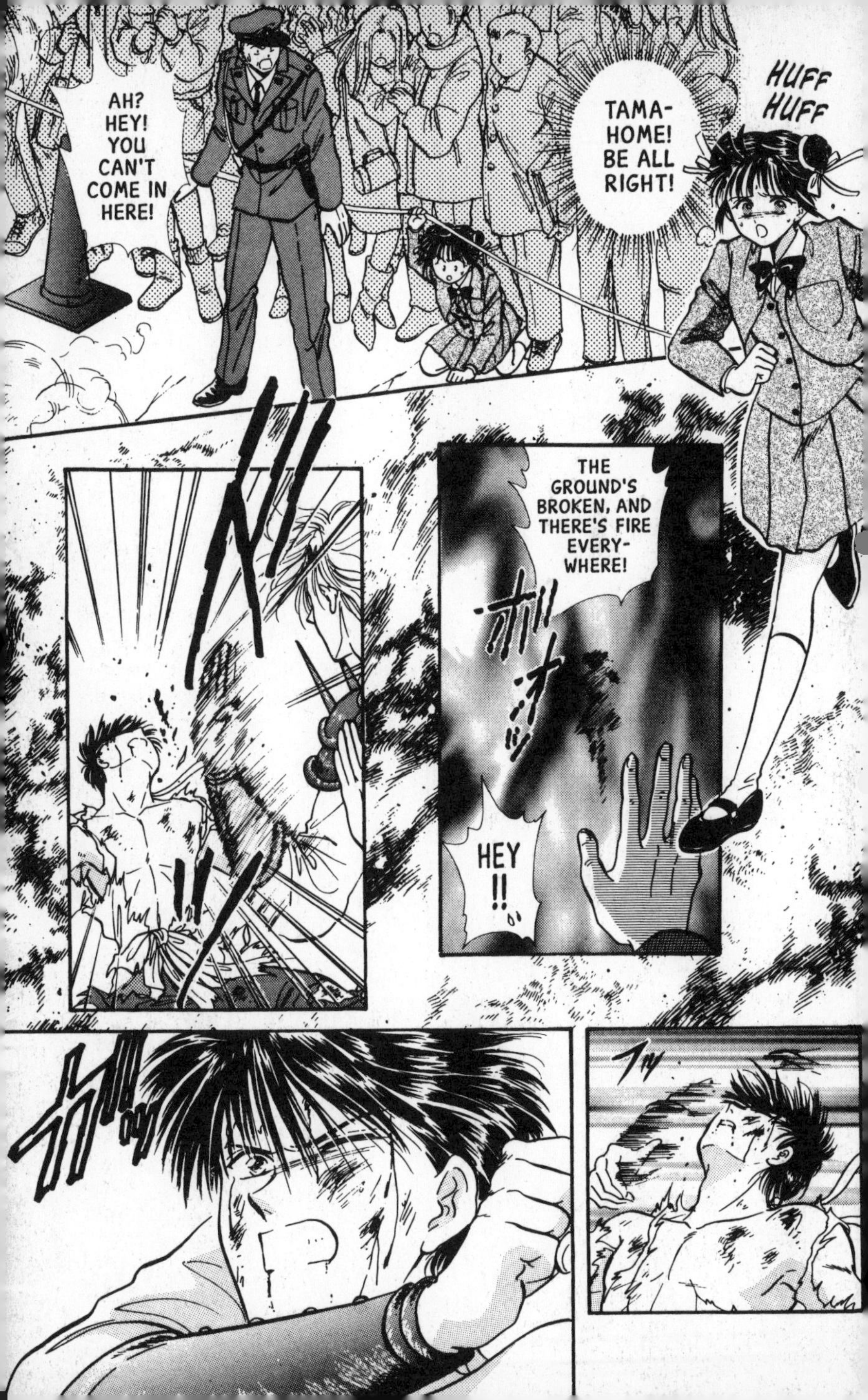
HUFF HUFF
TAMA-HOME! BE ALL RIGHT!
AH? HEY! YOU CAN'T COME IN HERE!
THE GROUND'S BROKEN, AND THERE'S FIRE EVERY-WHERE!
HEY !!

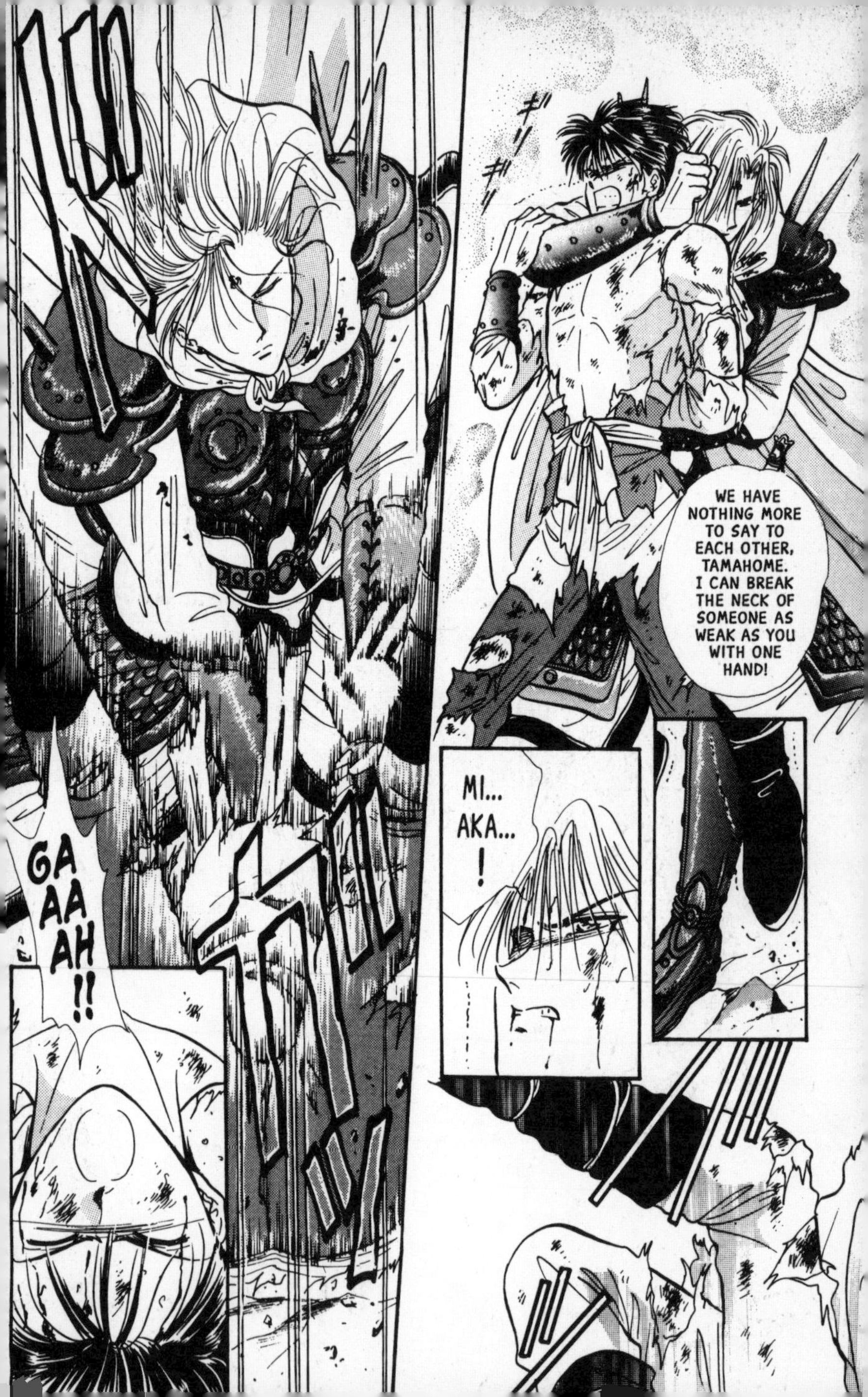
ギリギリ
WE HAVE NOTHING MORE TO SAY TO EACH OTHER, TAMAHOME. I CAN BREAK THE NECK OF SOMEONE AS WEAK AS YOU WITH ONE HAND!
MI... AKA... !
GAAAAH!!

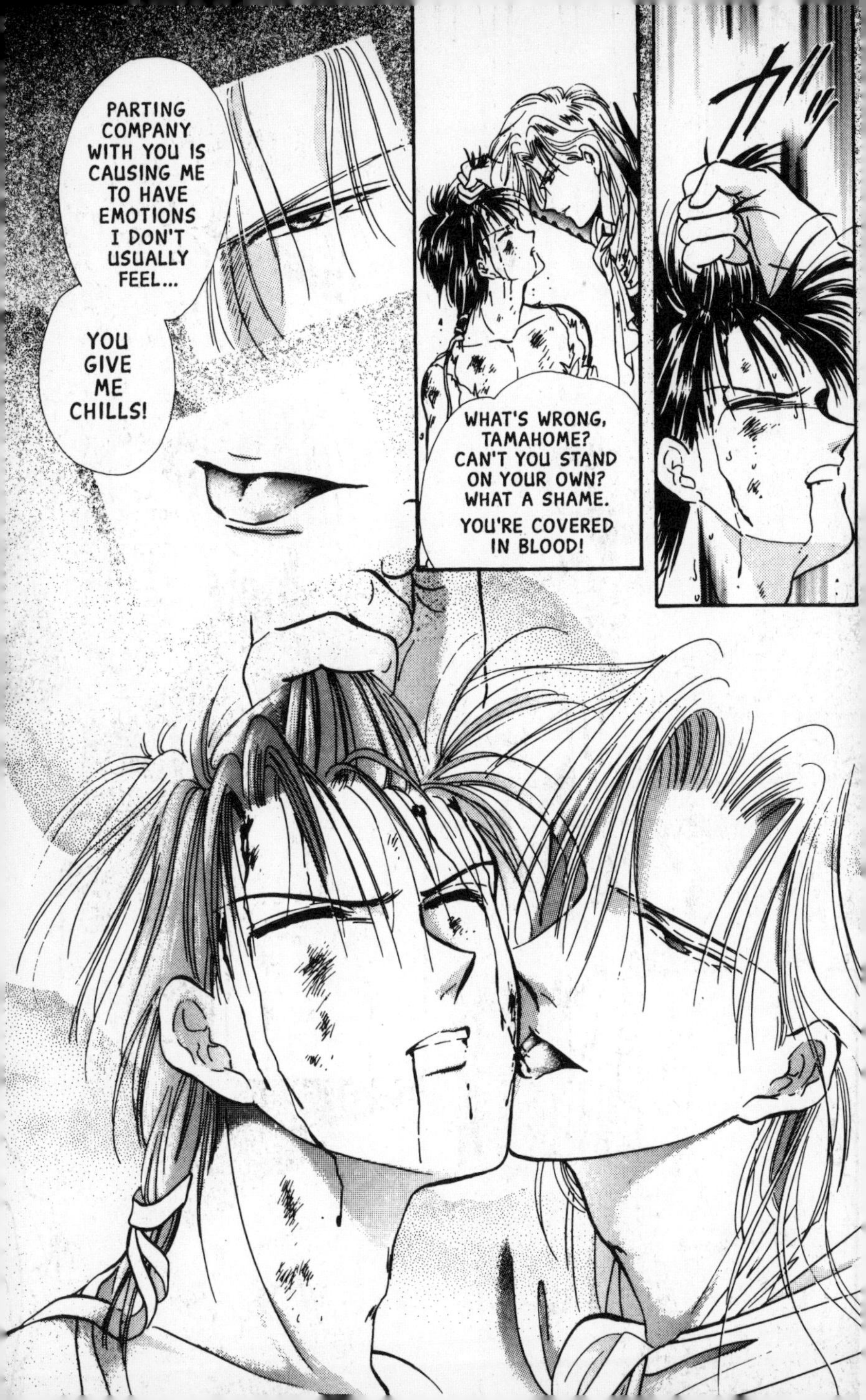
WHAT'S WRONG, TAMAHOME? CAN'T YOU STAND ON YOUR OWN? WHAT A SHAME.
YOU'RE COVERED IN BLOOD!
PARTING COMPANY WITH YOU IS CAUSING ME TO HAVE EMOTIONS I DON'T USUALLY FEEL...
YOU GIVE ME CHILLS!

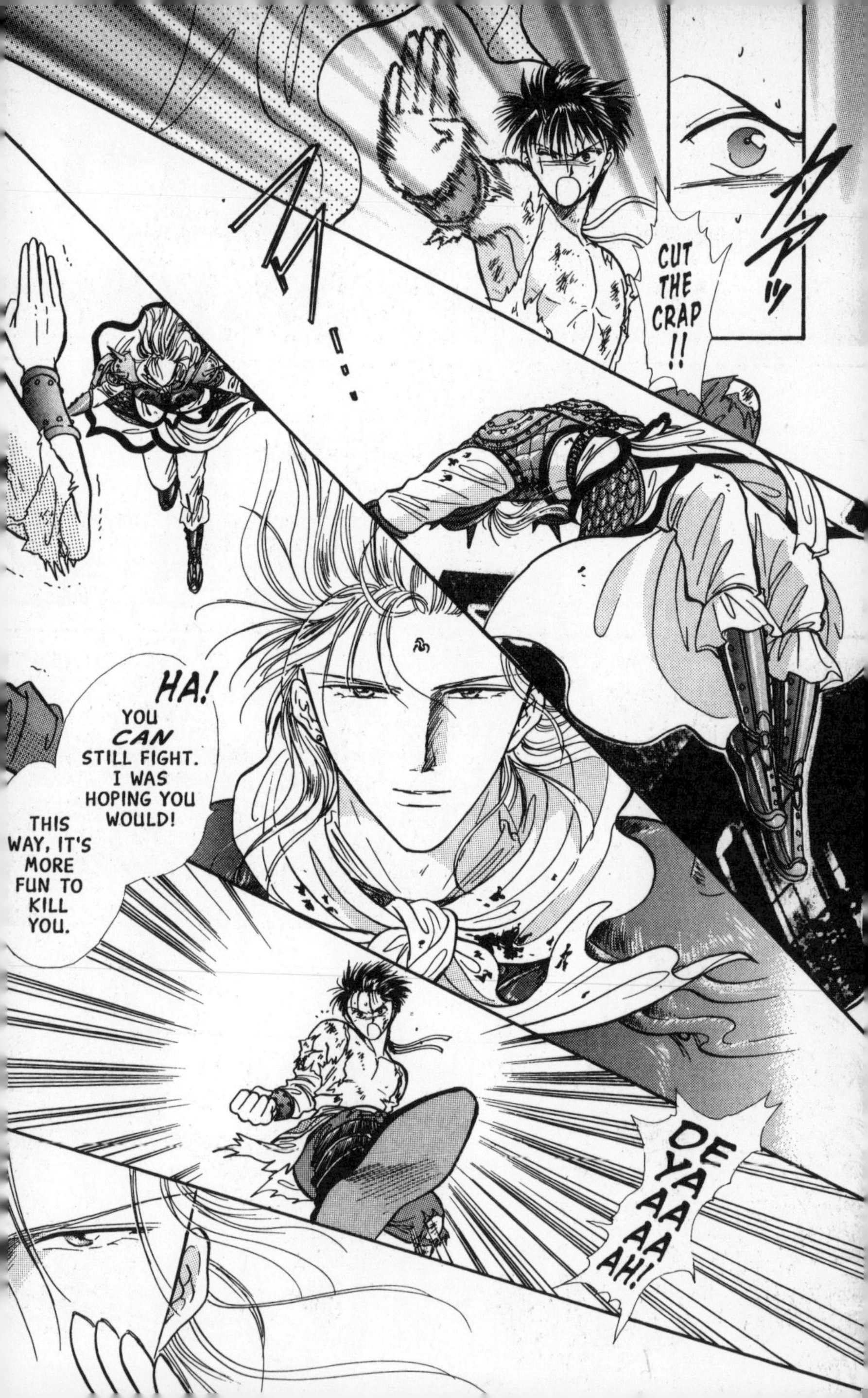
CUT THE CRAP!!
HA! YOU CAN STILL FIGHT. I WAS HOPING YOU WOULD!
THIS WAY, IT'S MORE FUN TO KILL YOU.
DE YAAAAAAH!

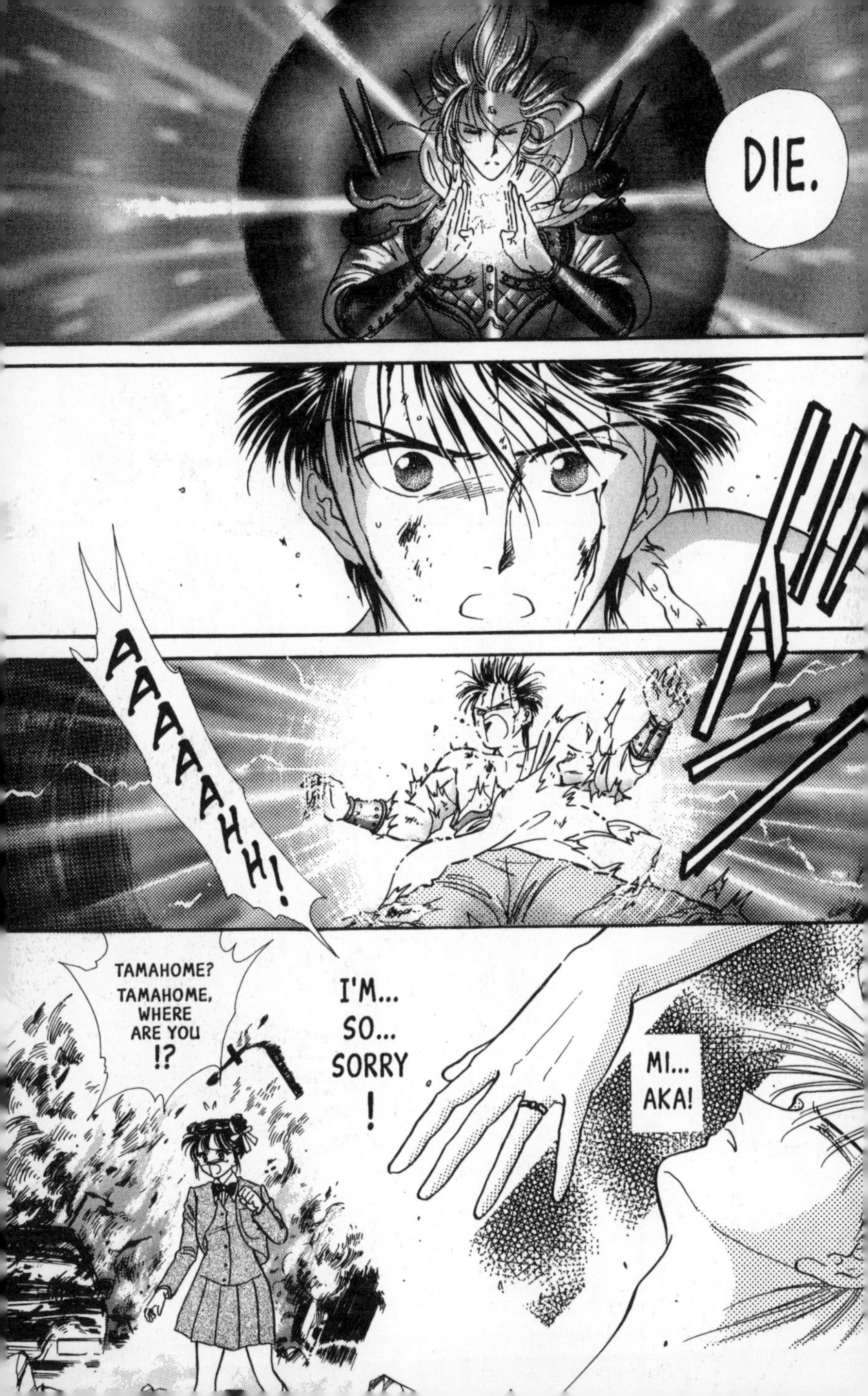
DIE.
AAAAAHH!
MI... AKA!
I'M... SO... SORRY!
TAMAHOME? TAMAHOME, WHERE ARE YOU!?

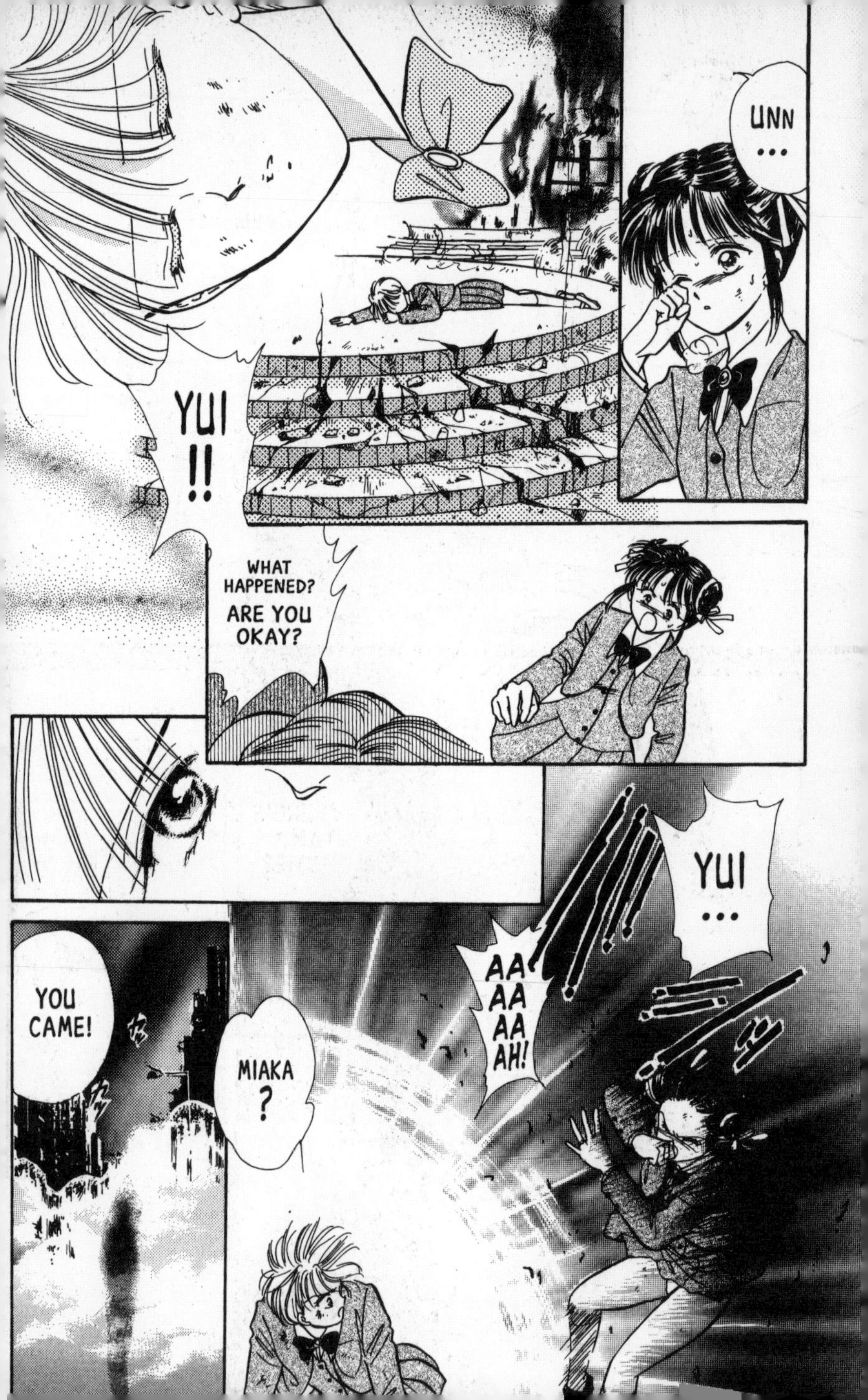

UNN...
YUI!!
WHAT HAPPENED? ARE YOU OKAY?
YUI...
AAAAAAAH!
MIAKA?
YOU CAME!

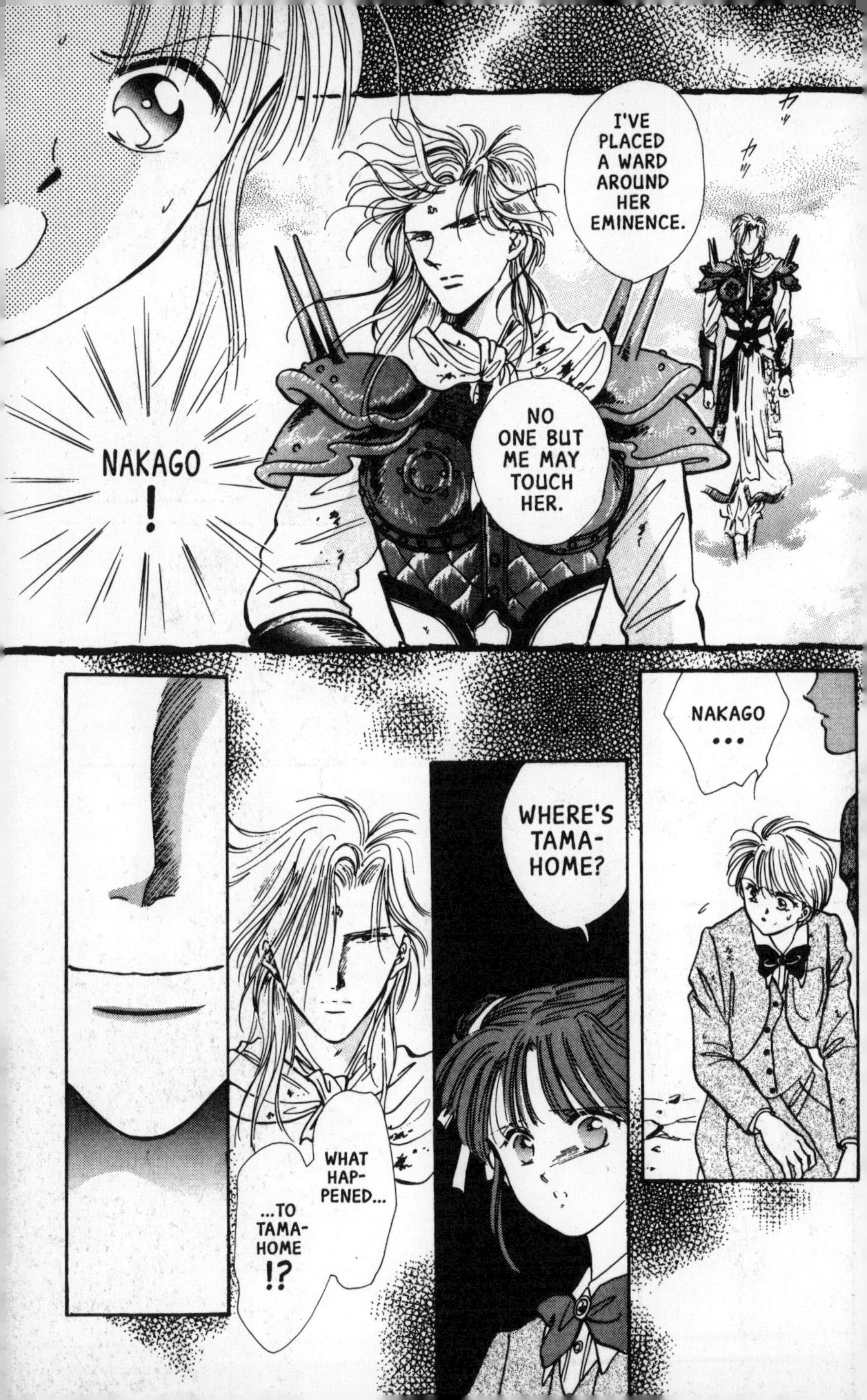
I'VE PLACED A WARD AROUND HER EMINENCE.
NO ONE BUT ME MAY TOUCH HER.
NAKAGO !
NAKAGO ...
WHERE'S TAMA-HOME?
WHAT HAP-PENED...
...TO TAMA-HOME !?

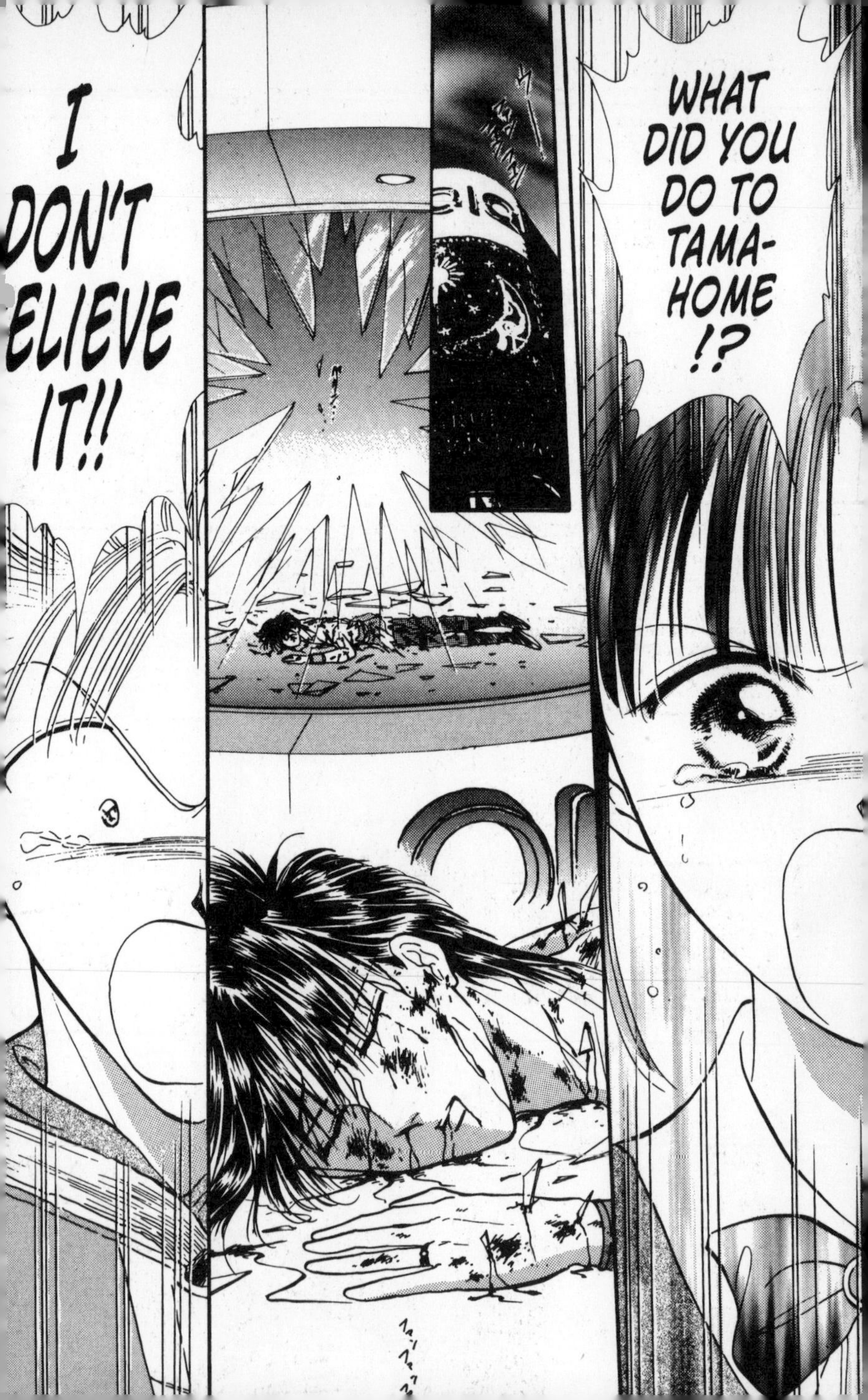
WHAT DID YOU DO TO TAMA-HOME !?
I DON'T ELIEVE IT!!

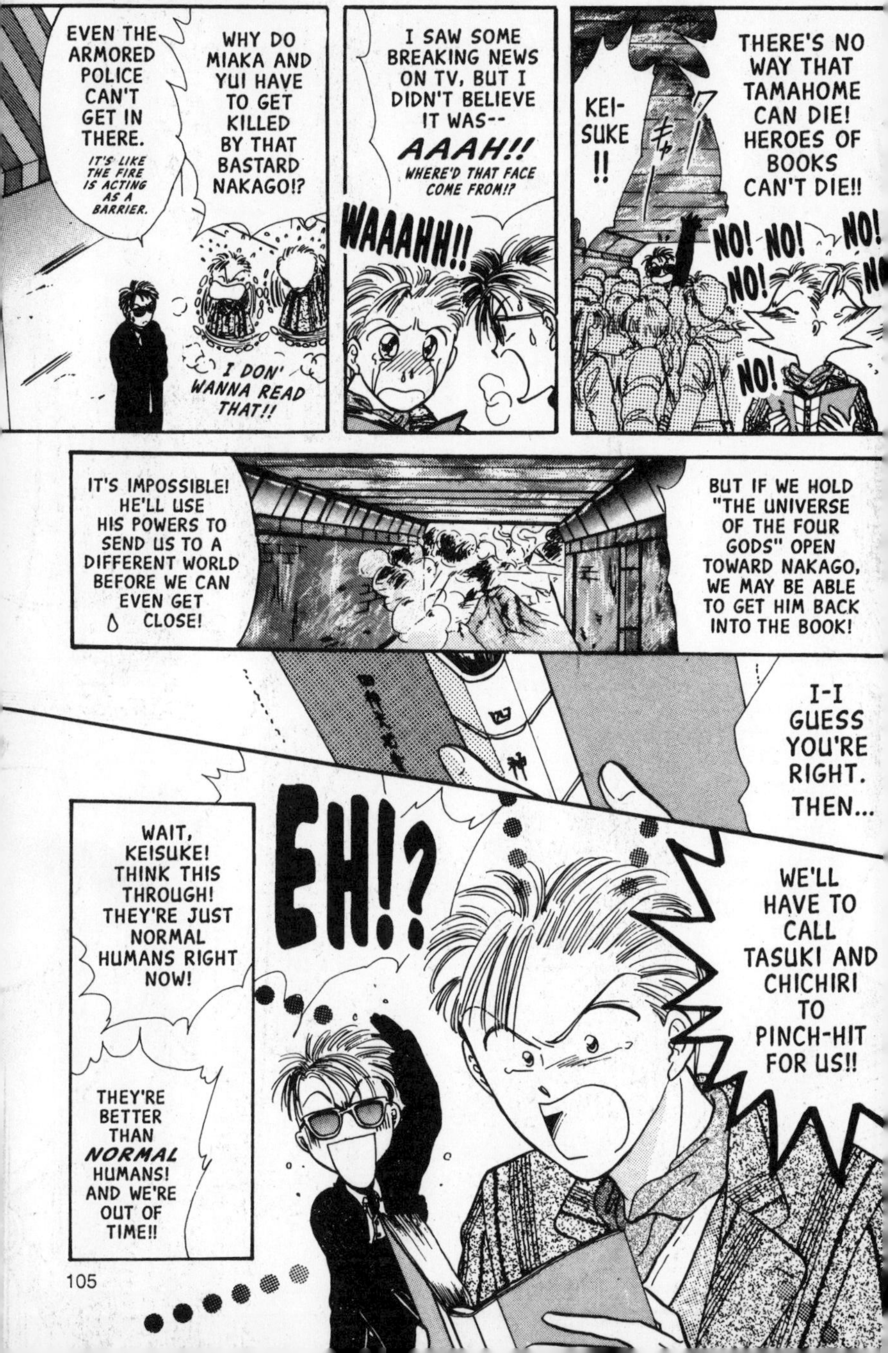
THERE'S NO WAY THAT TAMAHOME CAN DIE! HEROES OF BOOKS CAN'T DIE!!
KEI-SUKE !!
NO! NO! NO! NO! NO! NO!
I SAW SOME BREAKING NEWS ON TV, BUT I DIDN'T BELIEVE IT WAS-- AAAH!!
WHERE'D THAT FACE COME FROM!?
WAAAHH!!
WHY DO MIAKA AND YUI HAVE TO GET KILLED BY THAT BASTARD NAKAGO!?
EVEN THE ARMORED POLICE CAN'T GET IN THERE.
IT'S LIKE THE FIRE IS ACTING AS A BARRIER.
I DON' WANNA READ THAT!!
BUT IF WE HOLD "THE UNIVERSE OF THE FOUR GODS" OPEN TOWARD NAKAGO, WE MAY BE ABLE TO GET HIM BACK INTO THE BOOK!
IT'S IMPOSSIBLE! HE'LL USE HIS POWERS TO SEND US TO A DIFFERENT WORLD BEFORE WE CAN EVEN GET CLOSE!
I-I GUESS YOU'RE RIGHT. THEN...
WE'LL HAVE TO CALL TASUKI AND CHICHIRI TO PINCH-HIT FOR US!!
EH!?
WAIT, KEISUKE! THINK THIS THROUGH! THEY'RE JUST NORMAL HUMANS RIGHT NOW!
THEY'RE BETTER THAN NORMAL HUMANS! AND WE'RE OUT OF TIME!!

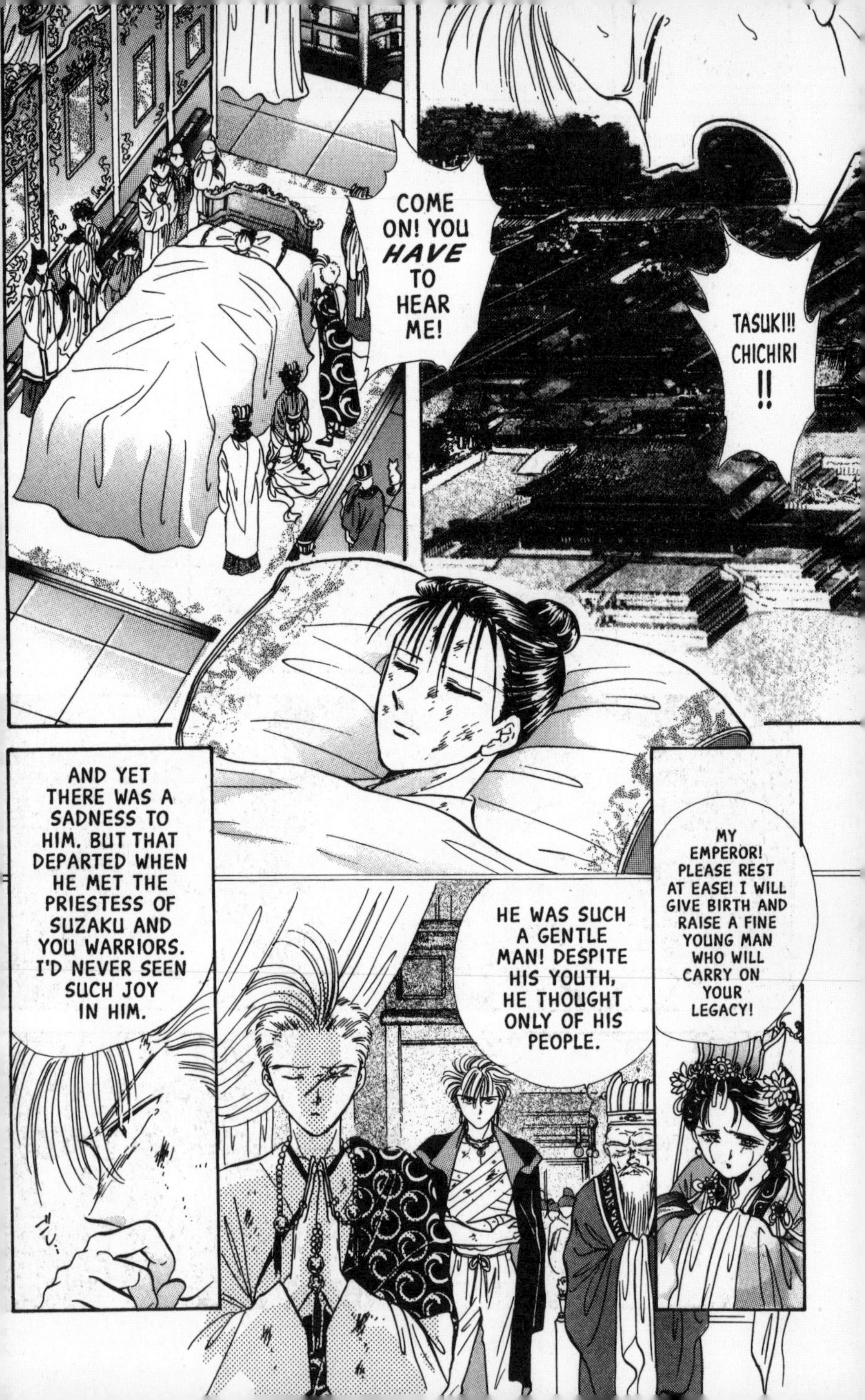
TASUKI!! CHICHIRI!!
COME ON! YOU HAVE TO HEAR ME!
MY EMPEROR! PLEASE REST AT EASE! I WILL GIVE BIRTH AND RAISE A FINE YOUNG MAN WHO WILL CARRY ON YOUR LEGACY!
HE WAS SUCH A GENTLE MAN! DESPITE HIS YOUTH, HE THOUGHT ONLY OF HIS PEOPLE.
AND YET THERE WAS A SADNESS TO HIM. BUT THAT DEPARTED WHEN HE MET THE PRIESTESS OF SUZAKU AND YOU WARRIORS. I'D NEVER SEEN SUCH JOY IN HIM.

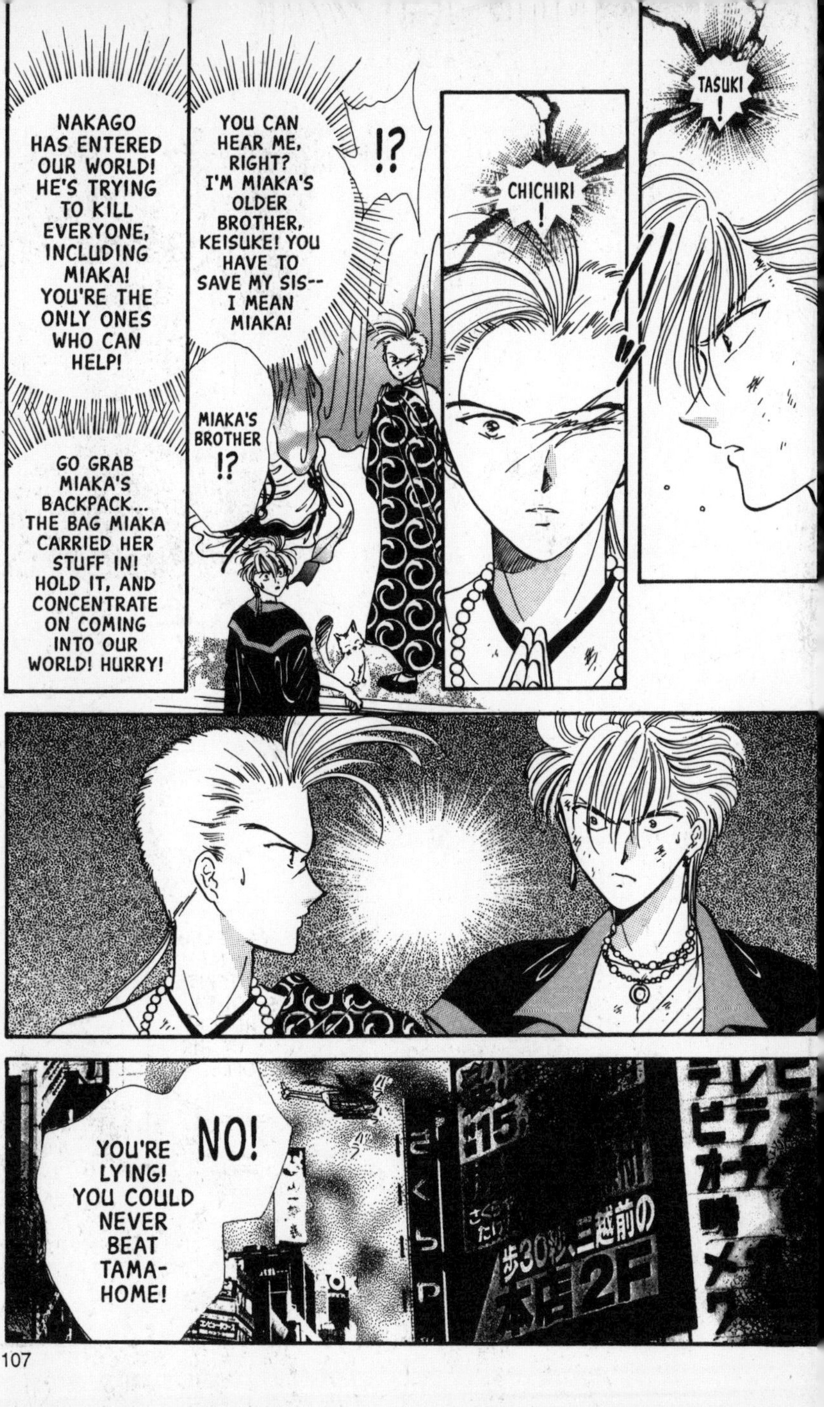
TASUKI!
CHICHIRI!
YOU CAN HEAR ME, RIGHT? I'M MIAKA'S OLDER BROTHER, KEISUKE! YOU HAVE TO SAVE MY SIS-- I MEAN MIAKA!
!?
MIAKA'S BROTHER !?
NAKAGO HAS ENTERED OUR WORLD! HE'S TRYING TO KILL EVERYONE, INCLUDING MIAKA! YOU'RE THE ONLY ONES WHO CAN HELP!
GO GRAB MIAKA'S BACKPACK... THE BAG MIAKA CARRIED HER STUFF IN! HOLD IT, AND CONCENTRATE ON COMING INTO OUR WORLD! HURRY!
NO!
YOU'RE LYING! YOU COULD NEVER BEAT TAMA-HOME!

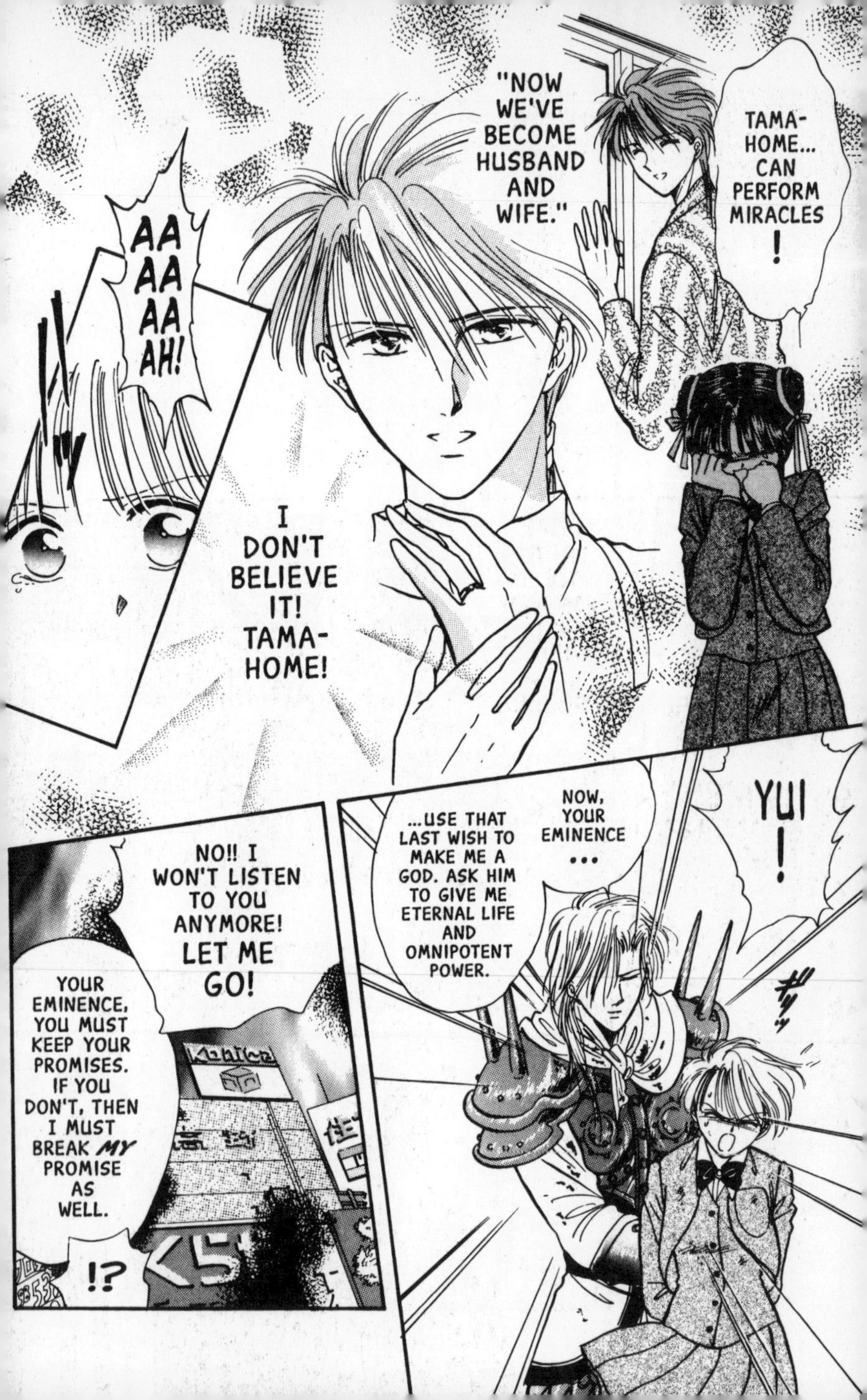

TAMA-HOME... CAN PERFORM MIRACLES!
"NOW WE'VE BECOME HUSBAND AND WIFE."
I DON'T BELIEVE IT! TAMA-HOME!
AAAAAAAH!
YUI!
NOW, YOUR EMINENCE...
...USE THAT LAST WISH TO MAKE ME A GOD. ASK HIM TO GIVE ME ETERNAL LIFE AND OMNIPOTENT POWER.
NO!! I WON'T LISTEN TO YOU ANYMORE! LET ME GO!
YOUR EMINENCE, YOU MUST KEEP YOUR PROMISES. IF YOU DON'T, THEN I MUST BREAK MY PROMISE AS WELL.
!?

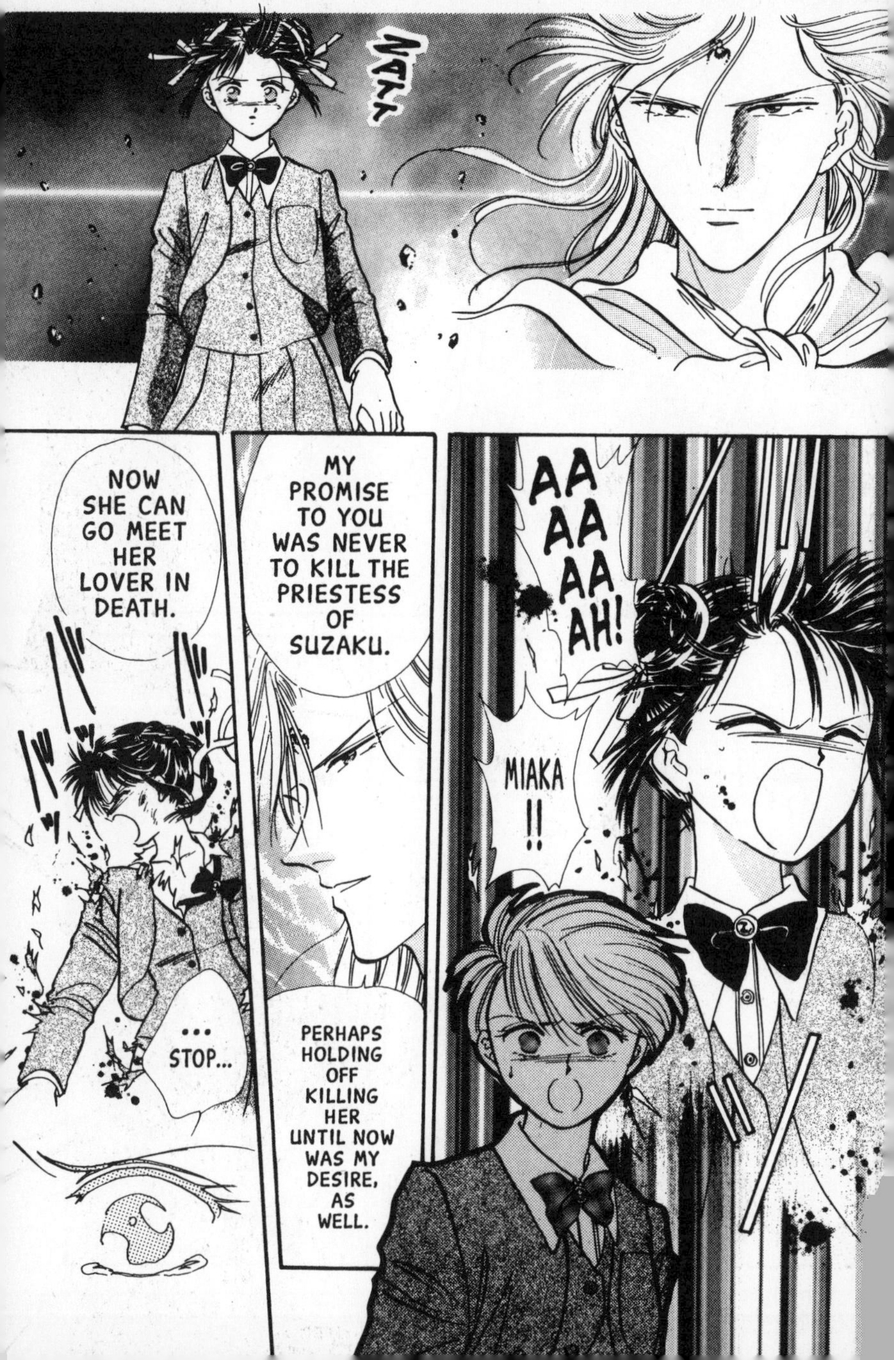
ZATT
AAAAAAAH!
MIAKA!!
MY PROMISE TO YOU WAS NEVER TO KILL THE PRIESTESS OF SUZAKU.
PERHAPS HOLDING OFF KILLING HER UNTIL NOW WAS MY DESIRE, AS WELL.
NOW SHE CAN GO MEET HER LOVER IN DEATH.
...STOP...

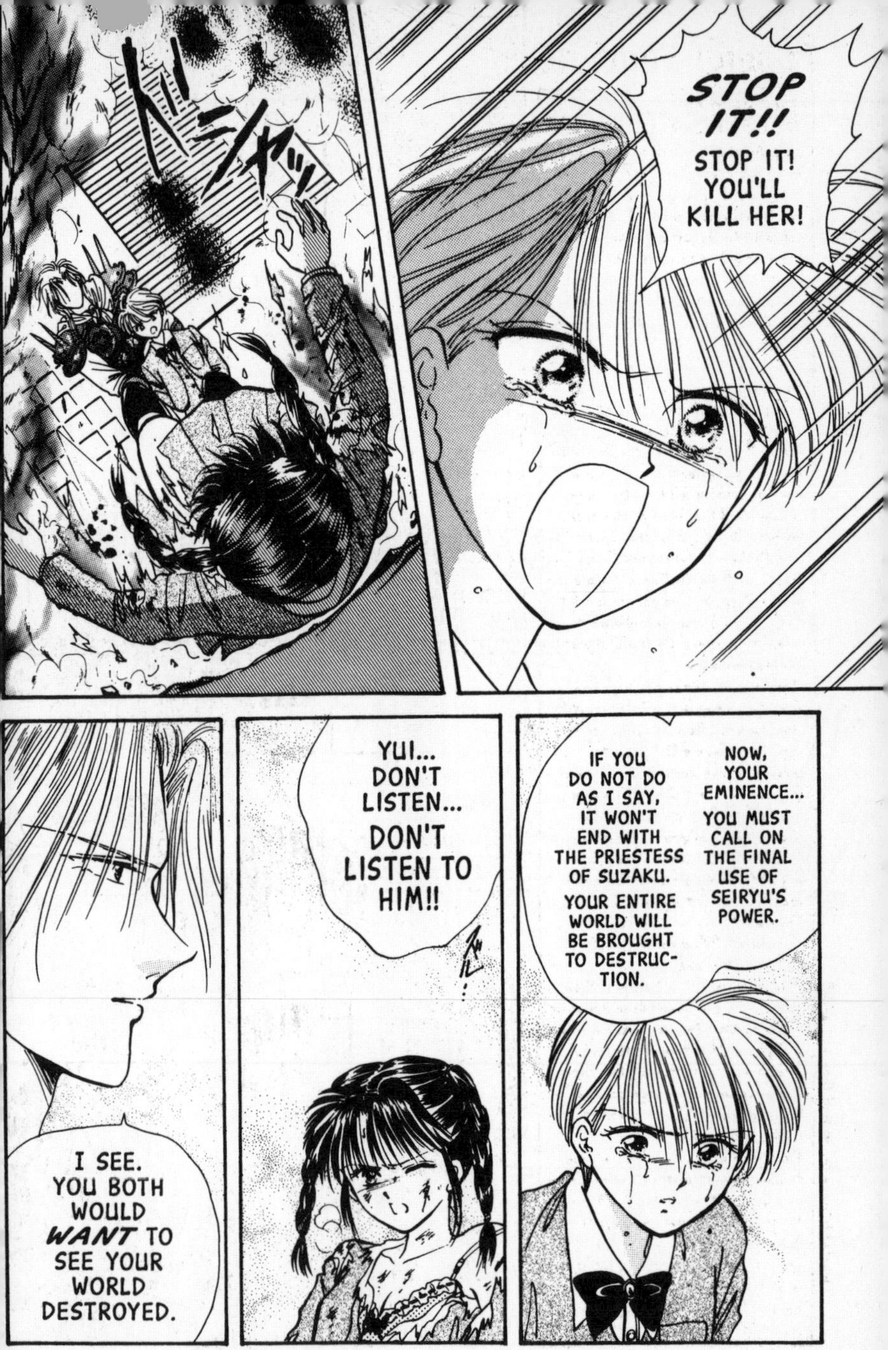
STOP IT!!
STOP IT! YOU'LL KILL HER!
NOW, YOUR EMINENCE... YOU MUST CALL ON THE FINAL USE OF SEIRYU'S POWER.
IF YOU DO NOT DO AS I SAY, IT WON'T END WITH THE PRIESTESS OF SUZAKU.
YOUR ENTIRE WORLD WILL BE BROUGHT TO DESTRUCTION.
YUI... DON'T LISTEN...
DON'T LISTEN TO HIM!!
I SEE. YOU BOTH WOULD *WANT* TO SEE YOUR WORLD DESTROYED.

THE "WHAT COULD HAVE BEEN" CORNER!

First: Nuriko's past. He was in Hotohori's inner seraglio, right? Actually, his little sister, Kang-Lin, wasn't supposed to die as a child; she was supposed to die just after she had been picked up to enter the seraglio. That's what my original set-up said. She fell in love with the Emperor (Hotohori), but she died in the accident soon after. Nuriko wanted his sister's wish fulfilled, so he took on women's clothes and entered the seraglio to take her place (they look exactly alike). Perfect, huh?

I thought so, but my editor said that it would be better if the character were an established long-time homosexual. And that seemed like such a reasonable suggestion that I just said, "I-I guess you're right," and went with the flow. That's Watase for you! And so, how he got himself into the Emperor's inner seraglio must remain a mystery. Oh, well! It was for laughs anyway!

And Chiriko. The reason why he didn't join up with the Celestial Warriors sooner... He got his chance to explain in Volume 11. But... My original set-up was to have Nakago capture him first! I mean, Nakago wouldn't let such an opportunity slide! And so, after the Amiboshi incident (that sounds strange...), the warriors would set out to rescue the real Chiriko. But my editor said, "You don't have to make everything so difficult!" And I said, "Yes, Sir!" ☺ *I'm so obedient!*

And in Volume 11, Subaru was there, right? It was my plan to use her powers to control time to make Chiriko 16.7 years old! I thought this would have been a great scene! But there was no room (in the page count or layout) to do it! (I had to resort to a bonus page only!)

I wanted to make the both of them younger! ➔

Another plan was to have the Celestial Warriors stop off on their journeys at a hot spring, and another was to include Hotohori taking a bath (all nude scenes!), but they didn't make it in. I had loads of comedy episodes! But if I can, I'll try to include them in Part 2!! ☺ *The nude scenes? No, I don't mean that!!*

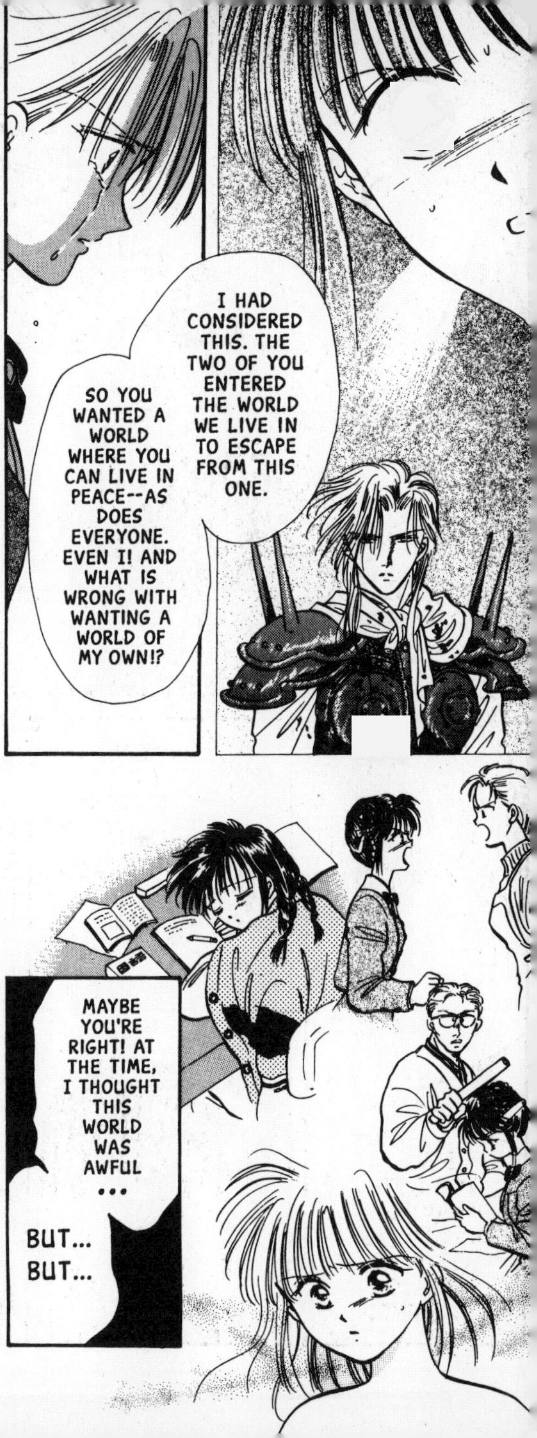
I HAD CONSIDERED THIS. THE TWO OF YOU ENTERED THE WORLD WE LIVE IN TO ESCAPE FROM THIS ONE.
SO YOU WANTED A WORLD WHERE YOU CAN LIVE IN PEACE--AS DOES EVERYONE. EVEN I! AND WHAT IS WRONG WITH WANTING A WORLD OF MY OWN!?
MAYBE YOU'RE RIGHT! AT THE TIME, I THOUGHT THIS WORLD WAS AWFUL...
BUT... BUT...

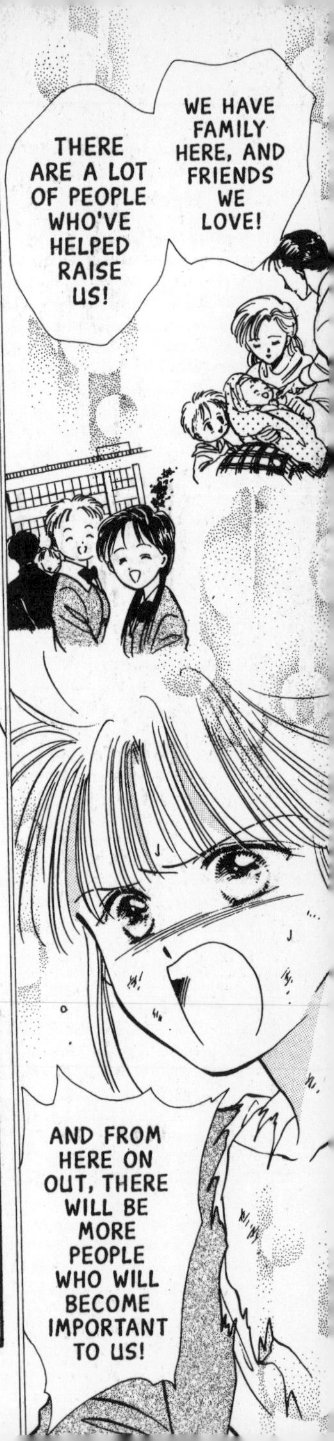
WE HAVE FAMILY HERE, AND FRIENDS WE LOVE!
THERE ARE A LOT OF PEOPLE WHO'VE HELPED RAISE US!
AND FROM HERE ON OUT, THERE WILL BE MORE PEOPLE WHO WILL BECOME IMPORTANT TO US!

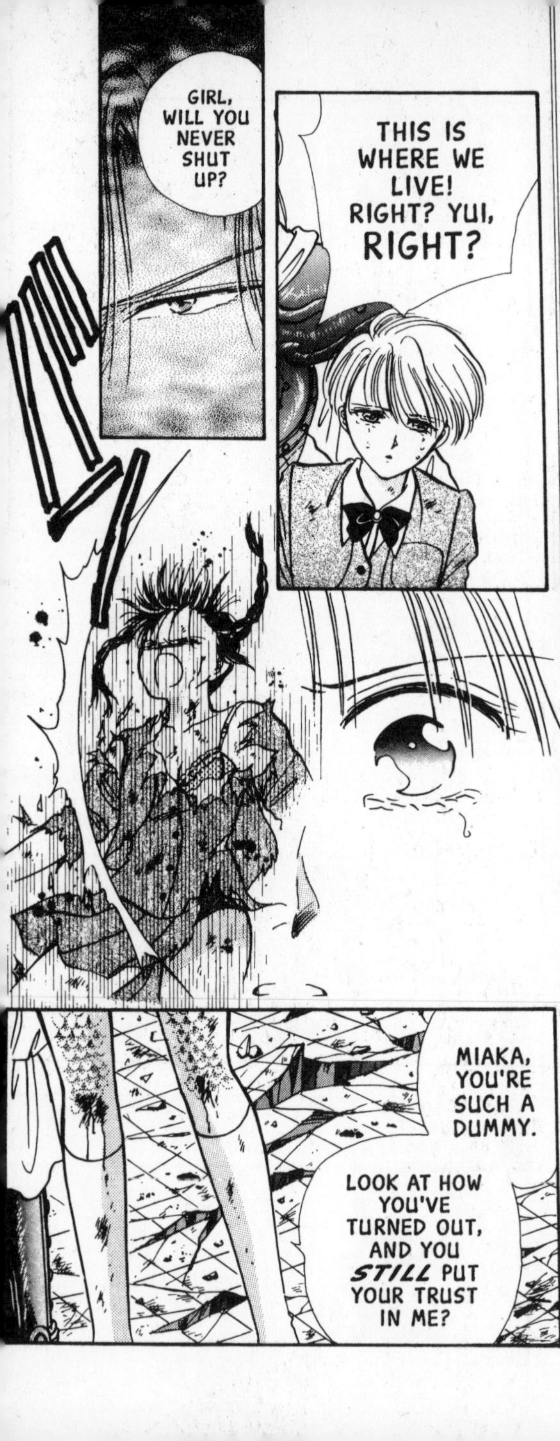
THIS IS WHERE WE LIVE! RIGHT? YUI, RIGHT?
GIRL, WILL YOU NEVER SHUT UP?
MIAKA, YOU'RE SUCH A DUMMY.
LOOK AT HOW YOU'VE TURNED OUT, AND YOU *STILL* PUT YOUR TRUST IN ME?

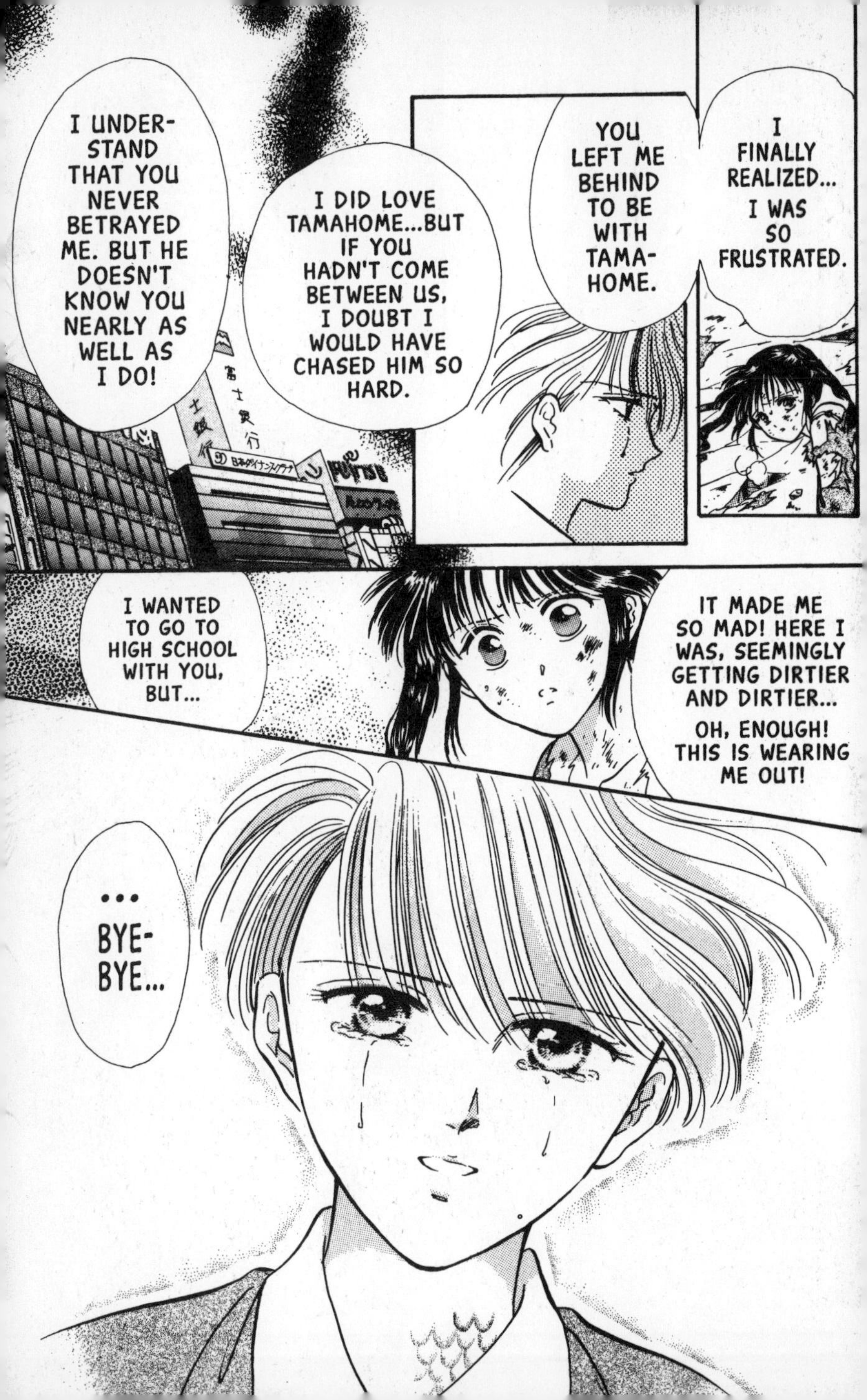
I FINALLY REALIZED... I WAS SO FRUSTRATED.
YOU LEFT ME BEHIND TO BE WITH TAMA-HOME.
I DID LOVE TAMAHOME...BUT IF YOU HADN'T COME BETWEEN US, I DOUBT I WOULD HAVE CHASED HIM SO HARD.
I UNDER-STAND THAT YOU NEVER BETRAYED ME. BUT HE DOESN'T KNOW YOU NEARLY AS WELL AS I DO!
IT MADE ME SO MAD! HERE I WAS, SEEMINGLY GETTING DIRTIER AND DIRTIER...
OH, ENOUGH! THIS IS WEARING ME OUT!
I WANTED TO GO TO HIGH SCHOOL WITH YOU, BUT...
... BYE-BYE...

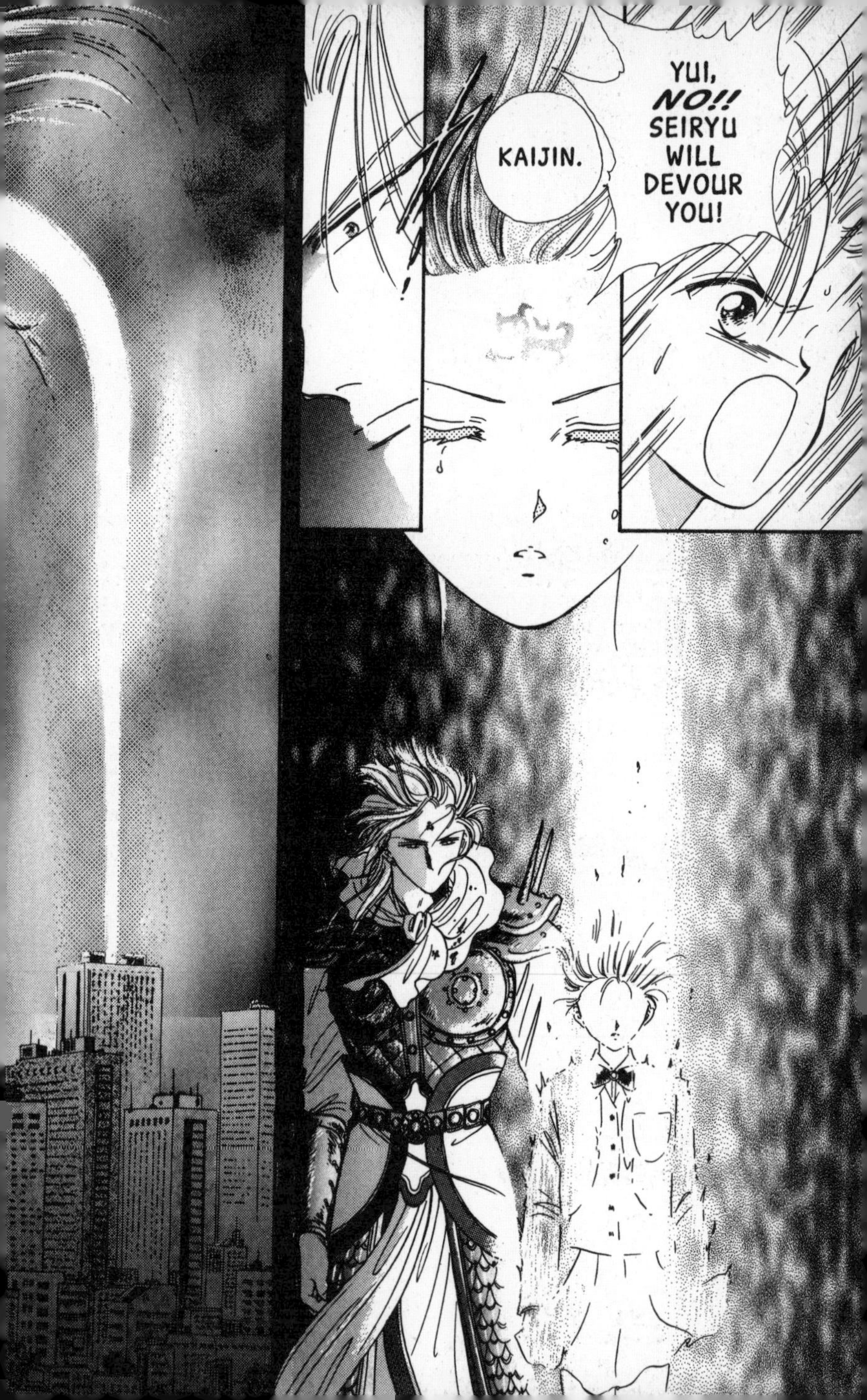
YUI, NO!! SEIRYU WILL DEVOUR YOU!
KAIJIN.

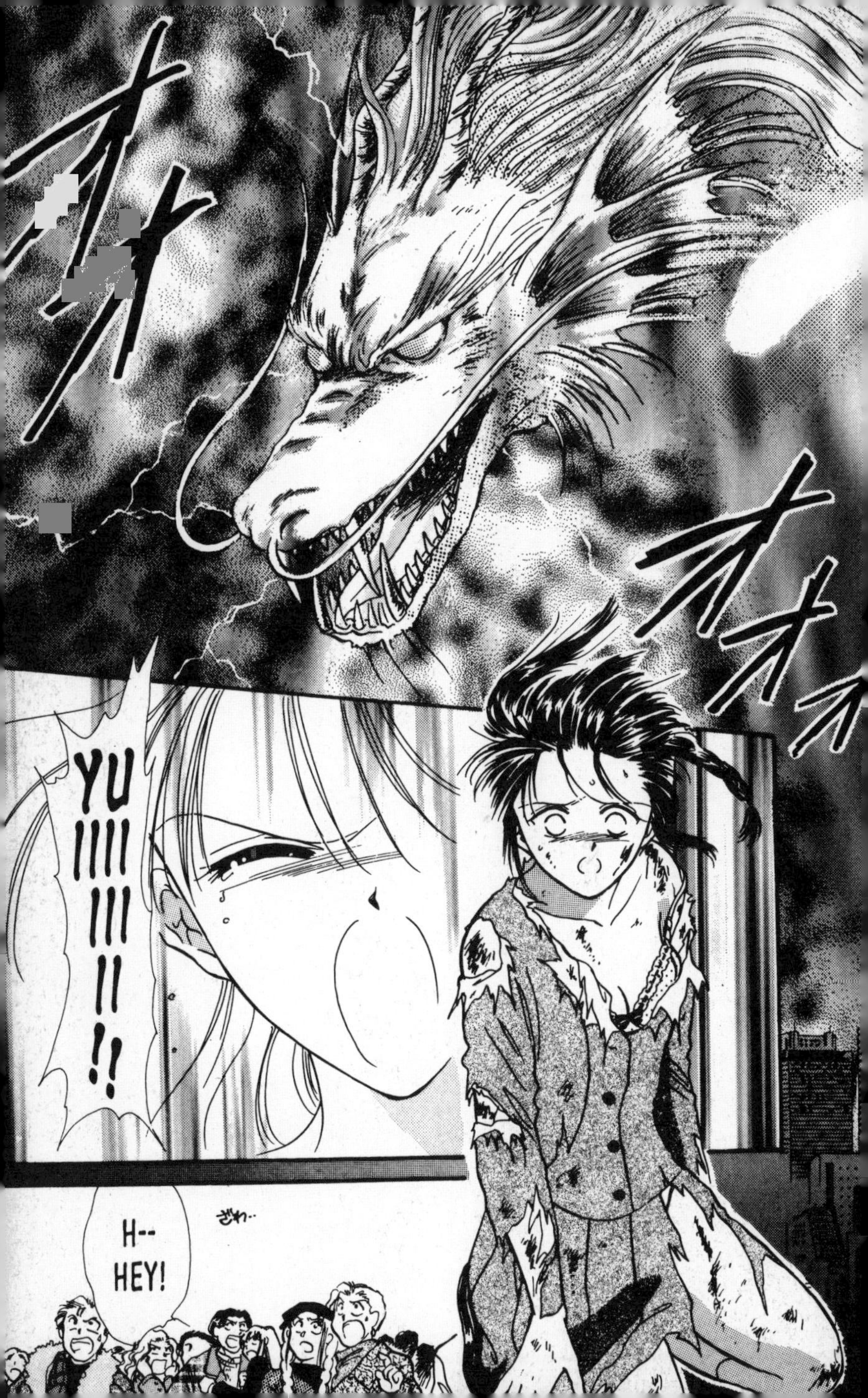
オオォ
YUIIIIIIIII!!
H-- HEY!
ざわ‥

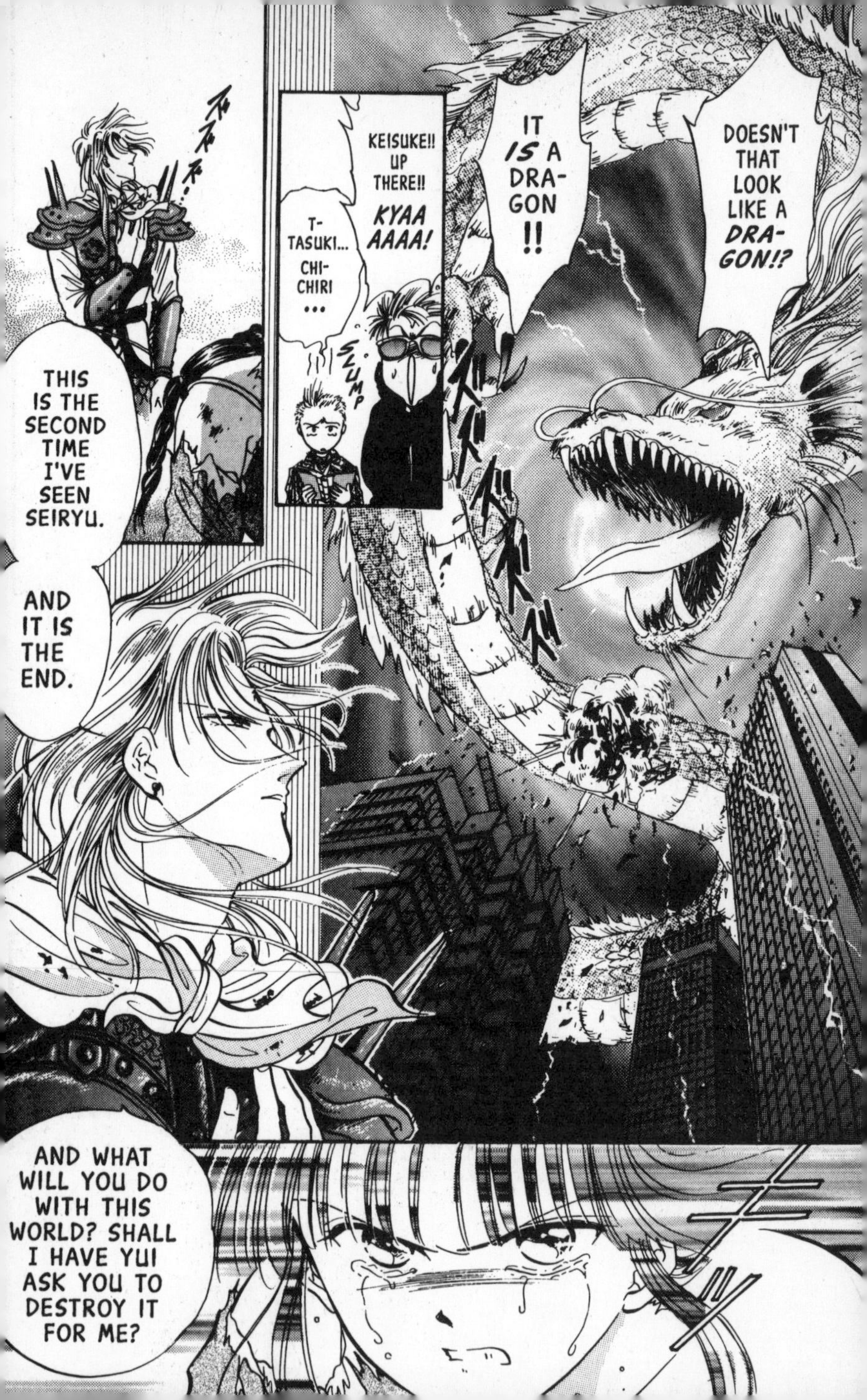
DOESN'T THAT LOOK LIKE A DRA-GON!?
IT IS A DRA-GON!!
KEISUKE!! UP THERE!!
KYAA AAAA!
T-TASUKI... CHI-CHIRI...
SLUMP
THIS IS THE SECOND TIME I'VE SEEN SEIRYU.
AND IT IS THE END.
AND WHAT WILL YOU DO WITH THIS WORLD? SHALL I HAVE YUI ASK YOU TO DESTROY IT FOR ME?

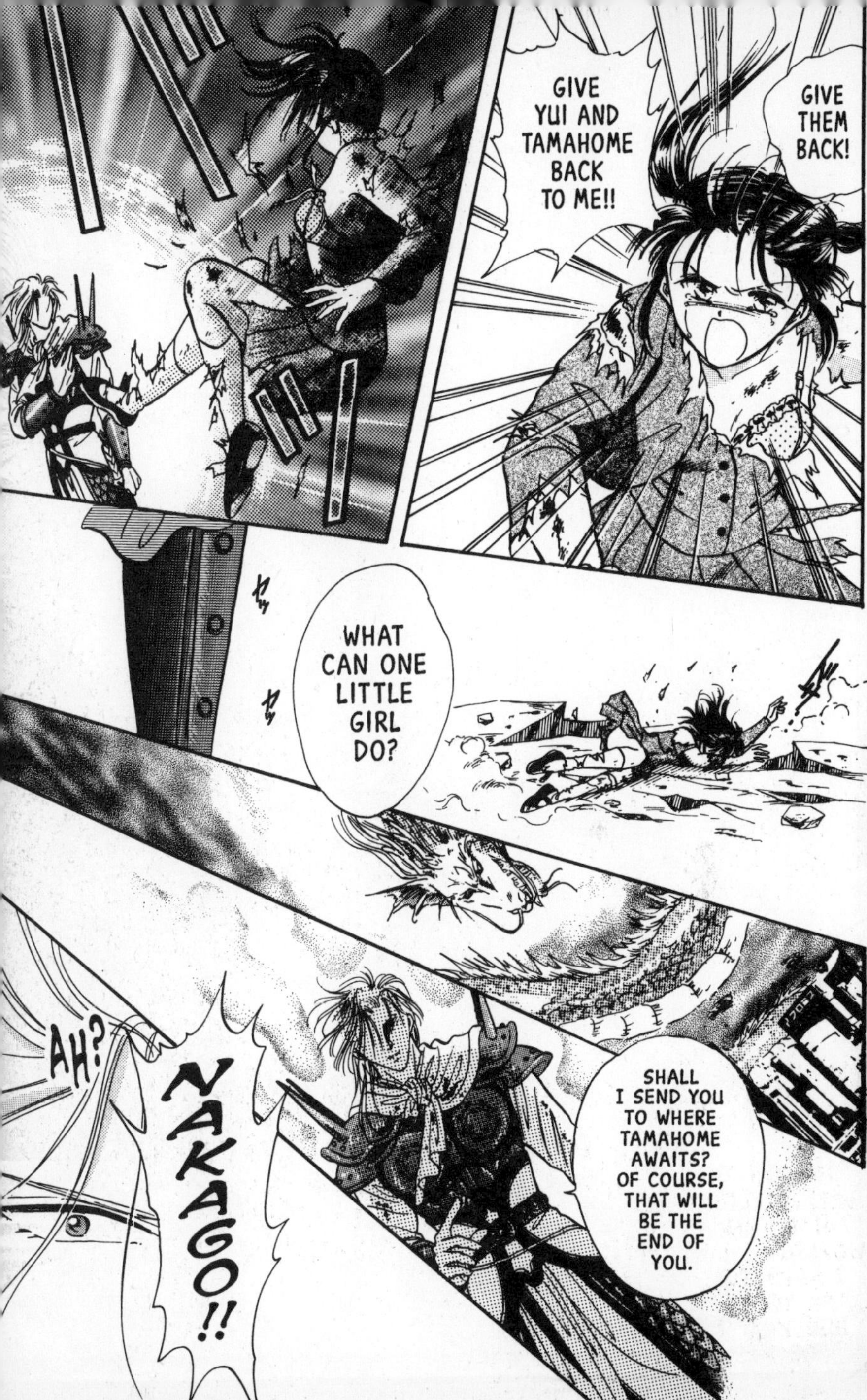
GIVE THEM BACK!
GIVE YUI AND TAMAHOME BACK TO ME!!
WHAT CAN ONE LITTLE GIRL DO?
SHALL I SEND YOU TO WHERE TAMAHOME AWAITS? OF COURSE, THAT WILL BE THE END OF YOU.
AH?
NAKAGO!!

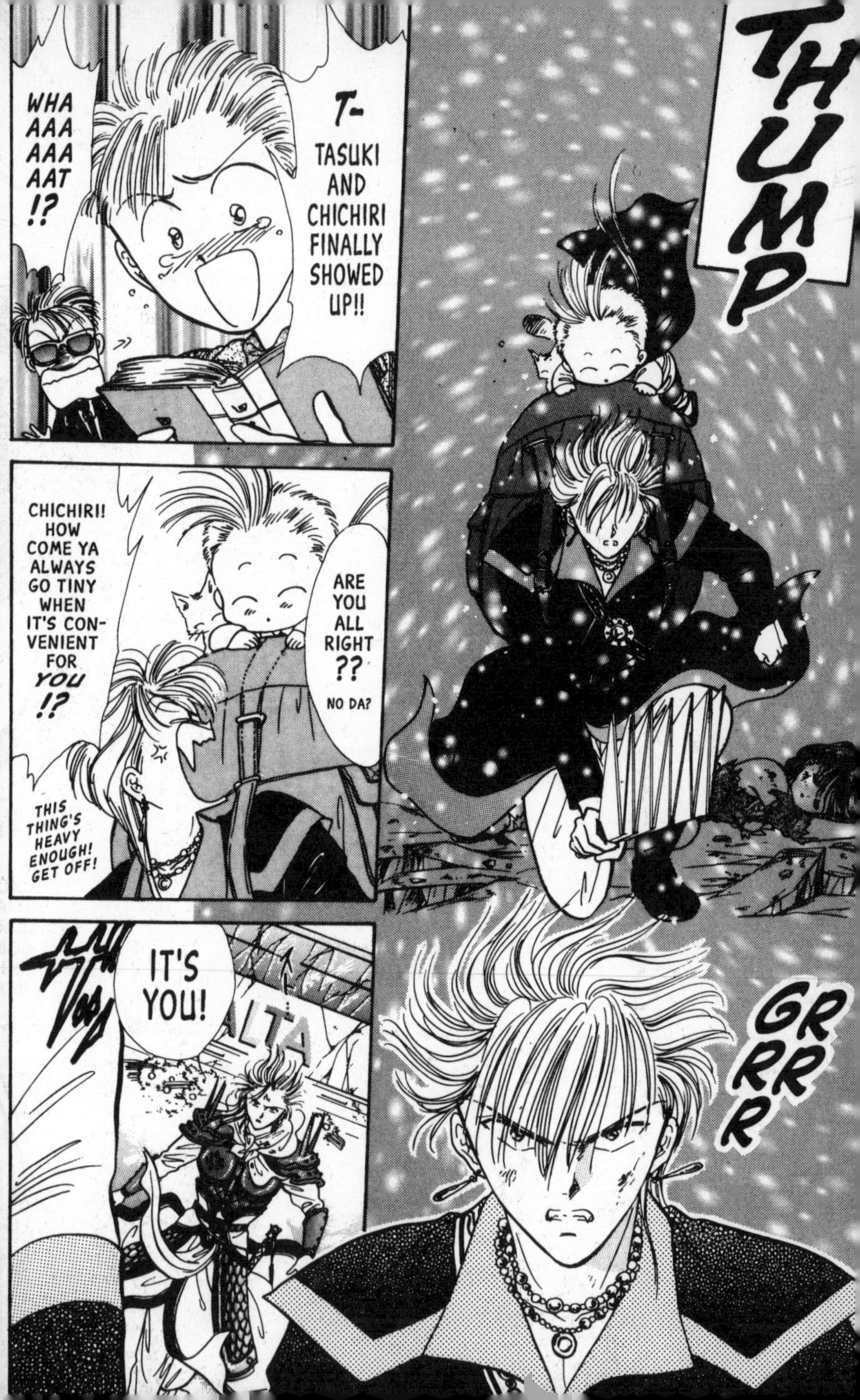
THUMP
GRRRR
T- TASUKI AND CHICHIRI FINALLY SHOWED UP!!
WHAAAAAAAAAAT!?
ARE YOU ALL RIGHT?? NO DA?
CHICHIRI! HOW COME YA ALWAYS GO TINY WHEN IT'S CONVENIENT FOR YOU!?
THIS THING'S HEAVY ENOUGH! GET OFF!
IT'S YOU!

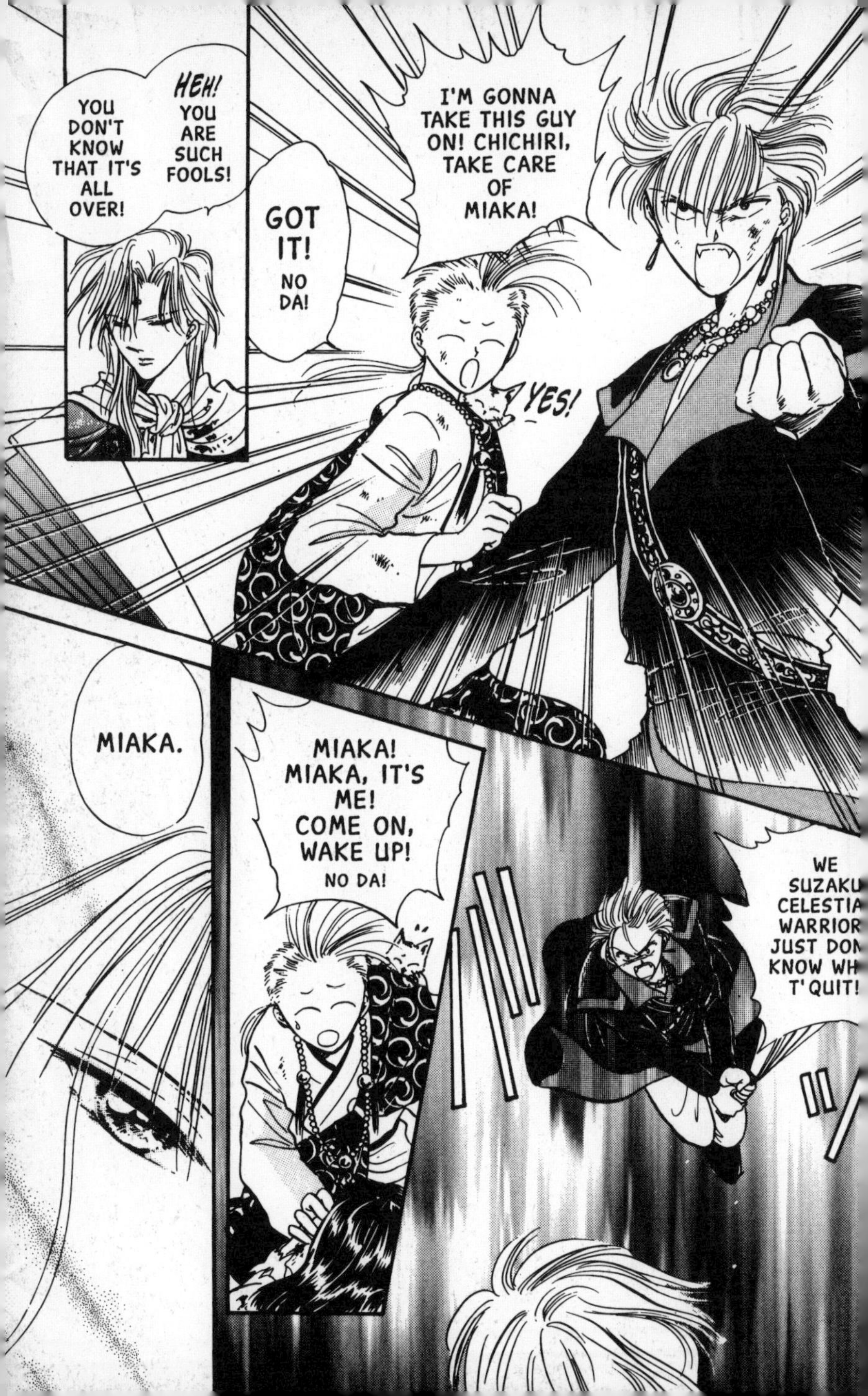
I'M GONNA TAKE THIS GUY ON! CHICHIRI, TAKE CARE OF MIAKA!
GOT IT! NO DA!
YES!
HEH! YOU ARE SUCH FOOLS!
YOU DON'T KNOW THAT IT'S ALL OVER!
WE SUZAKU CELESTIA WARRIOR JUST DON KNOW WH T' QUIT!
MIAKA! MIAKA, IT'S ME! COME ON, WAKE UP! NO DA!
MIAKA.

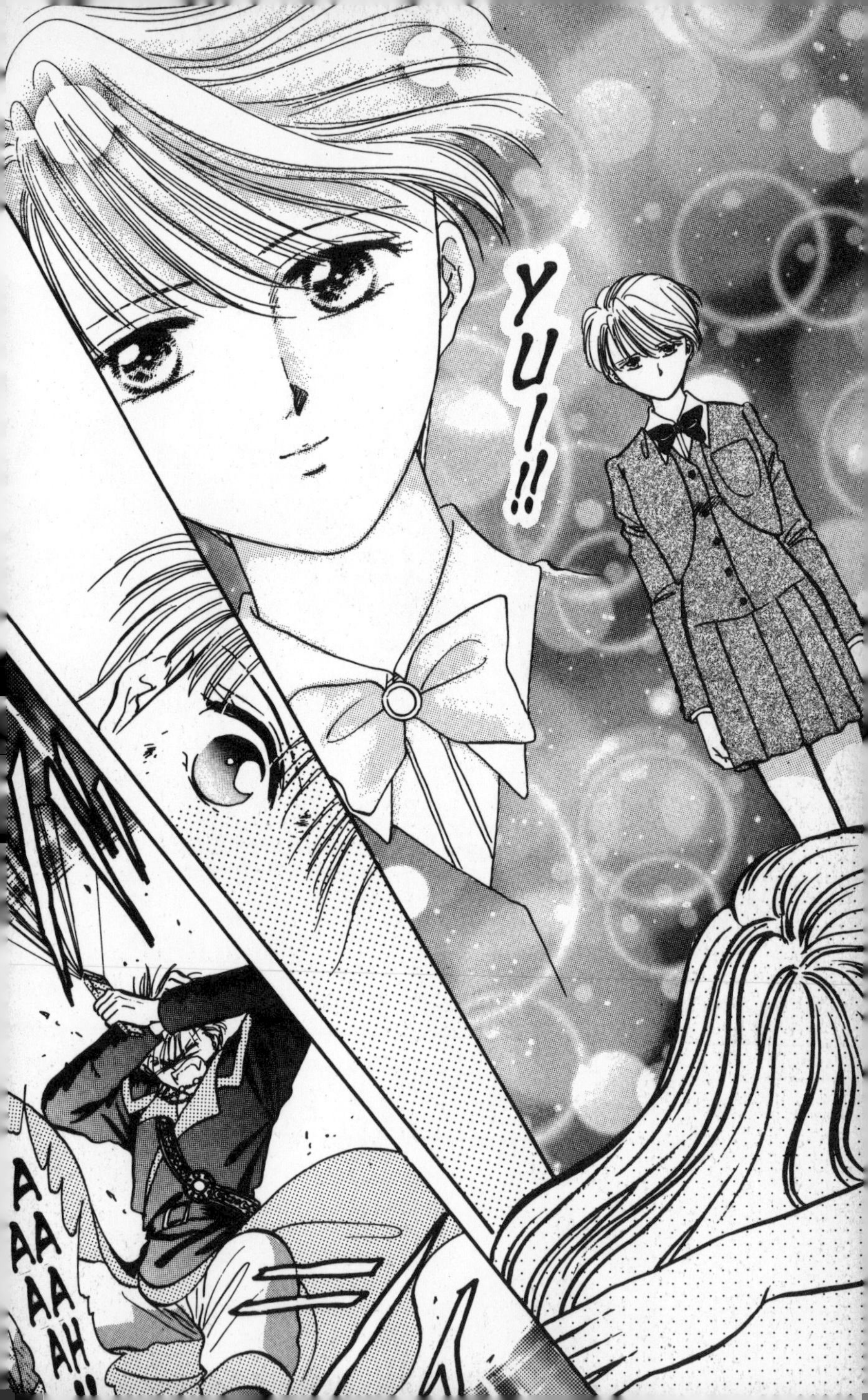
YUI!!!
AAAAAAH!!

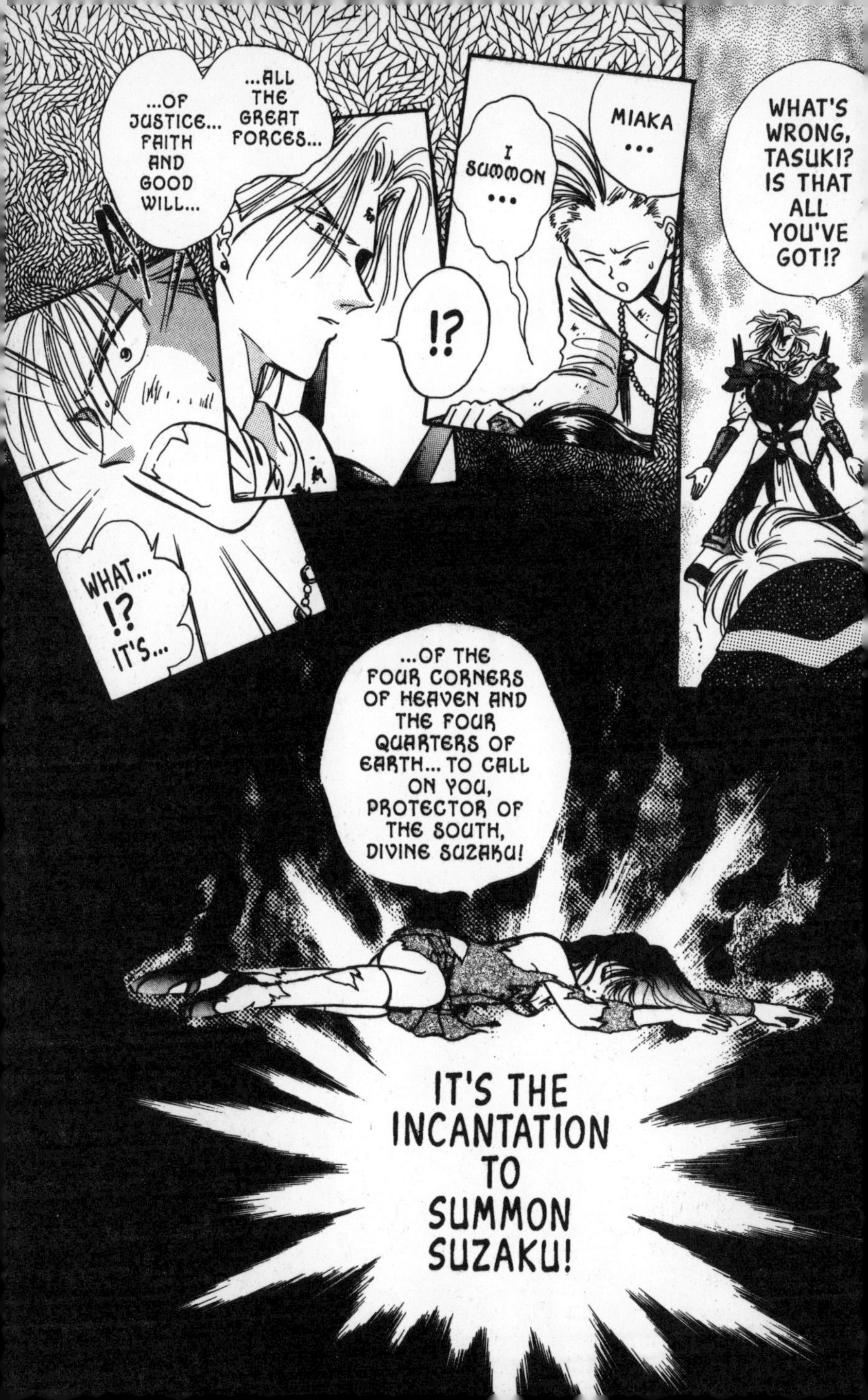
WHAT'S WRONG, TASUKI? IS THAT ALL YOU'VE GOT!?
MIAKA ...
I SUMMON ...
...ALL THE GREAT FORCES...
...OF JUSTICE... FAITH AND GOOD WILL...
!?
WHAT... !? IT'S...
...OF THE FOUR CORNERS OF HEAVEN AND THE FOUR QUARTERS OF EARTH... TO CALL ON YOU, PROTECTOR OF THE SOUTH, DIVINE SUZAKU!
IT'S THE INCANTATION TO SUMMON SUZAKU!

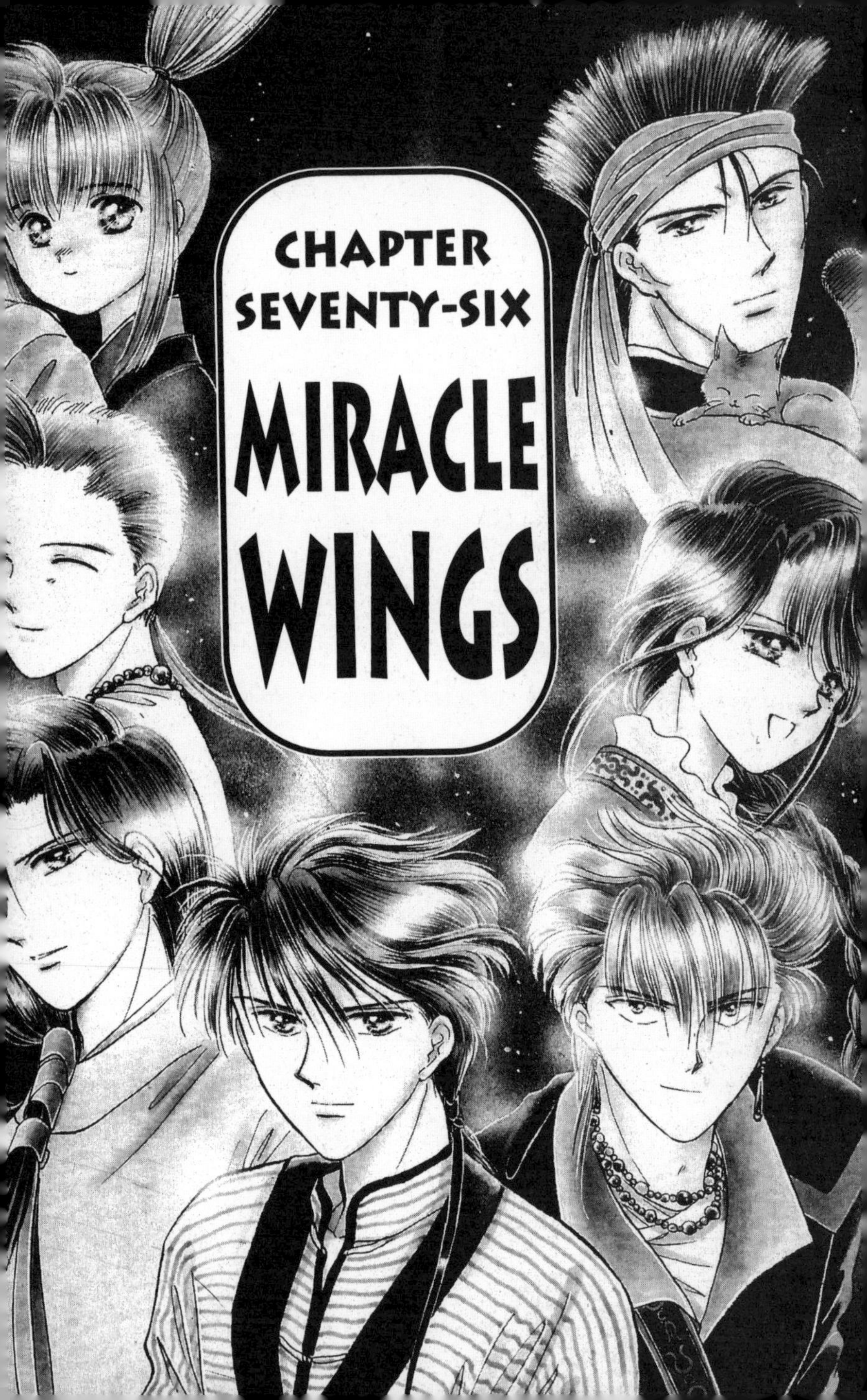
CHAPTER
SEVENTY-SIX
MIRACLE
WINGS

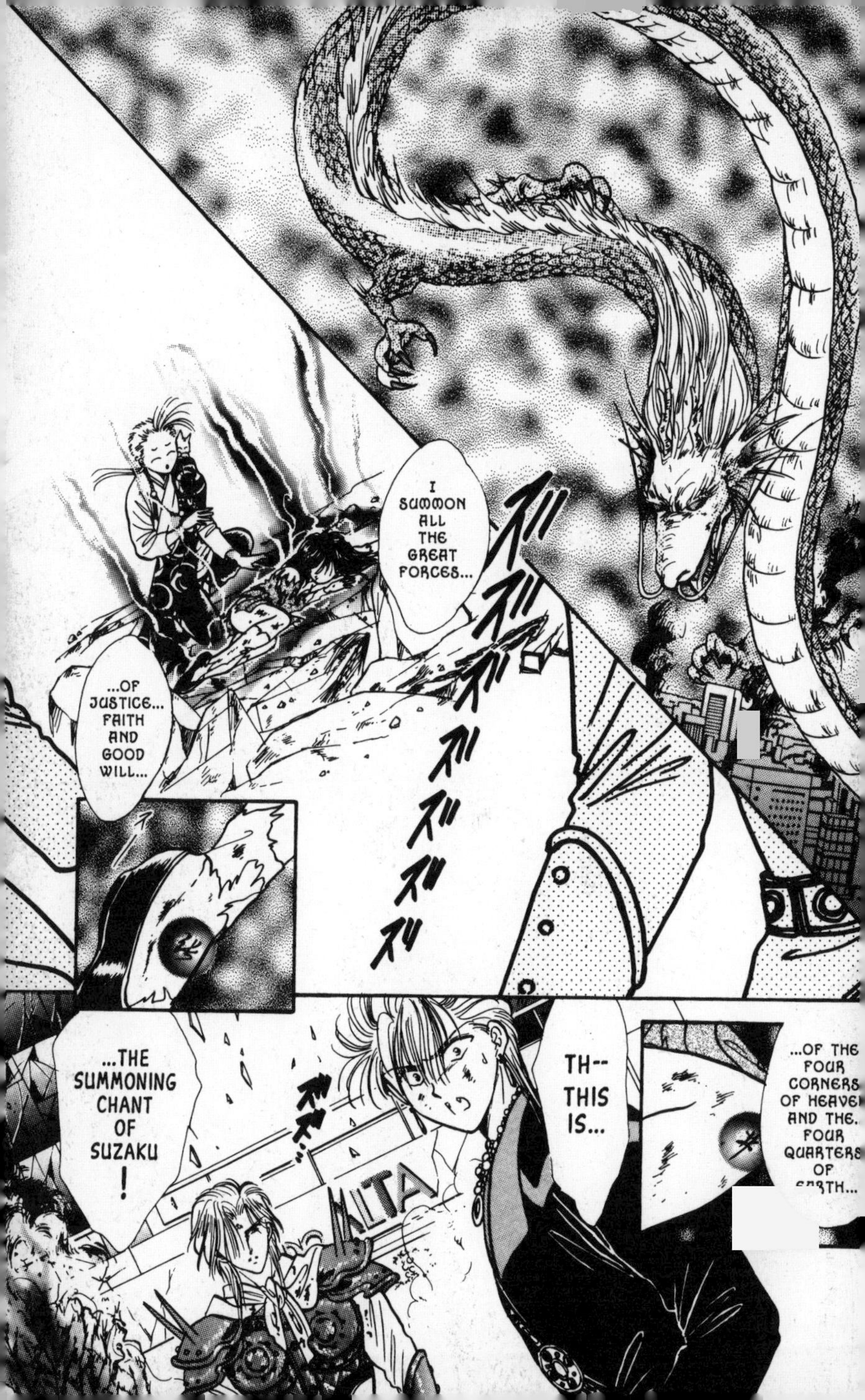
I SUMMON ALL THE GREAT FORCES...
...OF JUSTICE... FAITH AND GOOD WILL...
...OF THE FOUR CORNERS OF HEAVE AND THE FOUR QUARTERS OF
TH-- THIS IS...
...THE SUMMONING CHANT OF SUZAKU!
ALTA

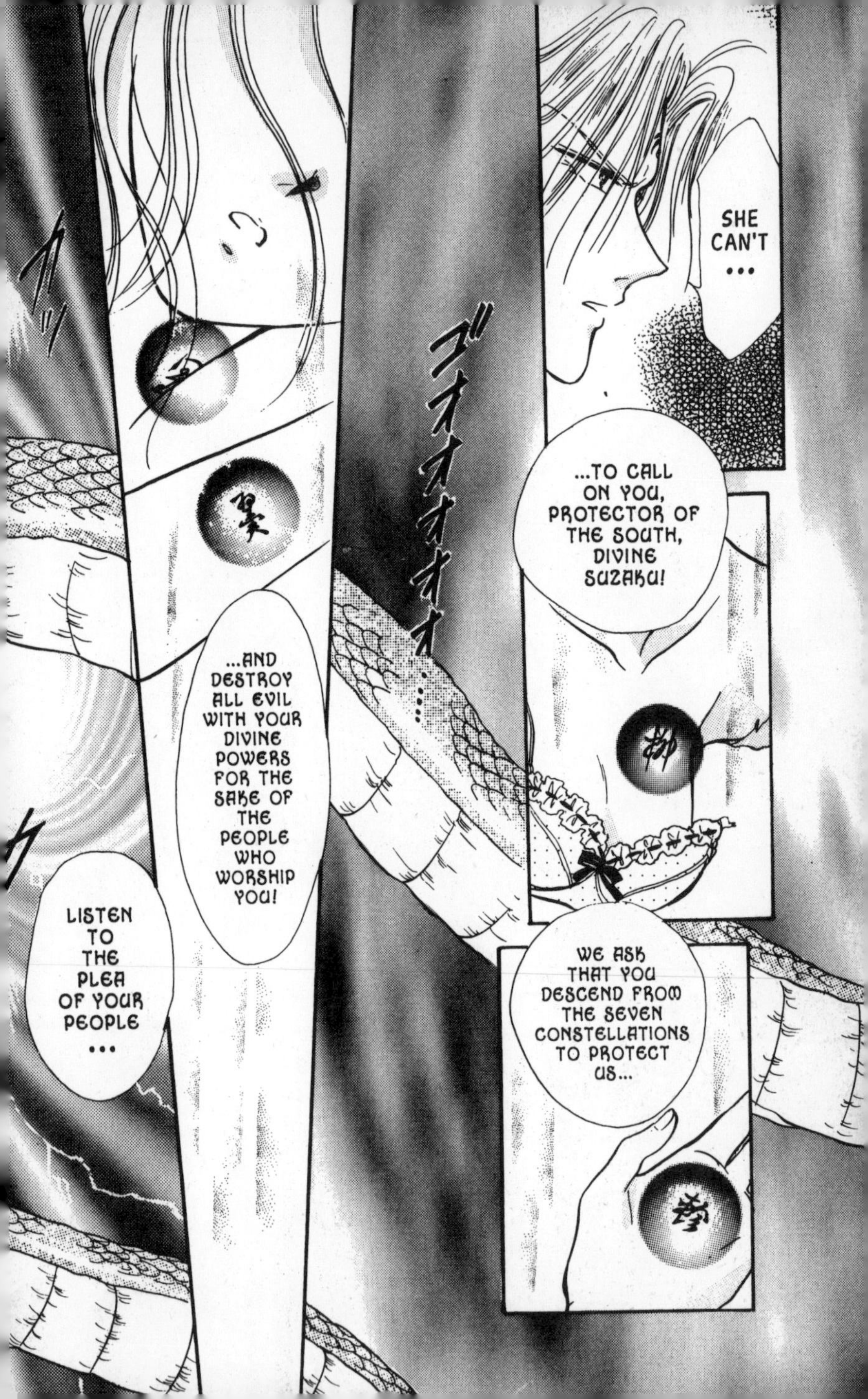
SHE CAN'T ...
...TO CALL ON YOU, PROTECTOR OF THE SOUTH, DIVINE SUZAKU!
WE ASK THAT YOU DESCEND FROM THE SEVEN CONSTELLATIONS TO PROTECT US...
...AND DESTROY ALL EVIL WITH YOUR DIVINE POWERS FOR THE SAKE OF THE PEOPLE WHO WORSHIP YOU!
LISTEN TO THE PLEA OF YOUR PEOPLE ...

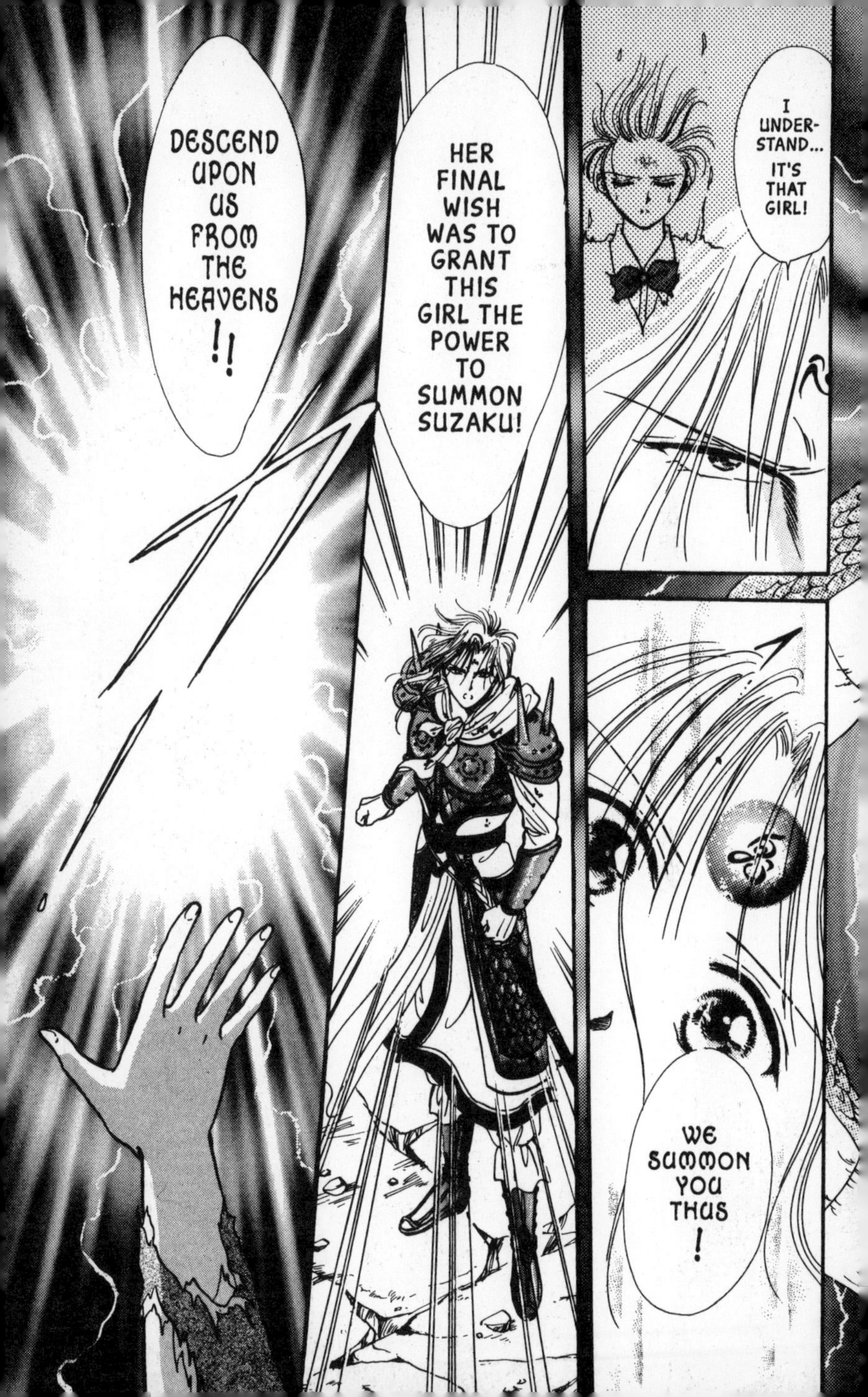
I UNDERSTAND... IT'S THAT GIRL!
WE SUMMON YOU THUS!
HER FINAL WISH WAS TO GRANT THIS GIRL THE POWER TO SUMMON SUZAKU!
DESCEND UPON US FROM THE HEAVENS!!

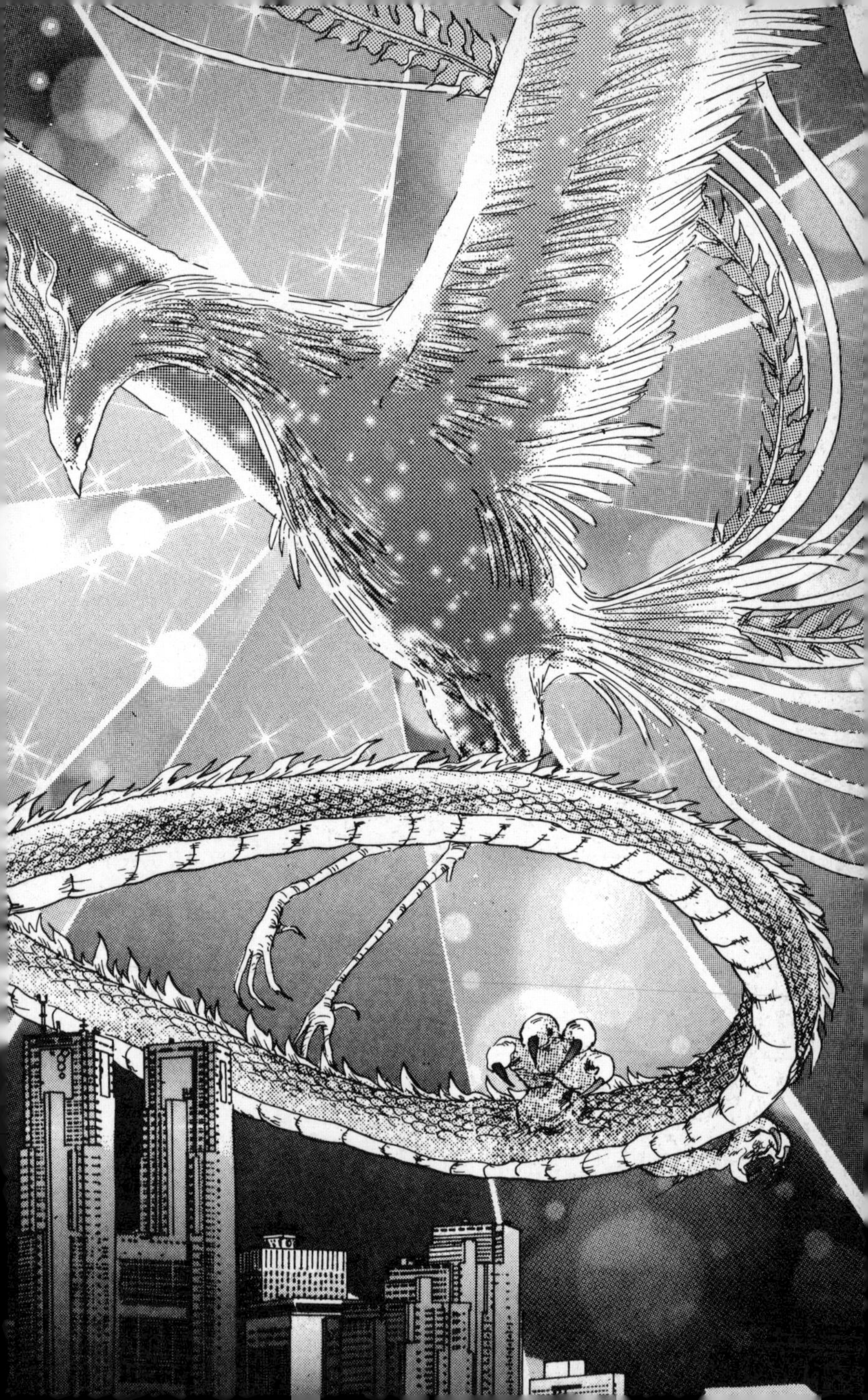

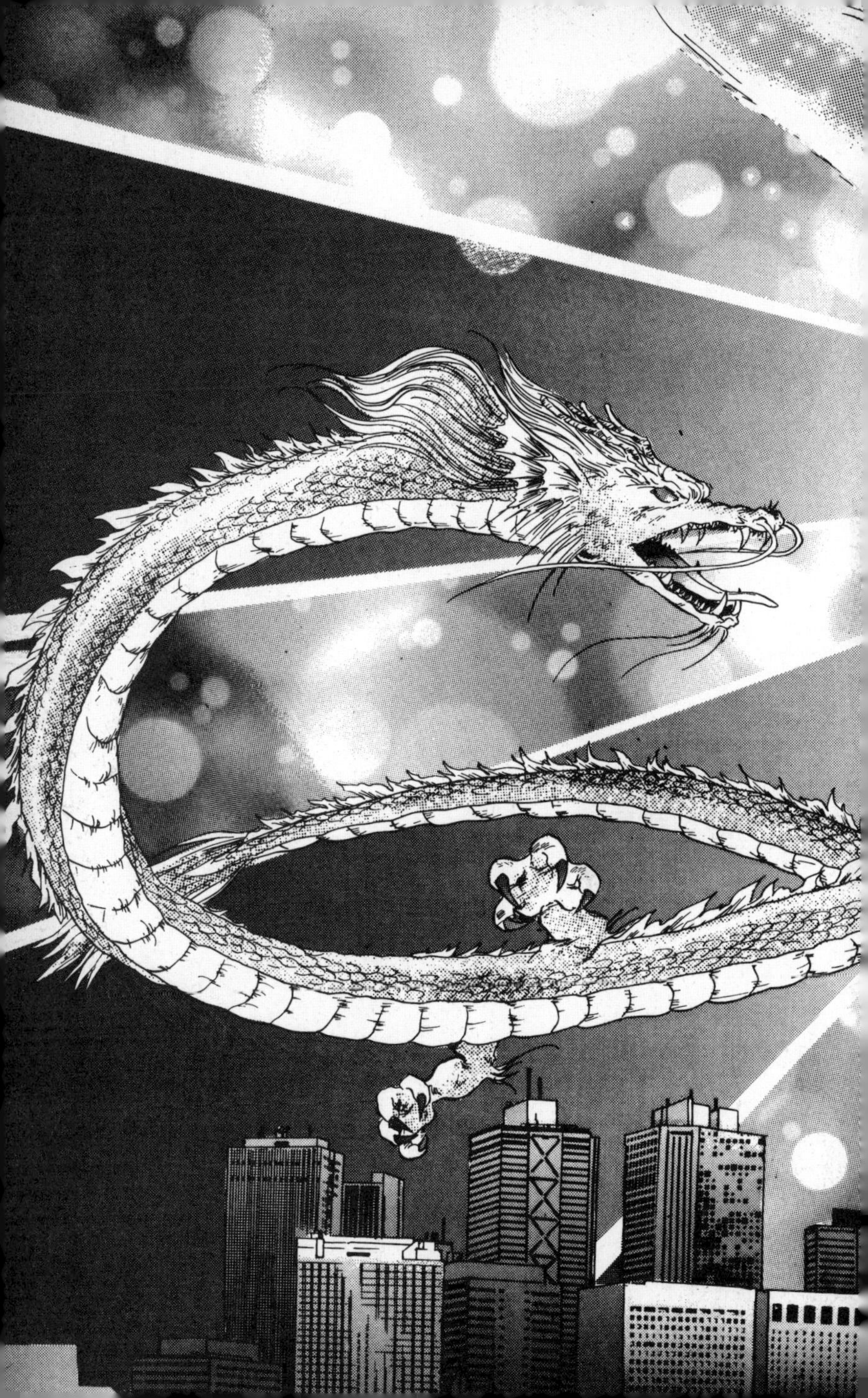

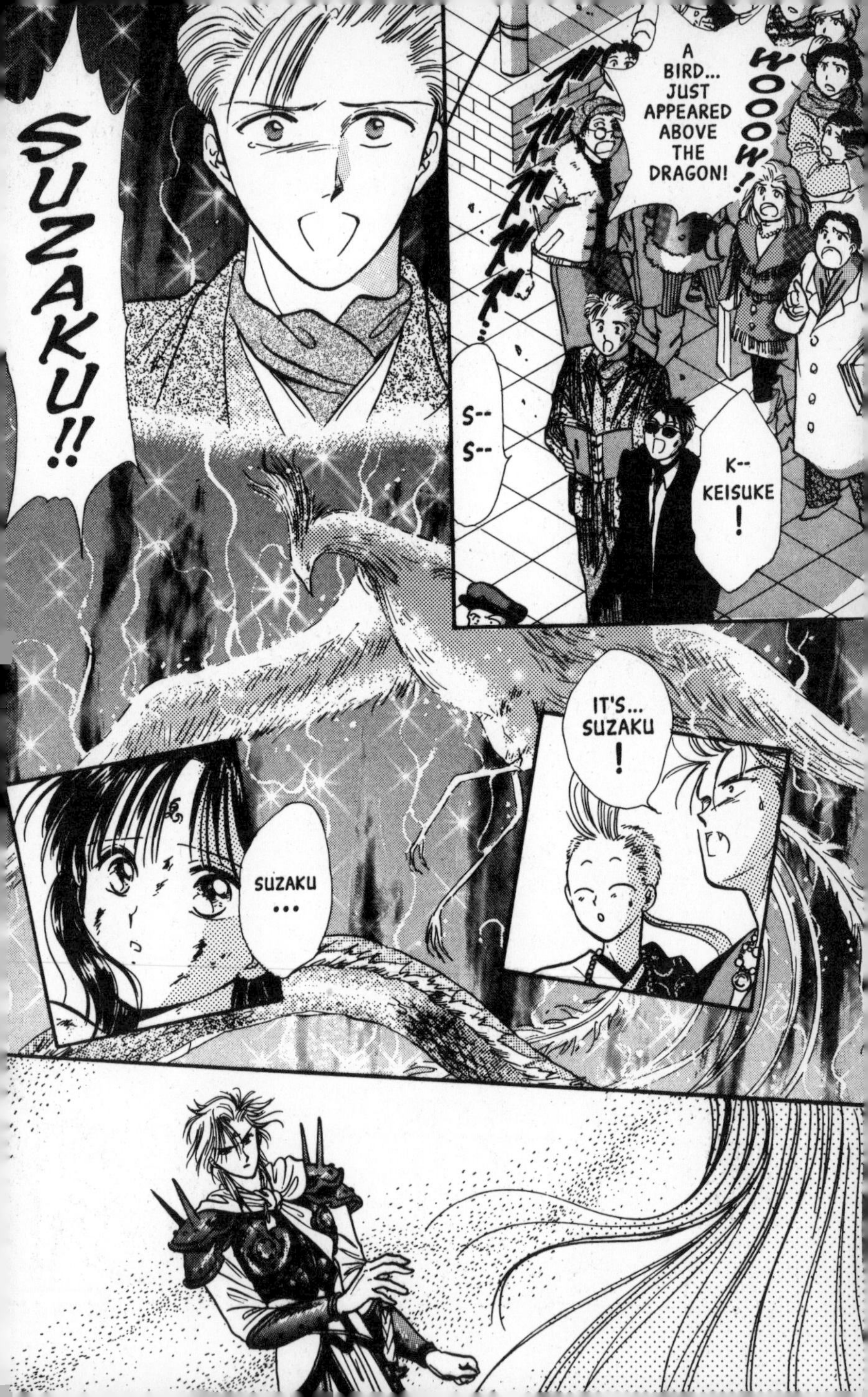
WOOOOW!
A BIRD... JUST APPEARED ABOVE THE DRAGON!
K-- KEISUKE!
S-- S--
SUZAKU!!
IT'S... SUZAKU!
SUZAKU...

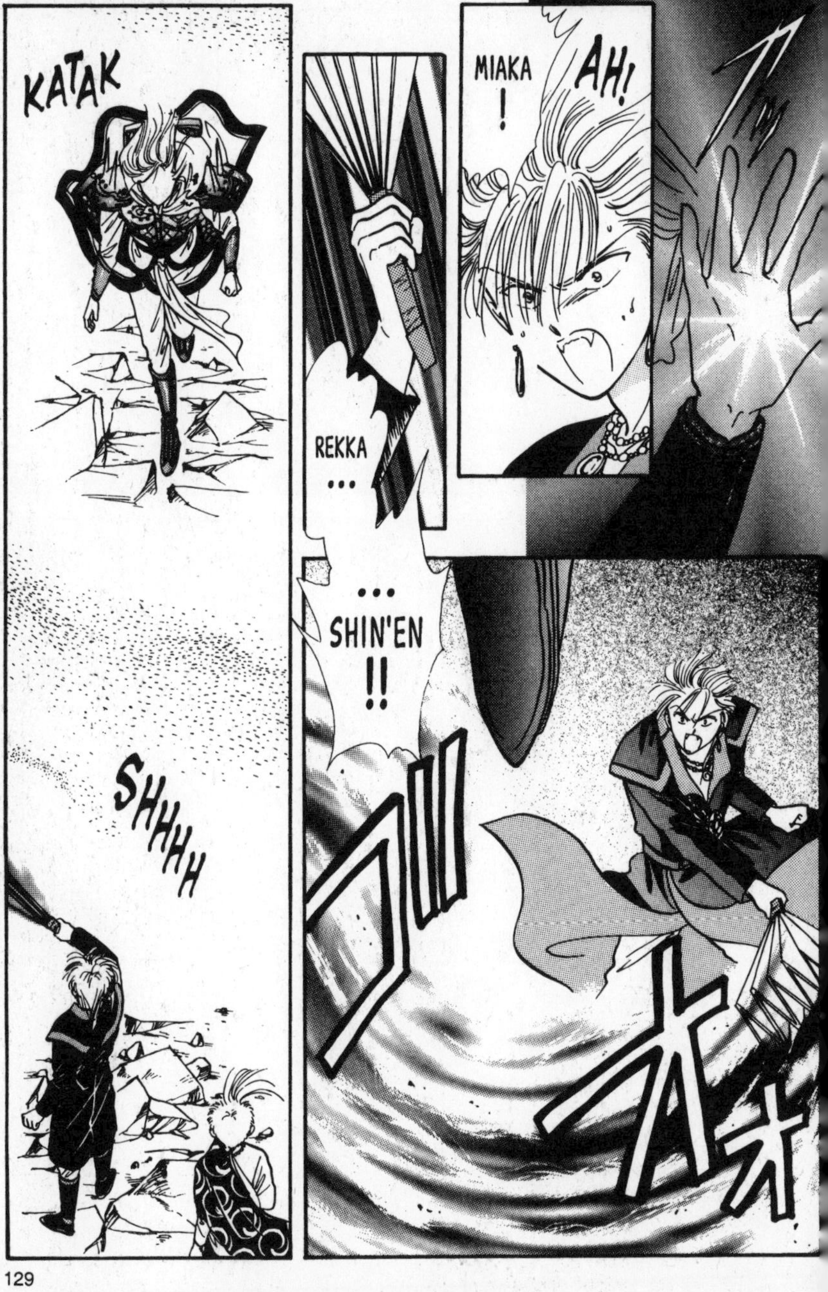
MIAKA !
AH!
REKKA ...
... SHIN'EN !!
KATAK
SHHHH

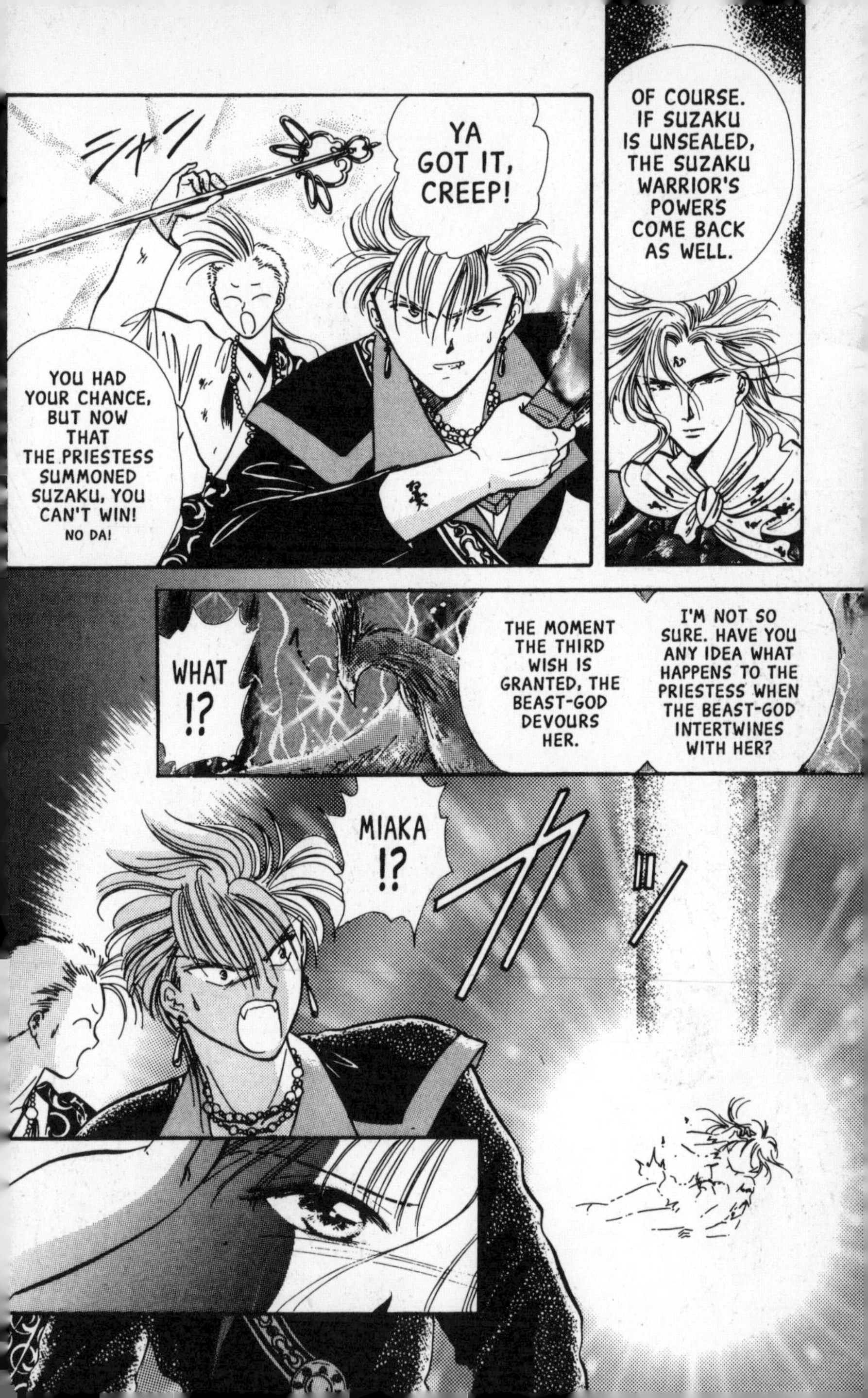

OF COURSE. IF SUZAKU IS UNSEALED, THE SUZAKU WARRIOR'S POWERS COME BACK AS WELL.
YA GOT IT, CREEP!
シャン
YOU HAD YOUR CHANCE, BUT NOW THAT THE PRIESTESS SUMMONED SUZAKU, YOU CAN'T WIN! NO DA!
I'M NOT SO SURE. HAVE YOU ANY IDEA WHAT HAPPENS TO THE PRIESTESS WHEN THE BEAST-GOD INTERTWINES WITH HER?
THE MOMENT THE THIRD WISH IS GRANTED, THE BEAST-GOD DEVOURS HER.
WHAT !?
MIAKA !?

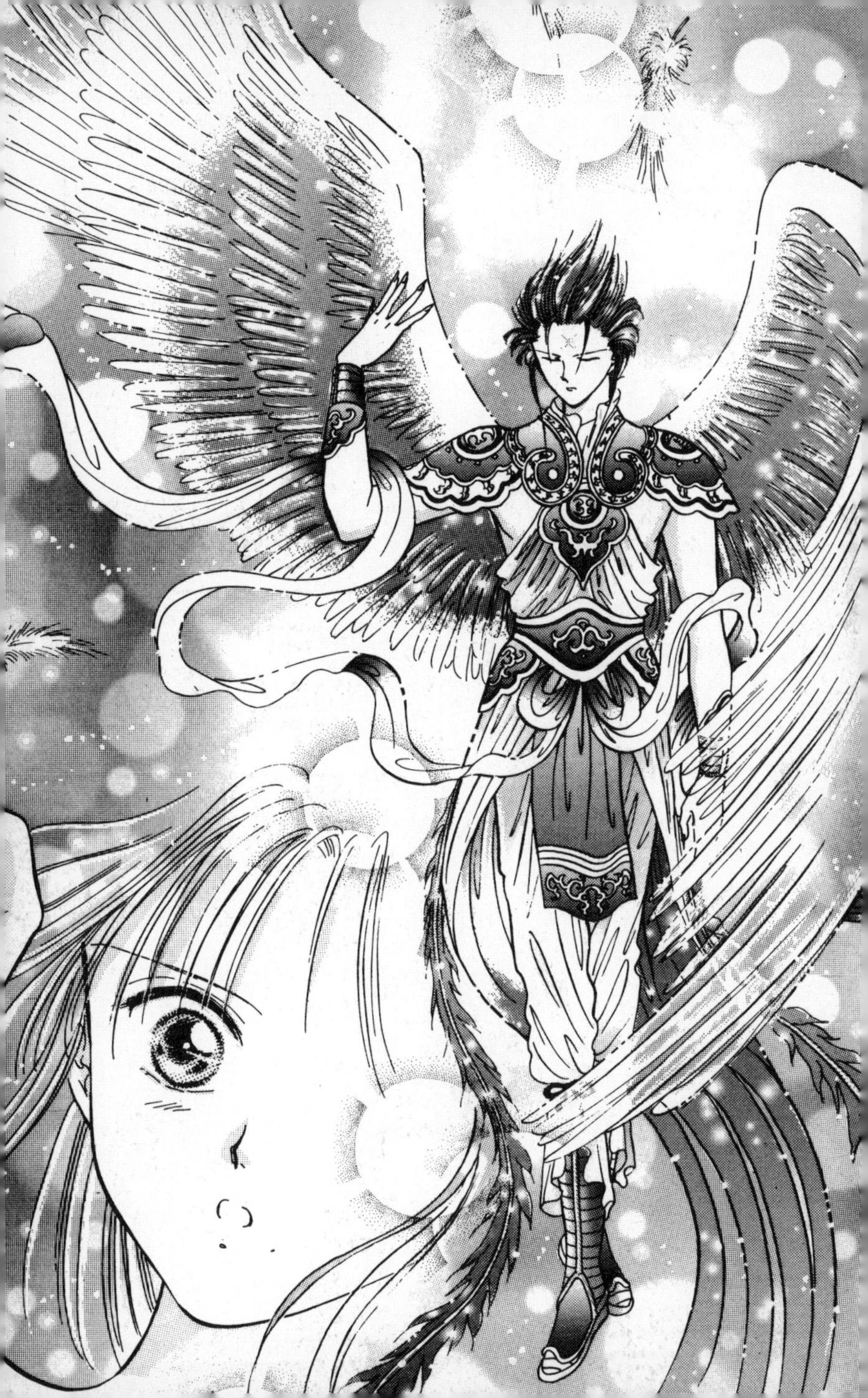

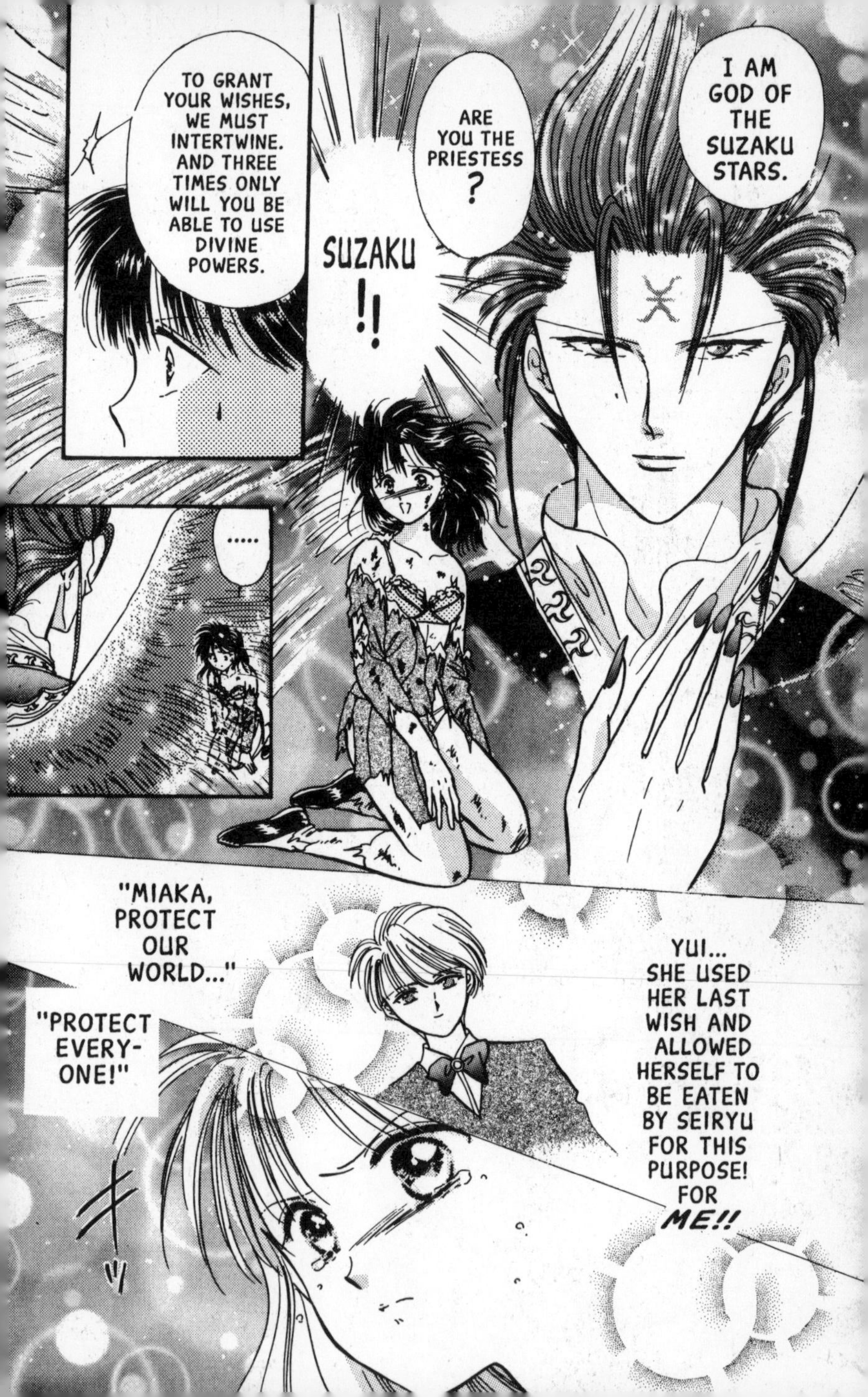
I AM GOD OF THE SUZAKU STARS.
ARE YOU THE PRIESTESS?
SUZAKU!!
TO GRANT YOUR WISHES, WE MUST INTERTWINE. AND THREE TIMES ONLY WILL YOU BE ABLE TO USE DIVINE POWERS.
.....
YUI... SHE USED HER LAST WISH AND ALLOWED HERSELF TO BE EATEN BY SEIRYU FOR THIS PURPOSE! FOR ME!!
"MIAKA, PROTECT OUR WORLD..."
"PROTECT EVERY-ONE!"

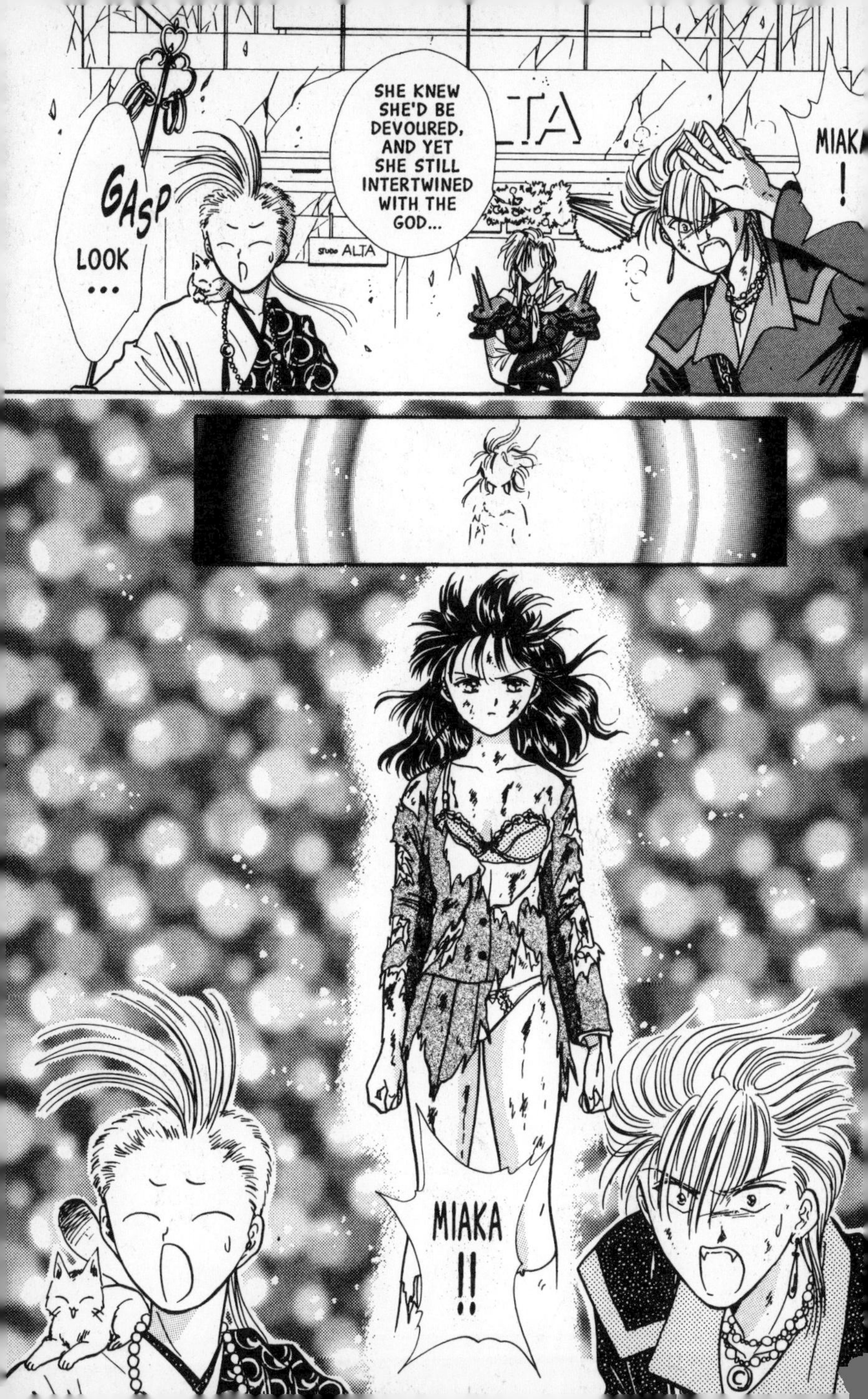
MIAKA!
SHE KNEW SHE'D BE DEVOURED, AND YET SHE STILL INTERTWINED WITH THE GOD...
GASP
LOOK...
STUDIO ALTA
MIAKA!!

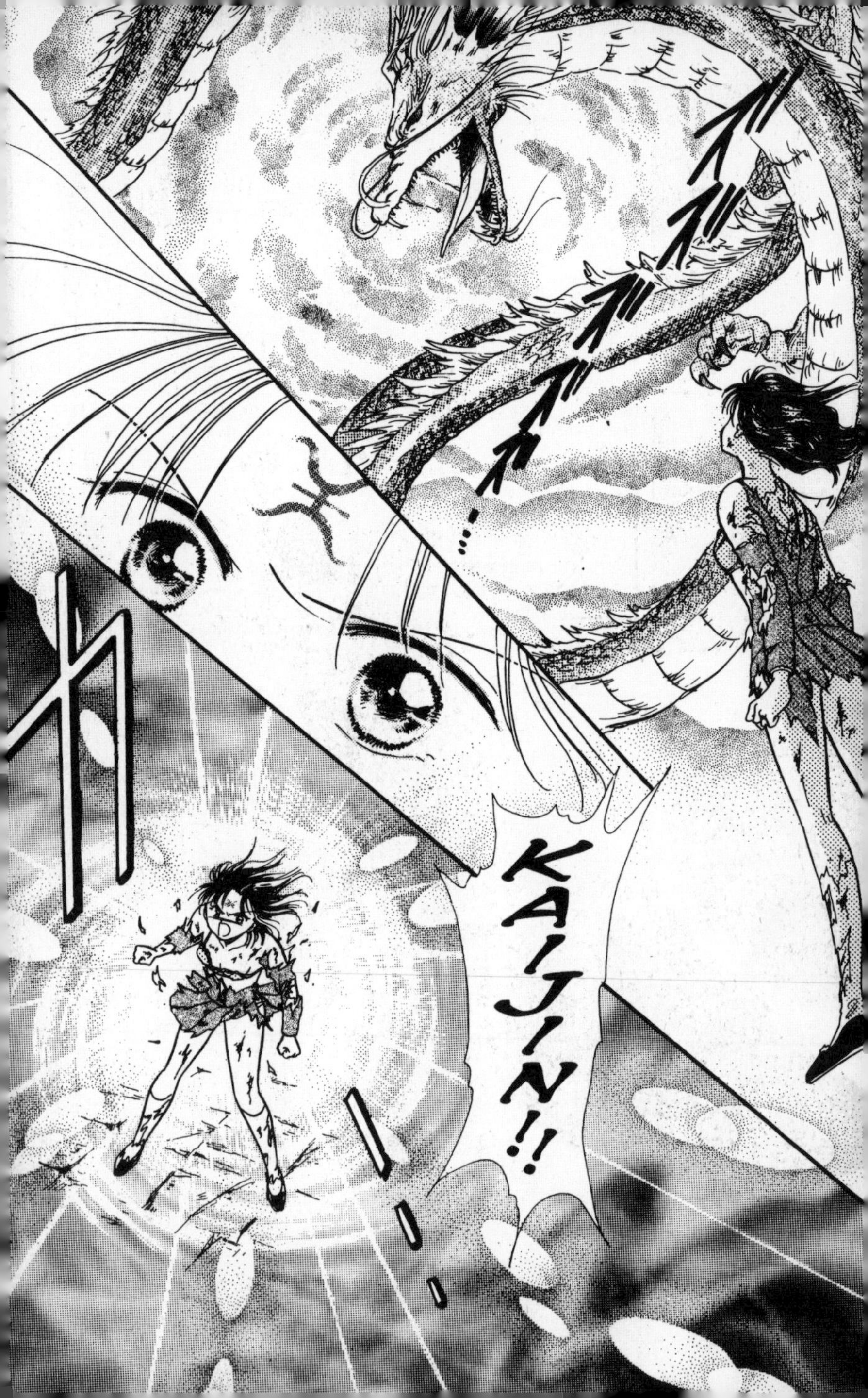
KAIJIN!!

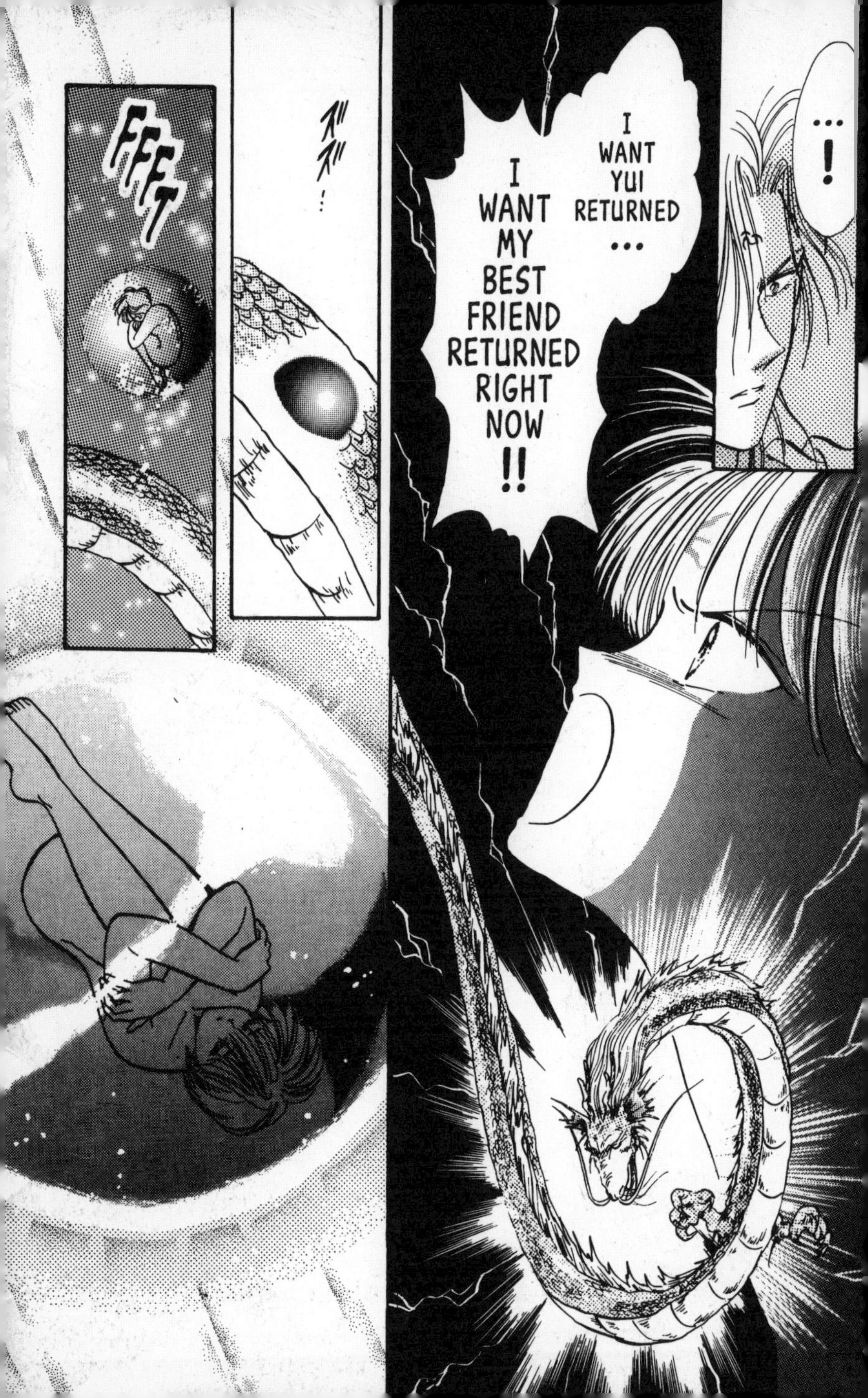
...!
I WANT YUI RETURNED...
I WANT MY BEST FRIEND RETURNED RIGHT NOW!!
ズズ!
FFFT

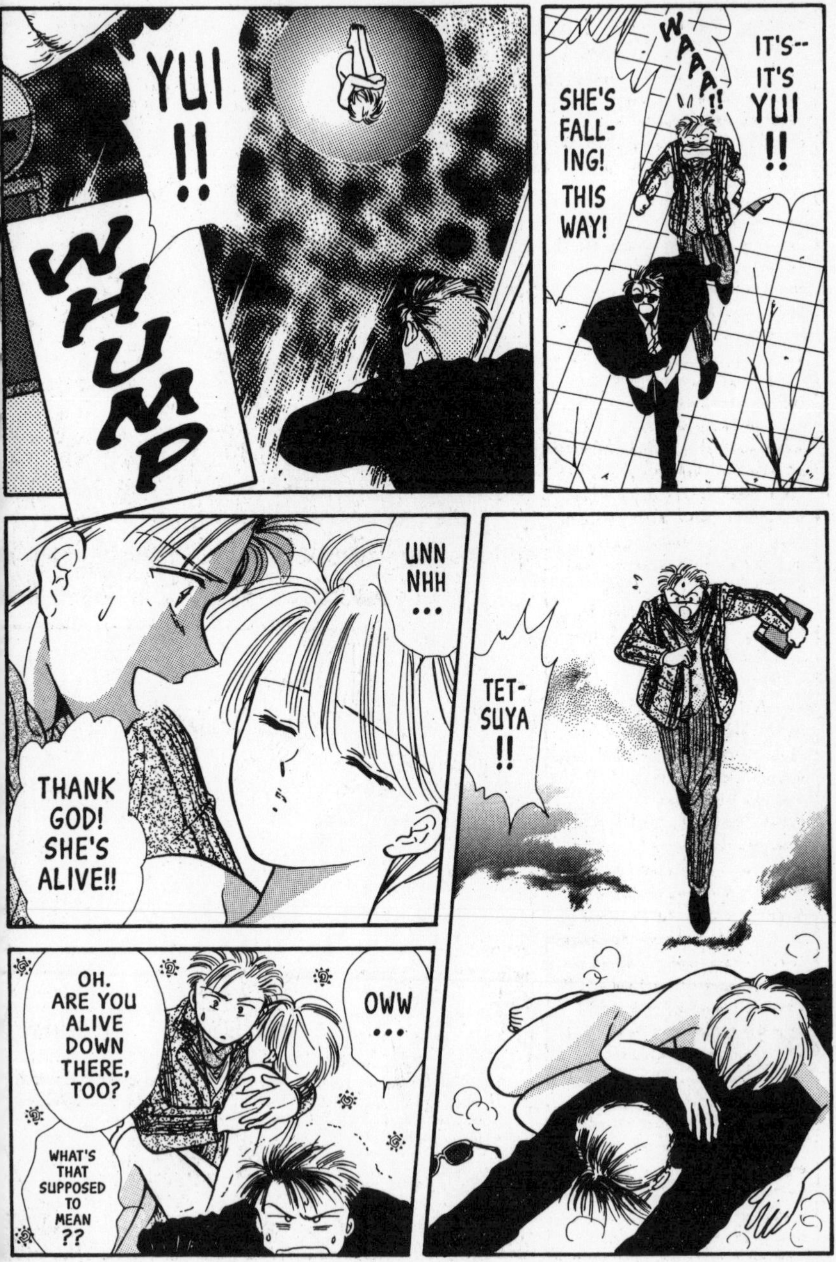
IT'S-- IT'S YUI!!
WAAAA!!
SHE'S FALLING! THIS WAY!
YUI!!
WHUMP
TET-SUYA!!
UNN NHH...
THANK GOD! SHE'S ALIVE!!
OWW...
OH. ARE YOU ALIVE DOWN THERE, TOO?
WHAT'S THAT SUPPOSED TO MEAN??

"WHAT I WOULD HAVE LIKED TO DRAW" CORNER

Fushigi Yûgi is a story that should be able to be enjoyed even by Japanese grade school students, and for that reason, it has to be a world as seen through the eyes of a third-year middle-school student, Miaka!

What I really wanted to draw was the world as seen through other points of view, as well; from the point of view of other people in the country, from a political point of view, and the point of view of those in power. Also, there was Nakago as a general. Yeah, he's cold, but he really knew what to do for his soldiers. They felt that he did right by them, and as a result, he was very popular (and a good fighter too), and they'd follow him anywhere. I also wanted to get into the past of the other generals. There was a character who was isolated by malicious slander. But if you try to put in too much, you lose focus on the story. And from the perspective of a third-year student in middle school, politics are boring. So we made enormous cuts in the story there. *I was somewhat happy about it. It saved me a lot of work!*

What else? In this story, the things that were the most fun (to draw) were the action (fight) scenes! Since this is a shōjo manga, I held back quite a bit, but I really love them! ♫♫

When I got to Chapters 74-77 *(this book)* I nearly broke out and said, "finally!!" *It was so fun...I was spellbound!* I did this for Nakago vs. Tamahome too, but for the Tasuki vs. Tamahome fight in Volume 5, I sketched entire fight scenes from rented Chinese Kung-Fu movies on video. Camera angles, movement right and left... (If I don't do research and work at it, I'll never learn!) Also, I kept the thought in my head how they would move if it were animated. The movements went round and round... *(I know, but I love it!!)*

And so I compiled an "Action Note" sketchbook with more than a hundred entries and sketches of movements. *But it was hard and wore me out!* Even now, when I find the time, I still add to it. If I want to get better, I have to work!!

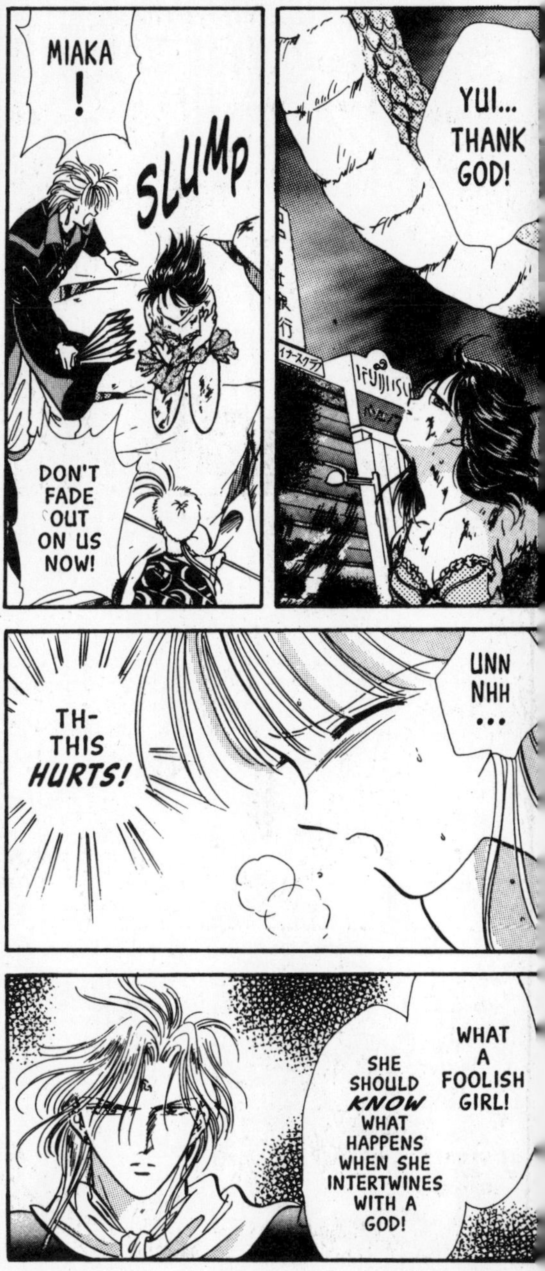
YUI... THANK GOD!
MIAKA!
SLUMP
DON'T FADE OUT ON US NOW!
UNN NHH...
TH-THIS *HURTS!*
WHAT A FOOLISH GIRL!
SHE SHOULD *KNOW* WHAT HAPPENS WHEN SHE INTERTWINES WITH A GOD!

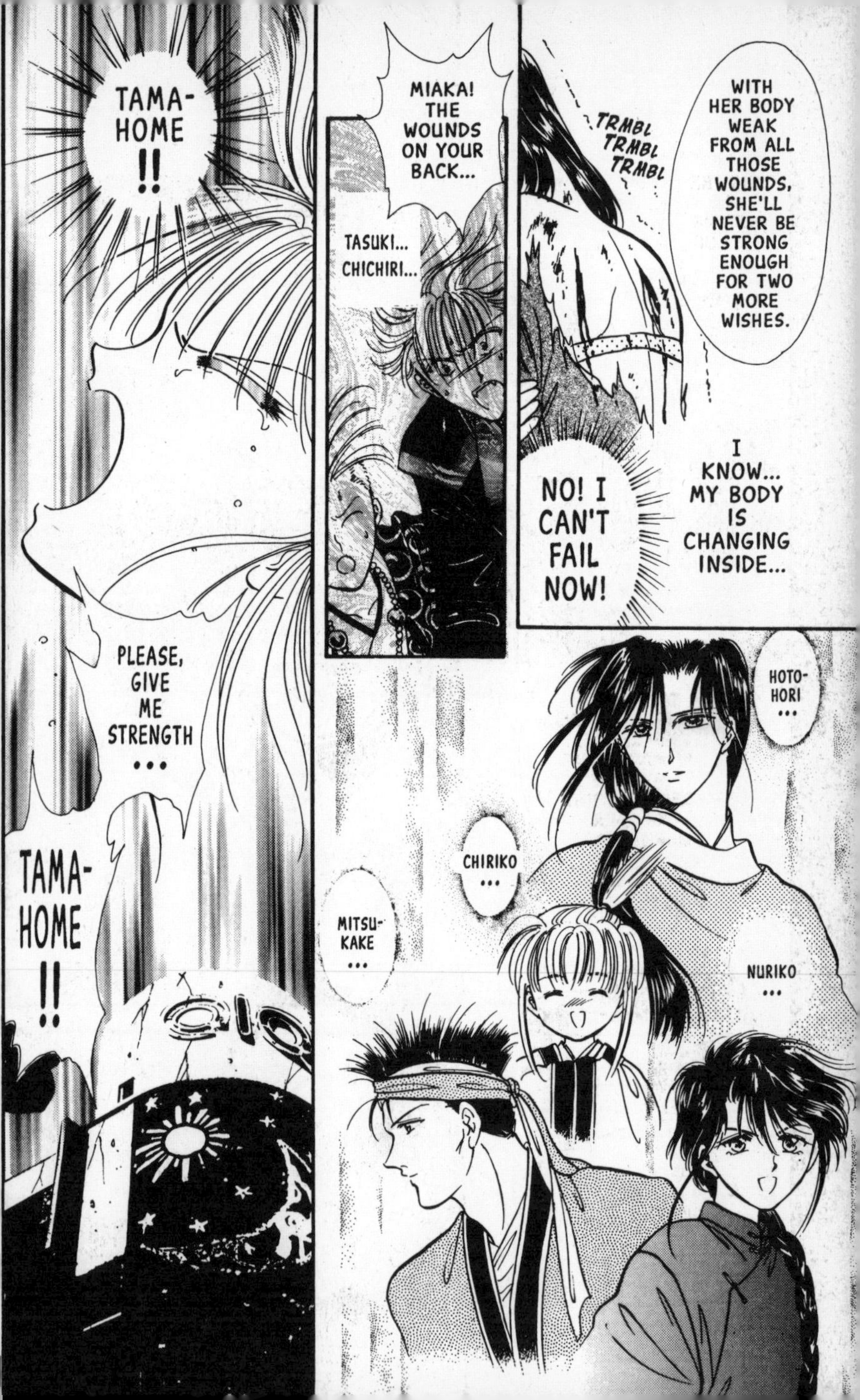
TRMBL TRMBL TRMBL
WITH HER BODY WEAK FROM ALL THOSE WOUNDS, SHE'LL NEVER BE STRONG ENOUGH FOR TWO MORE WISHES.
I KNOW... MY BODY IS CHANGING INSIDE...
NO! I CAN'T FAIL NOW!
MIAKA! THE WOUNDS ON YOUR BACK...
TASUKI... CHICHIRI...
HOTO-HORI...
NURIKO...
CHIRIKO...
MITSU-KAKE...
TAMA-HOME!!
PLEASE, GIVE ME STRENGTH...
TAMA-HOME!!

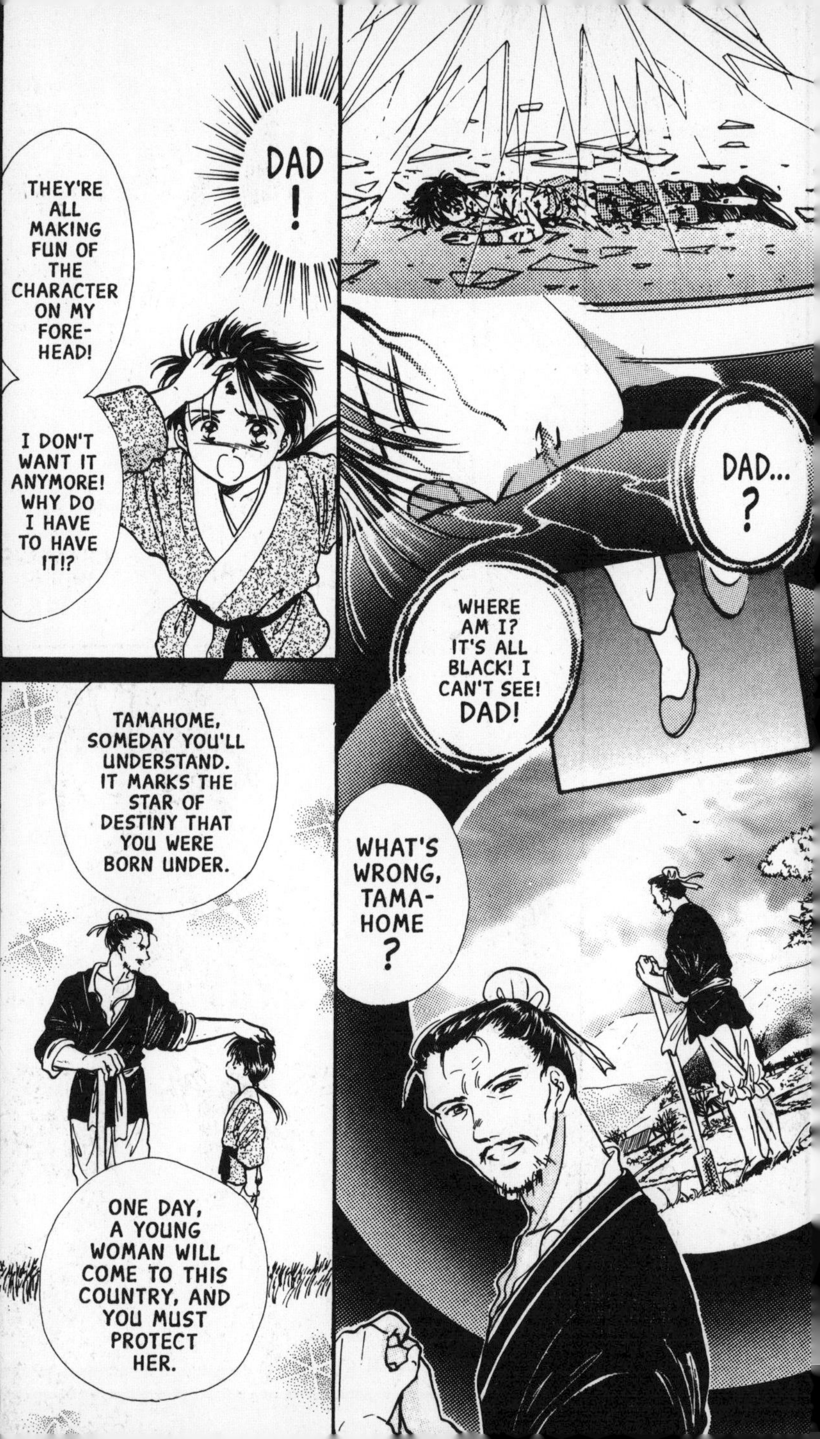
DAD...?
WHERE AM I? IT'S ALL BLACK! I CAN'T SEE! DAD!
WHAT'S WRONG, TAMAHOME?
DAD!
THEY'RE ALL MAKING FUN OF THE CHARACTER ON MY FOREHEAD!
I DON'T WANT IT ANYMORE! WHY DO I HAVE TO HAVE IT!?
TAMAHOME, SOMEDAY YOU'LL UNDERSTAND. IT MARKS THE STAR OF DESTINY THAT YOU WERE BORN UNDER.
ONE DAY, A YOUNG WOMAN WILL COME TO THIS COUNTRY, AND YOU MUST PROTECT HER.

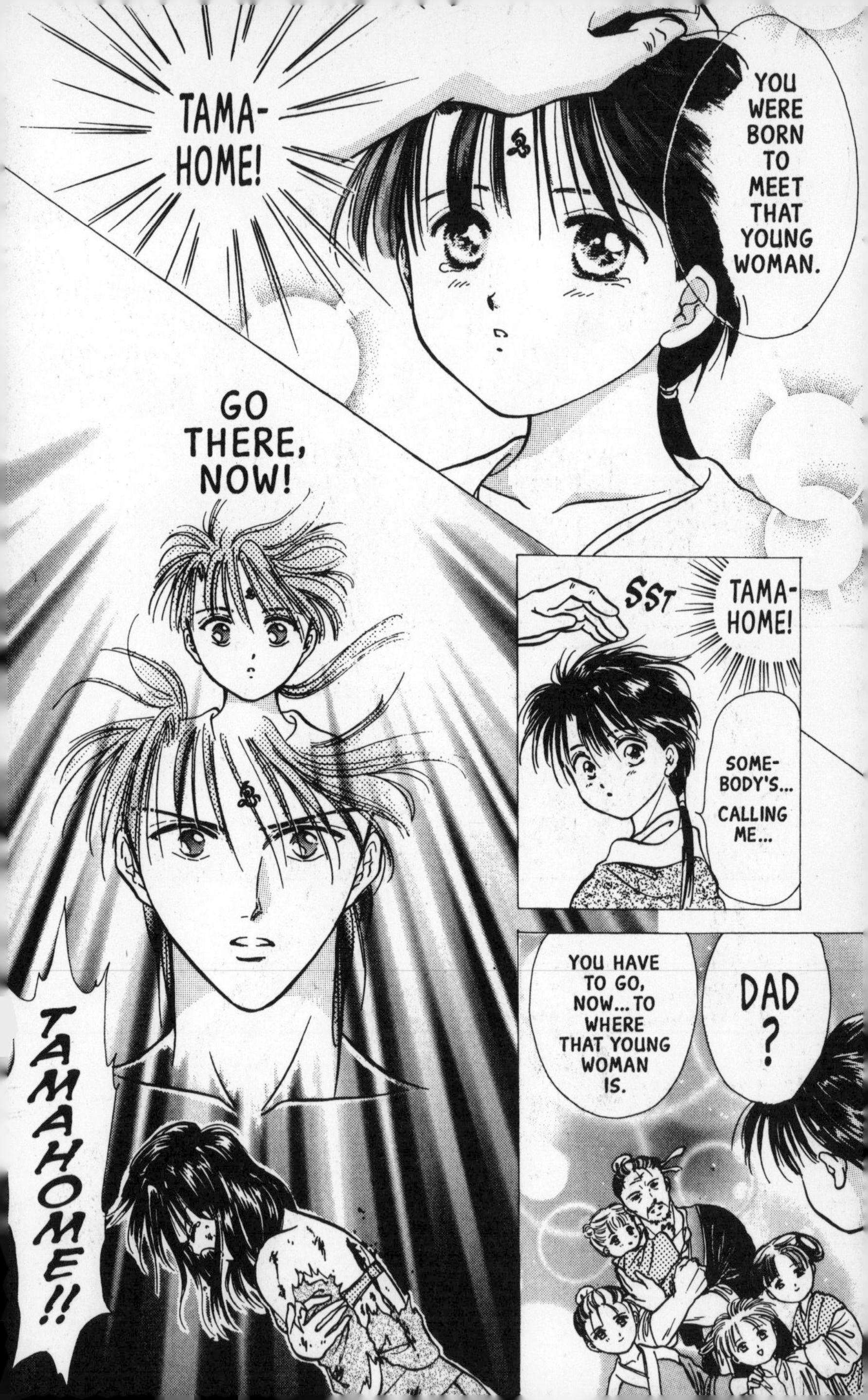
YOU WERE BORN TO MEET THAT YOUNG WOMAN.
TAMA-HOME!
TAMA-HOME!
SST
SOME-BODY'S... CALLING ME...
DAD?
YOU HAVE TO GO, NOW... TO WHERE THAT YOUNG WOMAN IS.
GO THERE, NOW!
TAMAHOME!!

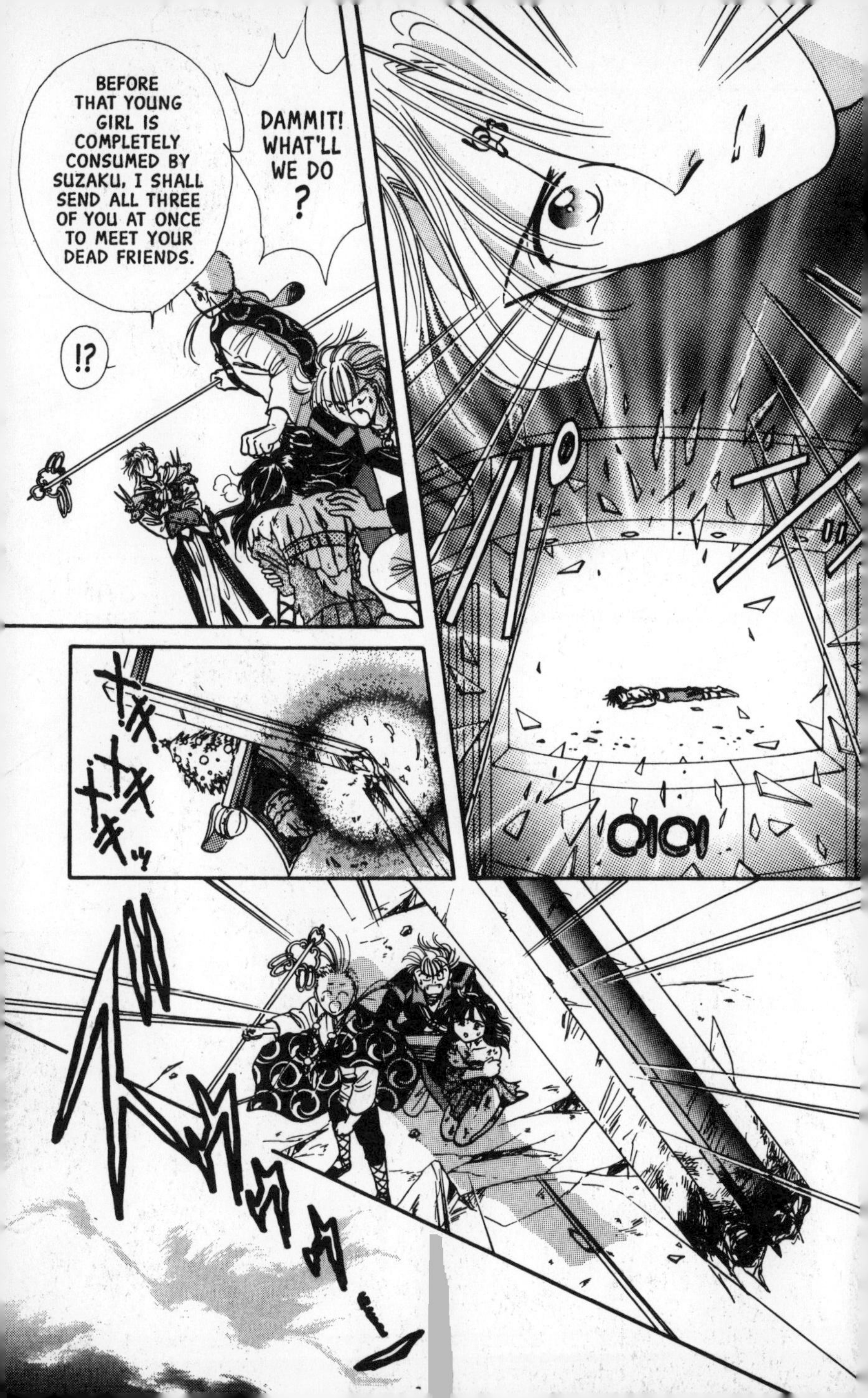
BEFORE THAT YOUNG GIRL IS COMPLETELY CONSUMED BY SUZAKU, I SHALL SEND ALL THREE OF YOU AT ONCE TO MEET YOUR DEAD FRIENDS.
DAMMIT! WHAT'LL WE DO?
!?

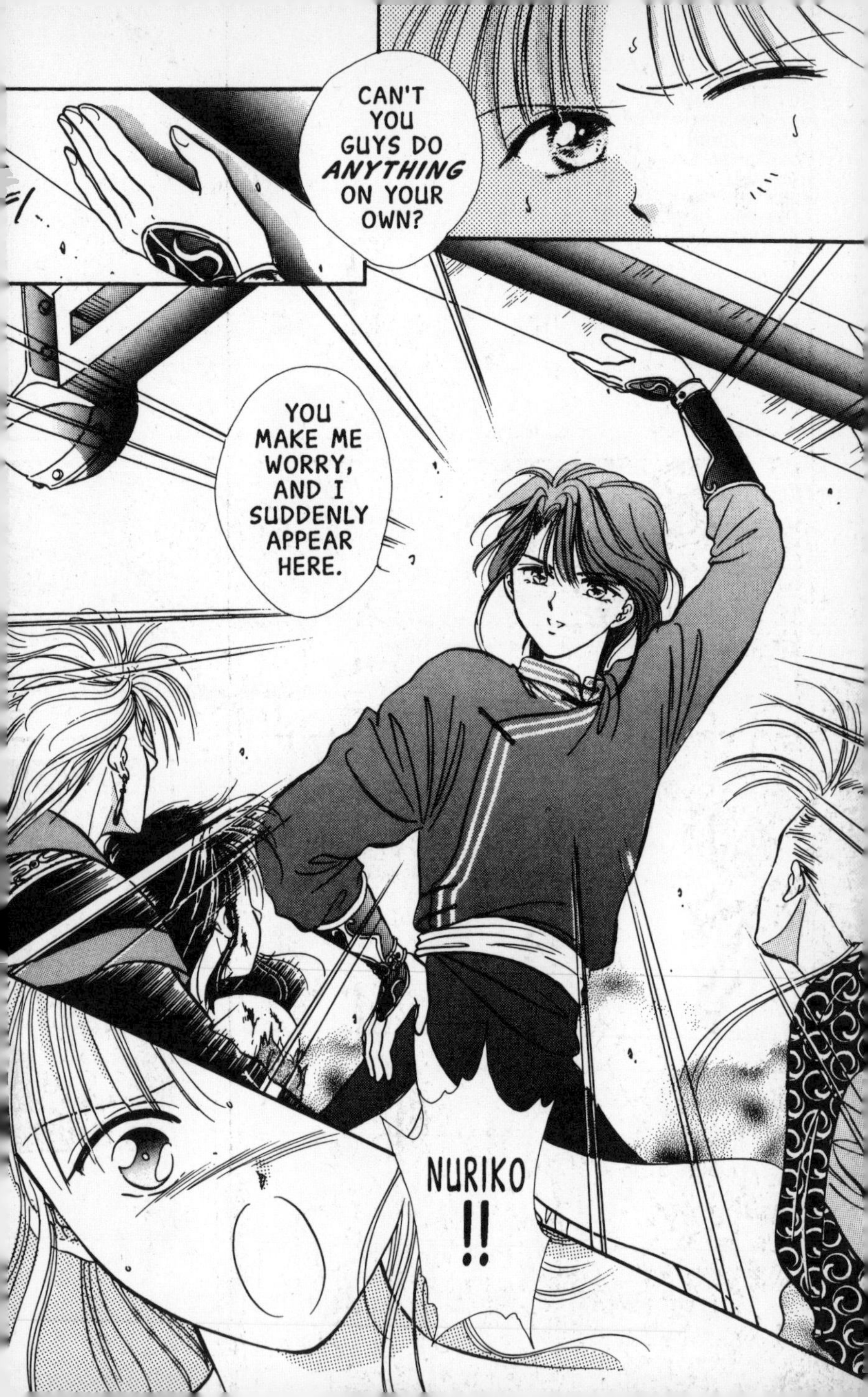
CAN'T YOU GUYS DO *ANYTHING* ON YOUR OWN?
YOU MAKE ME WORRY, AND I SUDDENLY APPEAR HERE.
NURIKO !!

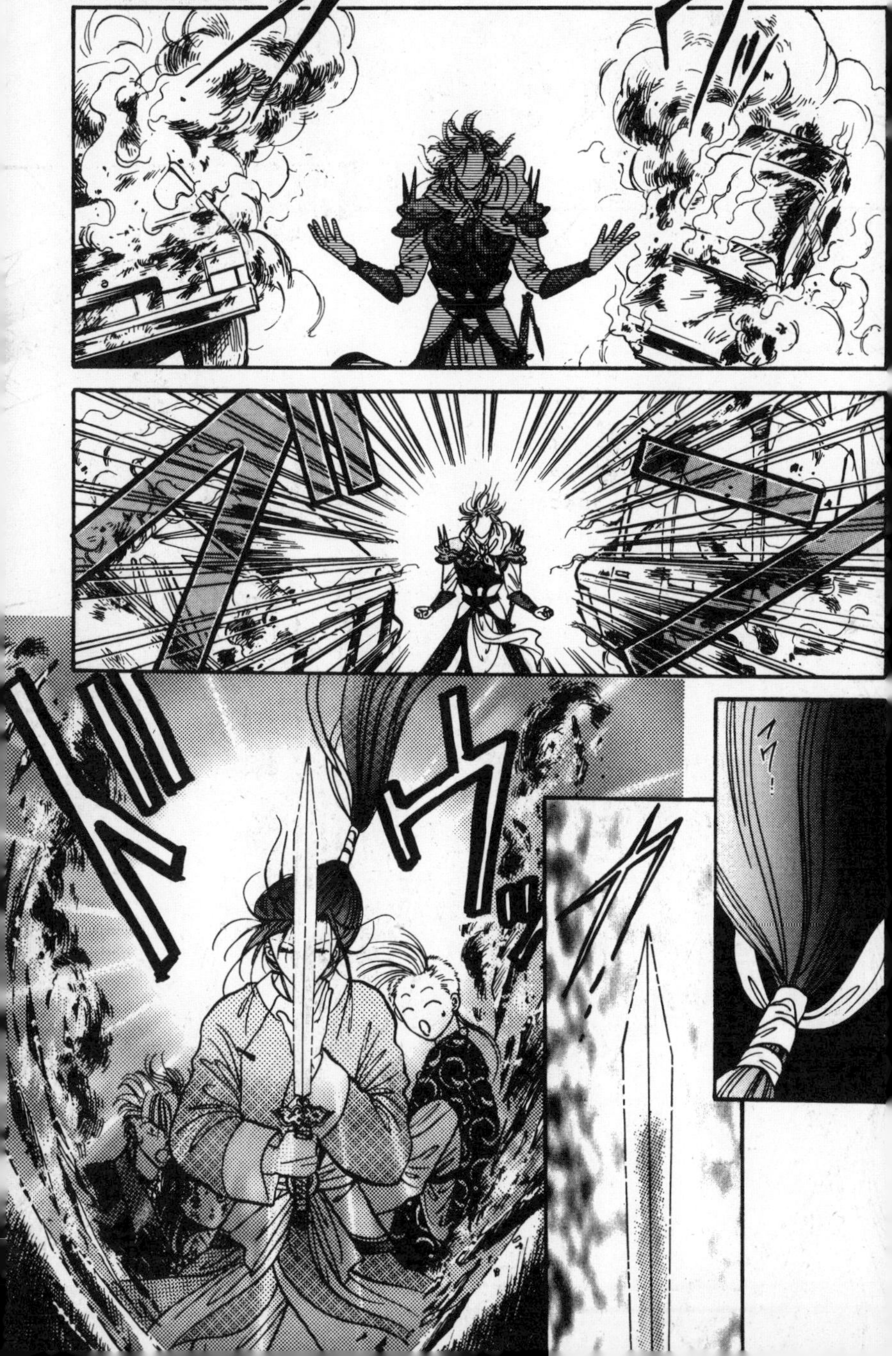

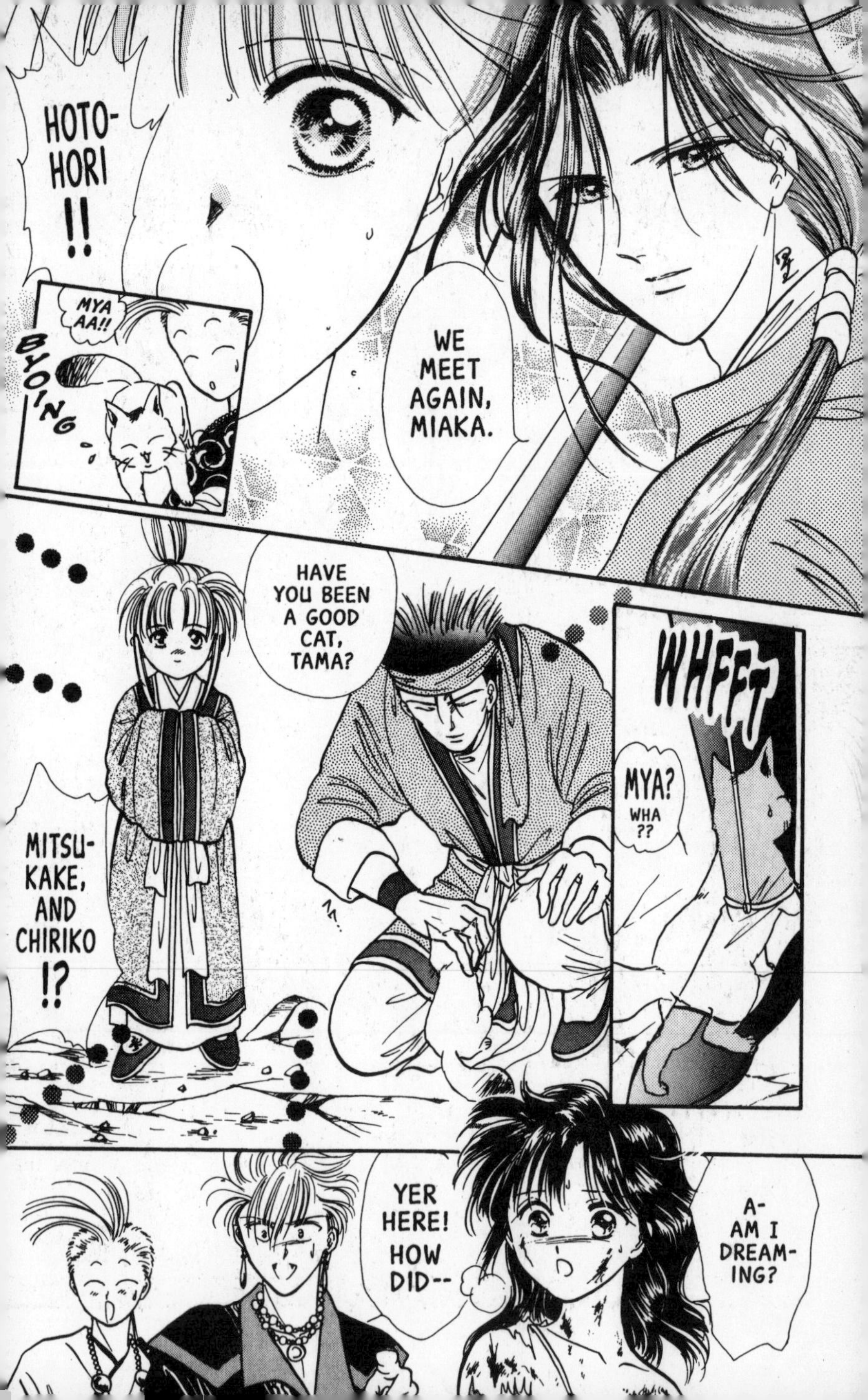
WE MEET AGAIN, MIAKA.
HOTO-HORI !!
MYA AA!!
BYOING
WHFFT
MYA? WHA ??
HAVE YOU BEEN A GOOD CAT, TAMA?
MITSU-KAKE, AND CHIRIKO !?
A- AM I DREAM-ING?
YER HERE! HOW DID--

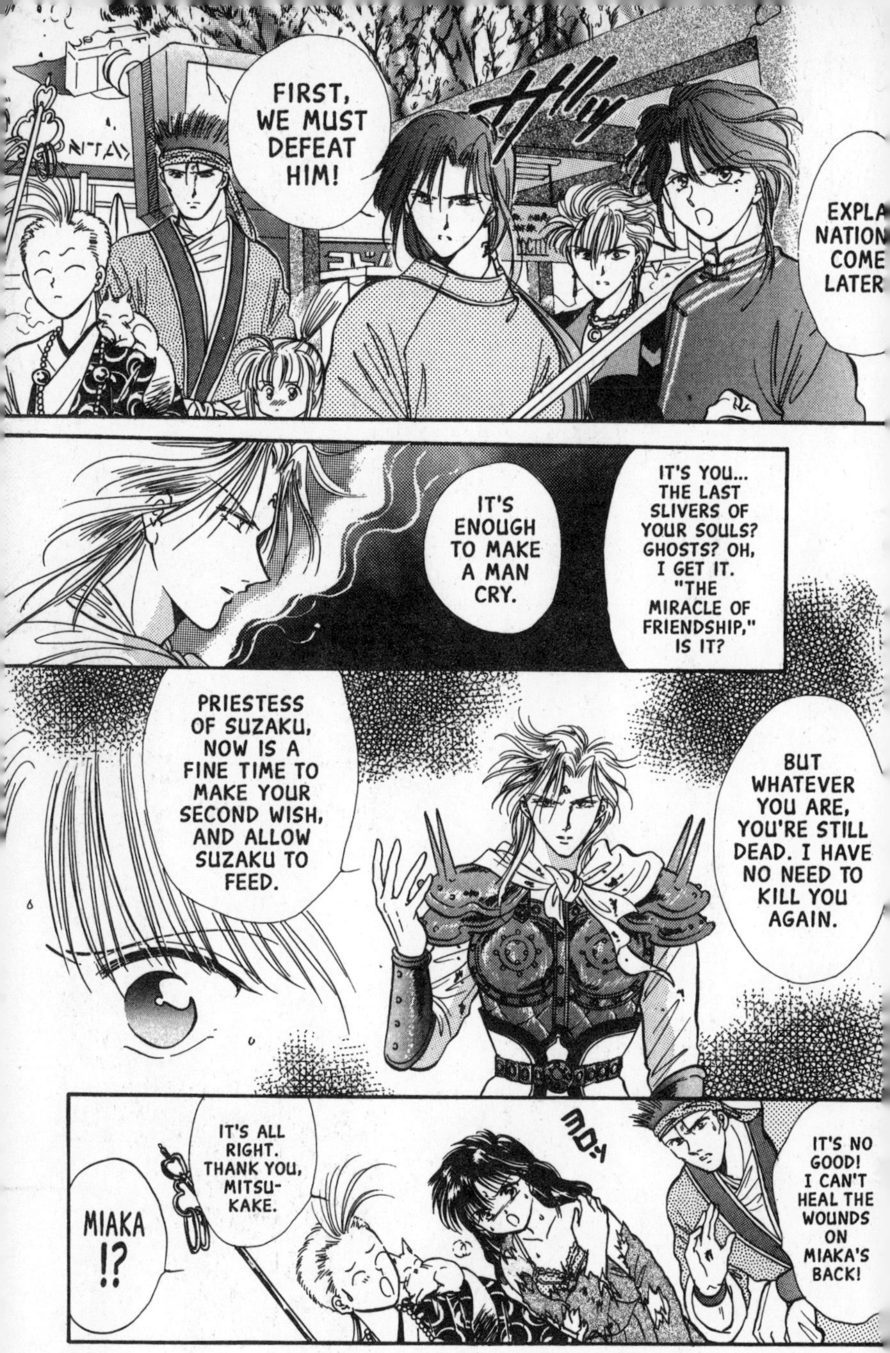
EXPLA NATION COME LATER
FIRST, WE MUST DEFEAT HIM!
IT'S YOU... THE LAST SLIVERS OF YOUR SOULS? GHOSTS? OH, I GET IT. "THE MIRACLE OF FRIENDSHIP," IS IT?
IT'S ENOUGH TO MAKE A MAN CRY.
BUT WHATEVER YOU ARE, YOU'RE STILL DEAD. I HAVE NO NEED TO KILL YOU AGAIN.
PRIESTESS OF SUZAKU, NOW IS A FINE TIME TO MAKE YOUR SECOND WISH, AND ALLOW SUZAKU TO FEED.
IT'S NO GOOD! I CAN'T HEAL THE WOUNDS ON MIAKA'S BACK!
IT'S ALL RIGHT. THANK YOU, MITSU-KAKE.
MIAKA !?

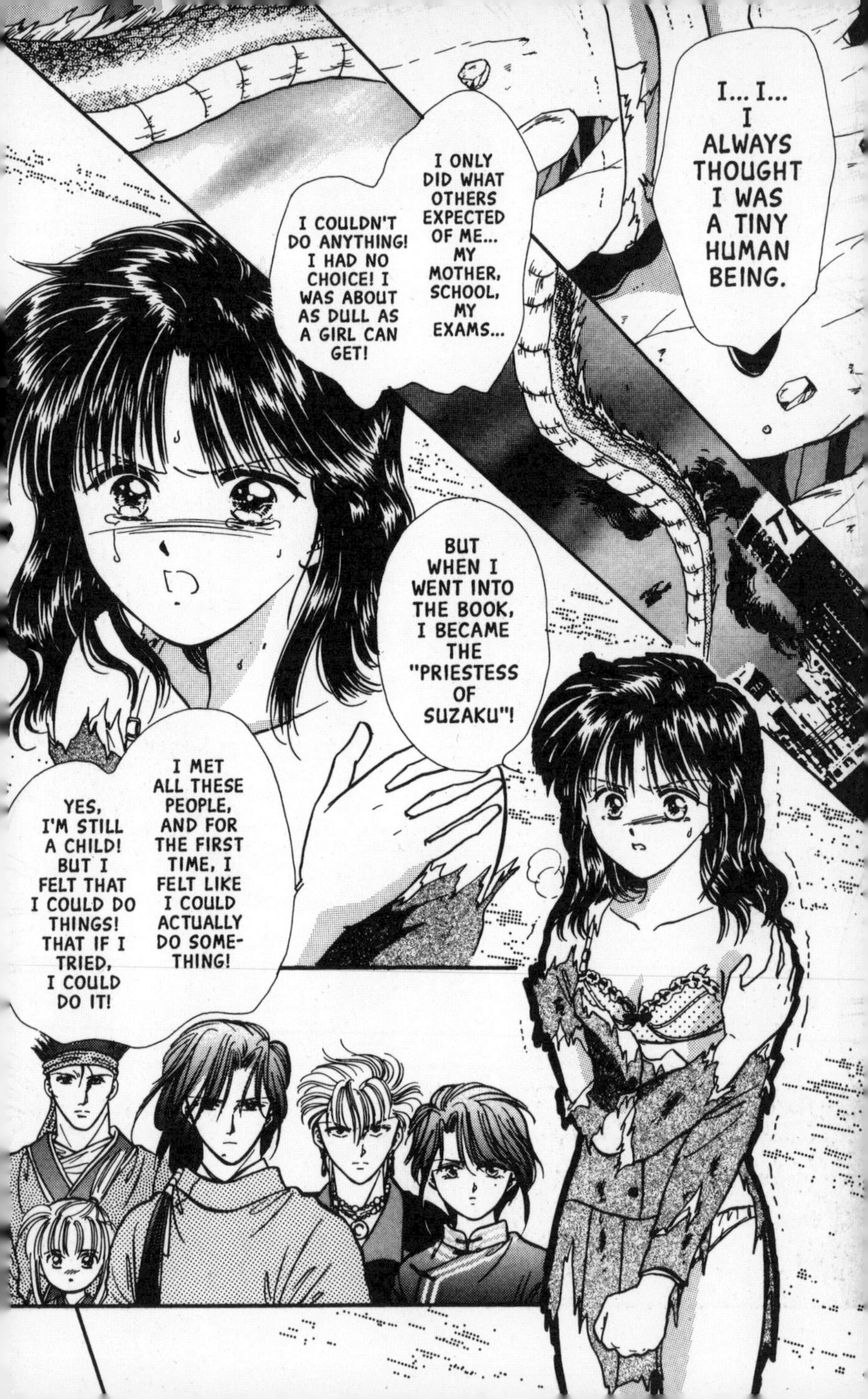
I... I... I ALWAYS THOUGHT I WAS A TINY HUMAN BEING.
I ONLY DID WHAT OTHERS EXPECTED OF ME... MY MOTHER, SCHOOL, MY EXAMS...
I COULDN'T DO ANYTHING! I HAD NO CHOICE! I WAS ABOUT AS DULL AS A GIRL CAN GET!
BUT WHEN I WENT INTO THE BOOK, I BECAME THE "PRIESTESS OF SUZAKU"!
I MET ALL THESE PEOPLE, AND FOR THE FIRST TIME, I FELT LIKE I COULD ACTUALLY DO SOME-THING!
YES, I'M STILL A CHILD! BUT I FELT THAT I COULD DO THINGS! THAT IF I TRIED, I COULD DO IT!

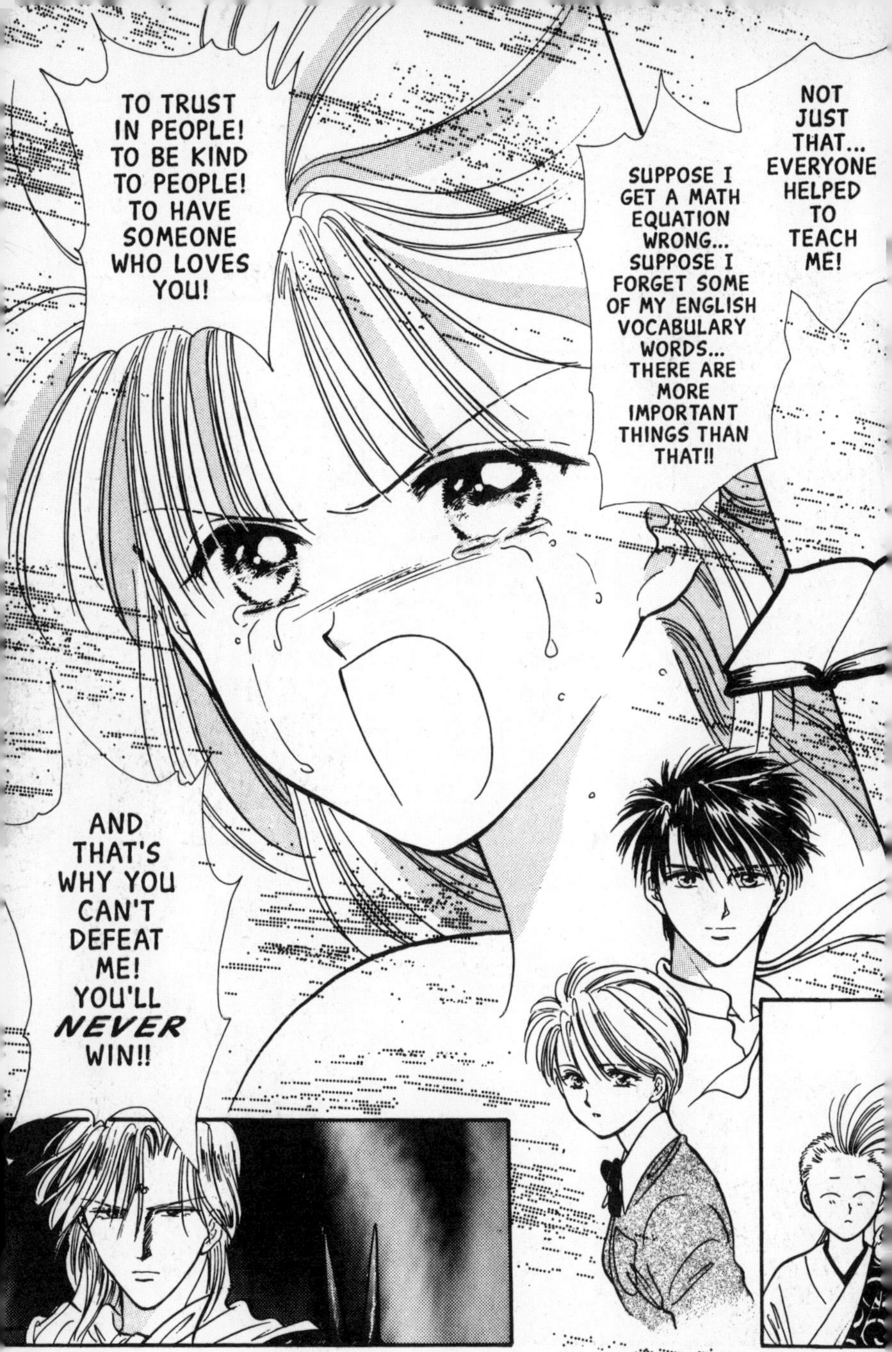
NOT JUST THAT... EVERYONE HELPED TO TEACH ME!
SUPPOSE I GET A MATH EQUATION WRONG... SUPPOSE I FORGET SOME OF MY ENGLISH VOCABULARY WORDS... THERE ARE MORE IMPORTANT THINGS THAN THAT!!
TO TRUST IN PEOPLE! TO BE KIND TO PEOPLE! TO HAVE SOMEONE WHO LOVES YOU!
AND THAT'S WHY YOU CAN'T DEFEAT ME! YOU'LL *NEVER* WIN!!

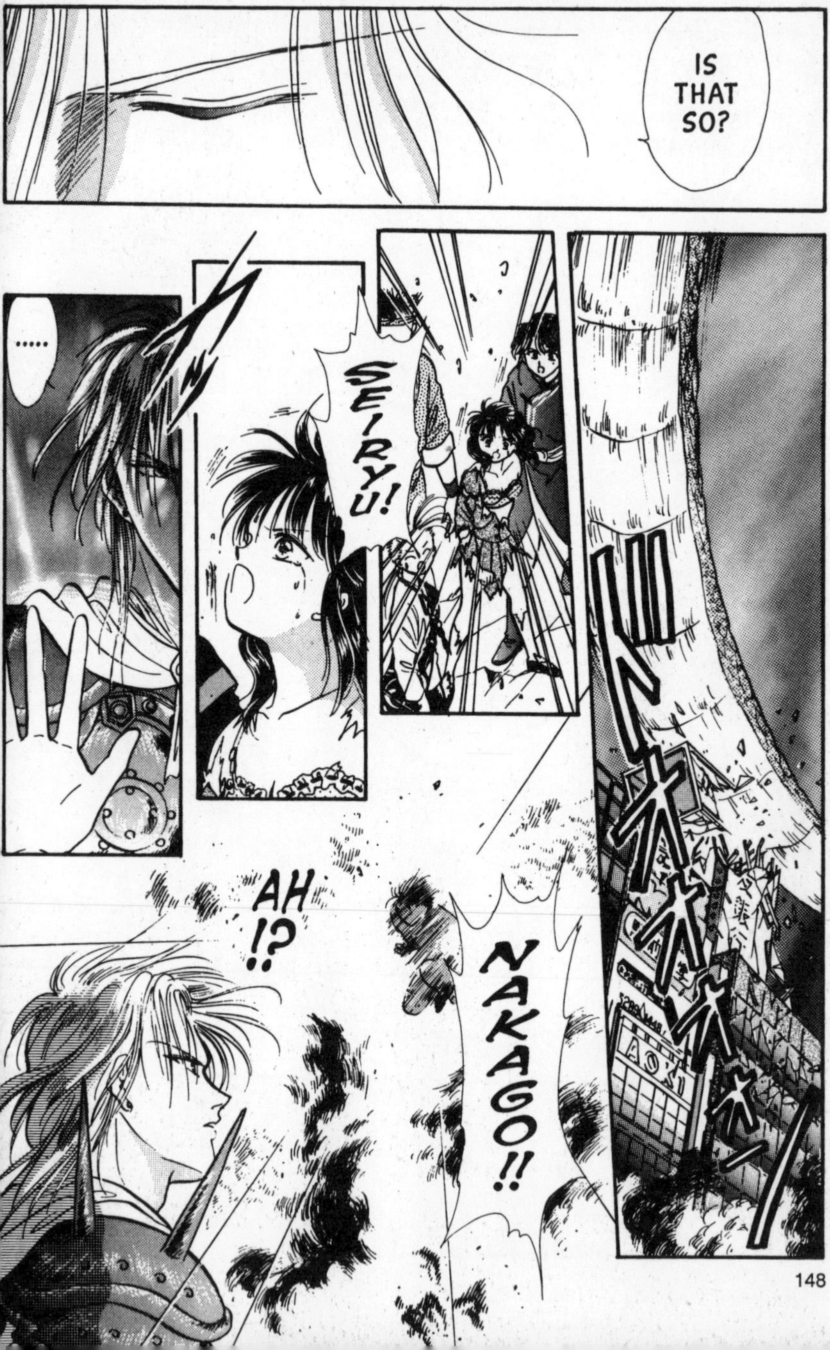
IS THAT SO?
SEIRYU!
......
NAKAGO!!
AH!?

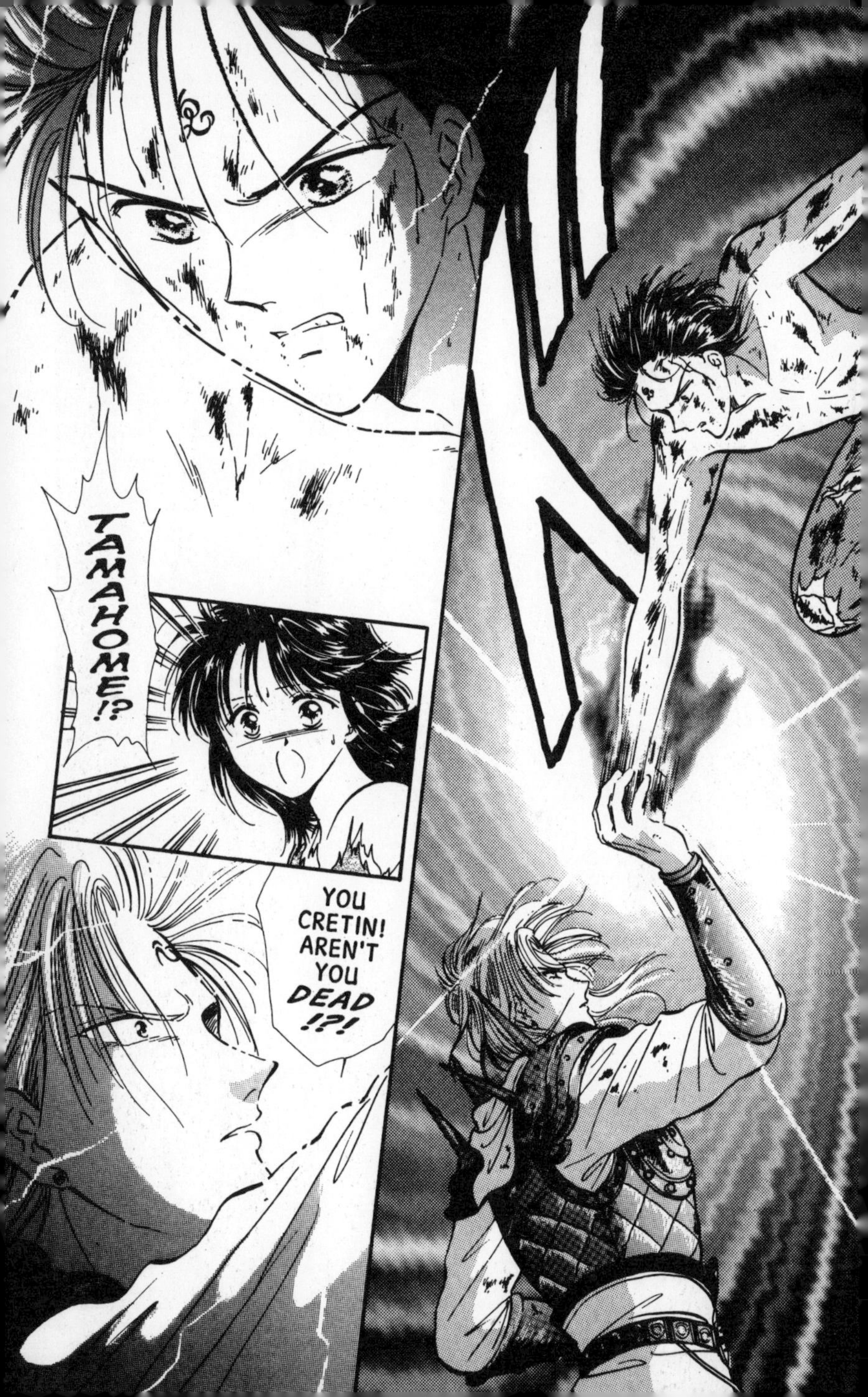
TAMAHOME!?
YOU CRETIN! AREN'T YOU DEAD !?!

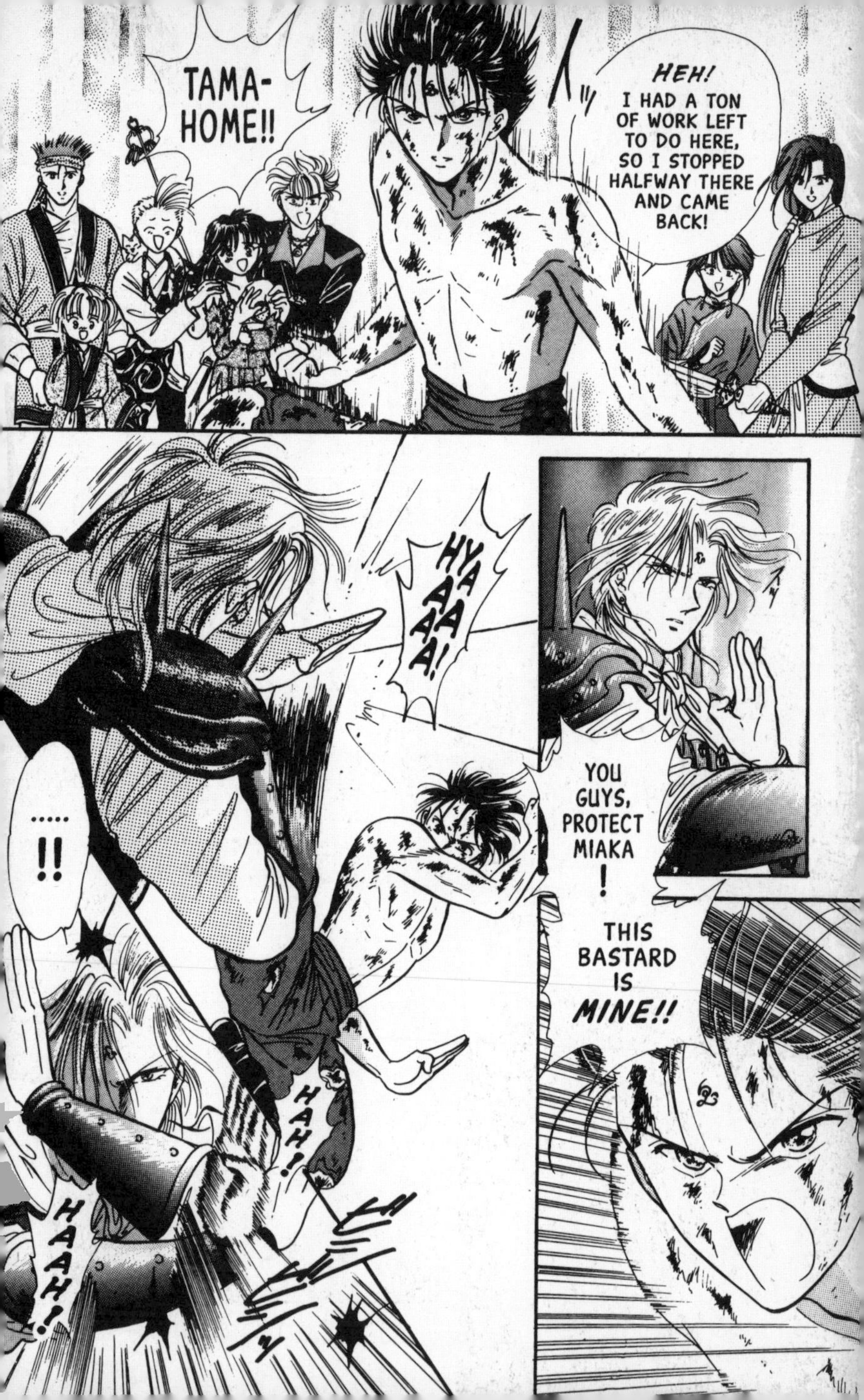
TAMA-HOME!!
HEH! I HAD A TON OF WORK LEFT TO DO HERE, SO I STOPPED HALFWAY THERE AND CAME BACK!
YOU GUYS, PROTECT MIAKA!
THIS BASTARD IS MINE!!
HYAAAAA!
.....!!
HAH!
HAAAH!

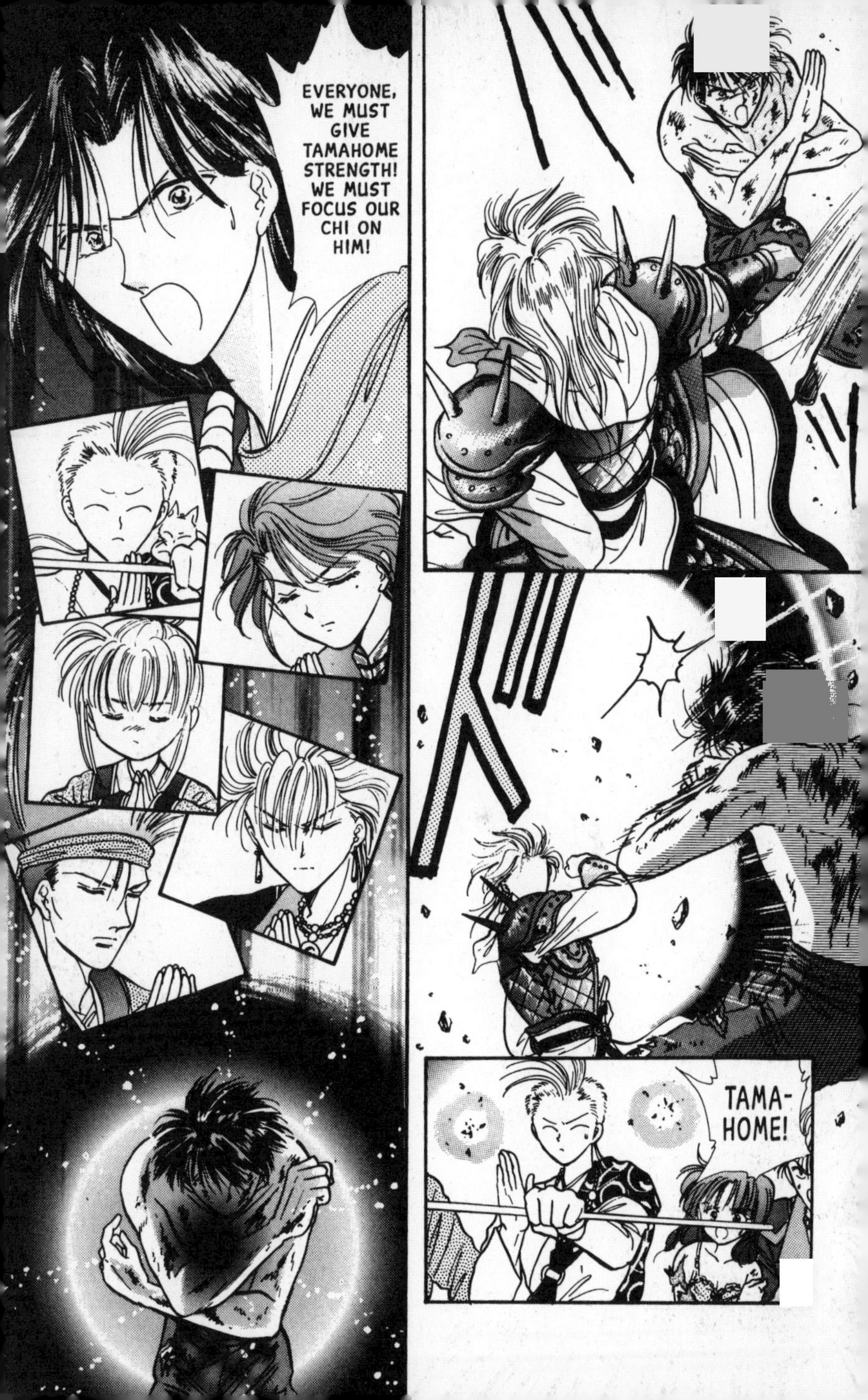
TAMA-HOME!
EVERYONE, WE MUST GIVE TAMAHOME STRENGTH! WE MUST FOCUS OUR CHI ON HIM!

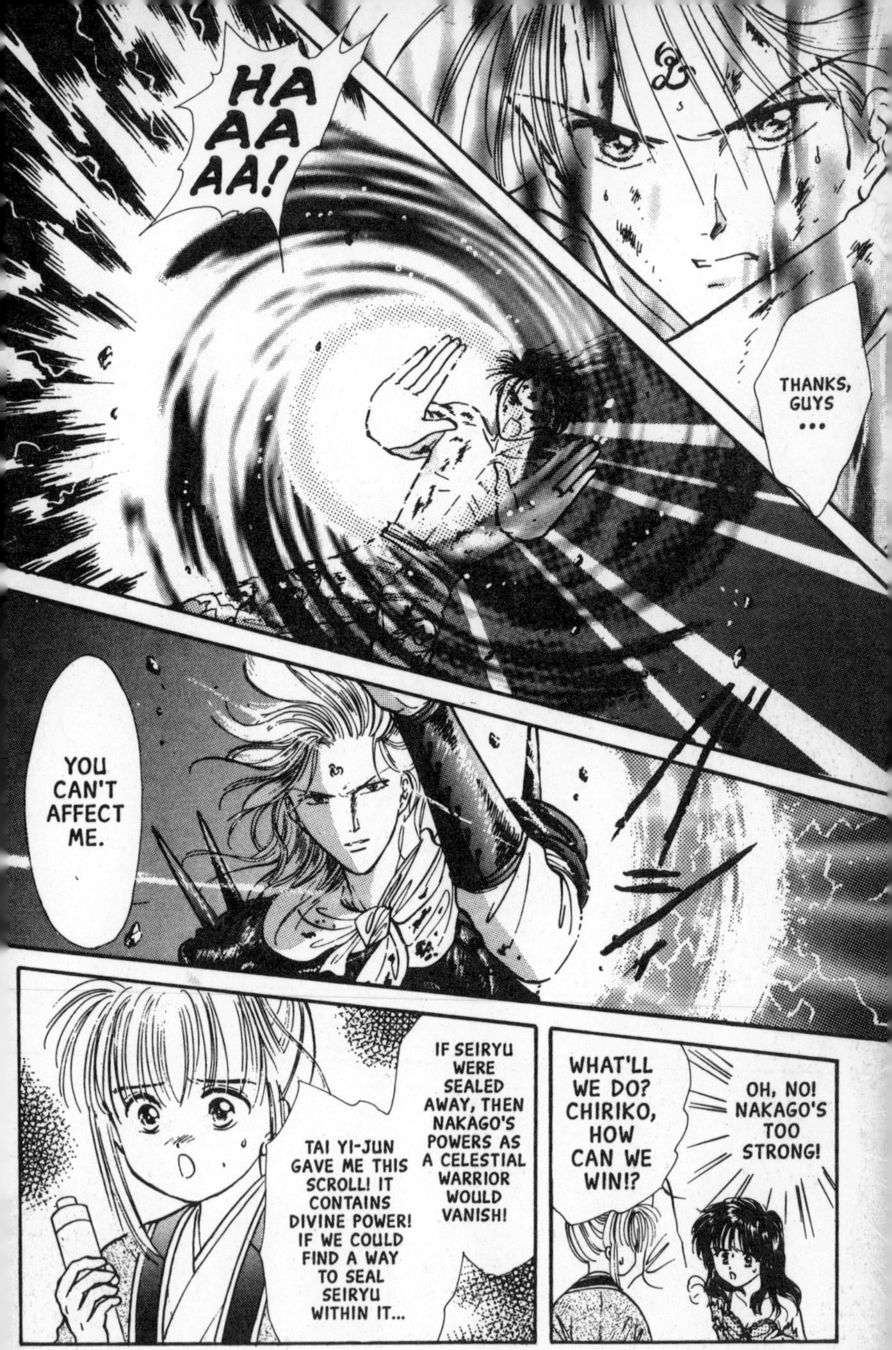
THANKS, GUYS ...
HA AA AA!
YOU CAN'T AFFECT ME.
OH, NO! NAKAGO'S TOO STRONG!
WHAT'LL WE DO? CHIRIKO, HOW CAN WE WIN!?
TAI YI-JUN GAVE ME THIS SCROLL! IT CONTAINS DIVINE POWER! IF WE COULD FIND A WAY TO SEAL SEIRYU WITHIN IT...
IF SEIRYU WERE SEALED AWAY, THEN NAKAGO'S POWERS AS A CELESTIAL WARRIOR WOULD VANISH!

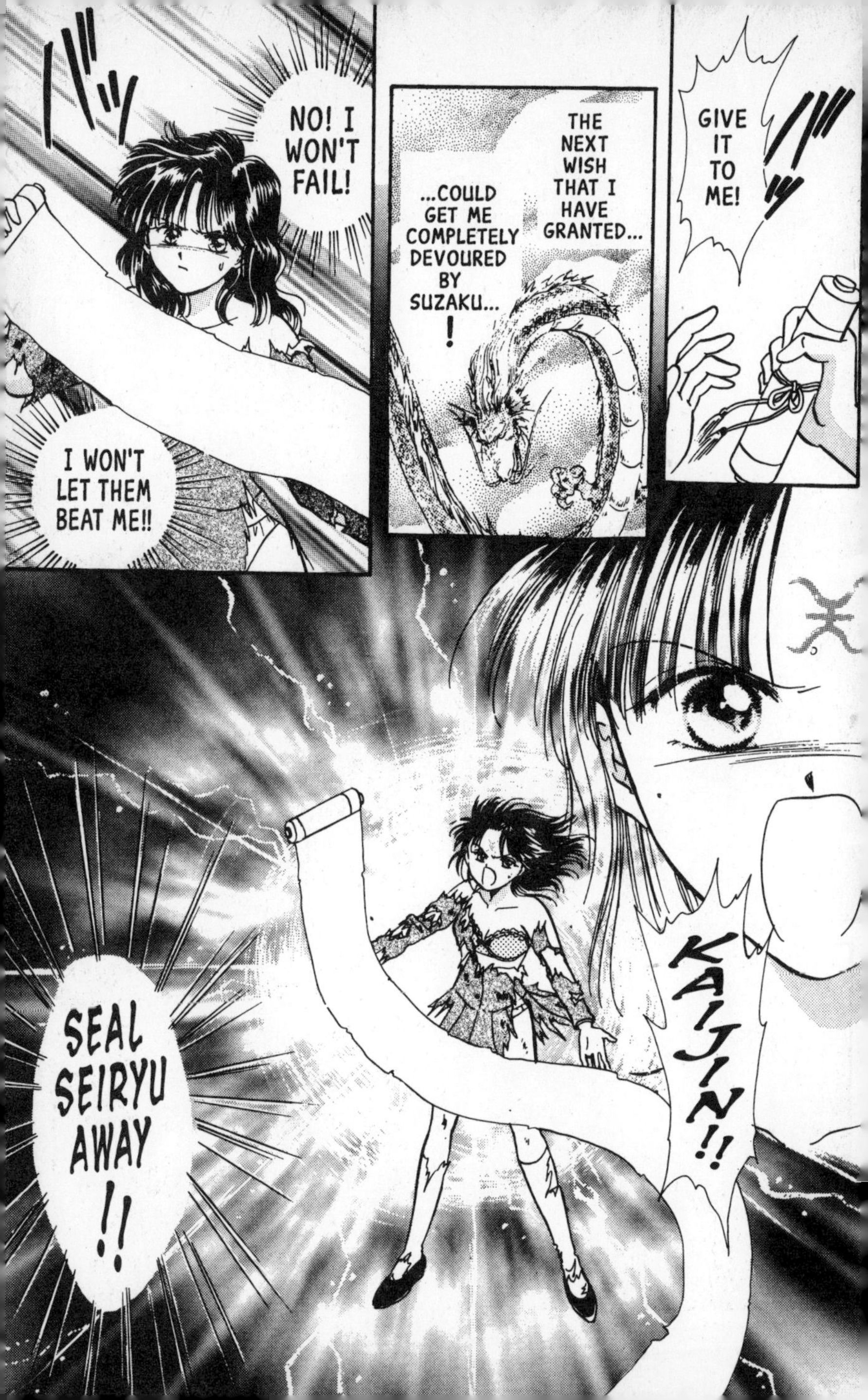
GIVE IT TO ME!
THE NEXT WISH THAT I HAVE GRANTED...
...COULD GET ME COMPLETELY DEVOURED BY SUZAKU...
!
NO! I WON'T FAIL!
I WON'T LET THEM BEAT ME!!
KAIJIN!!
SEAL SEIRYU AWAY!!

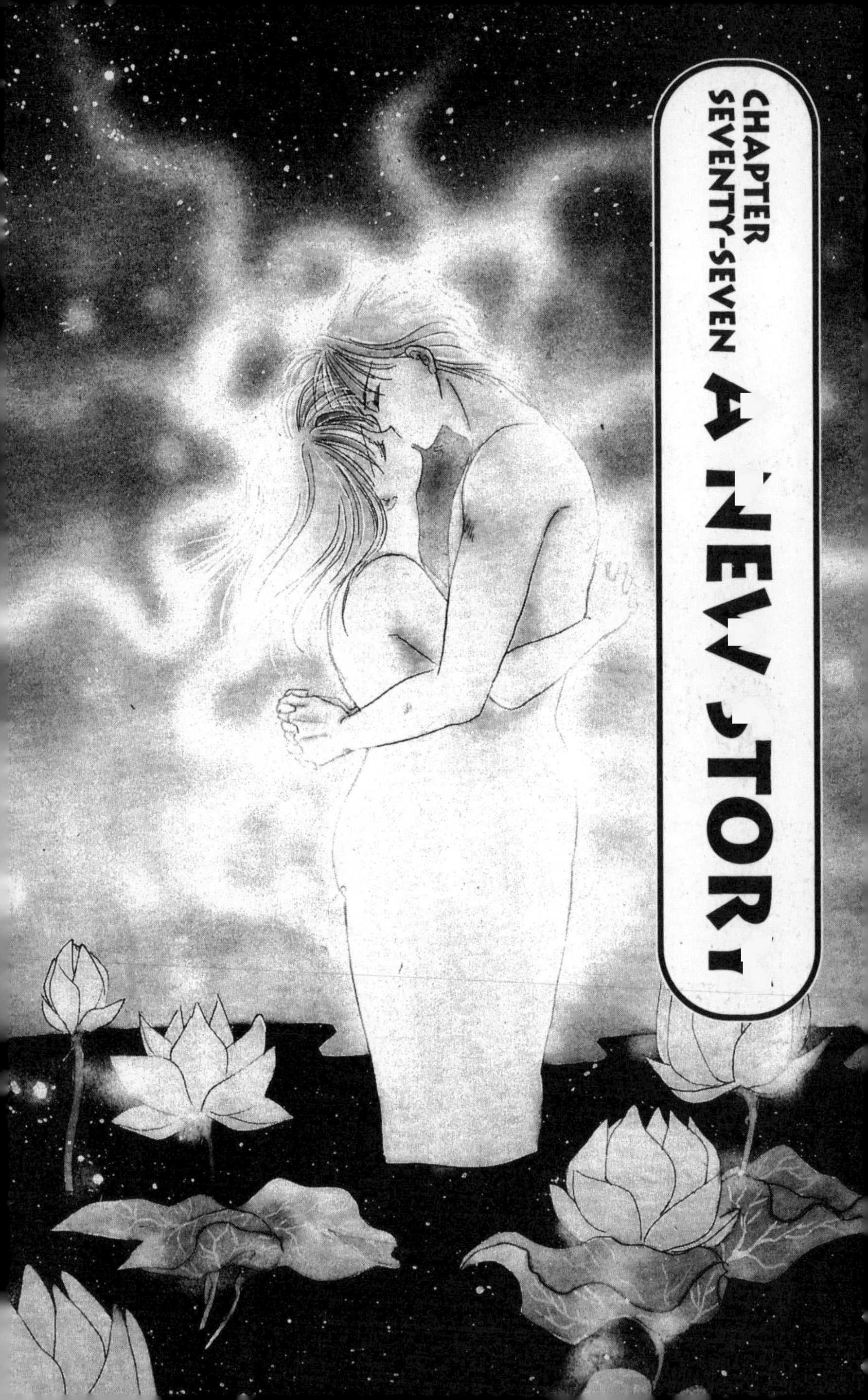
CHAPTER SEVENTY-SEVEN
A NEW STORY

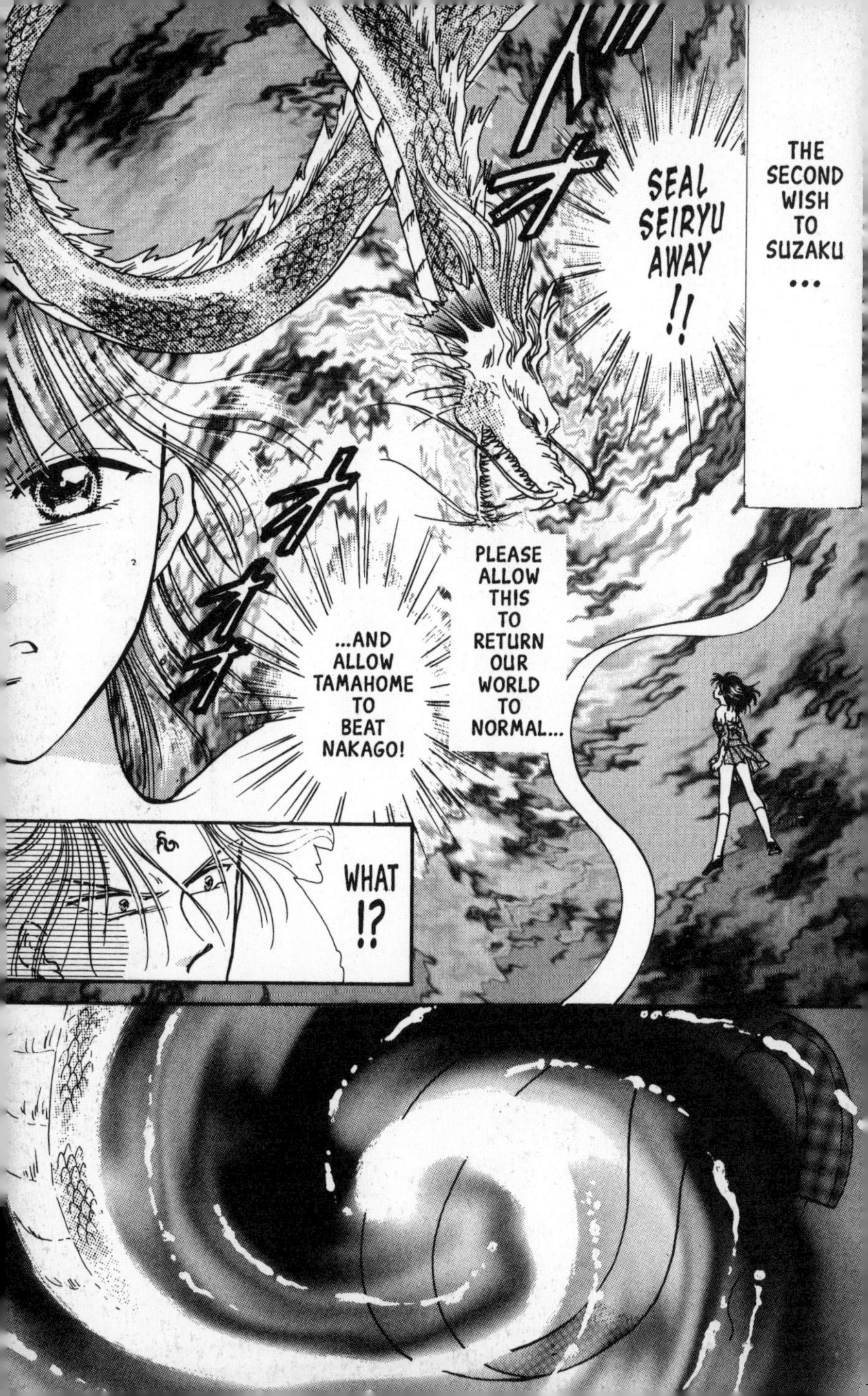
THE SECOND WISH TO SUZAKU...
SEAL SEIRYU AWAY!!
PLEASE ALLOW THIS TO RETURN OUR WORLD TO NORMAL...
...AND ALLOW TAMAHOME TO BEAT NAKAGO!
WHAT!?

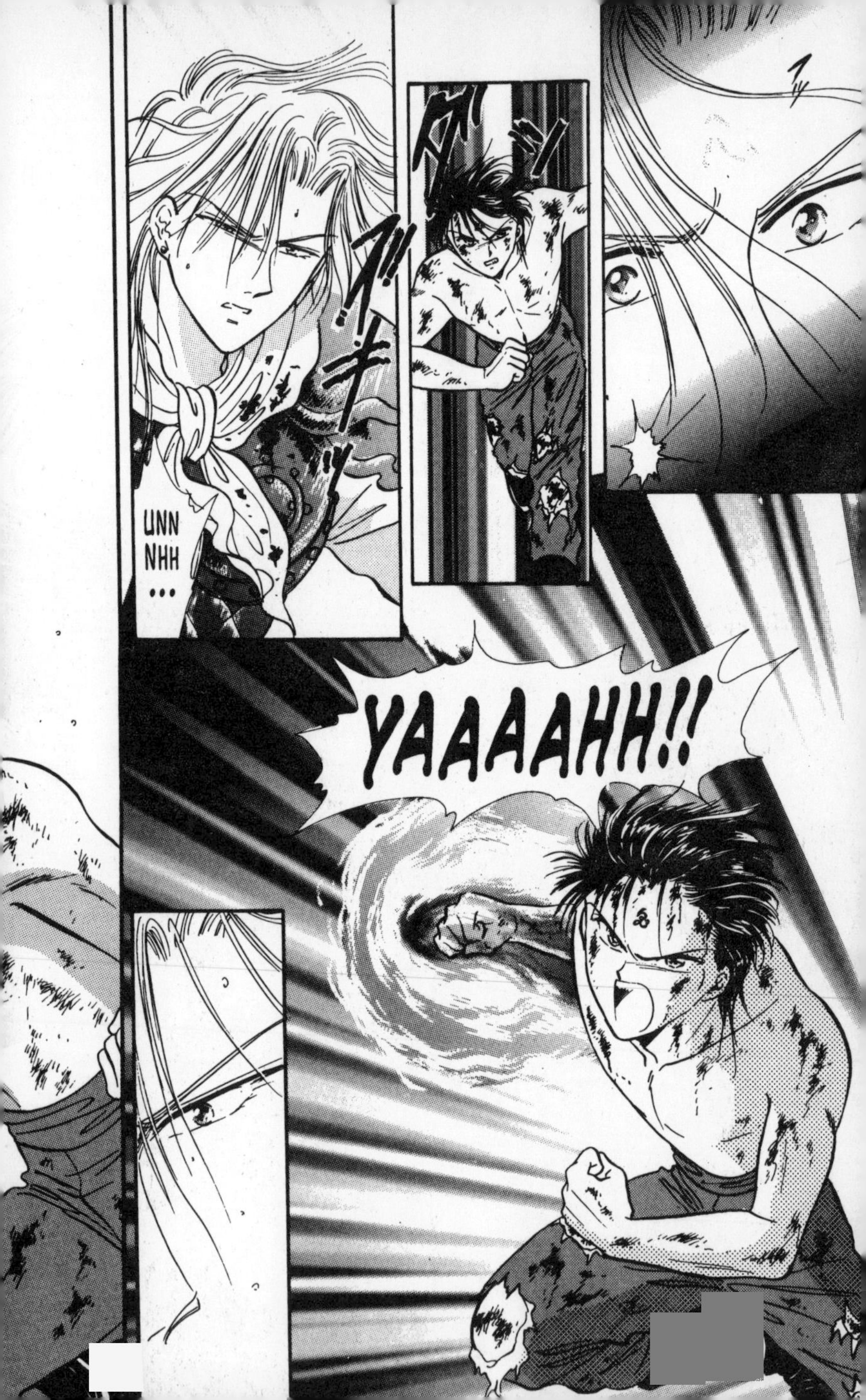
UNN NHH ...
YAAAAHH!!

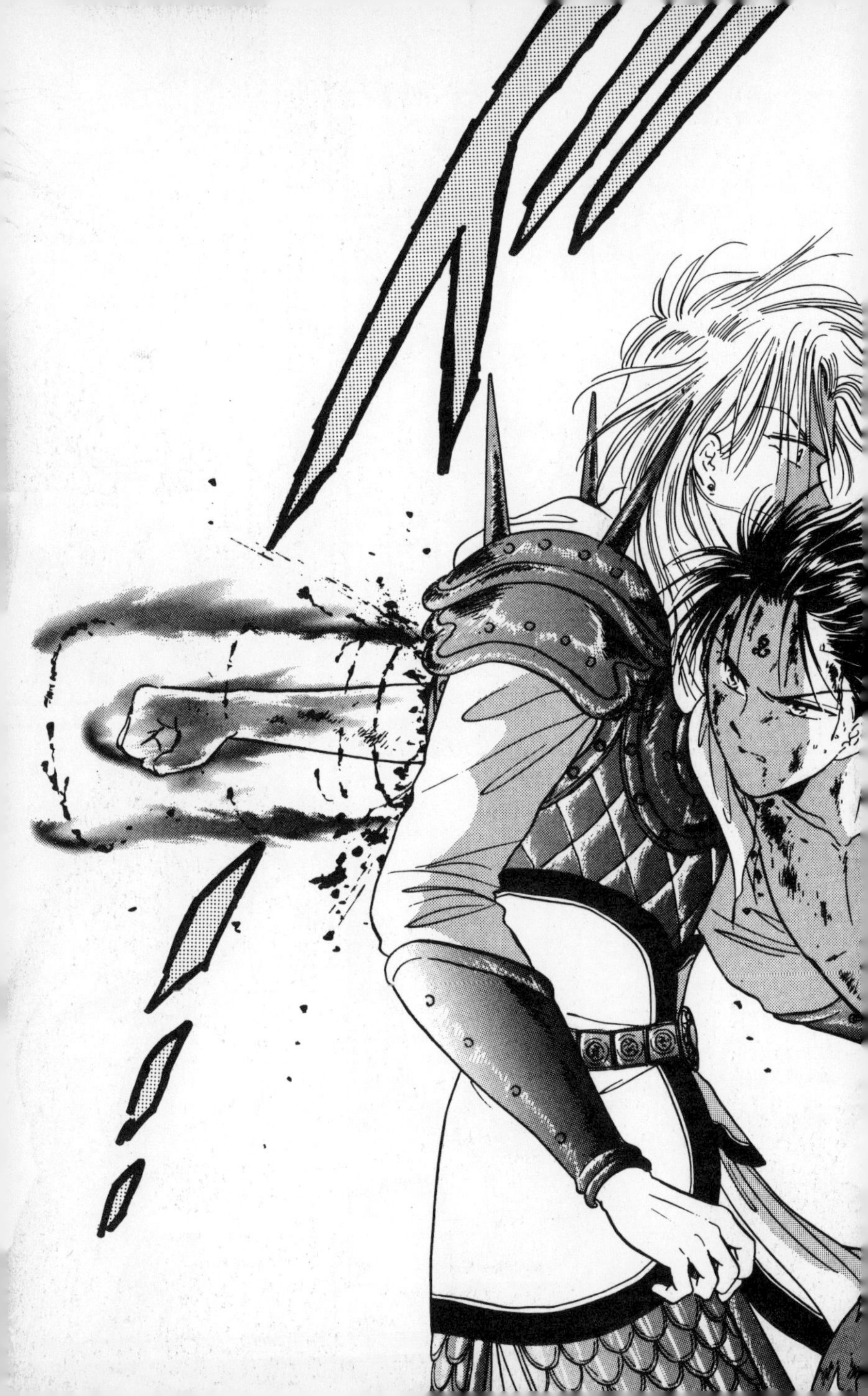

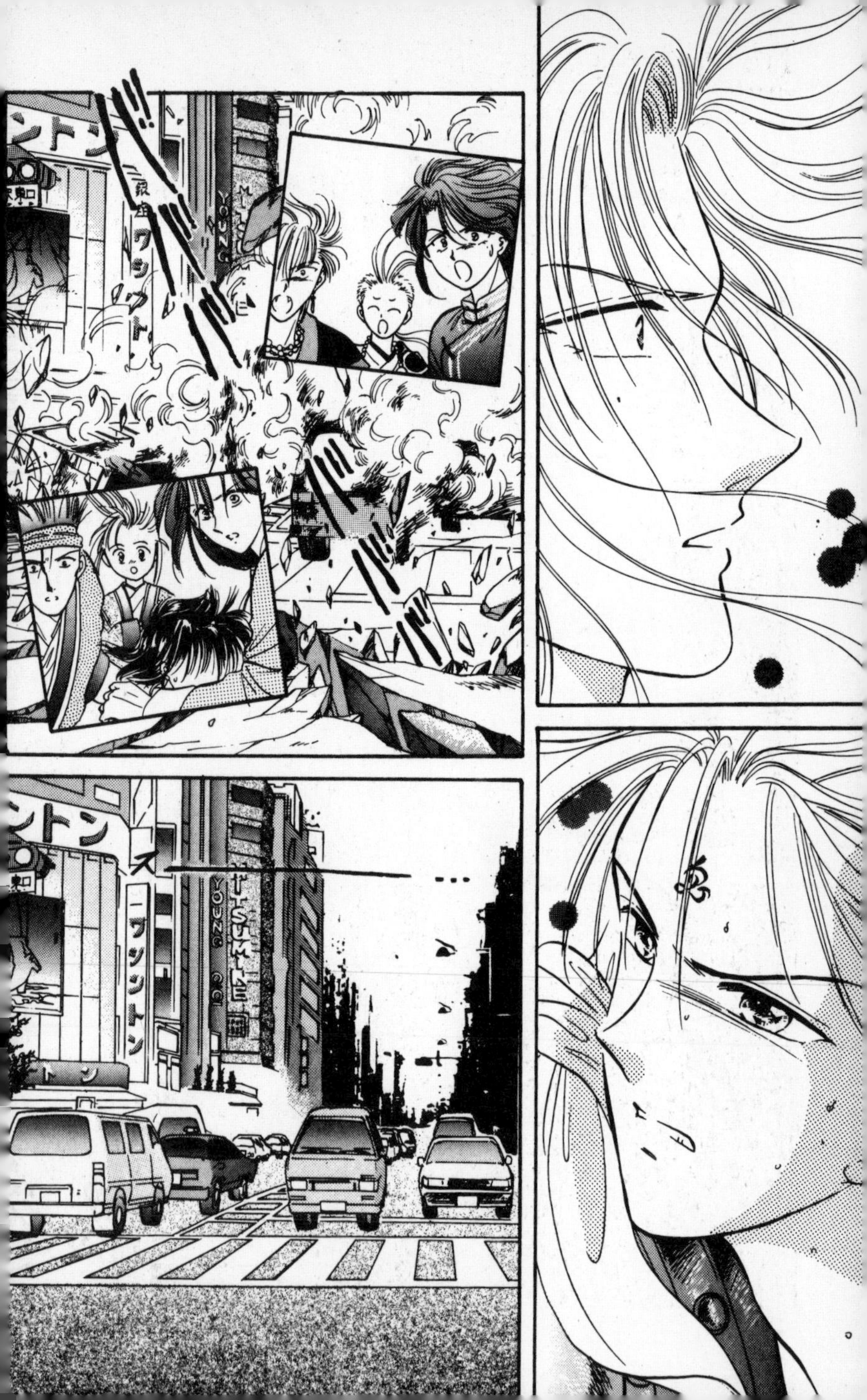
銀座ワシントン
YOUNG

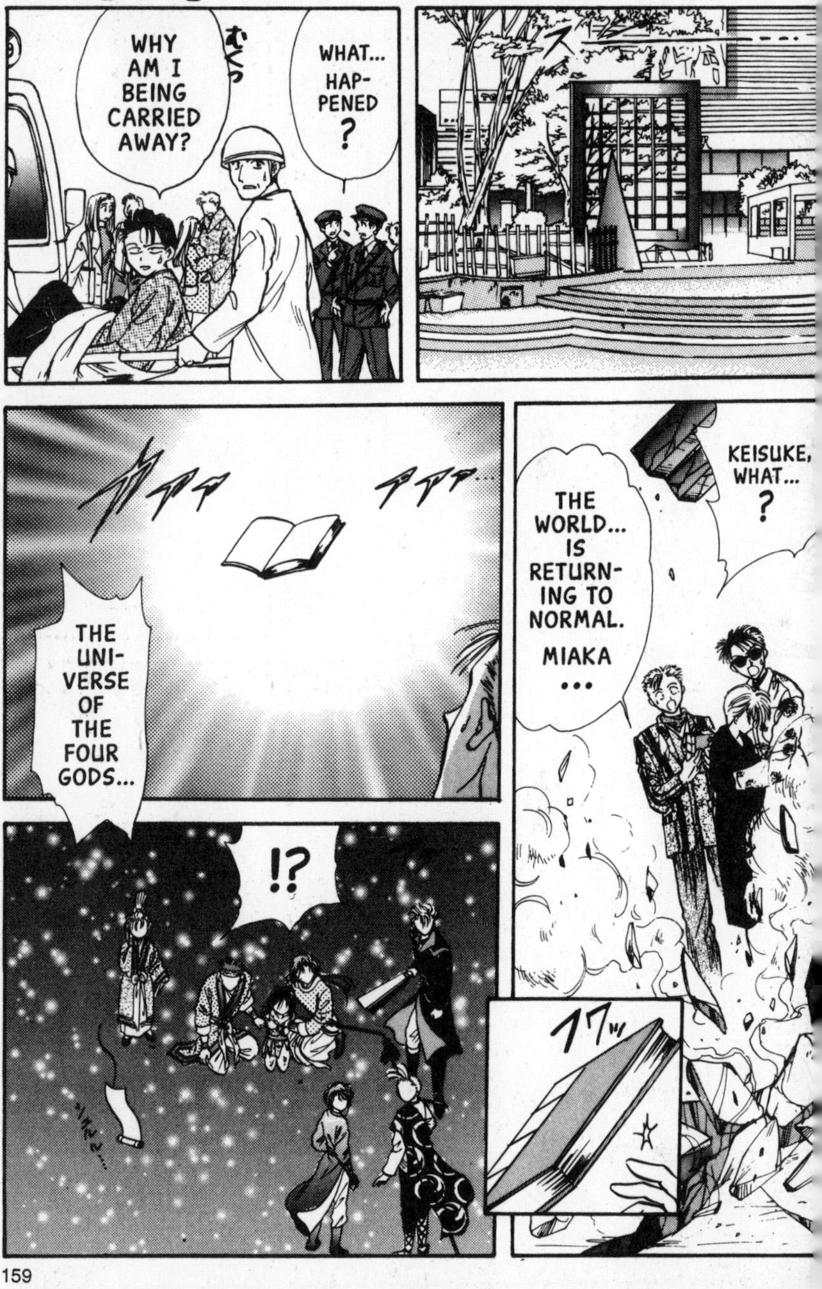
WHAT... HAPPENED?
むくっ
WHY AM I BEING CARRIED AWAY?
KEISUKE, WHAT...?
THE WORLD... IS RETURNING TO NORMAL.
MIAKA...
フワッ
THE UNIVERSE OF THE FOUR GODS...
!?

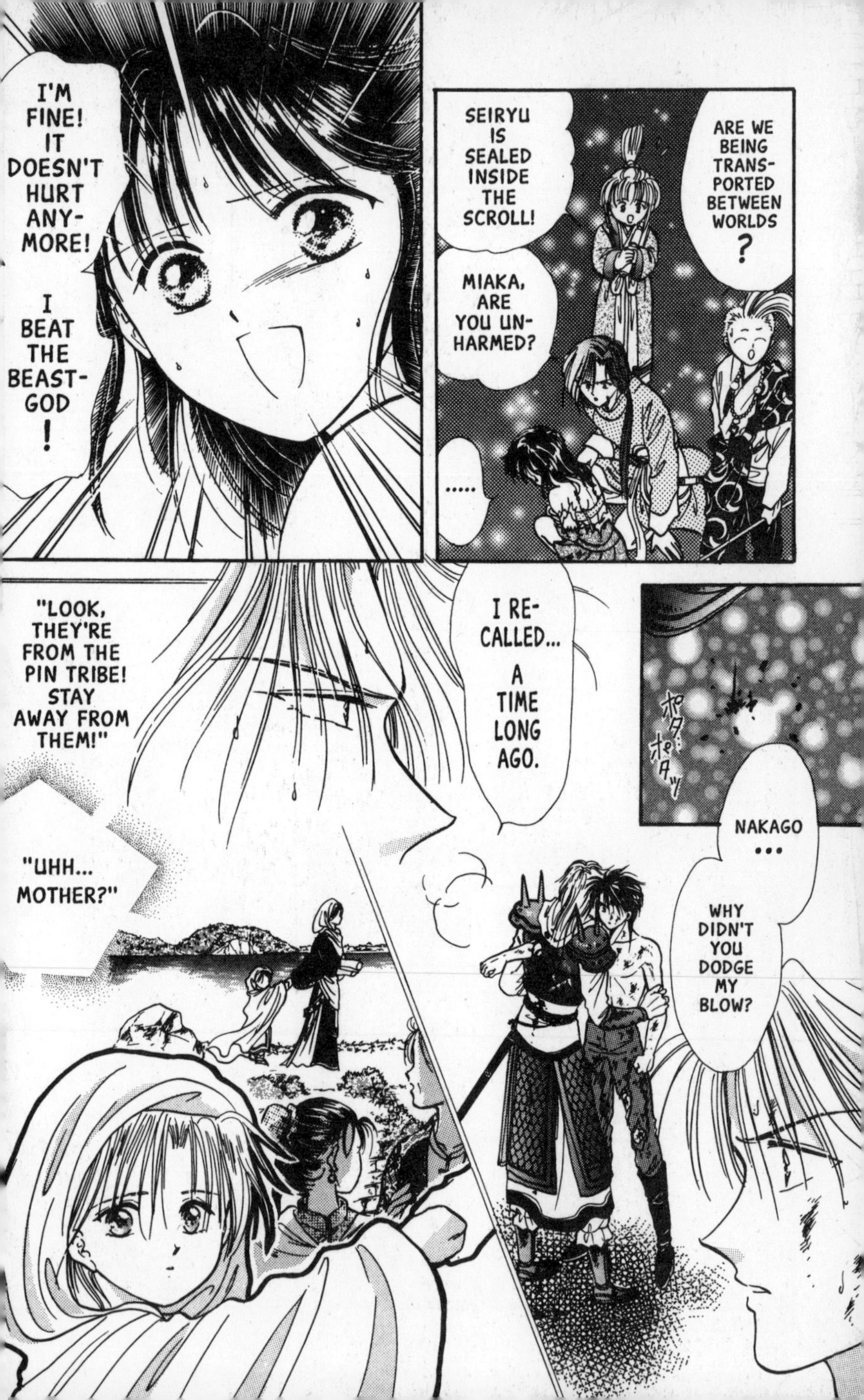
ARE WE BEING TRANSPORTED BETWEEN WORLDS?
SEIRYU IS SEALED INSIDE THE SCROLL!
MIAKA, ARE YOU UNHARMED?
.....
I'M FINE! IT DOESN'T HURT ANYMORE!
I BEAT THE BEAST-GOD!
ポタ ポタッ
NAKAGO...
WHY DIDN'T YOU DODGE MY BLOW?
I RECALLED... A TIME LONG AGO.
"LOOK, THEY'RE FROM THE PIN TRIBE! STAY AWAY FROM THEM!"
"UHH... MOTHER?"

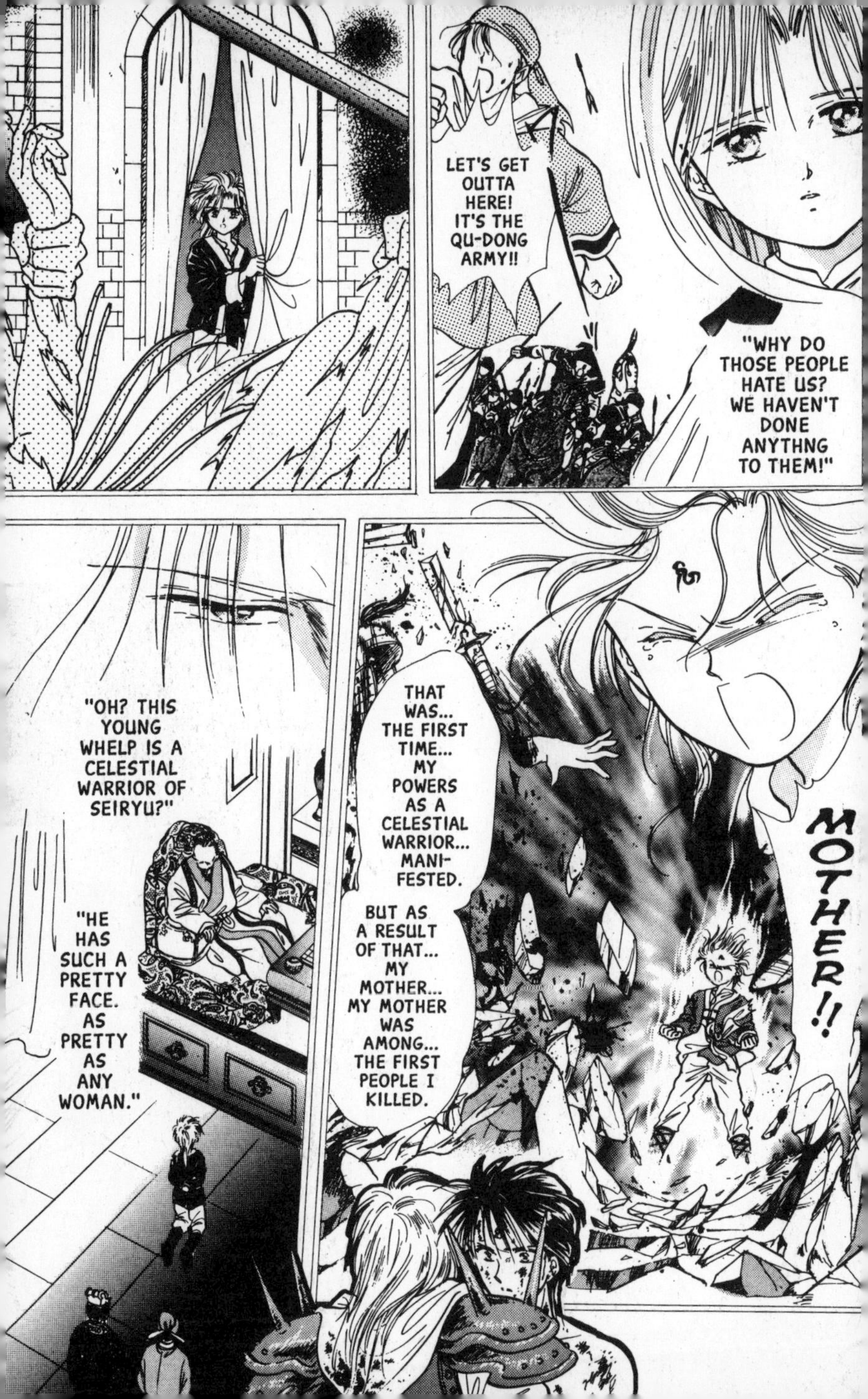
"WHY DO THOSE PEOPLE HATE US? WE HAVEN'T DONE ANYTHNG TO THEM!"
LET'S GET OUTTA HERE! IT'S THE QU-DONG ARMY!!
MOTHER!!
THAT WAS... THE FIRST TIME... MY POWERS AS A CELESTIAL WARRIOR... MANI-FESTED.
BUT AS A RESULT OF THAT... MY MOTHER... MY MOTHER WAS AMONG... THE FIRST PEOPLE I KILLED.
"OH? THIS YOUNG WHELP IS A CELESTIAL WARRIOR OF SEIRYU?"
"HE HAS SUCH A PRETTY FACE. AS PRETTY AS ANY WOMAN."

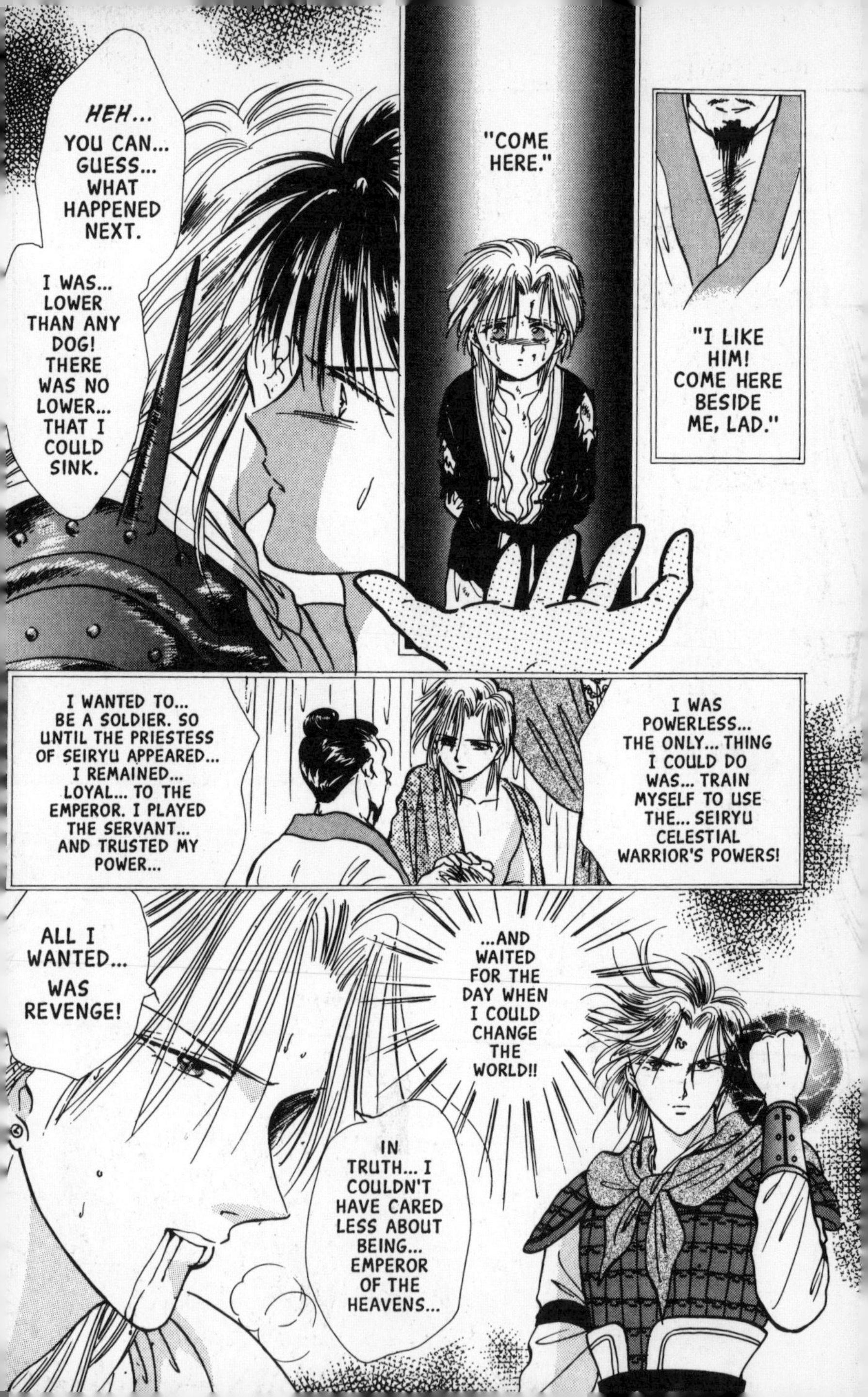
"I LIKE HIM! COME HERE BESIDE ME, LAD."
"COME HERE."
HEH... YOU CAN... GUESS... WHAT HAPPENED NEXT.
I WAS... LOWER THAN ANY DOG! THERE WAS NO LOWER... THAT I COULD SINK.
I WAS POWERLESS... THE ONLY... THING I COULD DO WAS... TRAIN MYSELF TO USE THE... SEIRYU CELESTIAL WARRIOR'S POWERS!
I WANTED TO... BE A SOLDIER. SO UNTIL THE PRIESTESS OF SEIRYU APPEARED... I REMAINED... LOYAL... TO THE EMPEROR. I PLAYED THE SERVANT... AND TRUSTED MY POWER...
...AND WAITED FOR THE DAY WHEN I COULD CHANGE THE WORLD!!
IN TRUTH... I COULDN'T HAVE CARED LESS ABOUT BEING... EMPEROR OF THE HEAVENS...
ALL I WANTED... WAS REVENGE!

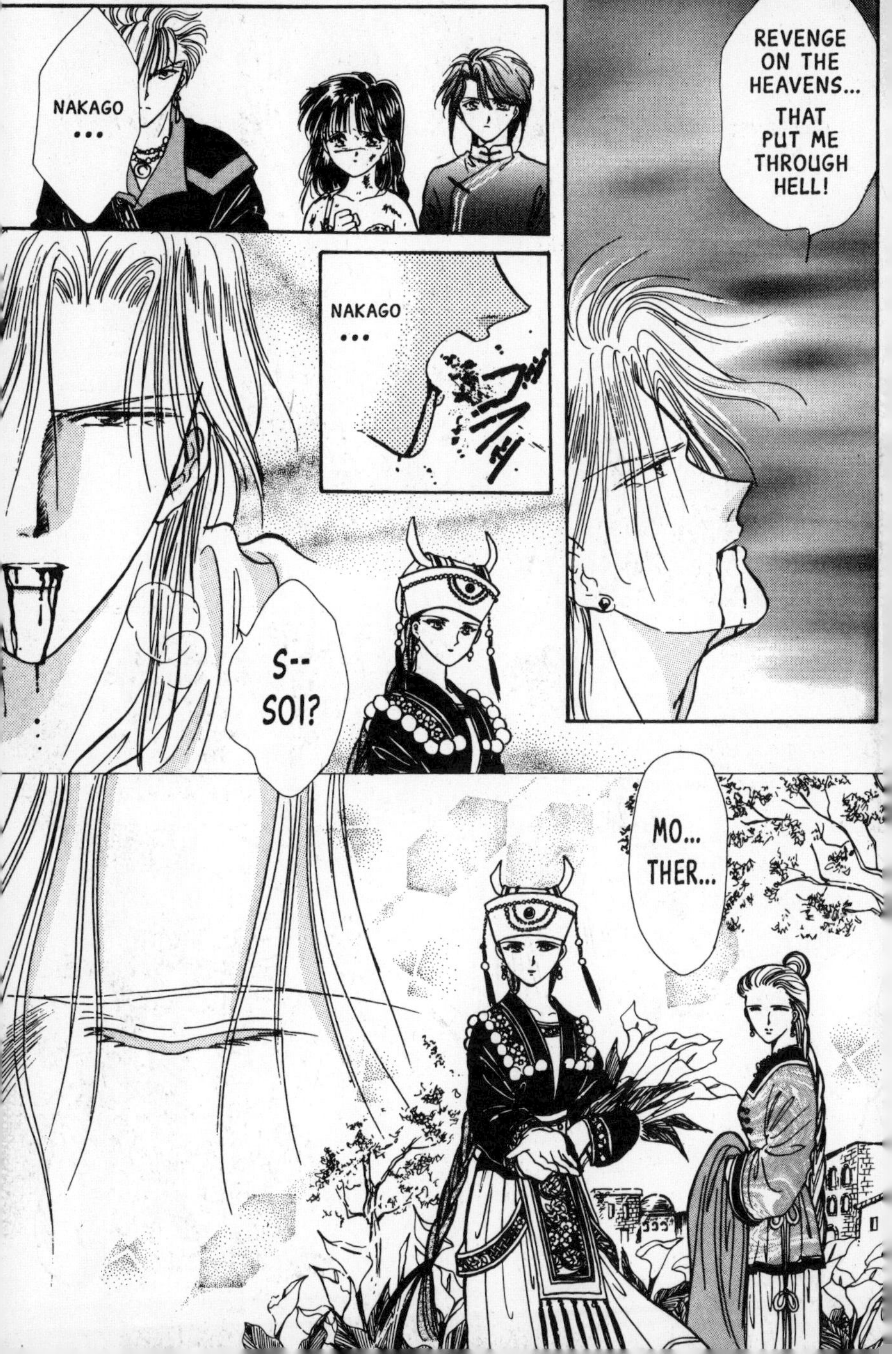
REVENGE ON THE HEAVENS... THAT PUT ME THROUGH HELL!
NAKAGO ...
NAKAGO ...
S-- SOI?
MO... THER...

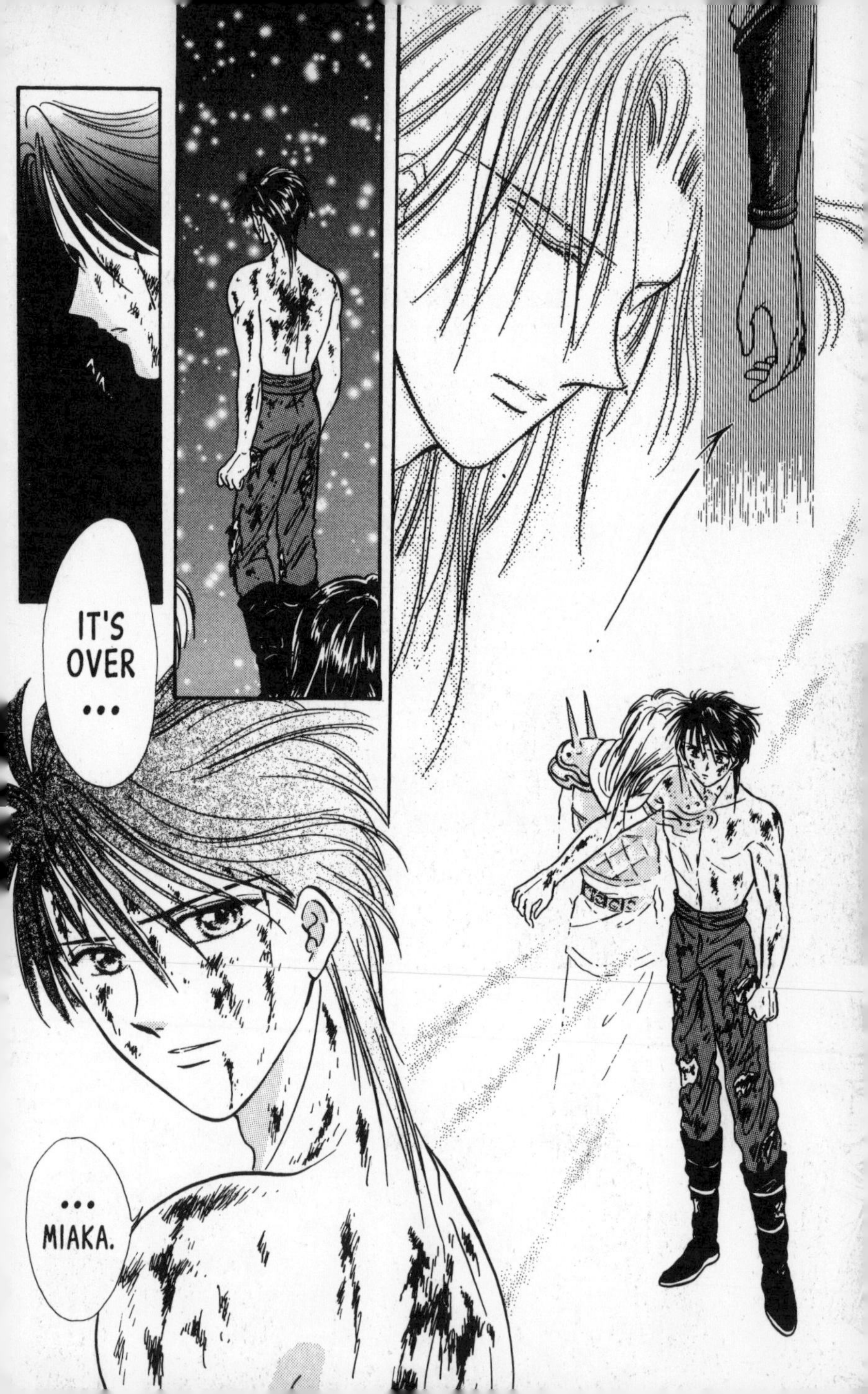
IT'S OVER ...
... MIAKA.

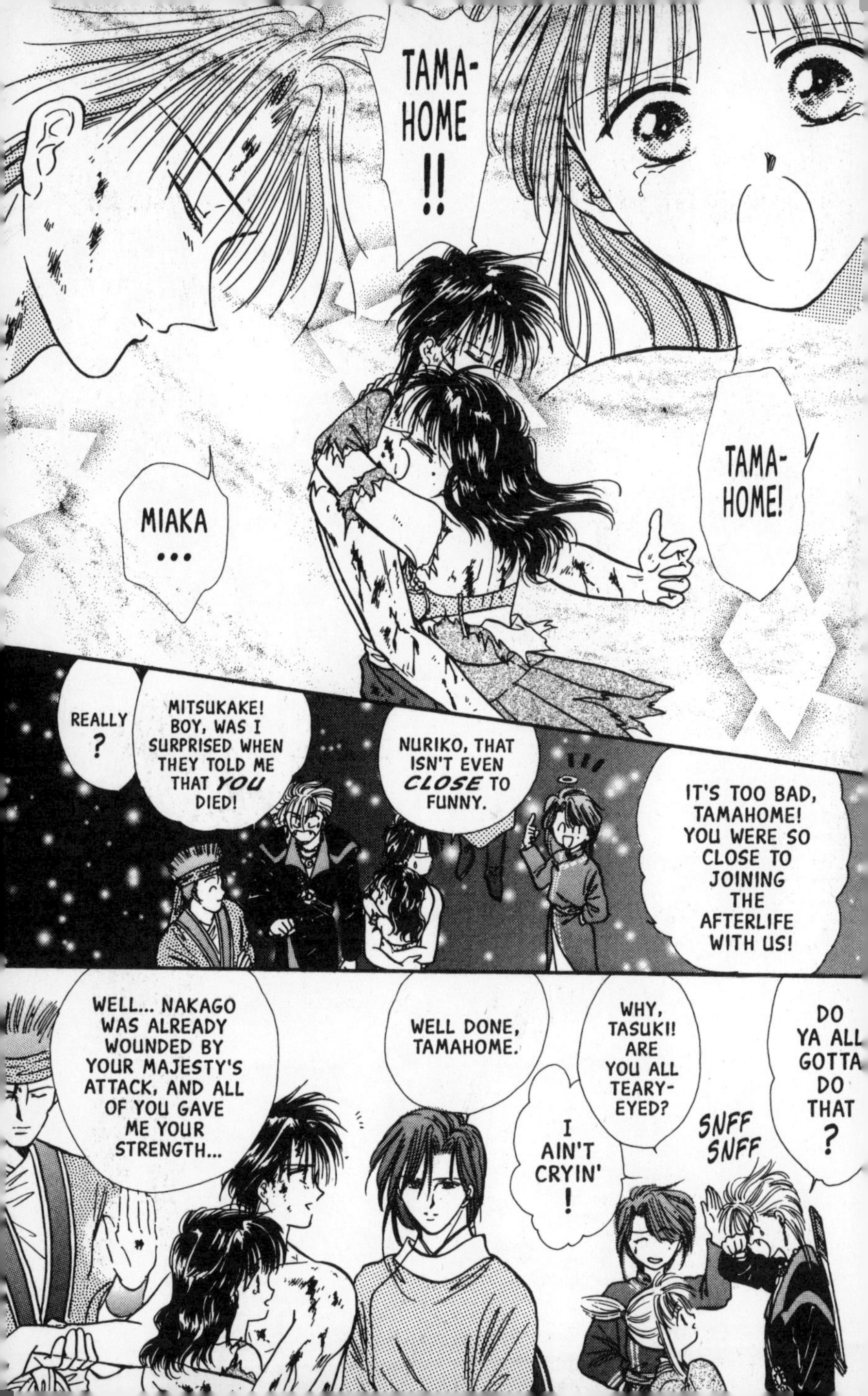
TAMA-HOME !!
TAMA-HOME!
MIAKA ...
IT'S TOO BAD, TAMAHOME! YOU WERE SO CLOSE TO JOINING THE AFTERLIFE WITH US!
NURIKO, THAT ISN'T EVEN CLOSE TO FUNNY.
MITSUKAKE! BOY, WAS I SURPRISED WHEN THEY TOLD ME THAT YOU DIED!
REALLY ?
DO YA ALL GOTTA DO THAT ?
SNFF SNFF
WHY, TASUKI! ARE YOU ALL TEARY-EYED?
I AIN'T CRYIN' !
WELL DONE, TAMAHOME.
WELL... NAKAGO WAS ALREADY WOUNDED BY YOUR MAJESTY'S ATTACK, AND ALL OF YOU GAVE ME YOUR STRENGTH...

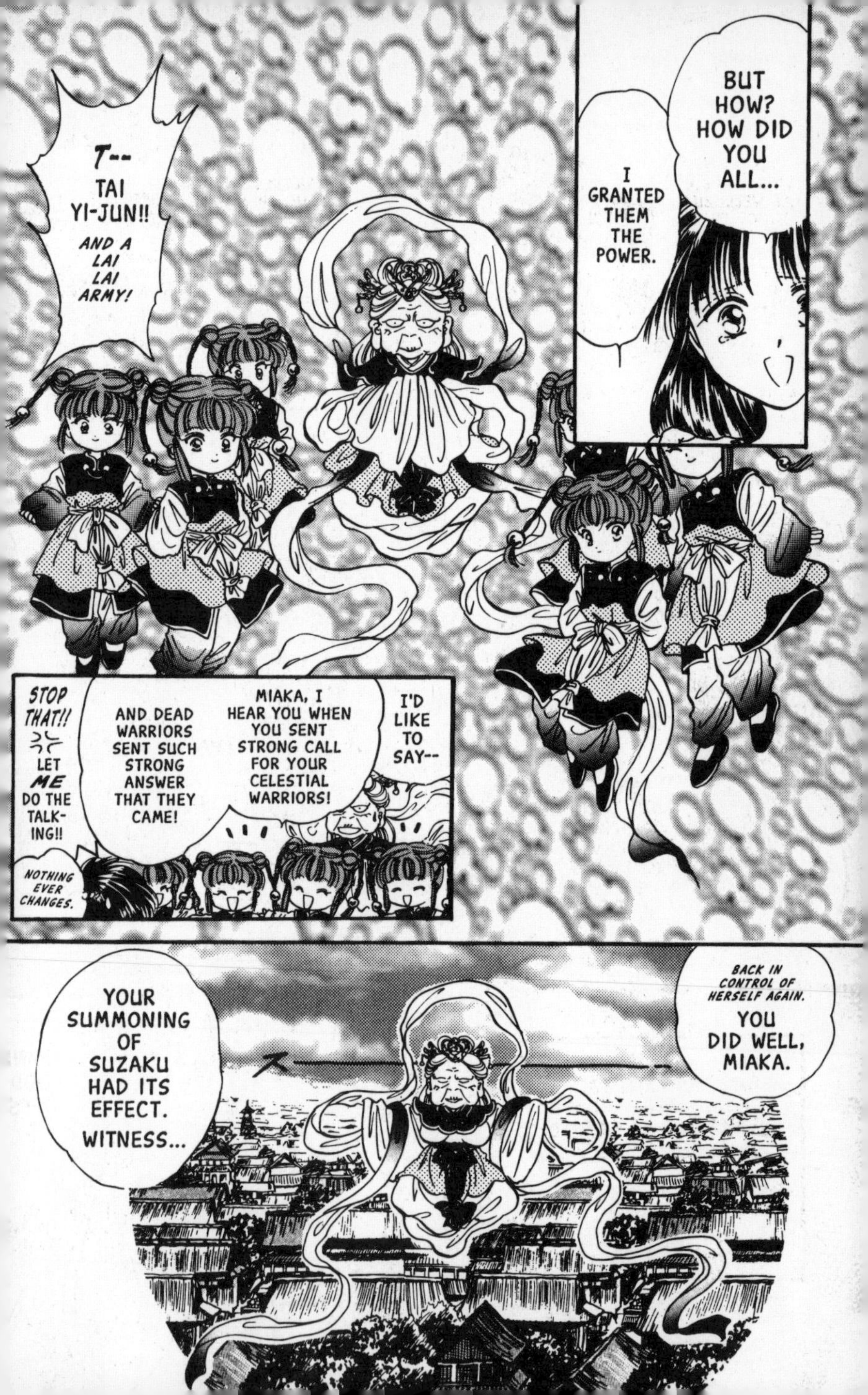
BUT HOW? HOW DID YOU ALL...
I GRANTED THEM THE POWER.
T-- TAI YI-JUN!!
AND A LAI LAI ARMY!
I'D LIKE TO SAY--
MIAKA, I HEAR YOU WHEN YOU SENT STRONG CALL FOR YOUR CELESTIAL WARRIORS!
AND DEAD WARRIORS SENT SUCH STRONG ANSWER THAT THEY CAME!
STOP THAT!! LET ME DO THE TALKING!!
NOTHING EVER CHANGES.
BACK IN CONTROL OF HERSELF AGAIN.
YOU DID WELL, MIAKA.
YOUR SUMMONING OF SUZAKU HAD ITS EFFECT. WITNESS...

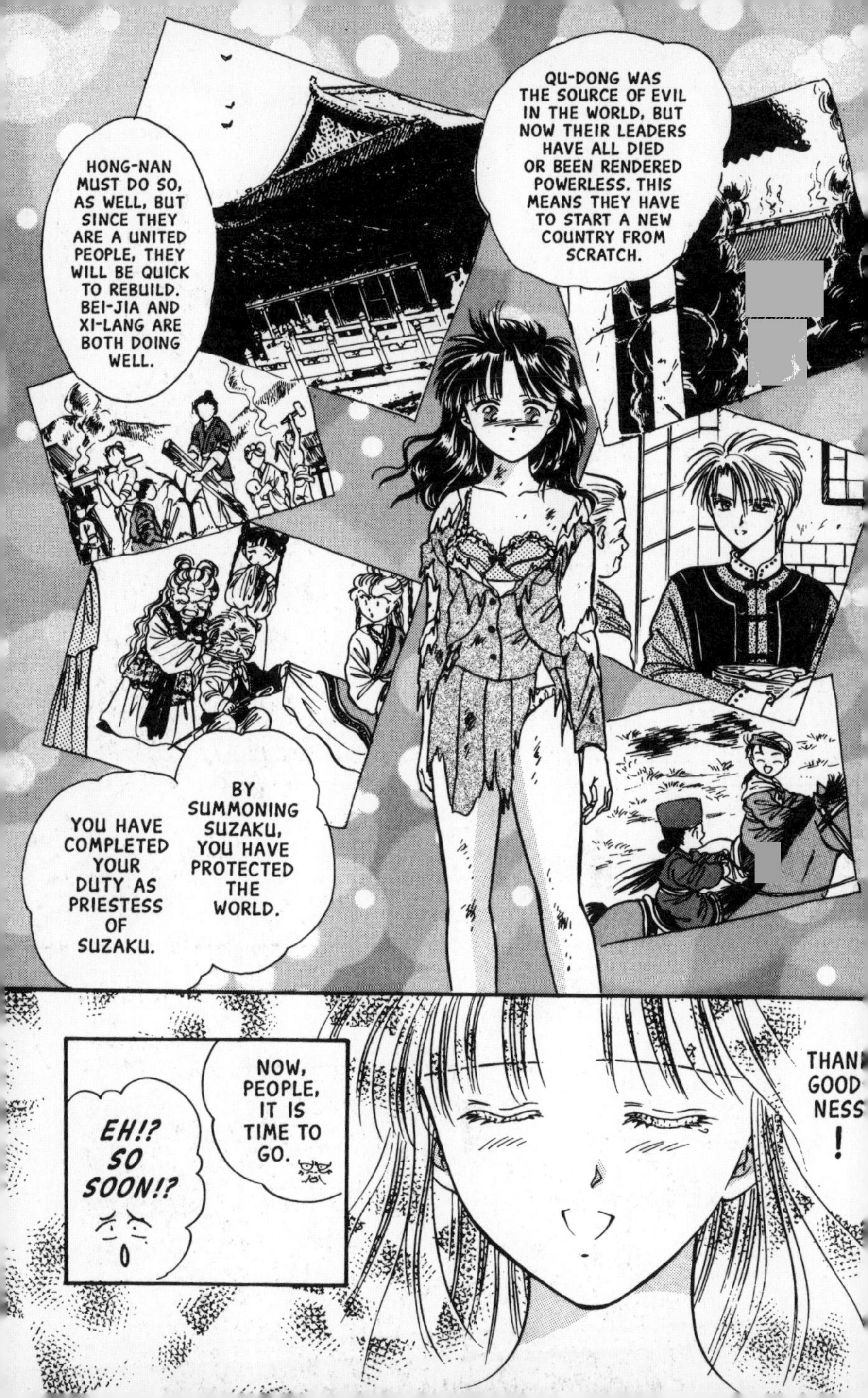
QU-DONG WAS THE SOURCE OF EVIL IN THE WORLD, BUT NOW THEIR LEADERS HAVE ALL DIED OR BEEN RENDERED POWERLESS. THIS MEANS THEY HAVE TO START A NEW COUNTRY FROM SCRATCH.
HONG-NAN MUST DO SO, AS WELL, BUT SINCE THEY ARE A UNITED PEOPLE, THEY WILL BE QUICK TO REBUILD. BEI-JIA AND XI-LANG ARE BOTH DOING WELL.
BY SUMMONING SUZAKU, YOU HAVE PROTECTED THE WORLD.
YOU HAVE COMPLETED YOUR DUTY AS PRIESTESS OF SUZAKU.
THAN GOODNESS !
NOW, PEOPLE, IT IS TIME TO GO.
EH!? SO SOON!?

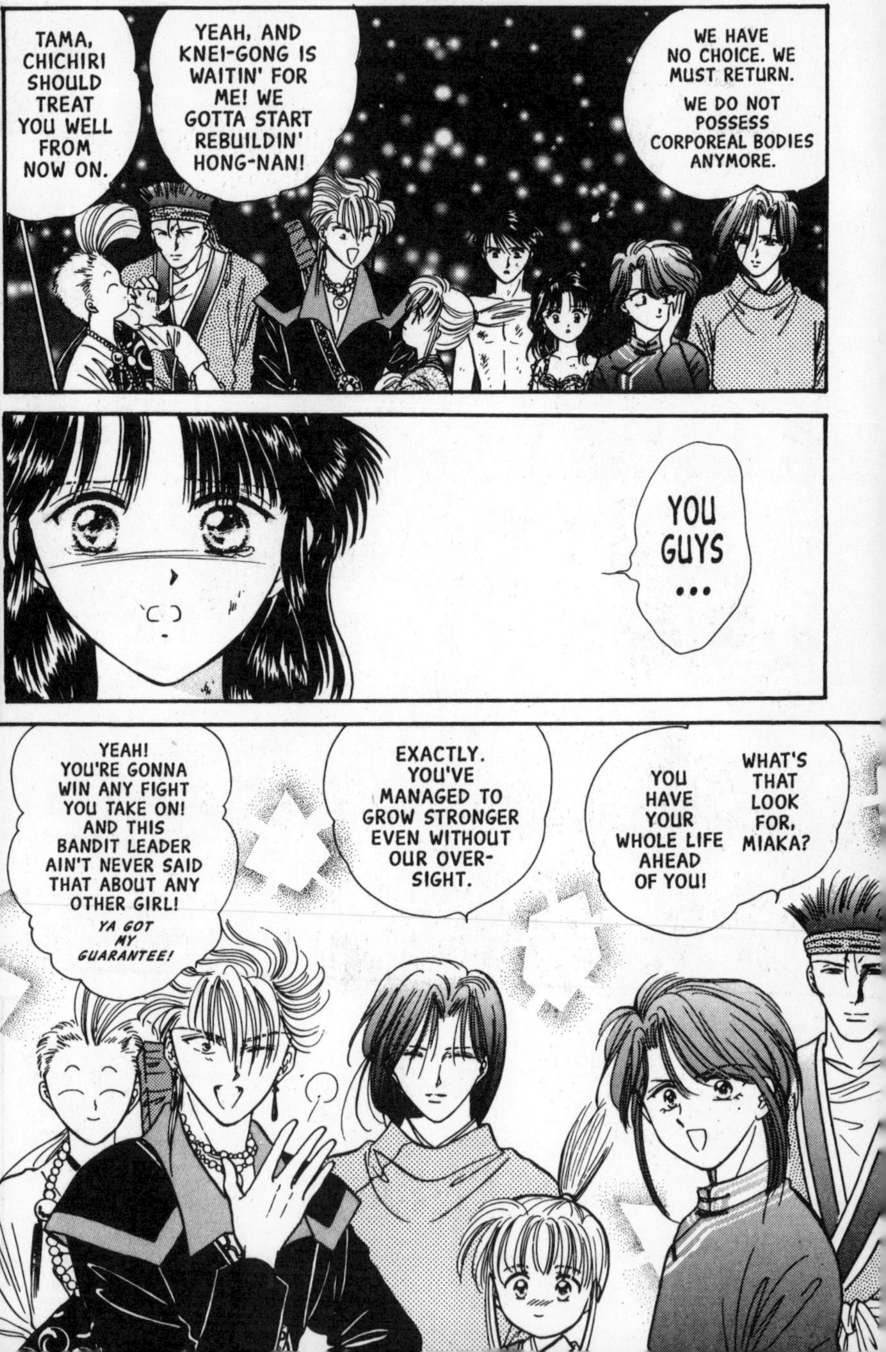
WE HAVE NO CHOICE. WE MUST RETURN.
WE DO NOT POSSESS CORPOREAL BODIES ANYMORE.
YEAH, AND KNEI-GONG IS WAITIN' FOR ME! WE GOTTA START REBUILDIN' HONG-NAN!
TAMA, CHICHIRI SHOULD TREAT YOU WELL FROM NOW ON.
YOU GUYS...
WHAT'S THAT LOOK FOR, MIAKA?
YOU HAVE YOUR WHOLE LIFE AHEAD OF YOU!
EXACTLY. YOU'VE MANAGED TO GROW STRONGER EVEN WITHOUT OUR OVER-SIGHT.
YEAH! YOU'RE GONNA WIN ANY FIGHT YOU TAKE ON! AND THIS BANDIT LEADER AIN'T NEVER SAID THAT ABOUT ANY OTHER GIRL!
YA GOT MY GUARANTEE!

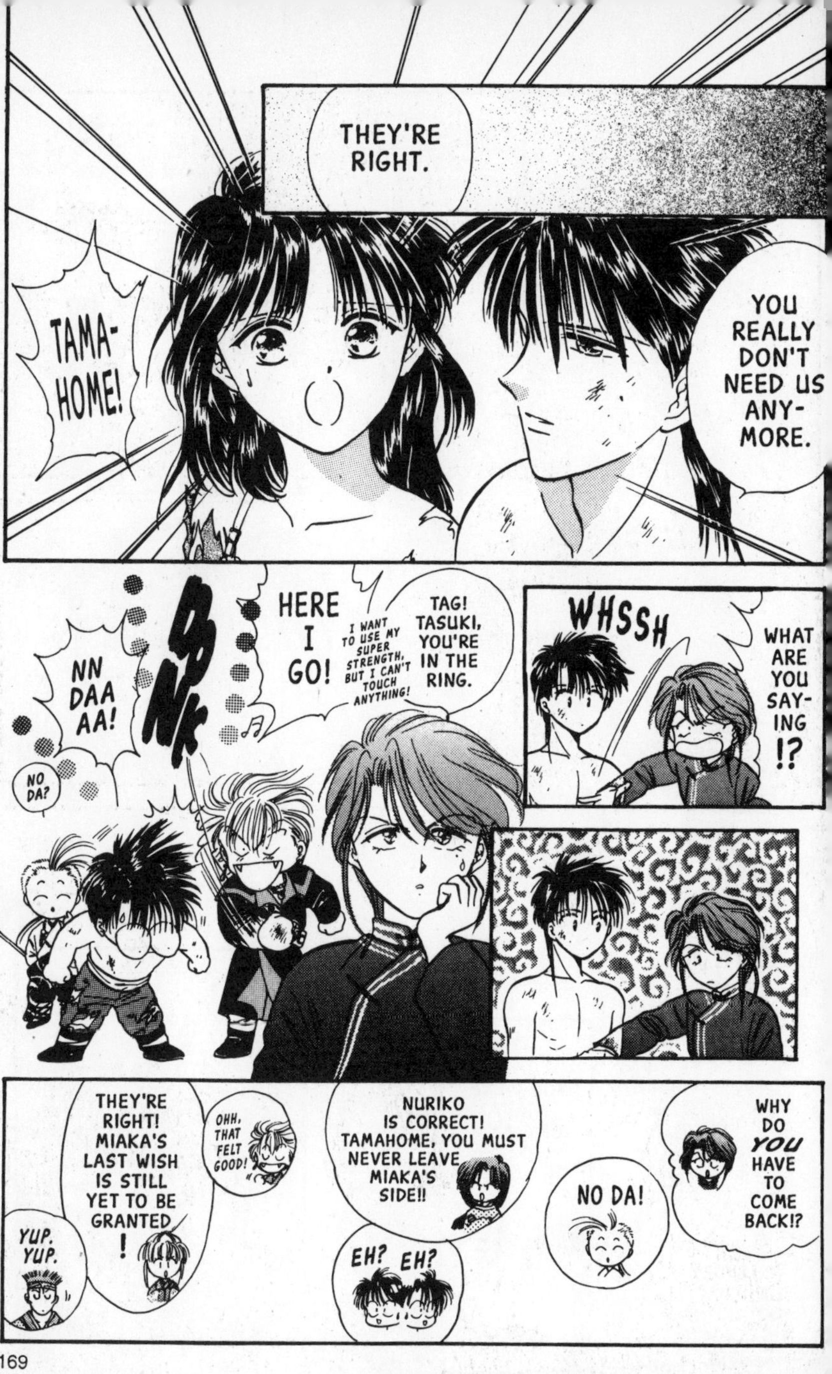

THEY'RE RIGHT.
YOU REALLY DON'T NEED US ANYMORE.
TAMA-HOME!
WHSSH
WHAT ARE YOU SAYING!?
TAG! TASUKI, YOU'RE IN THE RING.
I WANT TO USE MY SUPER STRENGTH, BUT I CAN'T TOUCH ANYTHING!
HERE I GO!
DONK
NN DAAAA!
NO DA?
WHY DO YOU HAVE TO COME BACK!?
NO DA!
NURIKO IS CORRECT! TAMAHOME, YOU MUST NEVER LEAVE MIAKA'S SIDE!!
EH? EH?
OHH, THAT FELT GOOD!
THEY'RE RIGHT! MIAKA'S LAST WISH IS STILL YET TO BE GRANTED!
YUP. YUP.

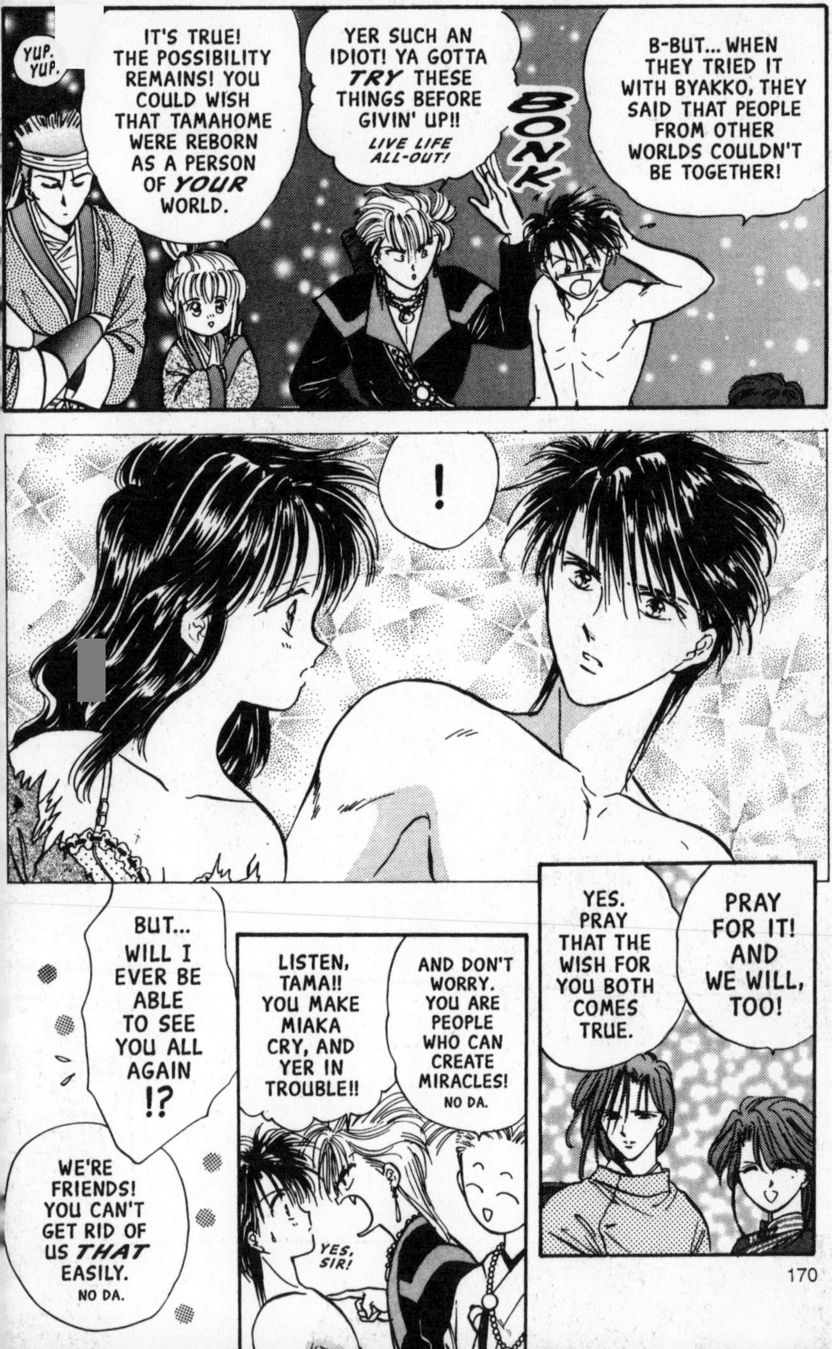
B-BUT... WHEN THEY TRIED IT WITH BYAKKO, THEY SAID THAT PEOPLE FROM OTHER WORLDS COULDN'T BE TOGETHER!
BONK
YER SUCH AN IDIOT! YA GOTTA TRY THESE THINGS BEFORE GIVIN' UP!!
LIVE LIFE ALL-OUT!
IT'S TRUE! THE POSSIBILITY REMAINS! YOU COULD WISH THAT TAMAHOME WERE REBORN AS A PERSON OF YOUR WORLD.
YUP. YUP.
!
PRAY FOR IT! AND WE WILL, TOO!
YES. PRAY THAT THE WISH FOR YOU BOTH COMES TRUE.
AND DON'T WORRY. YOU ARE PEOPLE WHO CAN CREATE MIRACLES! NO DA.
LISTEN, TAMA!! YOU MAKE MIAKA CRY, AND YER IN TROUBLE!!
YES, SIR!
BUT... WILL I EVER BE ABLE TO SEE YOU ALL AGAIN !?
WE'RE FRIENDS! YOU CAN'T GET RID OF US THAT EASILY. NO DA.

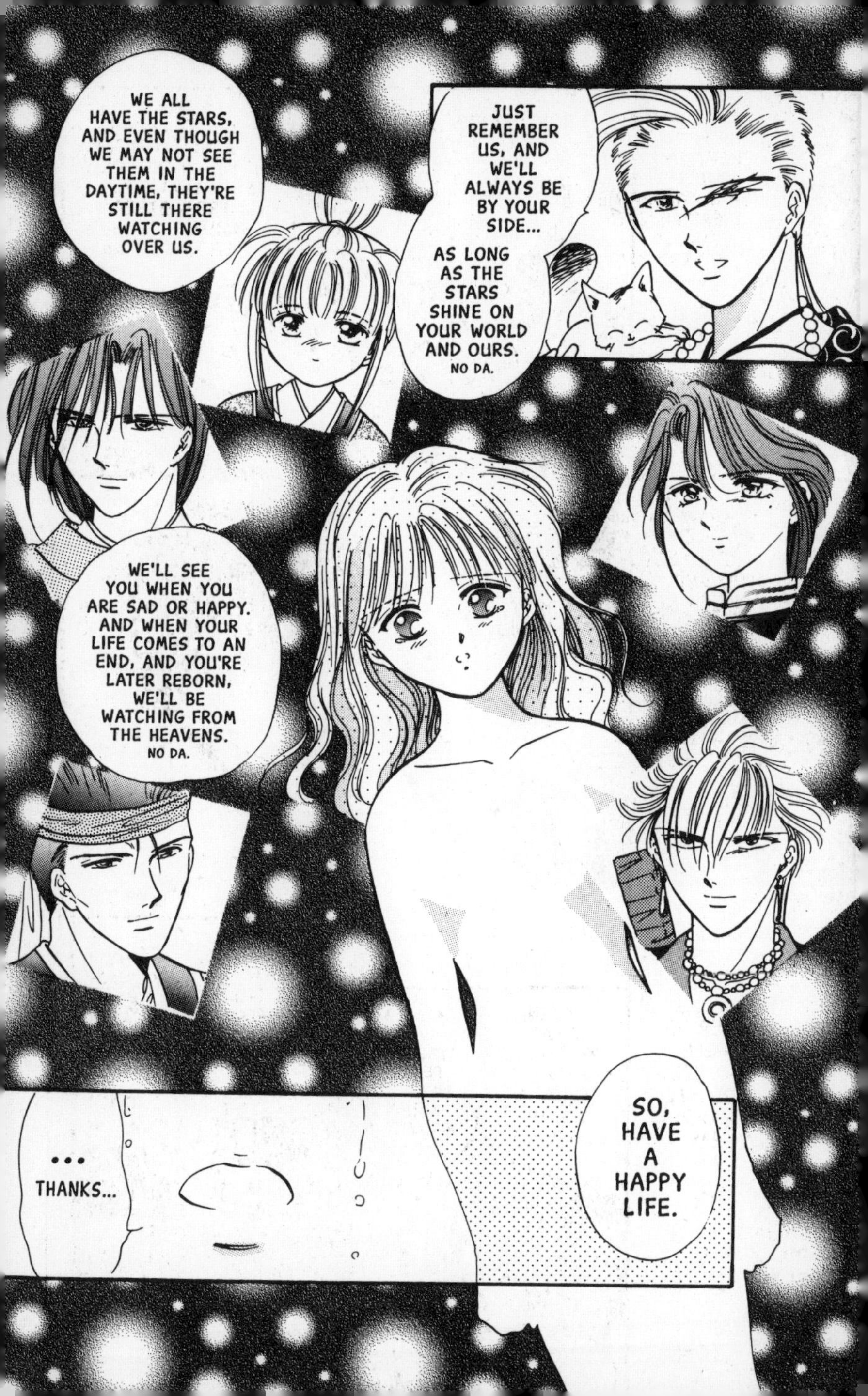
JUST REMEMBER US, AND WE'LL ALWAYS BE BY YOUR SIDE...
AS LONG AS THE STARS SHINE ON YOUR WORLD AND OURS. NO DA.
WE ALL HAVE THE STARS, AND EVEN THOUGH WE MAY NOT SEE THEM IN THE DAYTIME, THEY'RE STILL THERE WATCHING OVER US.
WE'LL SEE YOU WHEN YOU ARE SAD OR HAPPY. AND WHEN YOUR LIFE COMES TO AN END, AND YOU'RE LATER REBORN, WE'LL BE WATCHING FROM THE HEAVENS. NO DA.
SO, HAVE A HAPPY LIFE.
... THANKS...

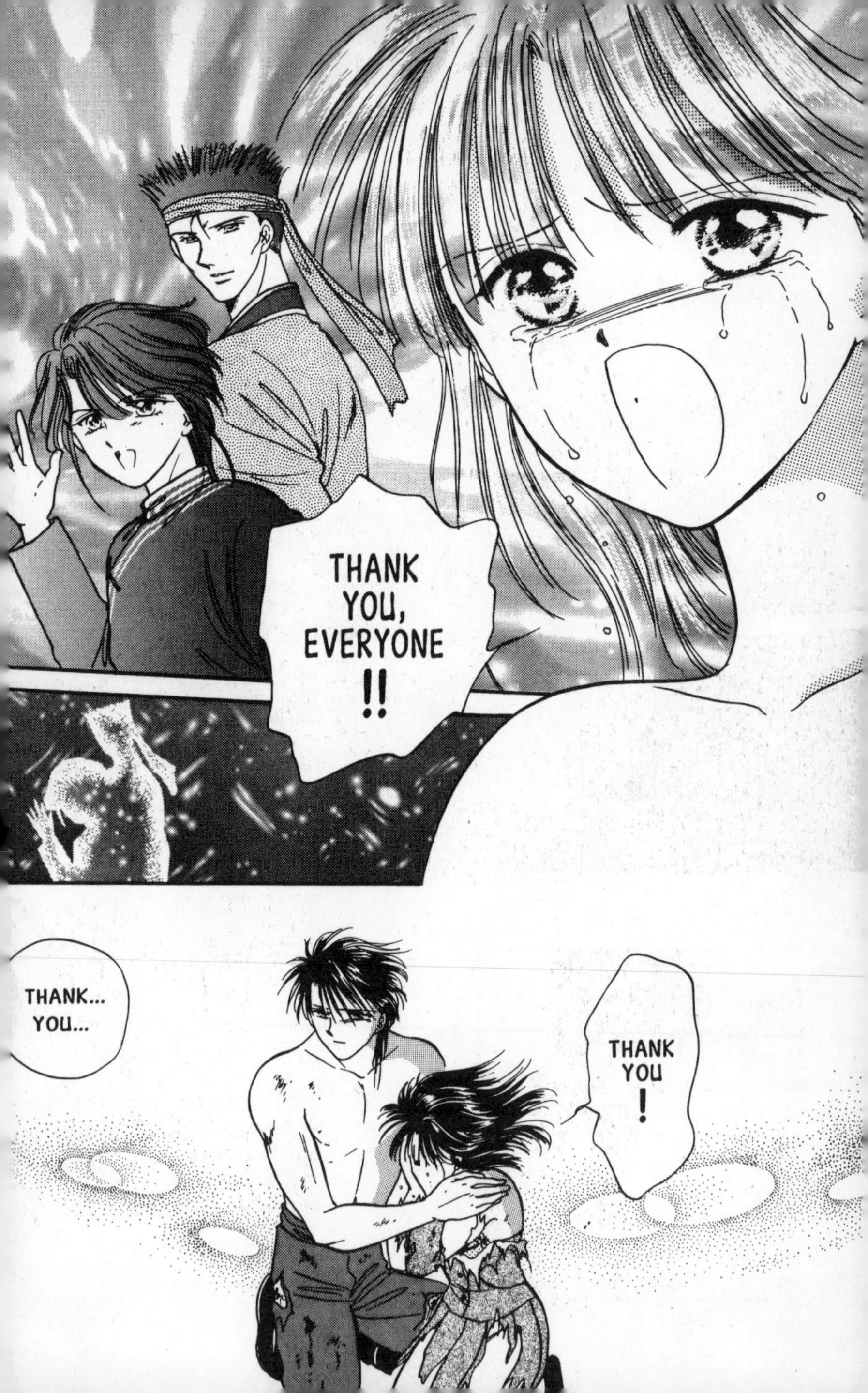
THANK YOU, EVERYONE !!
THANK YOU !
THANK... YOU...

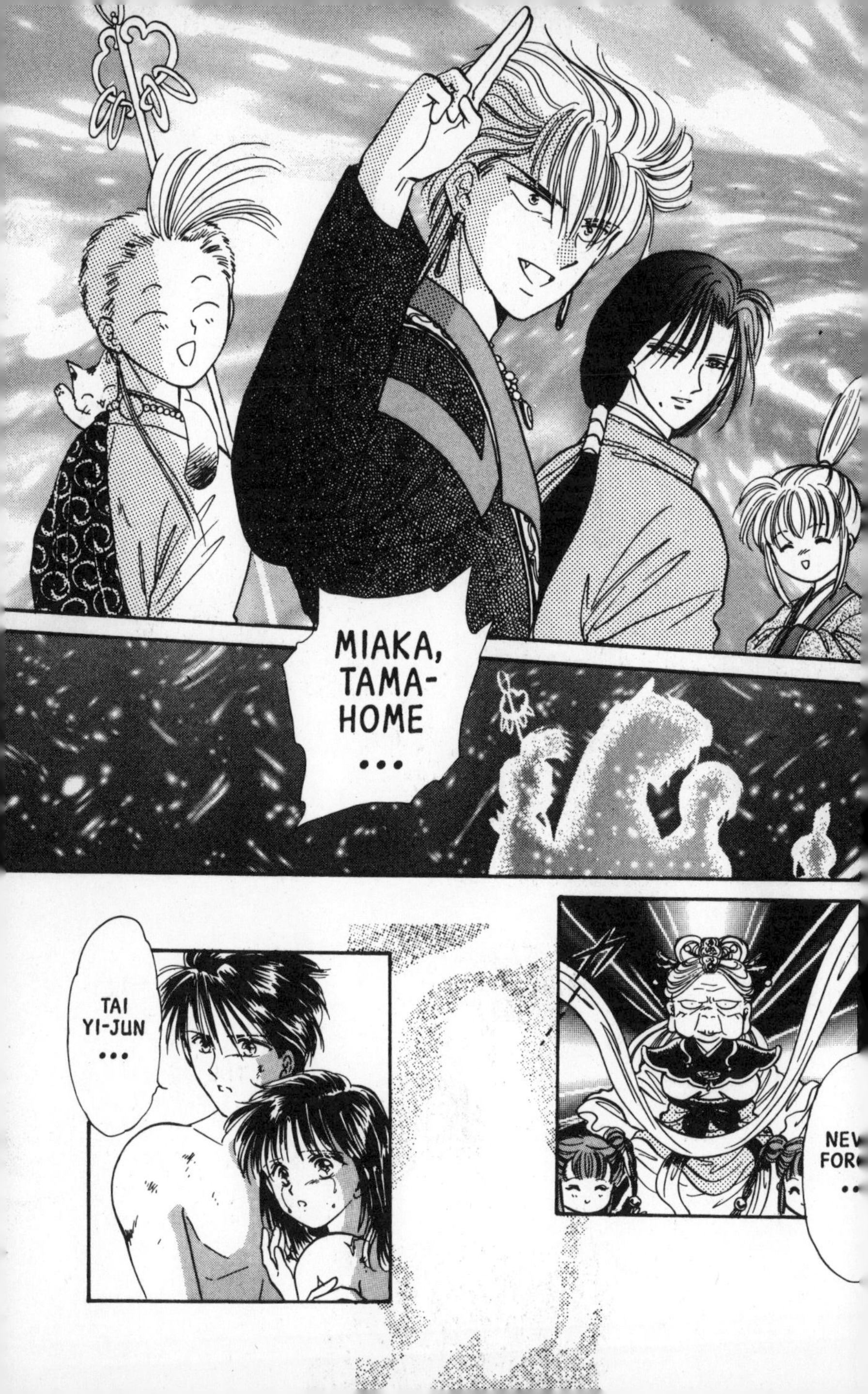
MIAKA, TAMA-HOME ...
NEV FOR ...
TAI YI-JUN ...

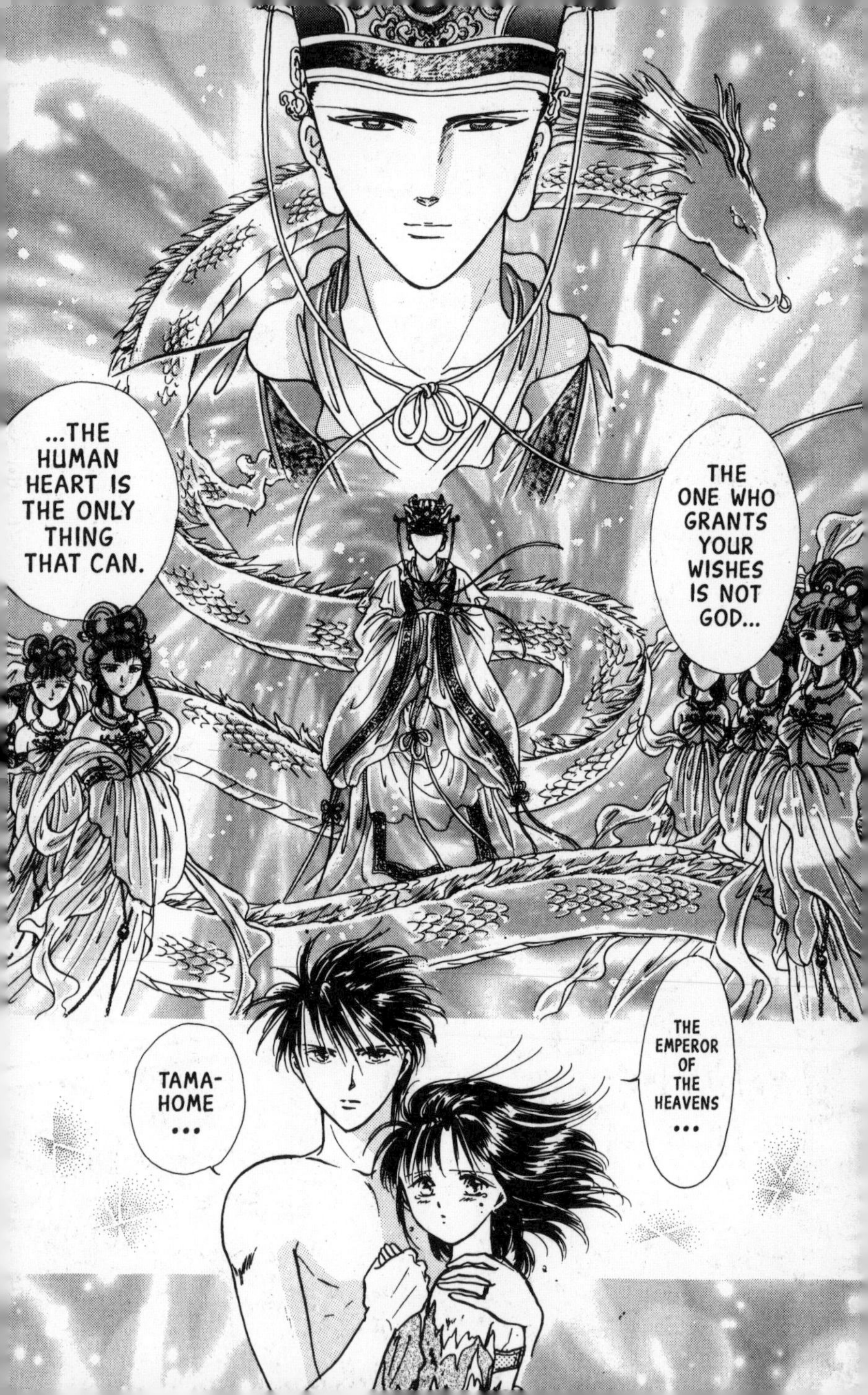
THE ONE WHO GRANTS YOUR WISHES IS NOT GOD...
...THE HUMAN HEART IS THE ONLY THING THAT CAN.
THE EMPEROR OF THE HEAVENS...
TAMA-HOME...

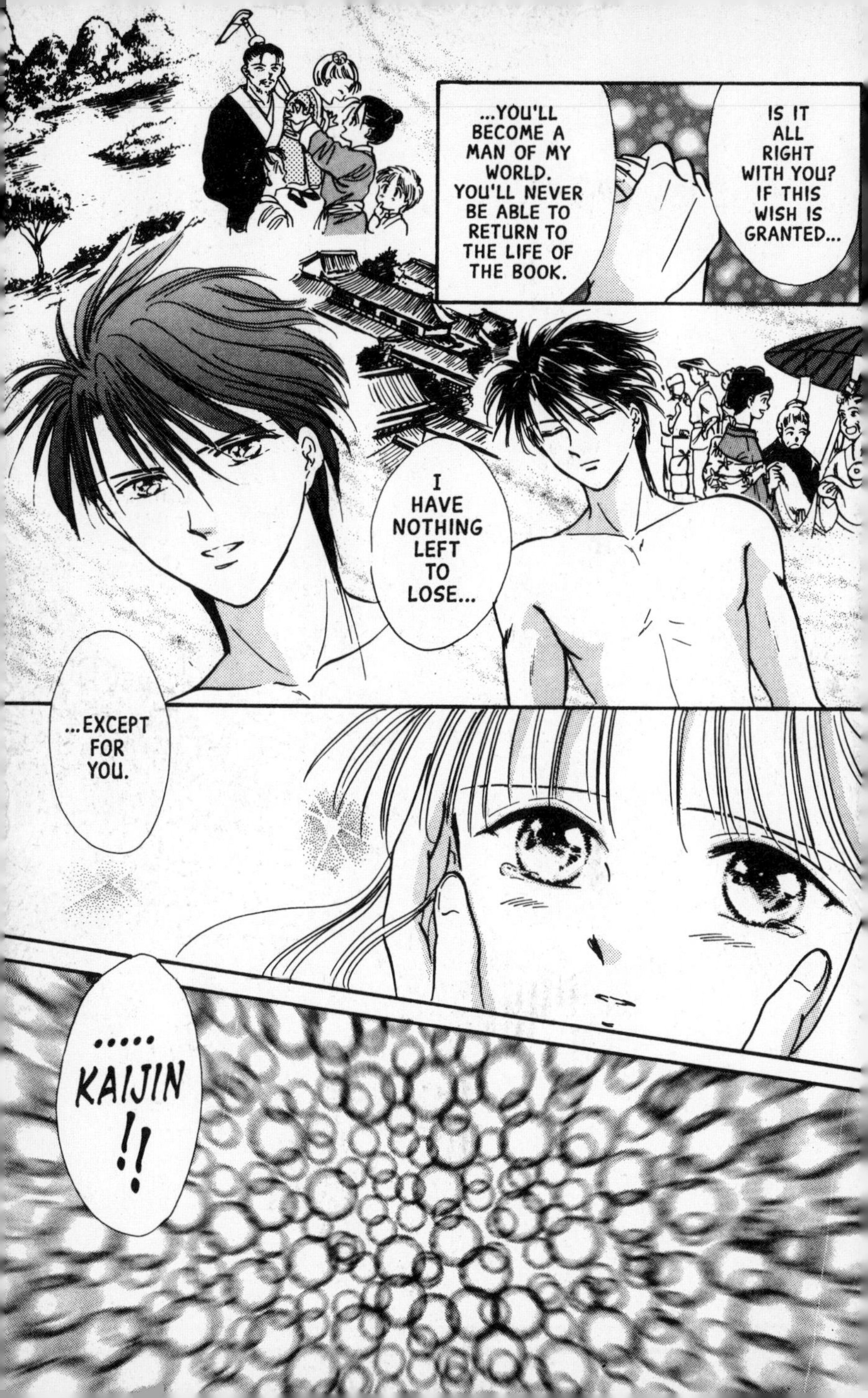
IS IT ALL RIGHT WITH YOU? IF THIS WISH IS GRANTED...
...YOU'LL BECOME A MAN OF MY WORLD.
YOU'LL NEVER BE ABLE TO RETURN TO THE LIFE OF THE BOOK.
I HAVE NOTHING LEFT TO LOSE...
...EXCEPT FOR YOU.
..... KAIJIN !!

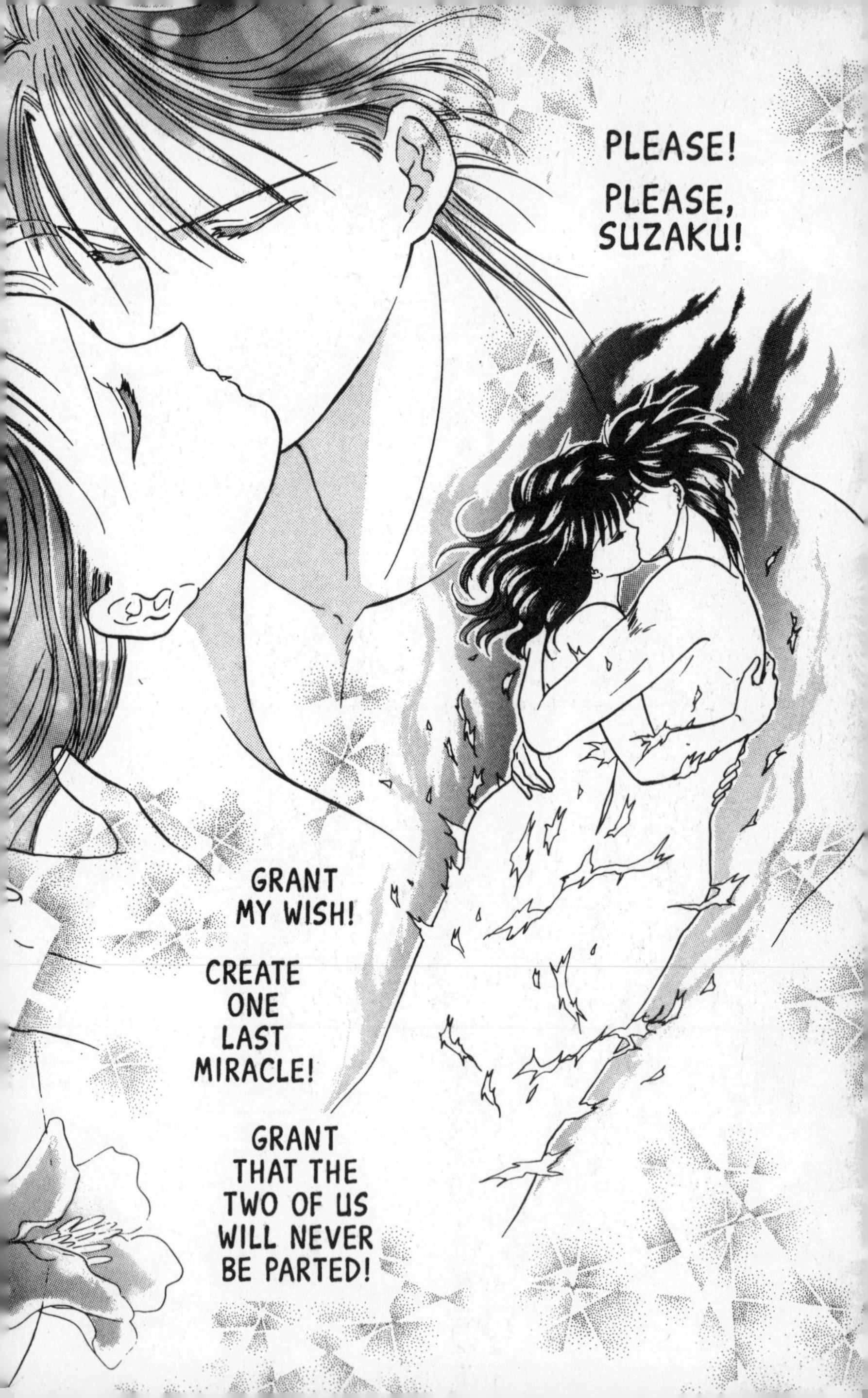
PLEASE!
PLEASE, SUZAKU!
GRANT MY WISH!
CREATE ONE LAST MIRACLE!
GRANT THAT THE TWO OF US WILL NEVER BE PARTED!

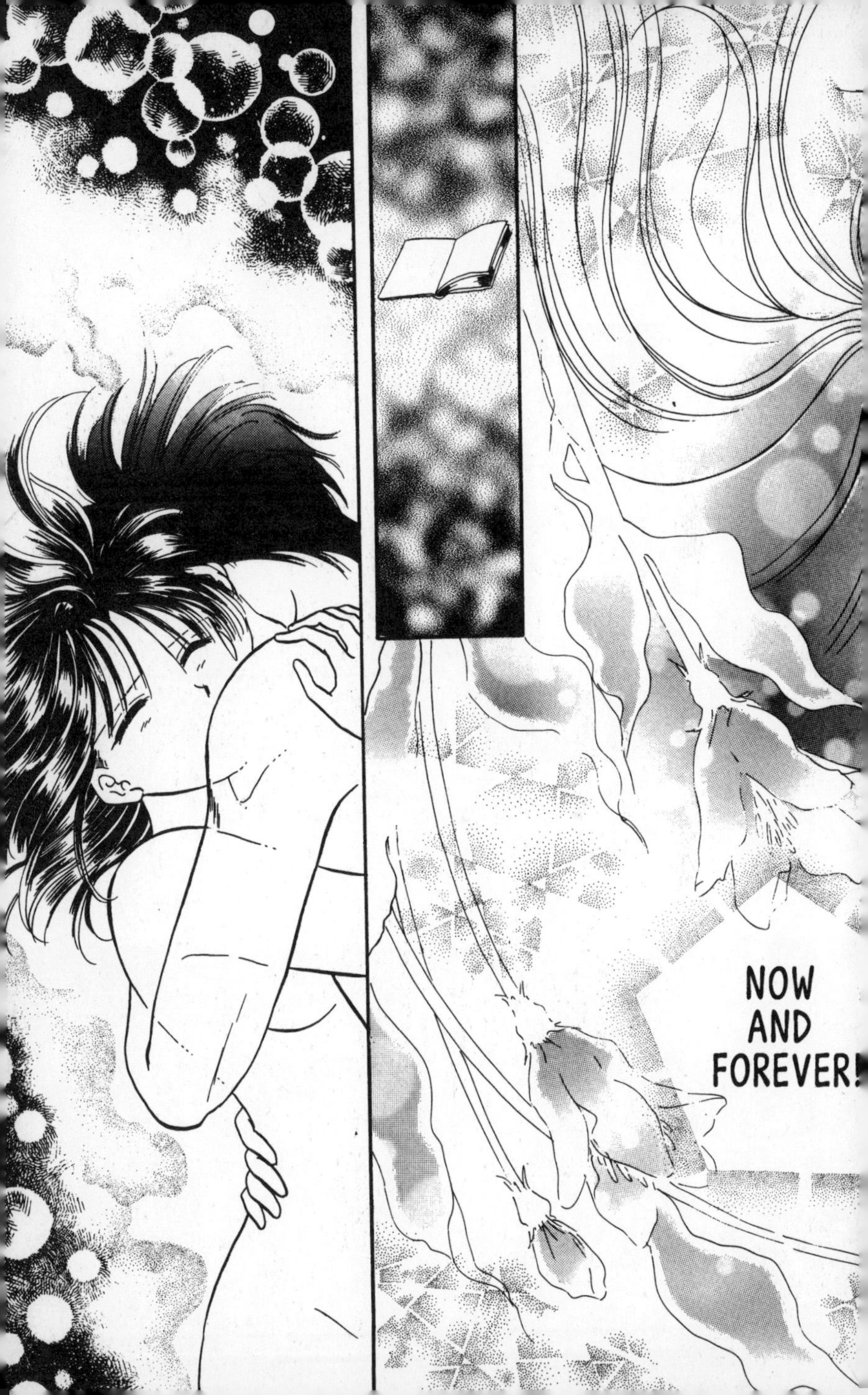
NOW AND FOREVER!

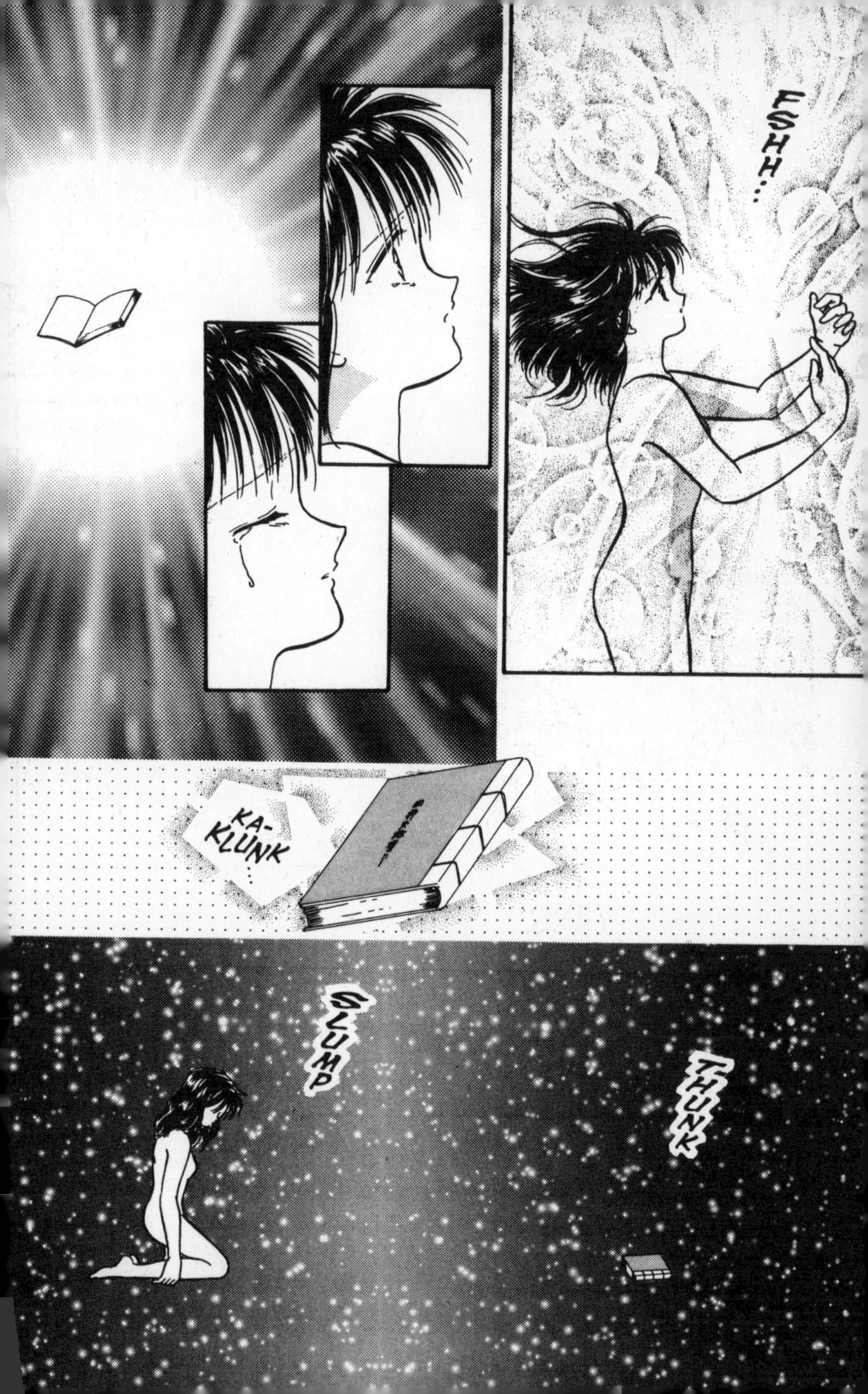
FSHH...
KA-KLUNK...
THUNK
SLUMP

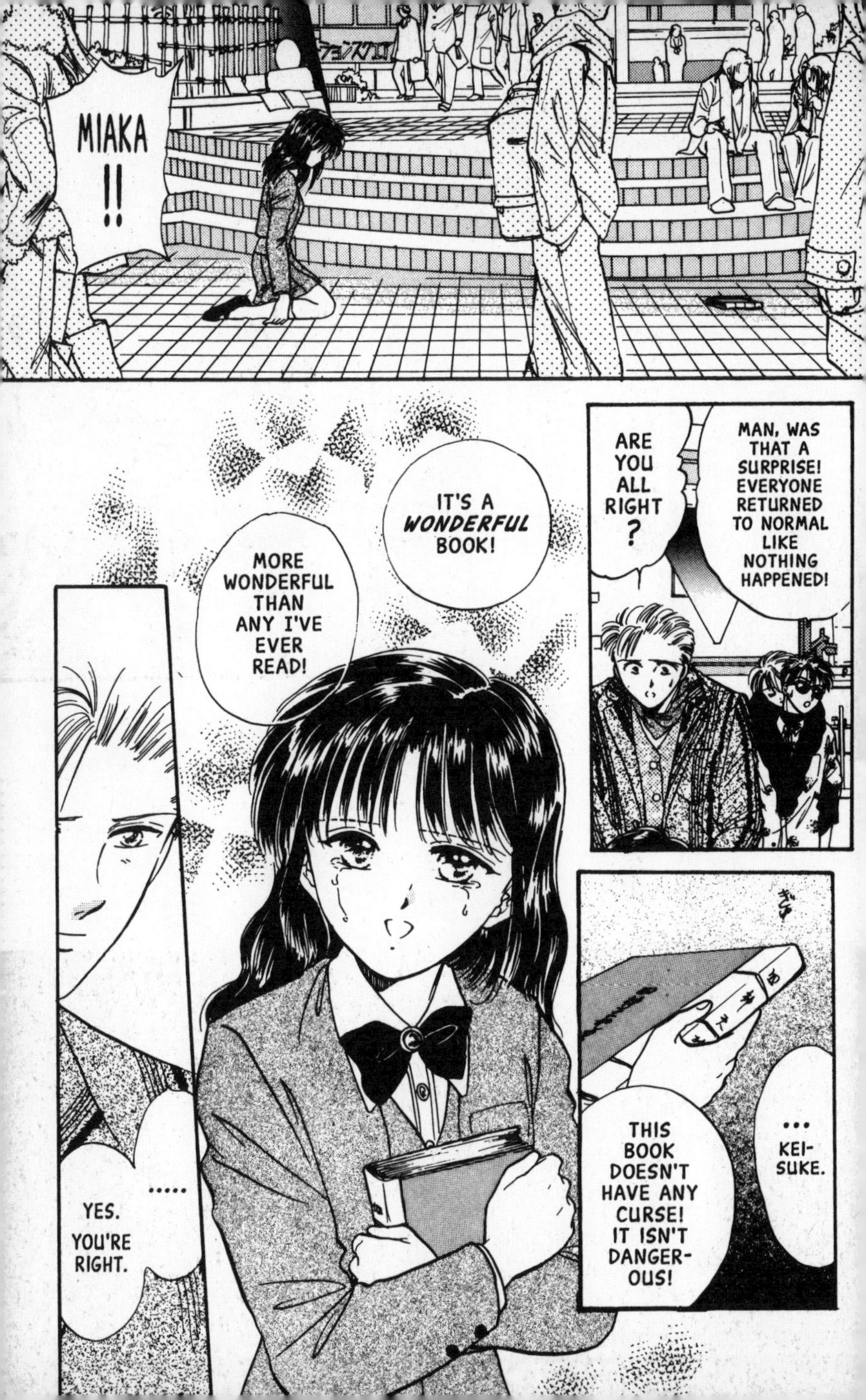
MIAKA !!
MAN, WAS THAT A SURPRISE! EVERYONE RETURNED TO NORMAL LIKE NOTHING HAPPENED!
ARE YOU ALL RIGHT?
... KEI-SUKE.
THIS BOOK DOESN'T HAVE ANY CURSE! IT ISN'T DANGER-OUS!
IT'S A *WONDERFUL* BOOK!
MORE WONDERFUL THAN ANY I'VE EVER READ!
.....
YES. YOU'RE RIGHT.

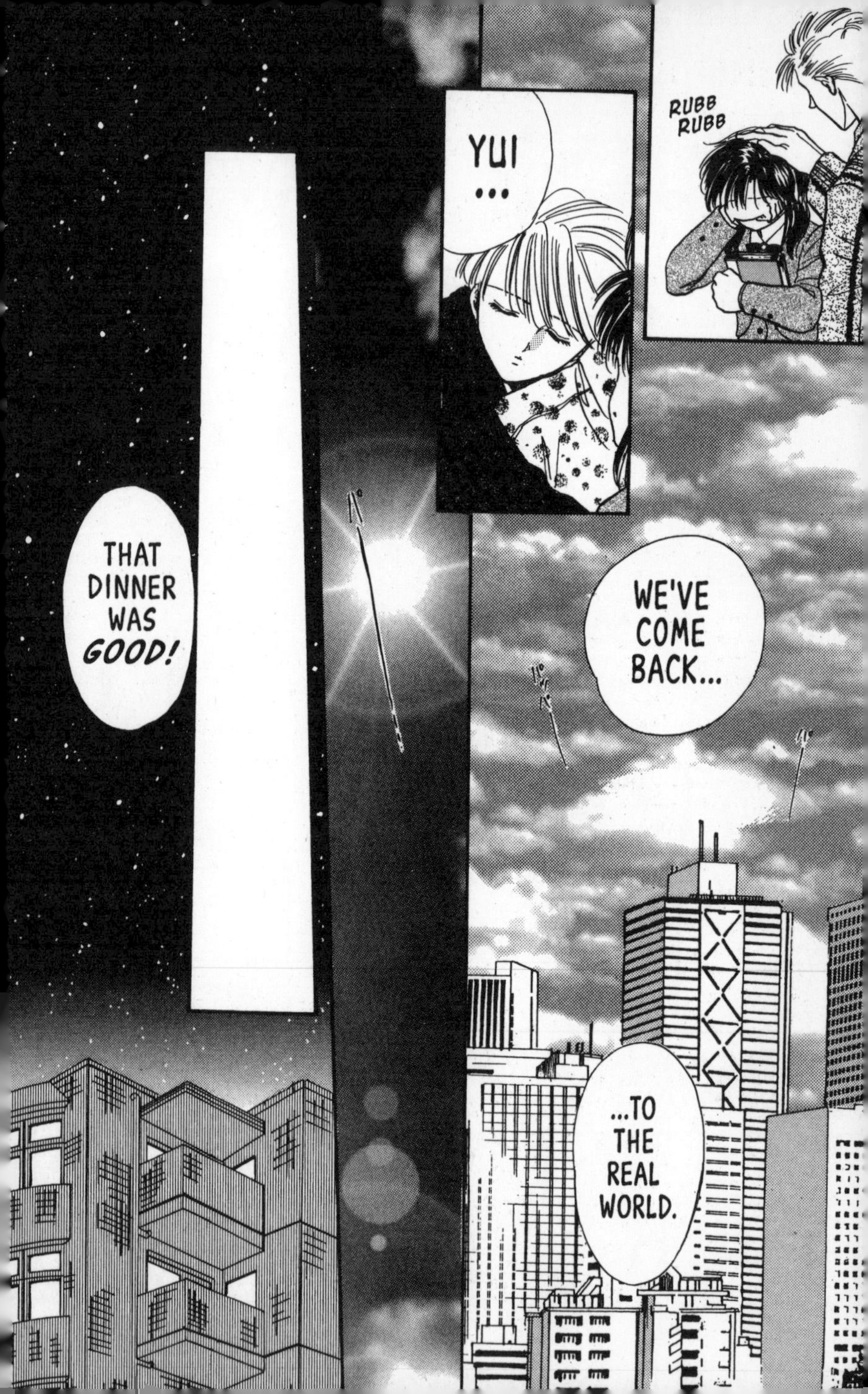
RUBB RUBB
YUI ...
WE'VE COME BACK...
...TO THE REAL WORLD.
THAT DINNER WAS *GOOD!*

Fushigi Yûgi ∾ 13

Now, I've received a lot of letters regarding Fushigi Yûgi! But I never expected the wonderful variety--like nothing I've ever seen! There are times when I've looked at them and thought to myself, "This is unfair!" ☺ But different people have different ways of interpreting things. I've had letters from everyone from grade-school-age kids to 38-year-old married women. Men, too! Really, a huge range of people! I expected the ones that say, "My brother reads it, too," but there were such a huge number of letters saying, "My mother is a fan, too," that I have to imagine it's a new age of manga.

There were also a surprising number of letters from people who went to their libraries to find "The Universe of the Four Gods." Even my editor said that there are so many people looking, "If there is a book like it, please let me know!" They even got requests from the libraries themselves. I was shocked! I made up "The Universe of the Four Gods." It doesn't exist! Neither does Mr. Okuda! "Fushigi Yûgi" takes place inside "The Universe of the Four Gods," and "The Universe of the Four Gods" can only be found inside "Fushigi Yûgi"! But the fact that I came this far is only because of you readers. Thank you so much!! My health has failed during its run, and there were times when I had to draw it all by myself. (Volume 9 was pretty much all me.) But I thought of you readers and did my best. There were times when nothing good ever seemed to happen, but at that time, my first thought would be, "I won't let them get me down!!" Now that Part 1 is over, all I see in my own work are defects, but still, I know that I tried my very best at the time, and I'm satisfied with that. Part 2 will be a continuation of the story, but there will be a whole new setting, and there will be new characters (and, of course, new villains)! And it's just possible that novels will come out covering the Priestesses of Genbu and Byakko. When!? And so, please continue to support Fushigi Yûgi!

And with that... 3/9

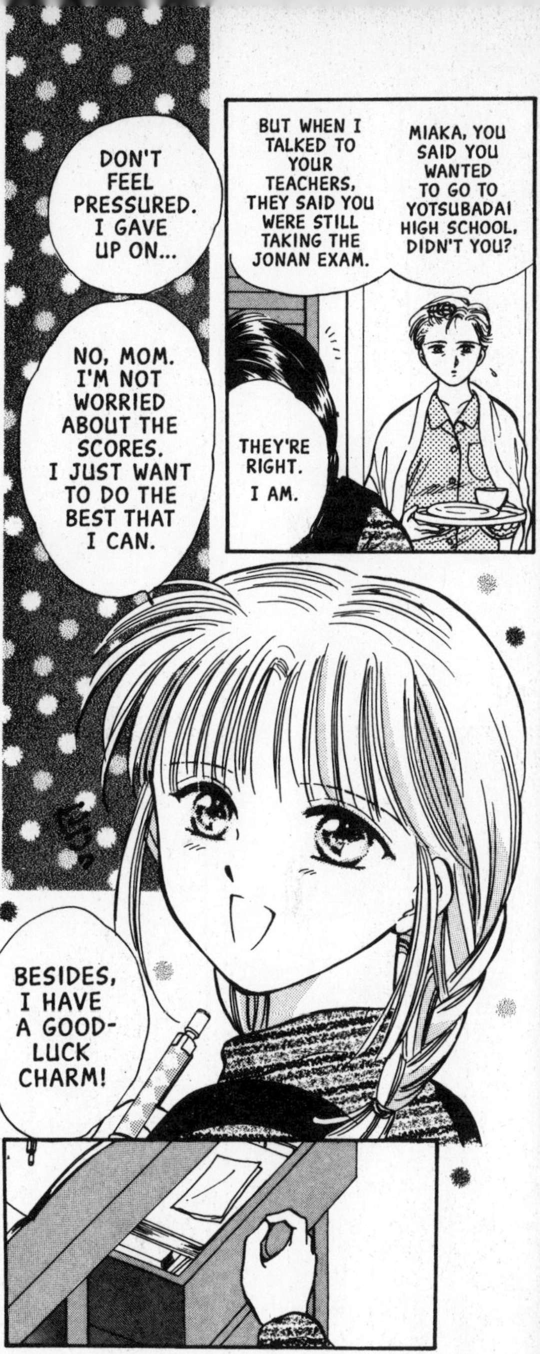
MIAKA, YOU SAID YOU WANTED TO GO TO YOTSUBADAI HIGH SCHOOL, DIDN'T YOU?
BUT WHEN I TALKED TO YOUR TEACHERS, THEY SAID YOU WERE STILL TAKING THE JONAN EXAM.
THEY'RE RIGHT.
I AM.
DON'T FEEL PRESSURED. I GAVE UP ON...
NO, MOM. I'M NOT WORRIED ABOUT THE SCORES. I JUST WANT TO DO THE BEST THAT I CAN.
BESIDES, I HAVE A GOOD-LUCK CHARM!

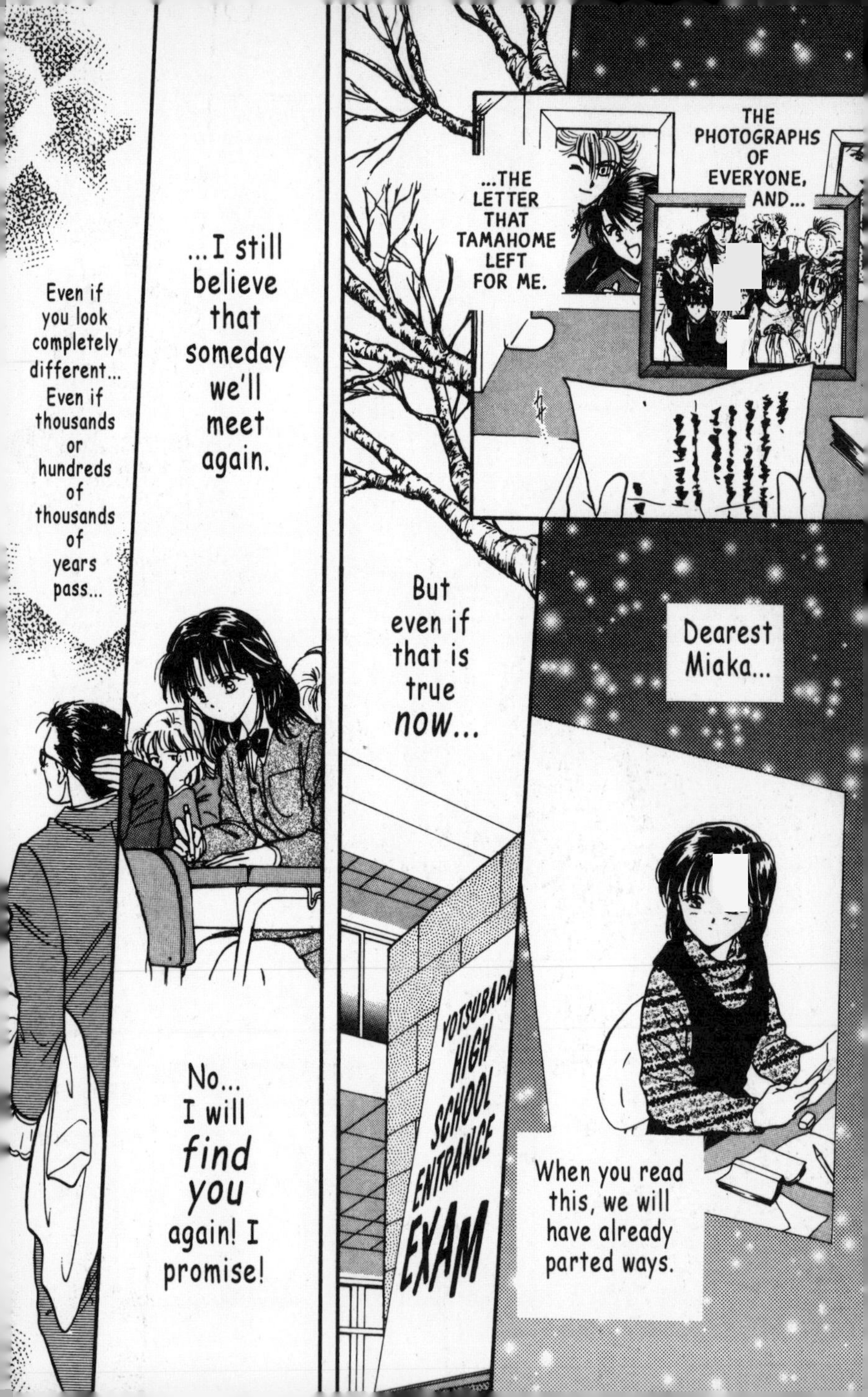
THE PHOTOGRAPHS OF EVERYONE, AND...
...THE LETTER THAT TAMAHOME LEFT FOR ME.
Dearest Miaka...
When you read this, we will have already parted ways.
But even if that is true now...
YOTSUBADA
HIGH SCHOOL ENTRANCE EXAM
...I still believe that someday we'll meet again.
No... I will find you again! I promise!
Even if you look completely different... Even if thousands or hundreds of thousands of years pass...

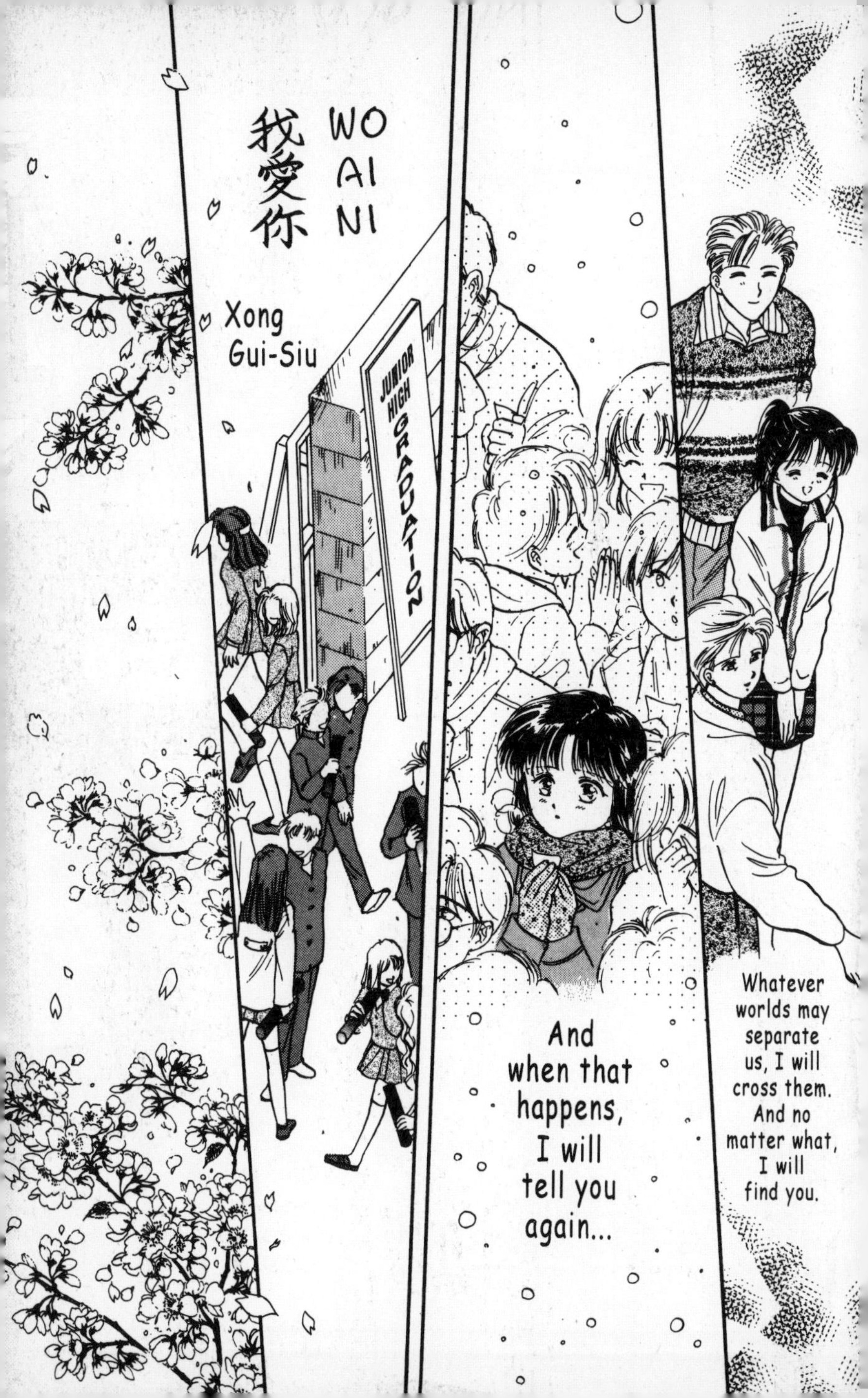
Whatever worlds may separate us, I will cross them. And no matter what, I will find you.
And when that happens, I will tell you again...
我愛你
WO AI NI
Xong Gui-Siu
JUNIOR HIGH GRADUATION

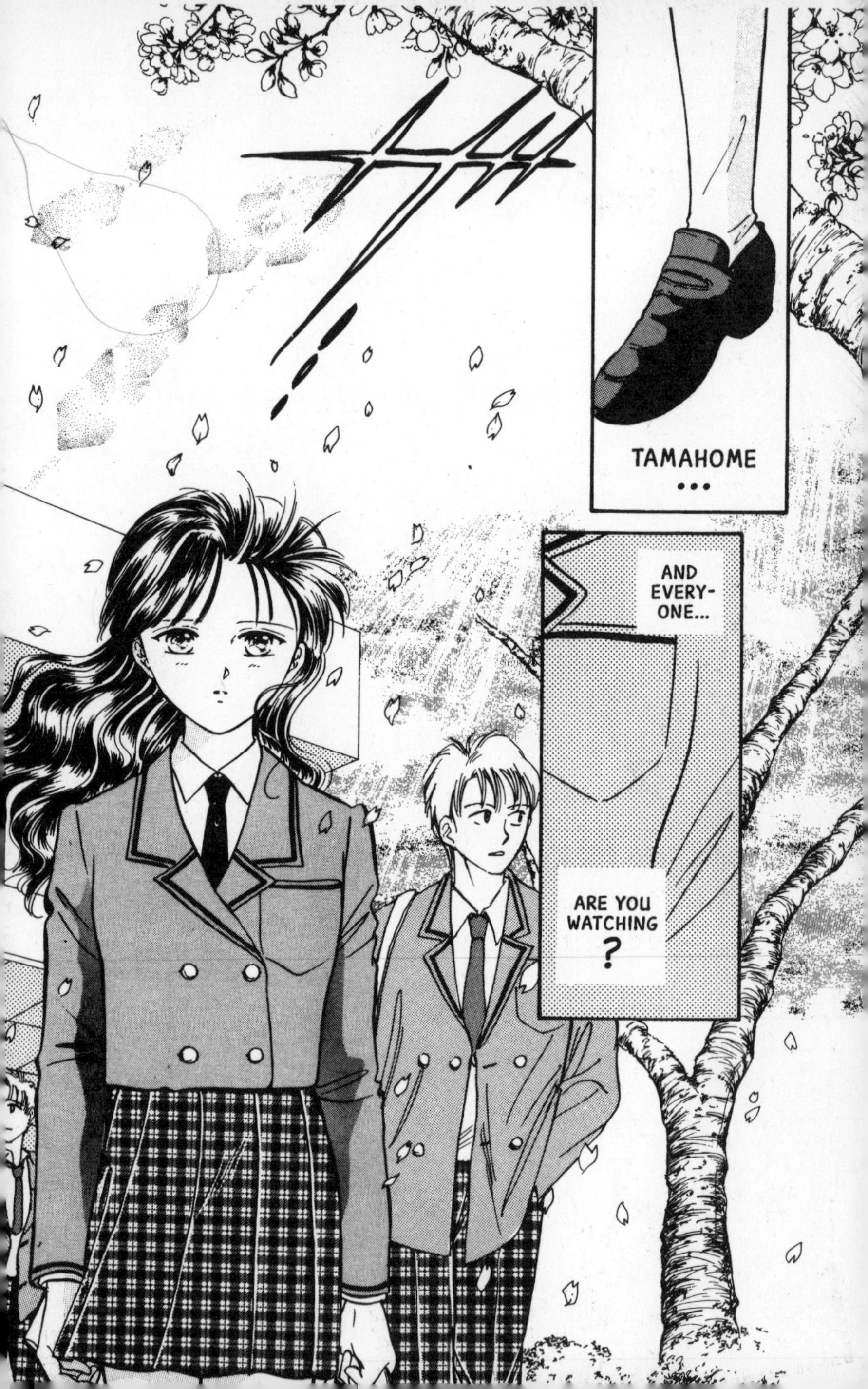
TAMAHOME
•••
AND EVERY-ONE...
ARE YOU WATCHING
?

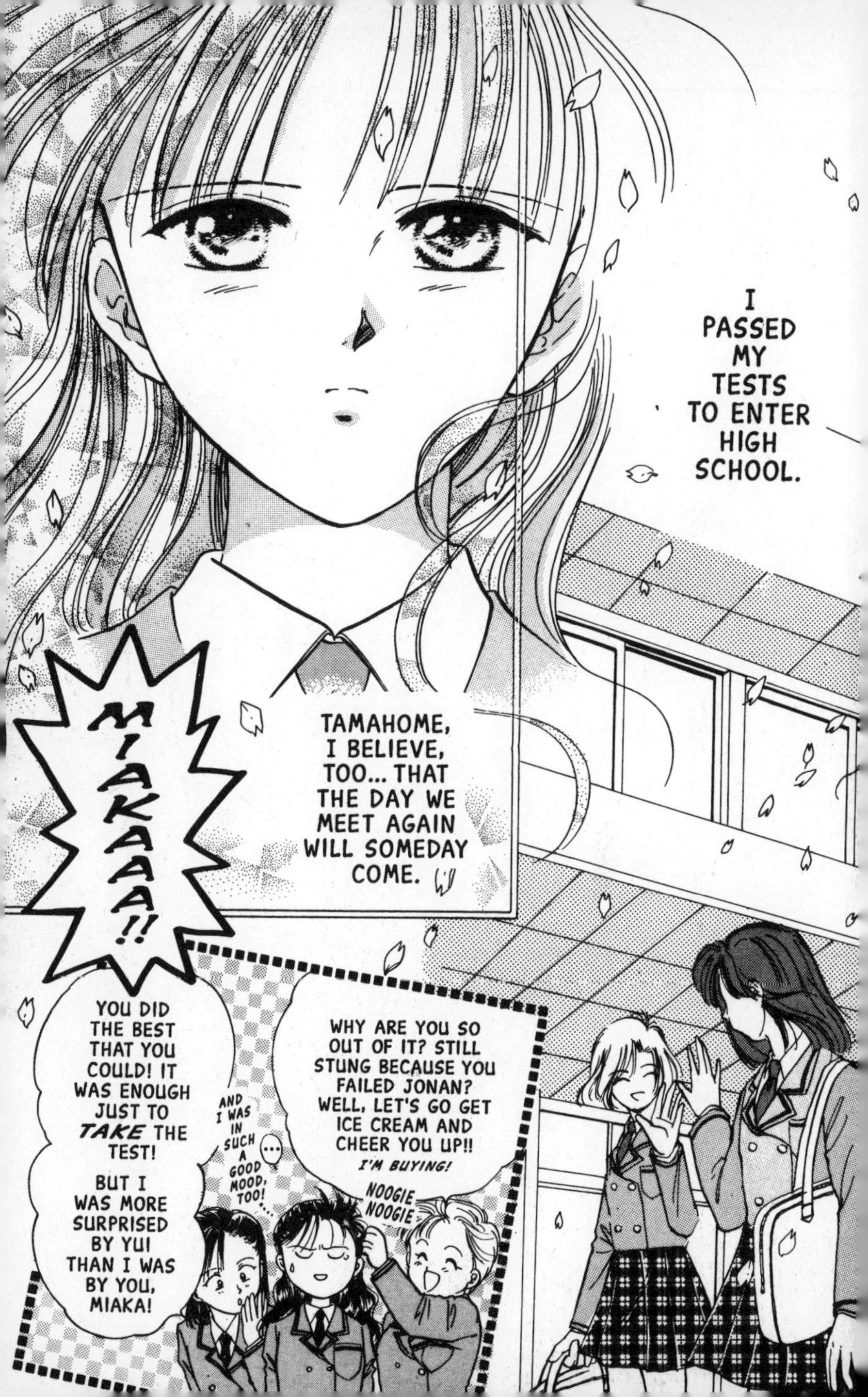
I PASSED MY TESTS TO ENTER HIGH SCHOOL.
TAMAHOME, I BELIEVE, TOO... THAT THE DAY WE MEET AGAIN WILL SOMEDAY COME.
MIAKAAAA!!
WHY ARE YOU SO OUT OF IT? STILL STUNG BECAUSE YOU FAILED JONAN? WELL, LET'S GO GET ICE CREAM AND CHEER YOU UP!!
I'M BUYING!
NOOGIE NOOGIE
AND I WAS IN SUCH A GOOD MOOD, TOO!
...
YOU DID THE BEST THAT YOU COULD! IT WAS ENOUGH JUST TO *TAKE* THE TEST!
BUT I WAS MORE SURPRISED BY YUI THAN I WAS BY YOU, MIAKA!

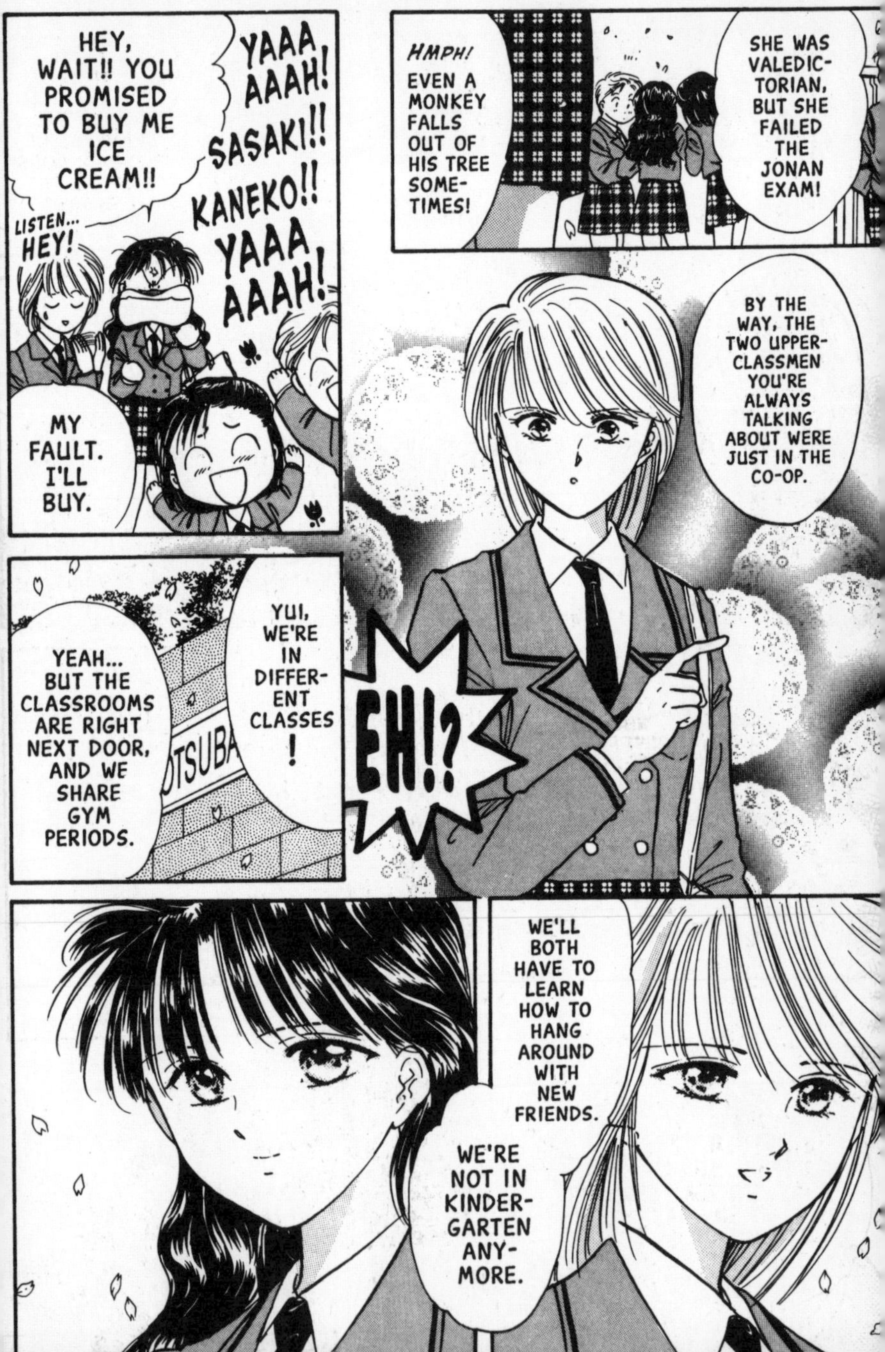
SHE WAS VALEDICTORIAN, BUT SHE FAILED THE JONAN EXAM!
HMPH! EVEN A MONKEY FALLS OUT OF HIS TREE SOMETIMES!
HEY, WAIT!! YOU PROMISED TO BUY ME ICE CREAM!!
YAAA AAAH! SASAKI!!
KANEKO!! YAAA AAAH!
LISTEN... HEY!
MY FAULT. I'LL BUY.
BY THE WAY, THE TWO UPPERCLASSMEN YOU'RE ALWAYS TALKING ABOUT WERE JUST IN THE CO-OP.
EH!?
YUI, WE'RE IN DIFFERENT CLASSES!
YEAH... BUT THE CLASSROOMS ARE RIGHT NEXT DOOR, AND WE SHARE GYM PERIODS.
OTSUBA
WE'LL BOTH HAVE TO LEARN HOW TO HANG AROUND WITH NEW FRIENDS.
WE'RE NOT IN KINDERGARTEN ANYMORE.

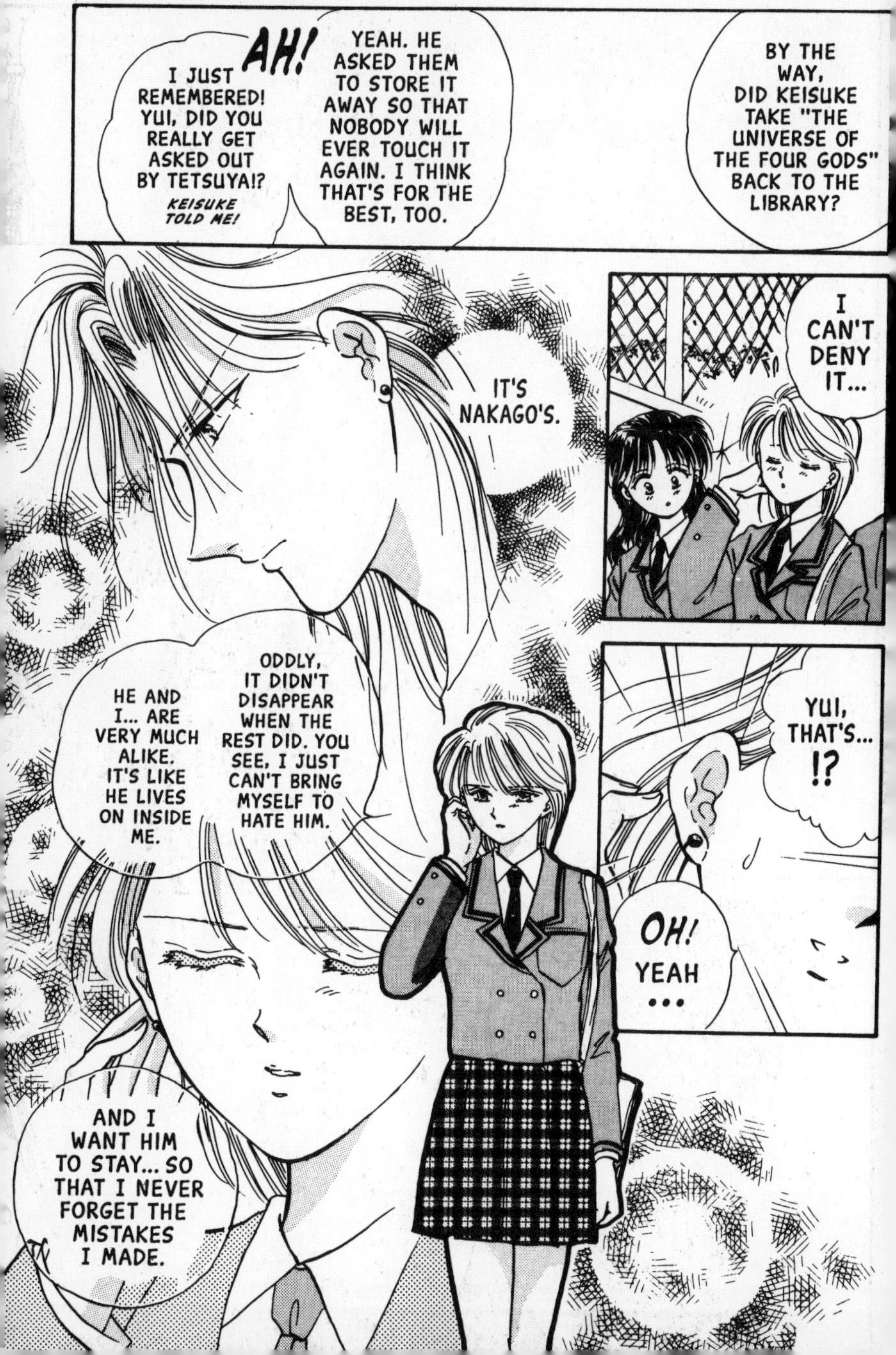
BY THE WAY, DID KEISUKE TAKE "THE UNIVERSE OF THE FOUR GODS" BACK TO THE LIBRARY?
YEAH. HE ASKED THEM TO STORE IT AWAY SO THAT NOBODY WILL EVER TOUCH IT AGAIN. I THINK THAT'S FOR THE BEST, TOO.
AH!
I JUST REMEMBERED! YUI, DID YOU REALLY GET ASKED OUT BY TETSUYA!?
KEISUKE TOLD ME!
I CAN'T DENY IT...
YUI, THAT'S... !?
OH! YEAH...
IT'S NAKAGO'S.
ODDLY, IT DIDN'T DISAPPEAR WHEN THE REST DID. YOU SEE, I JUST CAN'T BRING MYSELF TO HATE HIM.
HE AND I... ARE VERY MUCH ALIKE. IT'S LIKE HE LIVES ON INSIDE ME.
AND I WANT HIM TO STAY... SO THAT I NEVER FORGET THE MISTAKES I MADE.

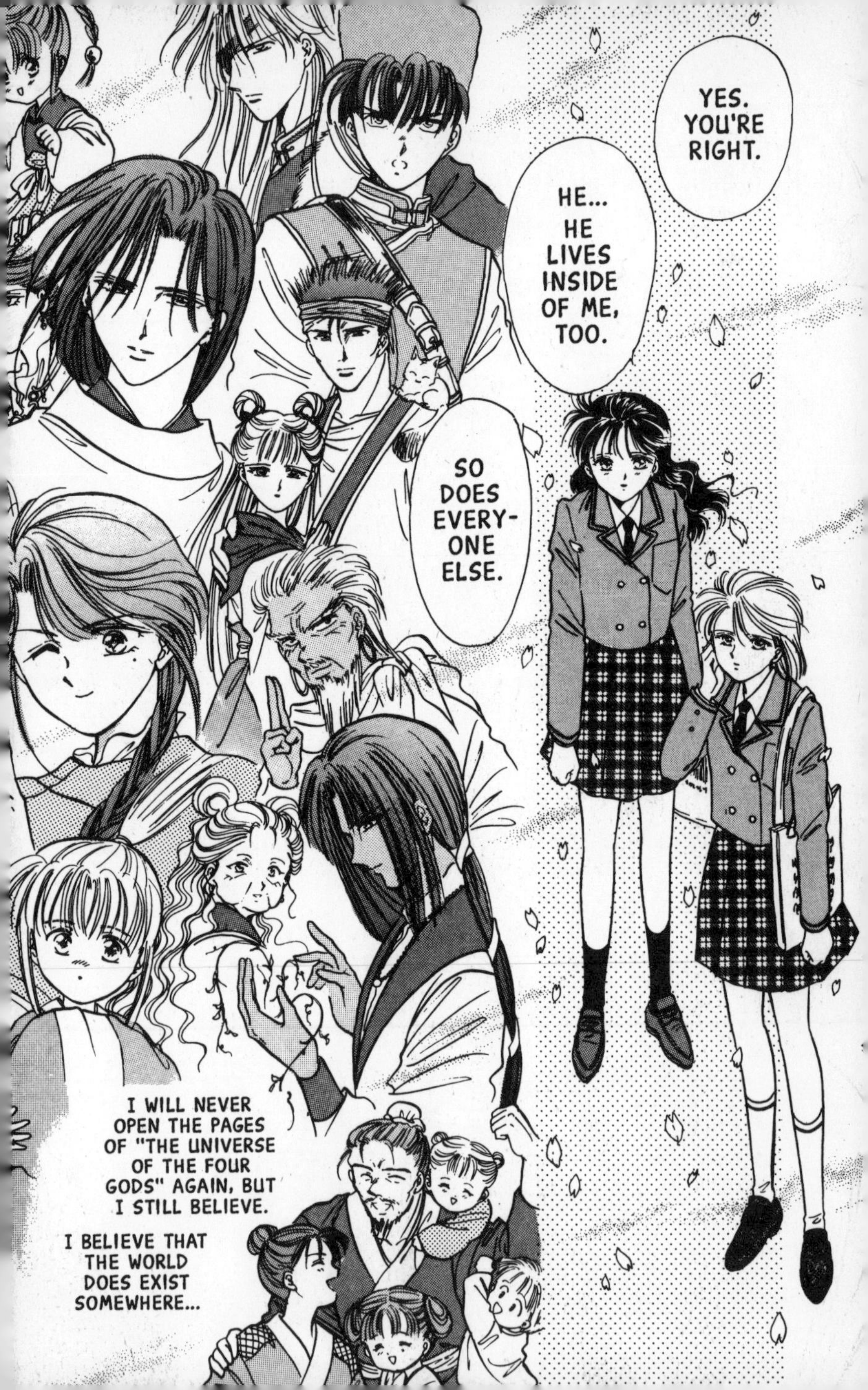
YES. YOU'RE RIGHT.
HE... HE LIVES INSIDE OF ME, TOO.
SO DOES EVERY-ONE ELSE.
I WILL NEVER OPEN THE PAGES OF "THE UNIVERSE OF THE FOUR GODS" AGAIN, BUT I STILL BELIEVE.
I BELIEVE THAT THE WORLD DOES EXIST SOMEWHERE...

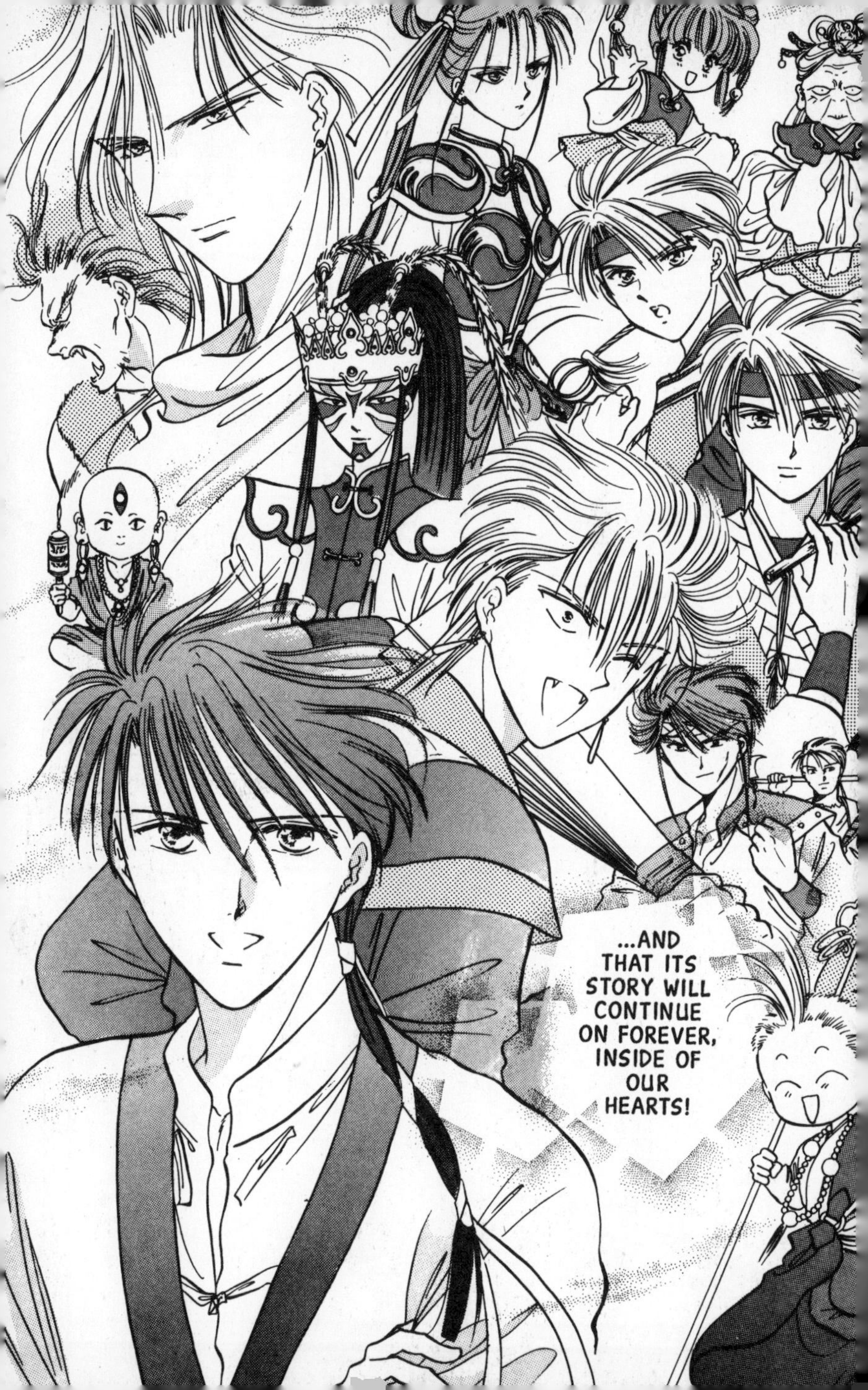
...AND THAT ITS STORY WILL CONTINUE ON FOREVER, INSIDE OF OUR HEARTS!

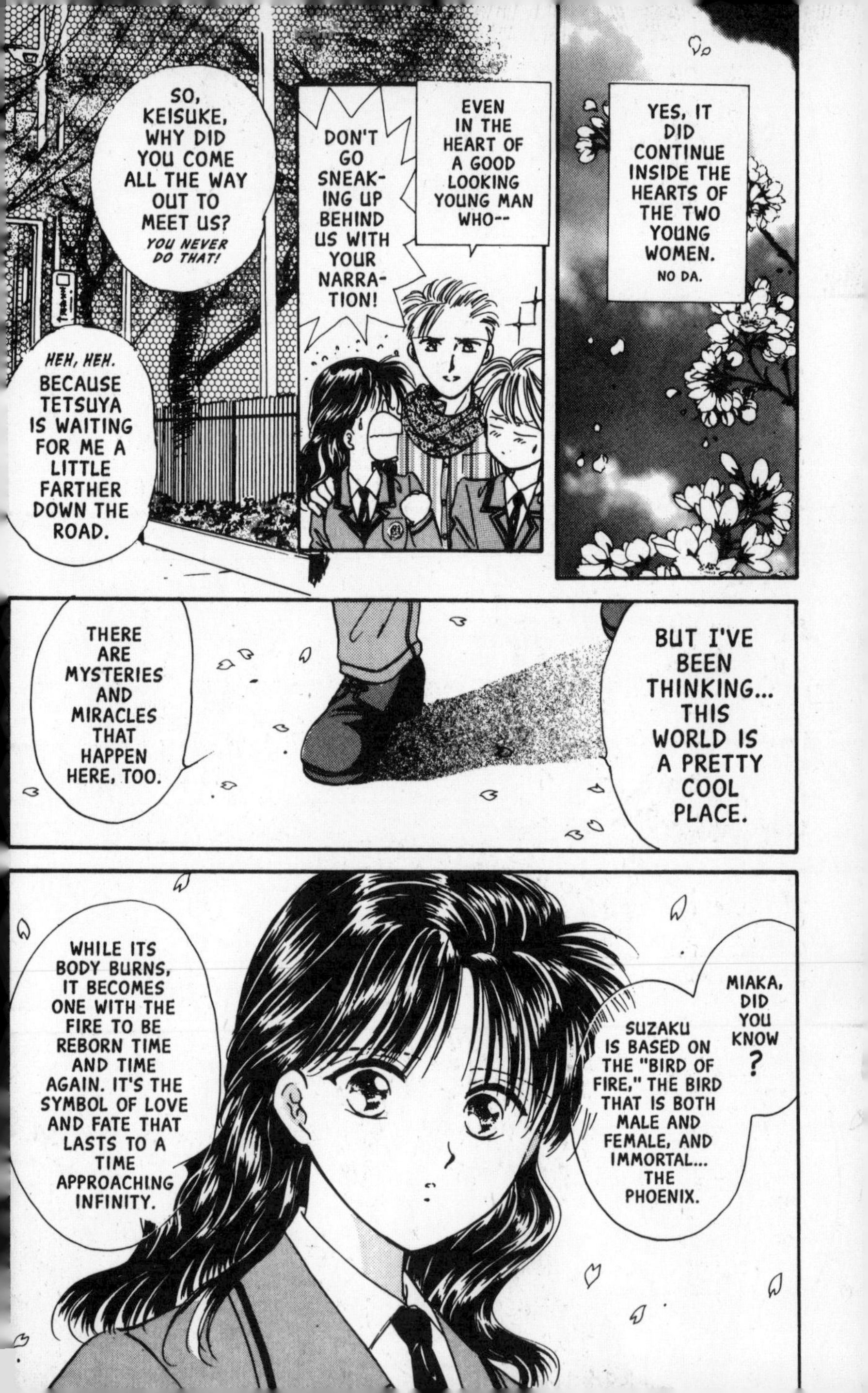
YES, IT DID CONTINUE INSIDE THE HEARTS OF THE TWO YOUNG WOMEN. NO DA.
EVEN IN THE HEART OF A GOOD LOOKING YOUNG MAN WHO--
DON'T GO SNEAK-ING UP BEHIND US WITH YOUR NARRA-TION!
SO, KEISUKE, WHY DID YOU COME ALL THE WAY OUT TO MEET US? YOU NEVER DO THAT!
HEH, HEH. BECAUSE TETSUYA IS WAITING FOR ME A LITTLE FARTHER DOWN THE ROAD.
BUT I'VE BEEN THINKING... THIS WORLD IS A PRETTY COOL PLACE.
THERE ARE MYSTERIES AND MIRACLES THAT HAPPEN HERE, TOO.
MIAKA, DID YOU KNOW ?
SUZAKU IS BASED ON THE "BIRD OF FIRE," THE BIRD THAT IS BOTH MALE AND FEMALE, AND IMMORTAL... THE PHOENIX.
WHILE ITS BODY BURNS, IT BECOMES ONE WITH THE FIRE TO BE REBORN TIME AND TIME AGAIN. IT'S THE SYMBOL OF LOVE AND FATE THAT LASTS TO A TIME APPROACHING INFINITY.

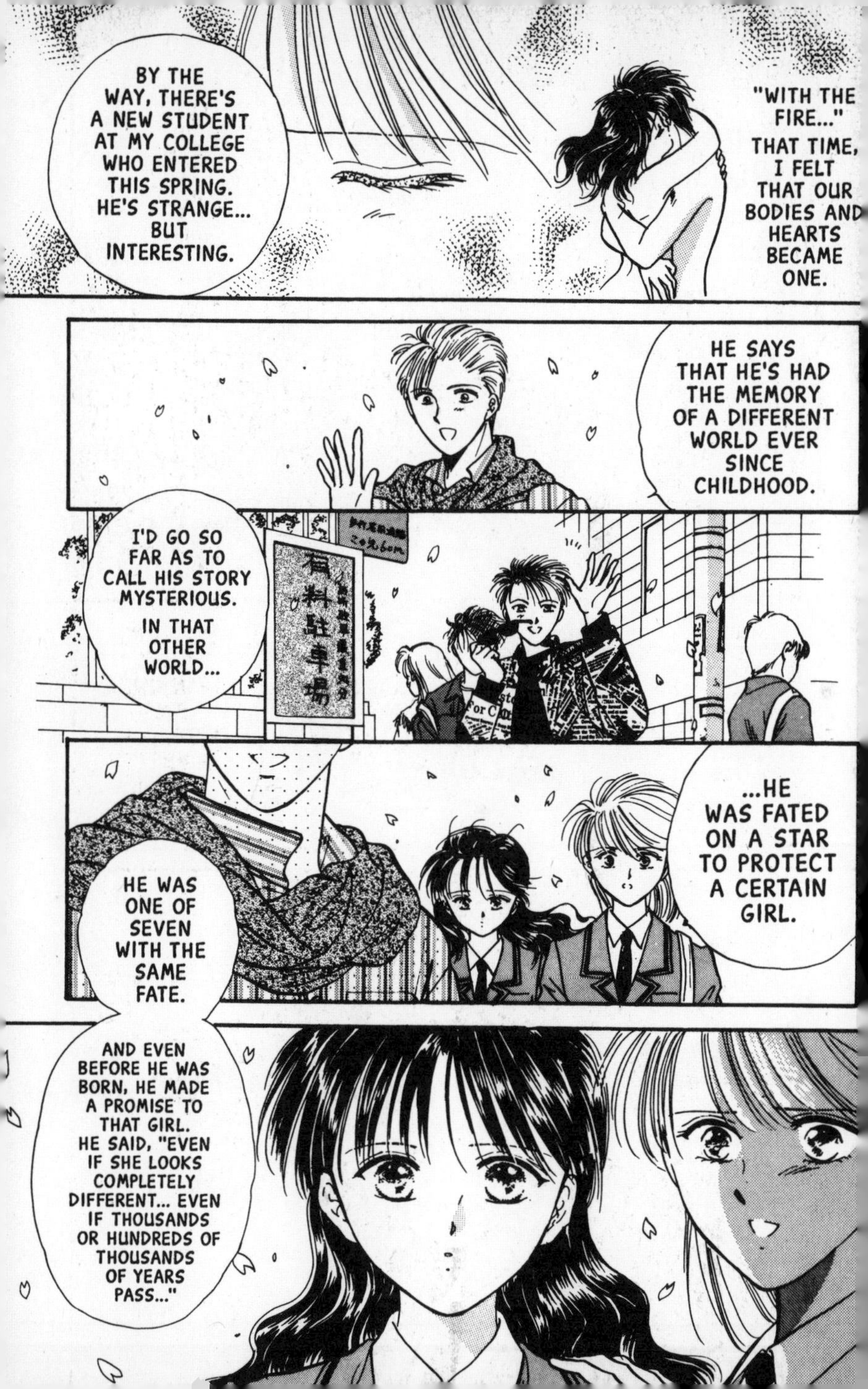
"WITH THE FIRE..." THAT TIME, I FELT THAT OUR BODIES AND HEARTS BECAME ONE.
BY THE WAY, THERE'S A NEW STUDENT AT MY COLLEGE WHO ENTERED THIS SPRING. HE'S STRANGE... BUT INTERESTING.
HE SAYS THAT HE'S HAD THE MEMORY OF A DIFFERENT WORLD EVER SINCE CHILDHOOD.
I'D GO SO FAR AS TO CALL HIS STORY MYSTERIOUS.
IN THAT OTHER WORLD...
有料駐車場
...HE WAS FATED ON A STAR TO PROTECT A CERTAIN GIRL.
HE WAS ONE OF SEVEN WITH THE SAME FATE.
AND EVEN BEFORE HE WAS BORN, HE MADE A PROMISE TO THAT GIRL. HE SAID, "EVEN IF SHE LOOKS COMPLETELY DIFFERENT... EVEN IF THOUSANDS OR HUNDREDS OF THOUSANDS OF YEARS PASS..."

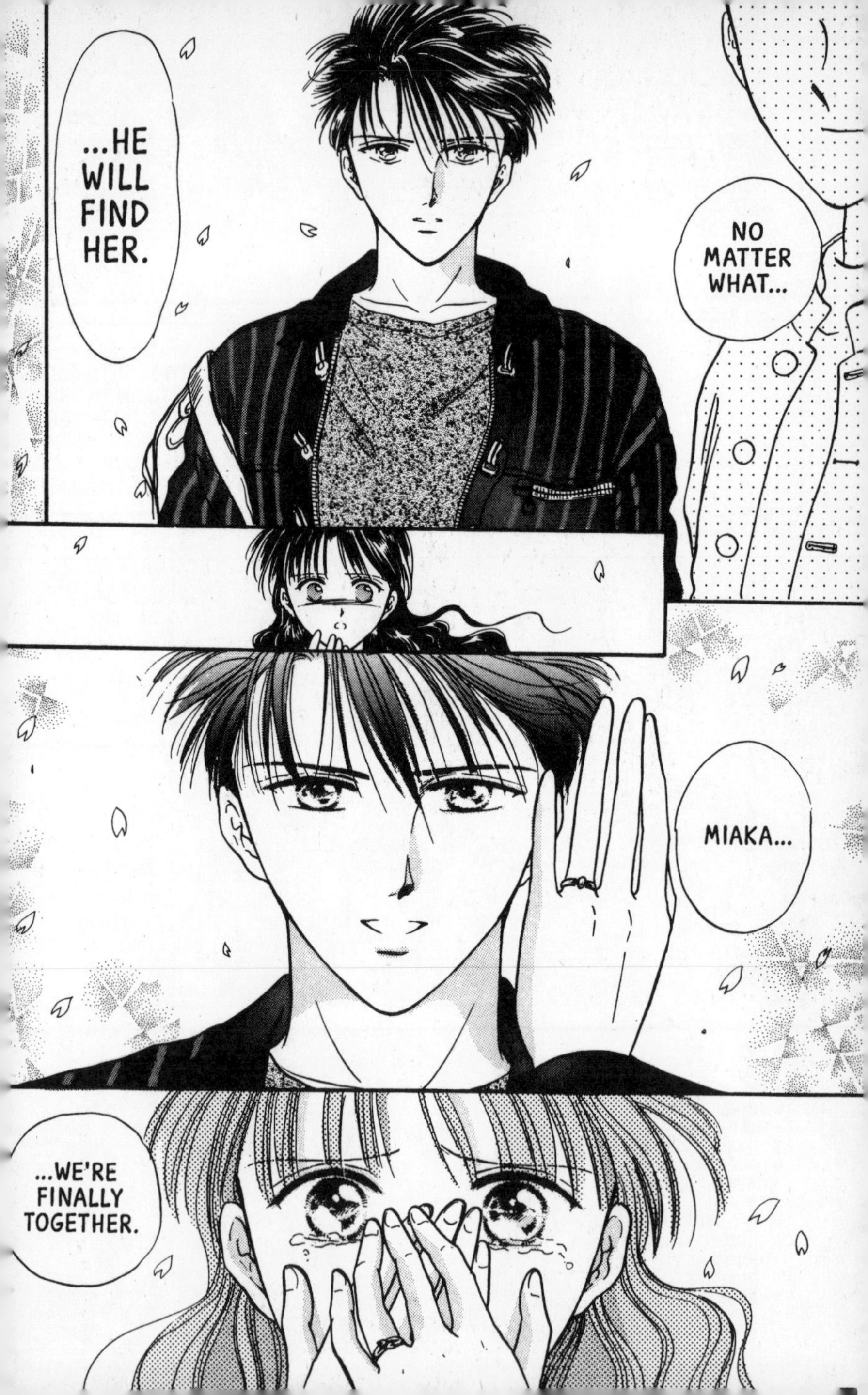
NO MATTER WHAT...
...HE WILL FIND HER.
MIAKA...
...WE'RE FINALLY TOGETHER.

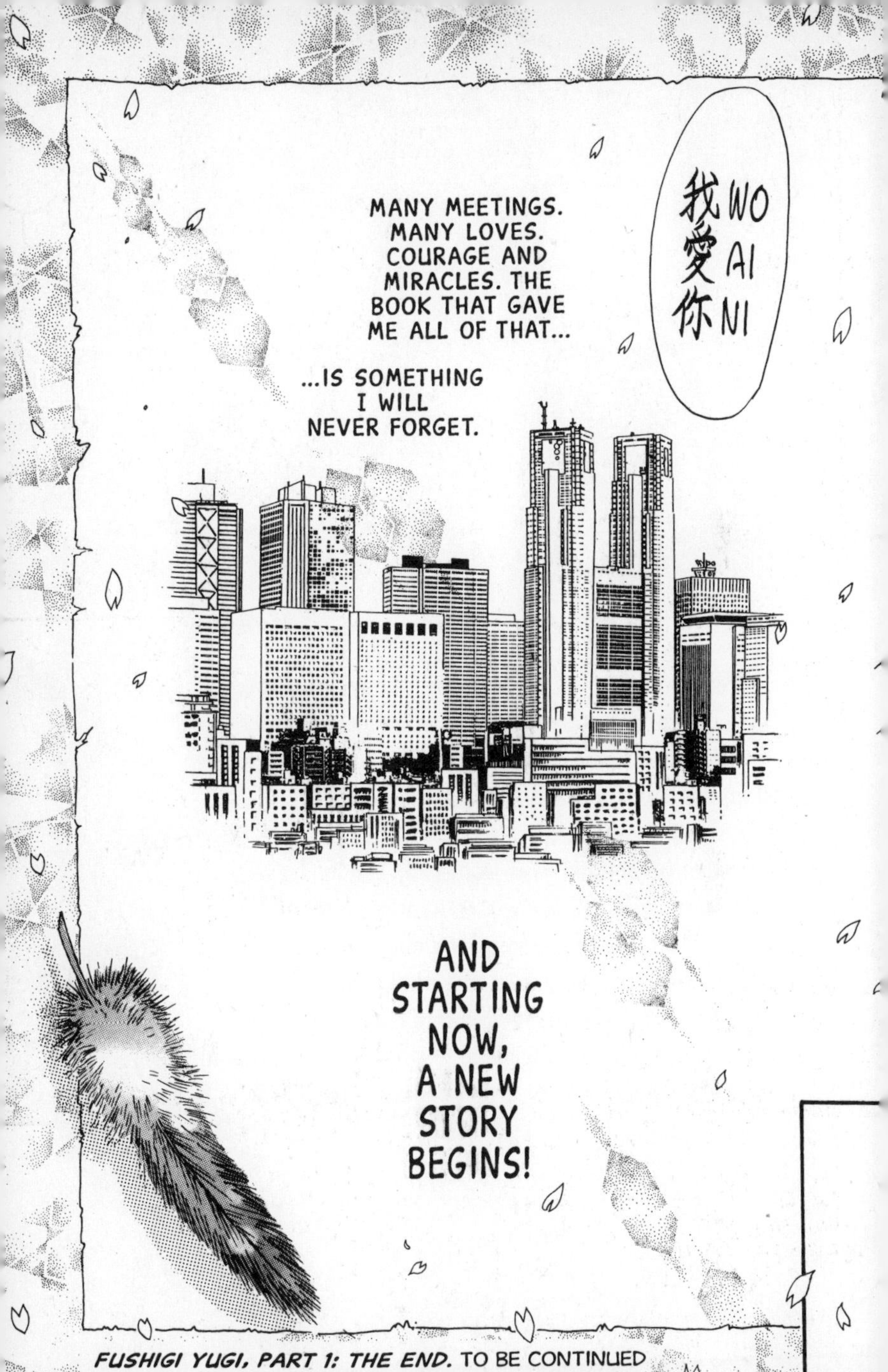
我愛你 WO AI NI
MANY MEETINGS. MANY LOVES. COURAGE AND MIRACLES. THE BOOK THAT GAVE ME ALL OF THAT...
...IS SOMETHING I WILL NEVER FORGET.
AND STARTING NOW, A NEW STORY BEGINS!

FUSHIGI YUGI, PART 1: THE END. TO BE CONTINUED IN ***PART 2,*** WHICH BEGINS IN ***VOLUME 14: PROPHET!***

ABOUT THE AUTHOR

Yû Watase was born on March 5 in a town near Osaka, Japan, and she was raised there before moving to Tokyo to follow her dream of creating manga. In the decade since her debut short story, PAJAMA DE OJAMA ("An Intrusion in Pajamas"), she has produced more than 50 compiled volumes of short stories and continuing series. Her latest series, ZETTAI KARESHI ("Absolute Boyfriend"), is currently running in the anthology magazine SHÔJO COMIC. Watase's long-running horror/romance story CERES: CELESTIAL LEGEND and her most recent completed series, ALICE 19TH, are now available in North America published by VIZ. She loves science fiction, fantasy and comedy.

The Fushigi Yûgi Guide to Sound Effects

Most of the sound effects in FUSHIGI YÛGI are the way Yû Watase created them, in their original Japanese.

We created this glossary for a page-by-page, panel-by-panel explanation of the action and background noises. By using this guide, you may even learn some Japanese.

The glossary lists page and panel number. For example, page 1, panel 3, would be listed as 1.3.

11.2 FX: GYURURURURURURU [zoom]
11.3 FX: BYU [throw]
11.4 FX: FU [dodge]
11.5 FX: DAN [leap]

12.1 FX: BA [pierce]

13.4 FX: PITA [stop]
13.5 FX: GAKUN [fall]
13.5 FX: DOSA [land]

14.1 FX: KORON [roll]
14.5 FX: DOSA [slump]

15.1 FX: SUUU [vanishing]
15.3 FX: ZAWA ZAWA [crowd noise]
15.3 FX: HA [alarm]
15.5 FX: PITA [stop]

16.2 FX: GOSHI [rub]
16.5 FX: WAAAA [shouting]

17.1 FX: HIHIIIIN [neighing]
17.3 FX: HYUUU [wind]

20.5 FX: KA [flash]

21.3 FX: DOHHH [burst]
21.4 FX: GU GU... [struggling]

24.2 FX: PISHA [shutting]
24.4 FX: GAKU GAKU GAKU [trembling]

27.2 FX: KASA... [grasp]

CHAPTER SEVENTY-THREE: THE CEREMONY

34.1 FX: CHI CHI [birds chirping]
34.2 FX: DAN [slam]
34.3 FX: BA [dash]
34.4 FX: KACHA [click]

CHAPTER SEVENTY-TWO: REQUIEM TO THE SKY

6.2 FX: ZAWA ZAWA [crowd murmuring]
6.4 FX: DOKA [blow]

7.1 FX: BYU [zoom]
7.2 FX: BISHI BISHI BISHI [hits]
7.3 FX: ZA [jump]
7.4 FX: GA [kick]

8.1 FX: ZUZAZAZA [sliding]
8.2 FX: DA [dash]
8.3 FX: GASHI [grab]
8.5 FX: DOKAKAKA [blows]

9.1 FX: GYURURURURURURU [spinning]
9.2 FX: GYUN [launch]
9.3 FX: GYURURURURURURU [spinning]
9.4 FX: GASHAAAN [crash]
9.5 FX: KU [float]

10.1 FX: GYUN [zoom]
10.1 FX: DA [dash]
10.4 FX: SHURURURURURURU [twirling]

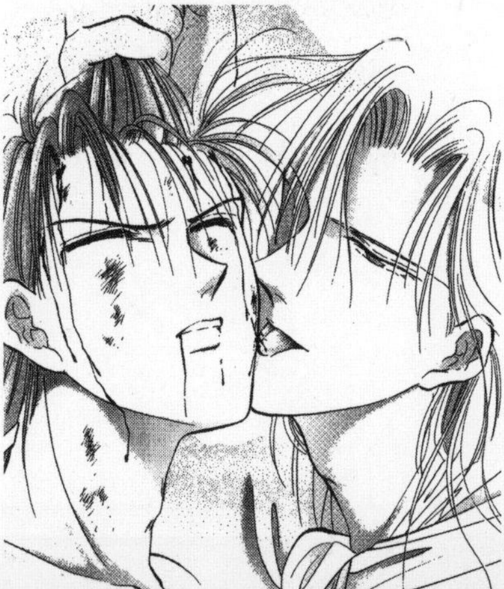

37.2 FX: NIKO [smile]
37.5 FX: ZAWA ZAWA [crowd noise]

38.2 FX: BA [snatch]
38.3 FX: ZAWA ZAWA [crowd noise]
39.2 FX: GASHAN [hanging up]
39.4 FX: DOON [bump]

41.1 FX: DOKI [heart beat]
41.2 FX: YORO [swaying]

42.2 FX: GYU… [squeeze]

44.6 FX: DA [dash]

45.3 FX: ZUKI [pain]
45.4 FX: ZUKIN ZUKIN ZUKIN [pain]

46-47.1 FX: UOOOOO [shouting]

48.4 FX: KA KA [footsteps]
48.4 FX: KA KA [footsteps]
48.5 FX: KA KA [footsteps]
48.6 FX: KA KA [footsteps]

49.3 FX: KAHHH [flash]
49.4 FX: BA [explosion]
49.5 FX: BISHA [splatter]

50.5 FX: HA [alarm]

51.2 FX: KASA… [place]

52.3 FX: GABA [recovering]
52.4 FX: BATAN [dropping]

57.2 FX: HA [alarm]

60.2 FX: SUUU [appearance]

CHAPTER SEVENTY-FOUR: EVEN IF IT TAKES MY LIFE

62.2 FX: KA [footstep]

64.4 FX: GABA [covering]

65.2 FX: BAN [door opening]
65.3 FX: BA [appearing]

67.3 FX: GYU [clench]

68.2 FX: NIKO [smile]
68.4 FX: KA KA [footsteps]

69.1 FX: SU [movement]

70.4 FX: BURU BURU [trembling]

71.2 FX: KA [footstep]
71.3 FX: KA KA [footsteps]
71.5 FX: ZUKA ZUKA [quick footfalls]
71.6 FX: HA [alarm]

72.2 FX: DO [explosion]
72.3 FX: KACHA [door opening]
72.4 FX: SORO [looking around]

73.1 FX: PIKU [twitch]

76.3 FX: TSUUN [emotional overload]
76.4 FX: BYUUU [smoke rising]

77.2 FX: DA [dash]
77.4 FX: BAN [explosion]
77.6 FX: BATA BATA [confusion]

78.1 FX: KA KA [footsteps]

80.4 FX: BAN [explosion]
80.5 FX: PARA PARA [debris falling]

81.1 FX: DA [running]

83.1 FX: BAN [explosion]
83.2 FX: ZUZUUUN [falling]

84.2 FX: KA [anger]
84.3 FX: ZURU [sliding down]

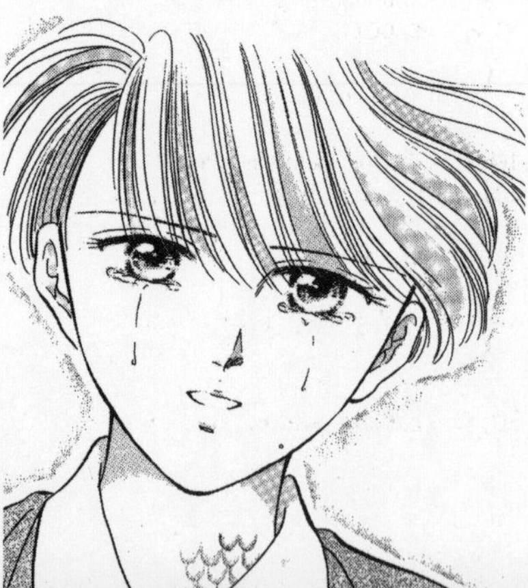

104.2 FX: UUUUU [siren]
104.2 FX: FAN FAN FAN [siren]
104.3 FX: PARIN [breaking glass]
104.4 FX: FAN FAN FAN [siren]

105.1 FX: WAAA [yelling]
105.1 FX: KYAAA [screaming]

107.6 FX: PARA PARA [rotors]

108.4 FX: HA [realization]
108.5 FX: GIRI [forced movement]

109.2 FX: BA [being hit]
109.2 FX: BA BA BA [hits]

110.2 FX: DOSHA [falling]
110.4 FX: ZURU [sliding]

112.4 FX: BARA [ripping]

114.2 FX: KA [flash]

115.1 FX: OOOOO [roaring]
115.4 FX: ZAWA… [crowd noise]

116.1 FX: ZUZUZUZUZU [rumbling]
116.3 FX: ZUZUZU [rumbling]
116.4 FX: KI [anger]

117.2 FX: BA [explosion]
117.3 FX: DOSA [crashing to earth]
117.3 FX: KA KA [footsteps]

118.5 FX: ZA [footfall]

119.3 FX: BA [dramatic movement]

120.4 FX: BASHI [an attack]

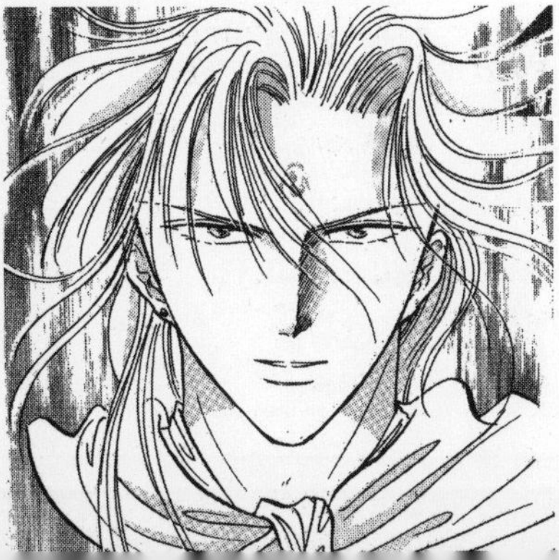

85.4 FX: KI [realization]

87.3 FX: BA [dramatic movement]

88.1 FX: DOO [explosion]

89.1 FX: GACHA [wires colliding]

90.3 FX: DA [dash]

91.1 FX: FU [vanishing]

92.1 FX: DOO [explosion]
92.3 FX: GASHAAAAN [sliding]

93.3 FX: FAN FAN FAN [sirens]
93.4 FX: FAN FAN FAN FAN [sirens]
93.5 FX: DOO [explosion]
93.6 FX: KA [footstep]

94.1 FX: KA KA KA KA [footsteps]
94.4 FX: DA [dash]

CHAPTER SEVENTY-FIVE: BYE-BYE

96.1 FX: BIIIBOOOO BIIIBOOO [sirens]
96.1 FX: PARA PARA PARA [rotors]
96.3 FX: SU [quick movement]
96.4 FX: BA [dramatic movement]

97.3 FX: BOO [flames]
97.4 FX: DOO [attack]
97.5 FX: FU [quick movement]
97.6 FX: GA [engulfing]

98.1 FX: GIRI GIRI [quivering]
98.4 FX: BA [dramatic movement]
98.5 FX: DOKA [slam]

99.1 FX: GA [grab]

100.1 FX: KAA [sudden awareness]
100.3 FX: FUWA [waft]

101.2 FX: DON [slam]

102.5 FX: BASHI [colliding]
102.6 FX: KA KA [footsteps]

103.1 FX: KA KA [footsteps]

151.1 FX: BA [dramatic movement]
151.2 FX: DO [explosion]

152.3 FX: BASHI [hitting the shield]

153.1 FX: BA [grab]
153.3 FX: BA [dramatic movement]

CHAPTER SEVENTY-SEVEN: A NEW STORY

155.2 FX: DOOOOOO [roaring]

156.1 FX: FU [disappearance]
156.2 FX: DA [dash]
156.3 FX: ZUKI [pain]

157.1 FX: DO [explosive force]

158.3 FX: BABABABABA [rumbling]
158.6 FX: SUUUUU [cleanly restored]

159.1 FX: SUUUUU [cleanly restored]
159.2 FX: MUKU [looking around]
159.4 FX: FUWA [float]
159.5 FX: KAAAAA [emitting light]
159.6 FX: FU [sudden appearance]
159.6 FX: SHULULU [rolling up]

160.3 FX: POTA POTA [dripping]

161.1 FX: WAAAA [shouts]

163.3 FX: GOFU [cough]

164.1 FX: SUUU [vanishing]
164.4 FX: FURA [release of energy]

173.4 FX: KA [flash]

179.3 FX: GYU [grip]

180.3 FX: BAAA [honking]
180.3 FX: BABAAA [honking]
180.4 FX: PAAAAA [bright light]

181.2 FX: NIKO [smile]

184.3 FX: ZA [sunshine]

121.4 FX: HA [alarm]

CHAPTER SEVENTY-SIX: MIRACLE WINGS

123.2 FX: ZUZUZUZUZUZU [rumbling]
123.4 FX: ZUZU [rumbling]

124.4 FX: GOOOOO [roaring]
124.6 FX: KA KA [flashes]

125.3 FX: FU [appearance]
125.5 FX: KAA [flash]

129.1 FX: KA [flash]
129.4 FX: GOOO [flames]

130.2 FX: SHAN [clanking]
130.4 FX: KA [flash]

132.5 FX: KI [sudden determination]

134.1 FX: ZUZUZUZUZU [rumbling]
134.3 FX: KA [flash]

135.3 FX: ZUZU [rumble]

141.1 FX: PAN [explosion]
141.3 FX: MEKI MEKI MEKI [creaking]
141.5 FX: ZUUUUUUN [falling]

142.2 FX: MIN [stopped]

143.1 FX: FUWA [spontaneous combustion]
143.2 FX: BUN [explosion]
143.3 FX: FUWA [wafting]
143.4 FX: KA [flash]
143.5 FX: DOO [flames parting]

144.4 FX: FUWA [wafting]

145.1 FX: ZA [sudden attention]
145.4 FX: YORO [wobble]

148.2 FX: DOOOON [crash]
148.5 FX: KA [flash]

149.1 FX: DO [slam]

150.1 FX: DO [landing]
150.2 FX: SU [sudden movement]
150.5 FX: BISHI BISHI [missed attacks]

EDITOR'S RECOMMENDATIONS

Did you like fushigi yûgi? Here's what VIZ recommends you try next:

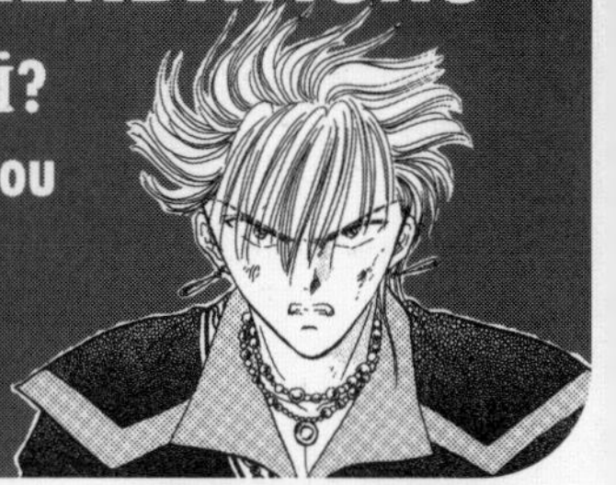

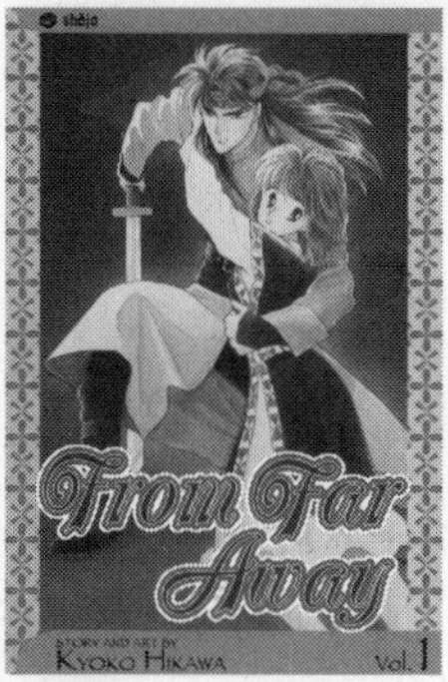
shôjo
From Far Away
STORY AND ART BY
KYOKO HIKAWA
Vol. 1

FROM FAR AWAY

On her way home from school one day, Noriko is unexpectedly plunged into a strange and extraordinary fantasy world. Her troubles compound exponentially when she is rescued and befriended by a handsome young man named Izark. He may be brave and courageous, but inside Izark lurks the darkest evil imaginable. And according to an ancient prophecy, Noriko possesses the power to unleash that evil. Now, inexorably bound together, these two unlikely allies must navigate a world both wondrous and hostile.

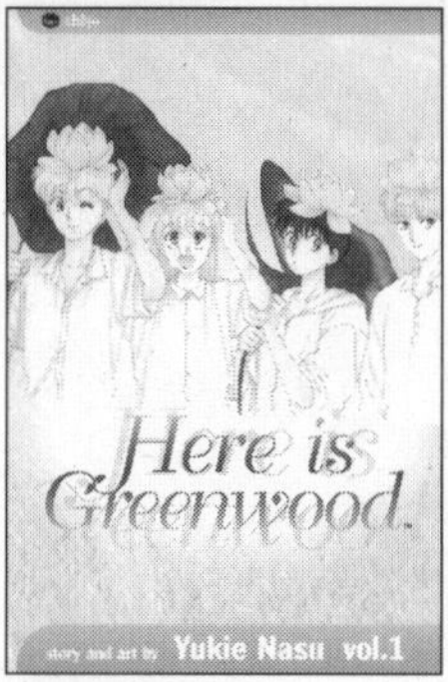
shôjo
Here is Greenwood
story and art by Yukie Nasu vol.1

HERE IS GREENWOOD

Kazuya nearly died in a serious car accident, but even before that, his life was going down the tubes. The woman he loves married his older brother, and the newlyweds came home to live with Kazuya's family. Kazuya decides to escape the house by attending Ryokuta Academy, an exclusive all-male boarding school. But his injuries from the car accident cause Kazuya to arrive at school a month late, so he is forced to live in Greenwood Dorm—the refuge for all the oddballs at Ryokuta. Things are very odd, indeed, when Kazuya is introduced to his new roommate, Shun Kisaragi, who seems to be...a girl!?

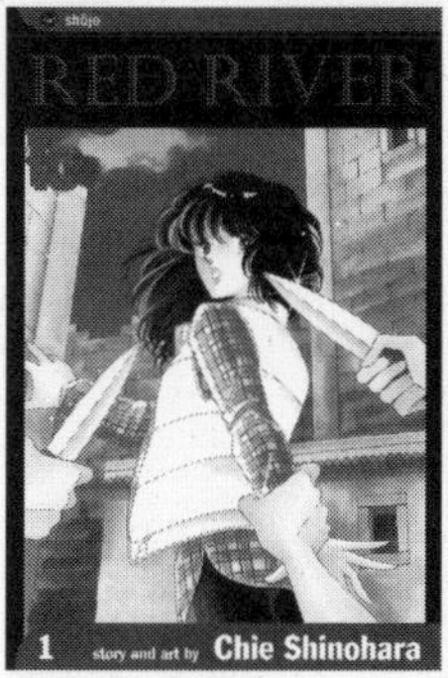
shôjo
RED RIVER
1 story and art by Chie Shinohara

RED RIVER

Yuri is ecstatic after passing her college entrance exam and having her first kiss with her childhood friend-turned-boyfriend. However, her luck soon changes. She starts to notice that water becomes agitated whenever she goes near it. One night, hands appear out of a puddle on the street and drag her into the water! Transported to an ancient village in the Middle East, she is then captured by armed troops and taken to the Queen's palace as a human sacrifice!

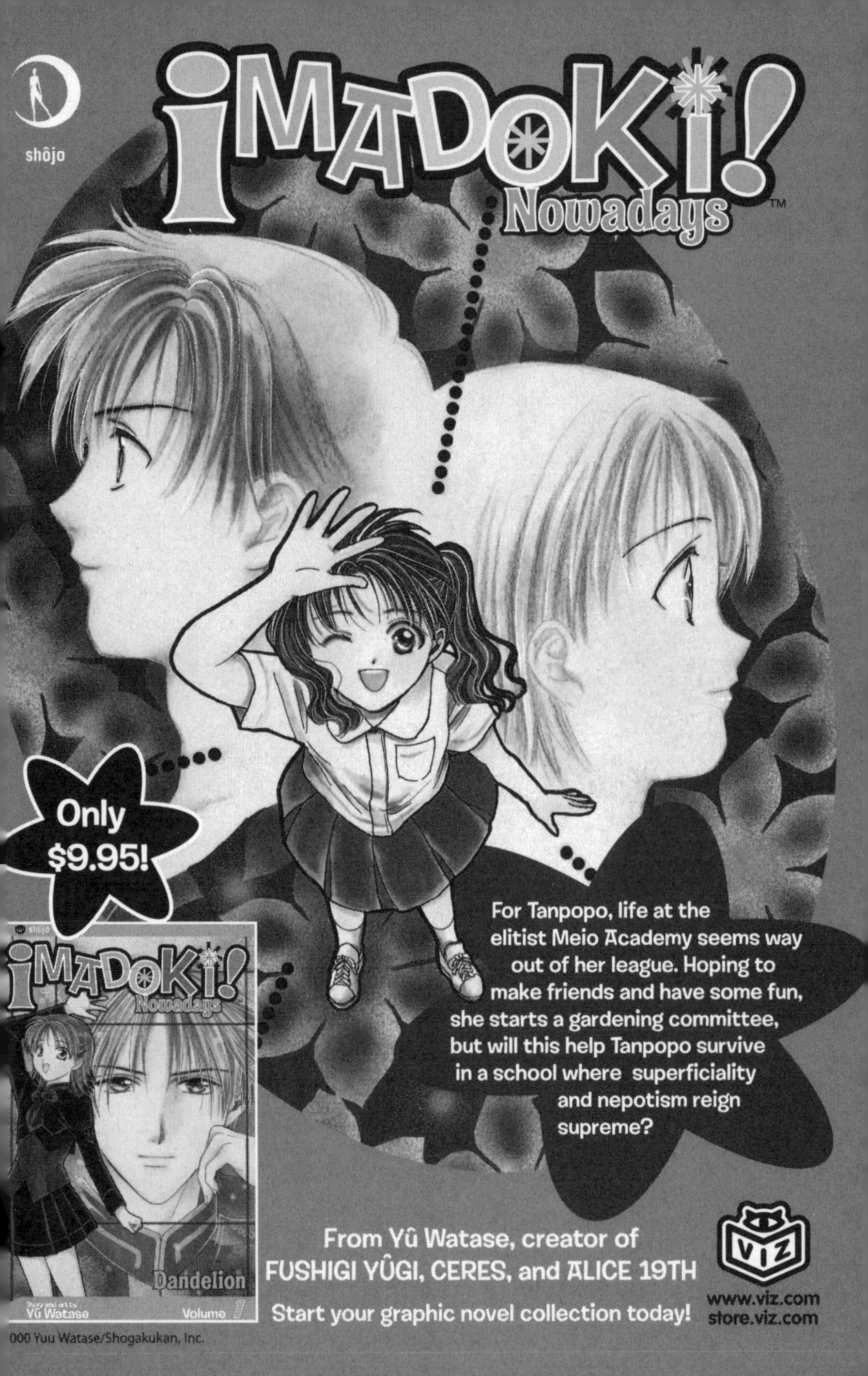
shôjo
IMADOKI!
Nowadays™
Only $9.95!
For Tanpopo, life at the elitist Meio Academy seems way out of her league. Hoping to make friends and have some fun, she starts a gardening committee, but will this help Tanpopo survive in a school where superficiality and nepotism reign supreme?
IMADOKI! Nowadays
Dandelion
Story and art by Yû Watase
Volume 1
From Yû Watase, creator of
FUSHIGI YÛGI, CERES, and ALICE 19TH
Start your graphic novel collection today!
VIZ
www.viz.com
store.viz.com

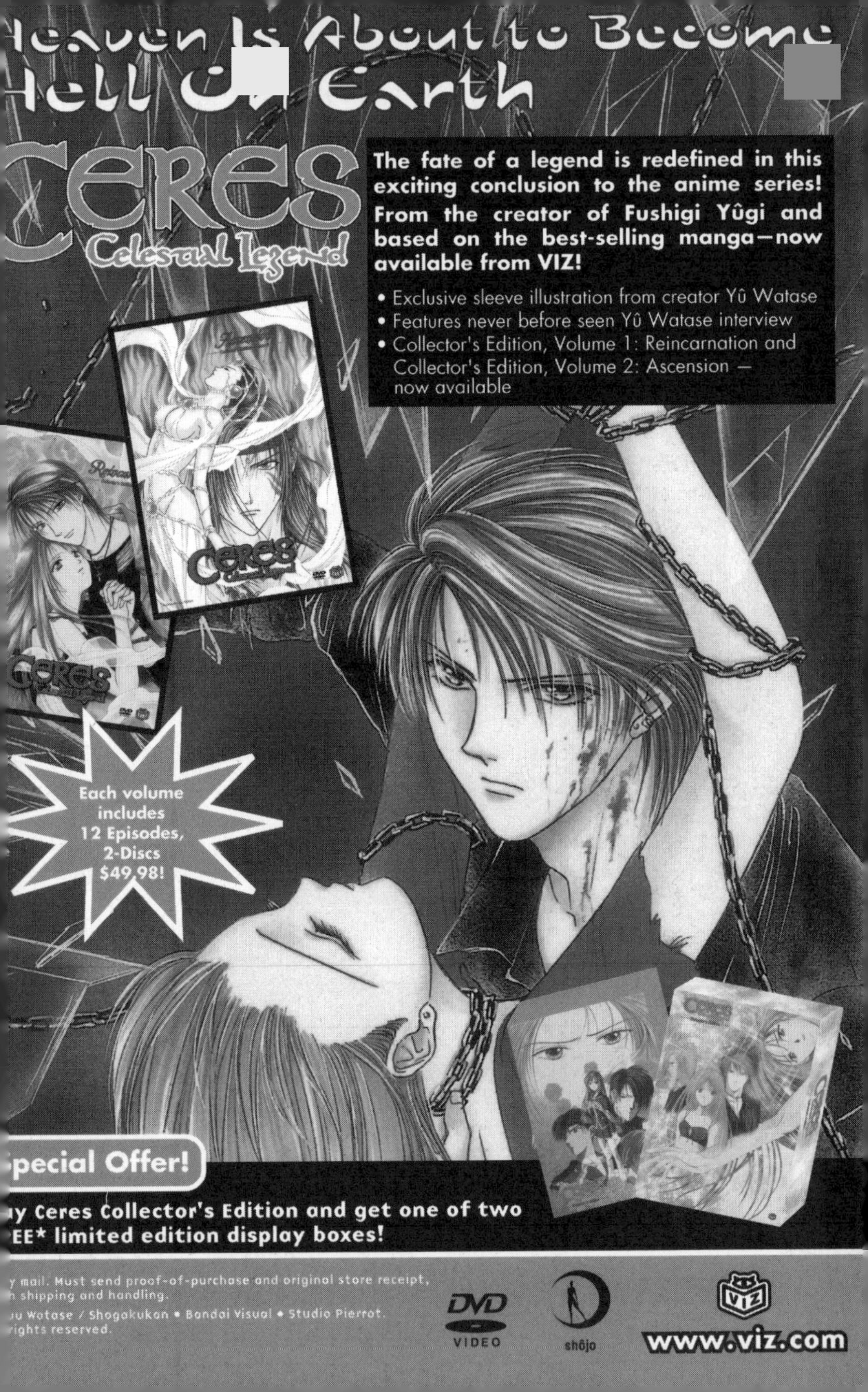

Heaven Is About to Become
Hell On Earth
Ceres
Celestial Legend
The fate of a legend is redefined in this exciting conclusion to the anime series! From the creator of Fushigi Yûgi and based on the best-selling manga—now available from VIZ!
• Exclusive sleeve illustration from creator Yû Watase
• Features never before seen Yû Watase interview
• Collector's Edition, Volume 1: Reincarnation and Collector's Edition, Volume 2: Ascension — now available
Each volume includes 12 Episodes, 2-Discs $49.98!
pecial Offer!
ıy Ceres Collector's Edition and get one of two
EE* limited edition display boxes!
y mail. Must send proof-of-purchase and original store receipt,
n shipping and handling.
u Watase / Shogakukan • Bandai Visual • Studio Pierrot.
rights reserved.
DVD VIDEO
shôjo
VIZ
www.viz.com

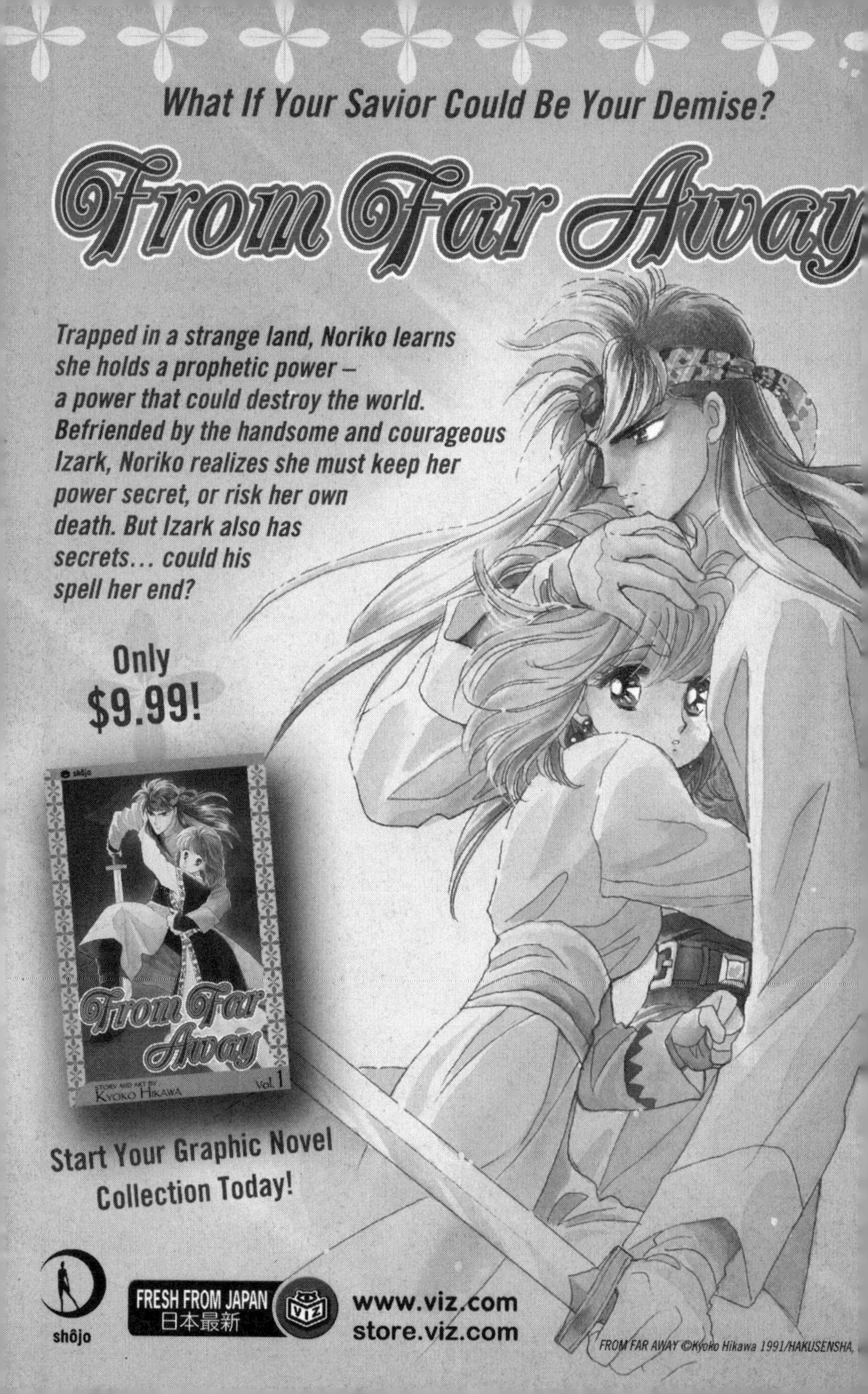
What If Your Savior Could Be Your Demise?
From Far Away
Trapped in a strange land, Noriko learns she holds a prophetic power – a power that could destroy the world. Befriended by the handsome and courageous Izark, Noriko realizes she must keep her power secret, or risk her own death. But Izark also has secrets… could his spell her end?
Only $9.99!
From Far Away
Story and Art by Kyoko Hikawa
Vol. 1
Start Your Graphic Novel Collection Today!
shôjo
FRESH FROM JAPAN 日本最新
VIZ
www.viz.com
store.viz.com
FROM FAR AWAY ©Kyoko Hikawa 1991/HAKUSENSHA,

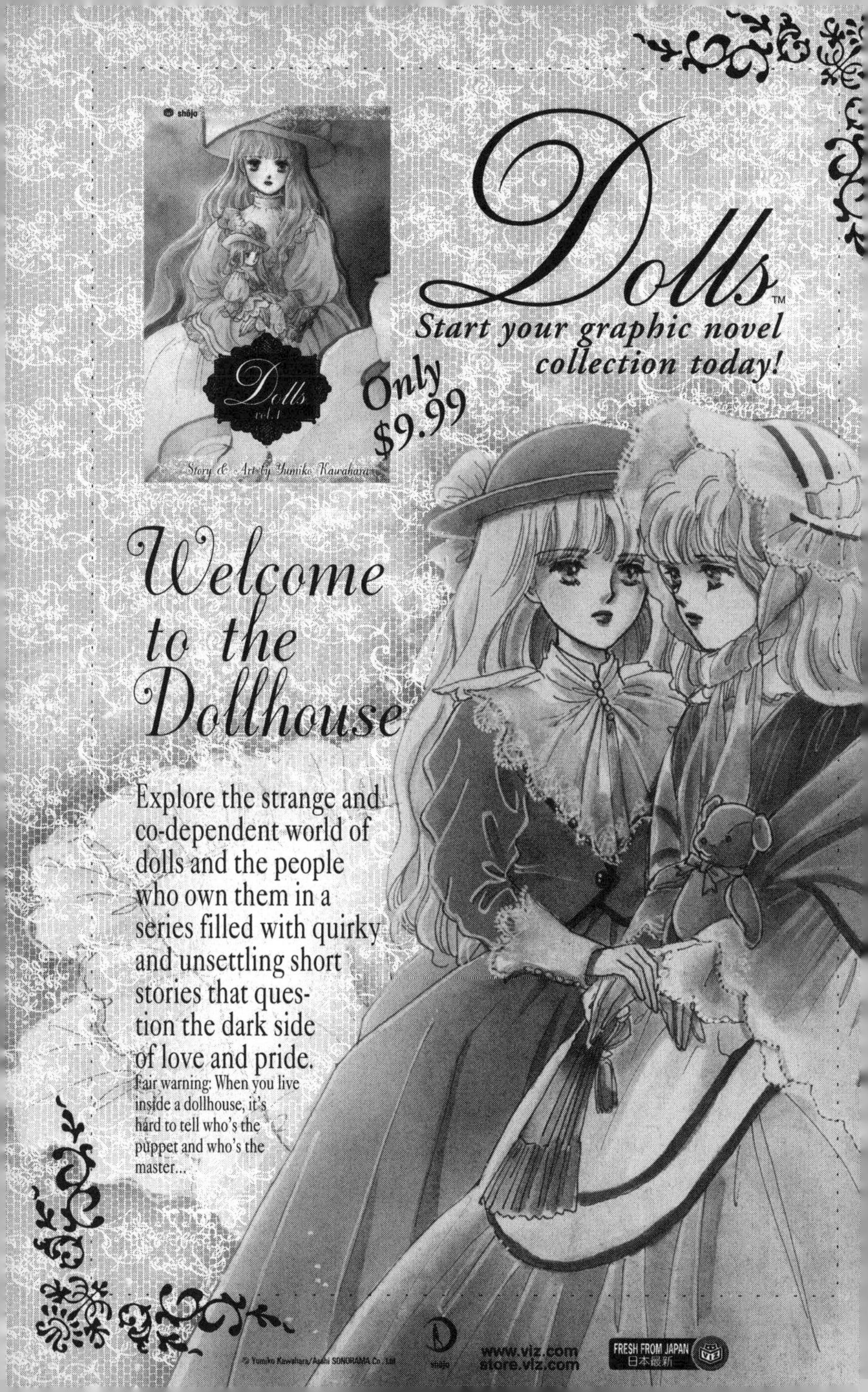
shōjo
Dolls vol.1
Story & Art by Yumiko Kawahara
Dolls™
Start your graphic novel collection today!
Only $9.99
Welcome to the Dollhouse
Explore the strange and co-dependent world of dolls and the people who own them in a series filled with quirky and unsettling short stories that question the dark side of love and pride.
Fair warning: When you live inside a dollhouse, it's hard to tell who's the puppet and who's the master...
© Yumiko Kawahara/Asahi SONORAMA Co., Ltd.
shōjo
www.viz.com
store.viz.com
FRESH FROM JAPAN
日本最新
VIZ

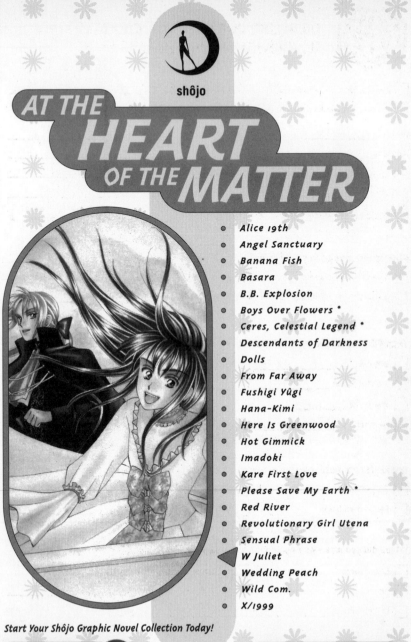

COMPLETE OUR SURVEY AND LET US KNOW WHAT YOU THINK!

☐ Please do NOT send me information about VIZ products, news and events, special offers, or other information.

☐ Please do NOT send me information from VIZ's trusted business partners.

Name: _____

Address: _____

City:_____ State:_____ Zip:_____

E-mail: _____

☐ Male ☐ Female   Date of Birth (mm/dd/yyyy): ___/___/_____ (Under 13? Parental consent required)

What race/ethnicity do you consider yourself? (please check one)

☐ Asian/Pacific Islander   ☐ Black/African American   ☐ Hispanic/Latino

☐ Native American/Alaskan Native   ☐ White/Caucasian   ☐ Other:_____

What VIZ product did you purchase? (check all that apply and indicate title purchased)

☐ DVD/VHS _____

☐ Graphic Novel_____

☐ Magazines _____

☐ Merchandise _____

Reason for purchase: (check all that apply)

☐ Special offer   ☐ Favorite title   ☐ Gift

☐ Recommendation   ☐ Other_____

Where did you make your purchase? (please check one)

☐ Comic store   ☐ Bookstore   ☐ Mass/Grocery Store

☐ Newsstand   ☐ Video/Video Game Store ☐ Other:_____

☐ Online (site:_____)

What other VIZ properties have you purchased/own? _____

_____

How many anime and/or manga titles have you purchased in the last year? How many were VIZ titles? (please check one from each column)

ANIME	MANGA	VIZ
☐ None	☐ None	☐ None
☐ 1-4	☐ 1-4	☐ 1-4
☐ 5-10	☐ 5-10	☐ 5-10
☐ 11+	☐ 11+	☐ 11+

I find the pricing of VIZ products to be: (please check one)

☐ Cheap ☐ Reasonable ☐ Expensive

What genre of manga and anime would you like to see from VIZ? (please check two)

☐ Adventure ☐ Comic Strip ☐ Science Fiction ☐ Fighting

☐ Horror ☐ Romance ☐ Fantasy ☐ Sports

What do you think of VIZ's new look?

☐ Love It ☐ It's OK ☐ Hate It ☐ Didn't Notice ☐ No Opinion

Which do you prefer? (please check one)

☐ Reading right-to-left

☐ Reading left-to-right

Which do you prefer? (please check one)

☐ Sound effects in English

☐ Sound effects in Japanese with English captions

☐ Sound effects in Japanese only with a glossary at the back

THANK YOU! Please send the completed form to:

NJW Research
42 Catharine St.
Poughkeepsie, NY 12601

All information provided will be used for internal purposes only. We promise not to sell or otherwise divulge your information.